HUGO GROTIUS – THEOLOGIAN

ESSAYS IN HONOUR OF
G.H.M. POSTHUMUS MEYJES

STUDIES IN THE HISTORY
OF
CHRISTIAN THOUGHT

EDITED BY

HEIKO A. OBERMAN, Tucson, Arizona

IN COOPERATION WITH

HENRY CHADWICK, Cambridge
JAROSLAV PELIKAN, New Haven, Connecticut
BRIAN TIERNEY, Ithaka, New York
ARJO VANDERJAGT, Groningen

VOLUME LV

HENK J.M. NELLEN AND EDWIN RABBIE (EDS.)

HUGO GROTIUS – THEOLOGIAN

HUGO GROTIUS
THEOLOGIAN

ESSAYS IN HONOUR OF
G.H.M. POSTHUMUS MEYJES

EDITED BY

HENK J.M. NELLEN

AND

EDWIN RABBIE

E.J. BRILL
LEIDEN · NEW YORK · KÖLN
1994

The paper in this book meets the guidelines for permanence and durability of the Committee on Production Guidelines for Book Longevity of the Council on Library Resources.

BR
350
.G7
H84
1994

Library of Congress Cataloging-in-Publication Data

Hugo Grotius, theologian : essays in honour of G.H.M. Posthumus Meyjes
/ edited by Henk J.M. Nellen and Edwin Rabbie.
    p   cm. — (Studies in the history of Christian Thought, ISSN
0081-8607 ; v. 55)
    English and French.
    Partial proceedings of a colloquium held in Leiden and Haarlem,
June 3–5, 1992.
    Includes bibliographical references (p. xxx–xxx) and indexes.
    ISBN 9004100008 (alk. paper)
    1. Theology—16th century—Congresses.   2. Grotius, Hugo,
1583–1645—Congresses.   I. Posthumus Meyjes, G.H.M. (Guillaume
Henri Marie)   II. Nellen, Henk J.M., 1949–   III. Rabbie, Edwin,
1957– .   IV. Series.
BR350.G7H84   1994
230'.092—dc20   93-46252
                                              CIP

Die Deutsche Bibliothek - CIP-Einheitsaufnahme

Hugo Grotius, theologian : essays in honour of G. H. M.
Posthumus Meyjes / ed. by Henk J. M. Nellen and Edwin
Rabbie. – Leiden ; New York ; Köln : Brill, 1994
    (Studies in the history of Christian thought ; Vol. 55)
    ISBN 90–04–10000–8
NE: Nellen, Henk J. M. [Hrsg.]; Posthumus Meyjes, Guillaume H.
    M.: Festschrift; GT

ISSN 0081-8607
ISBN 90 04 10000 8

© *Copyright 1994 by E.J. Brill, Leiden, The Netherlands*

*All rights reserved. No part of this publication may be reproduced, translated, stored in
a retrieval system, or transmitted in any form or by any means, electronic,
mechanical, photocopying, recording or otherwise, without prior written
permission from the publisher.*

*Authorization to photocopy items for internal or personal
use is granted by E.J. Brill provided that
the appropriate fees are paid directly to The Copyright
Clearance Center, 222 Rosewood Drive, Suite 910
Danvers MA 01923, USA.
Fees are subject to change.*

PRINTED IN THE NETHERLANDS

CONTENTS

PART THREE
THE INFLUENCE OF GROTIUS' THEOLOGICAL THOUGHT

BIBLIOGRAPHIES AND INDEXES

PREFACE

In 1984 Professor Guillaume H.M. Posthumus Meyjes discovered among the manuscripts of the Amsterdam University Library a theological work of Hugo Grotius that for a long time had been considered lost, the early work *Meletius sive de iis quae inter christianos conveniunt epistola*, dating from the year 1611. It was this remarkable discovery that breathed new life into the interest in Grotius' theological works. As a member of the supervising committee of the then Grotius Institute of the Royal Netherlands Academy of Arts and Sciences Posthumus Meyjes took the lead in broadening the Institute's programme of scholarly editions. The committee decided to initiate a new series of Hugo Grotius' theological works, in addition to the current series of correspondence and Latin poetry. This was an obvious choice, since there can be no doubt that in Grotius' œuvre his theological works take a prominent position both in extent and influence. This becomes clear from the monumental edition of the *Opera theologica*, which was published in 1679 in four huge folio volumes, and from the fact that Grotius' most frequently printed work is not the famous *De iure belli ac pacis* (1625), but his apology of Christianity *De veritate religionis christianae* (1627), which has been printed over a hundred and fifty times.

In 1988 the *Meletius*, edited by Posthumus Meyjes, was published. At the same time, the Grotius Institute put the finishing touches to the first volume of the new series *Hugo Grotius, Opera theologica*. When this volume, containing the *Defensio fidei catholicae de satisfactione Christi adversus Faustum Socinum Senensem* (1617), was published in 1990, Grotius' two earliest theological works became available for the first time in critical editions with English translations, extensive introductions and commentaries. It was decided to continue with Grotius' two most important works on the relationship between church and state, *Ordinum Hollandiae ac Westfrisiae pietas* (1613) and *De imperio summarum potestatum circa sacra* (1647). On 1 January 1992 the Grotius Institute became the Grotius Department of the "Constantijn Huygens Institute for text editions and intellectual history" of the Royal Netherlands Academy of Arts and Sciences. Within this new framework plans have been developed to further extend the series of theological works to include the already mentioned tract *De veritate* and Grotius' most controversial polemical work *Verantwoordingh* (*Apologeticus*, 1622).

In 1985 Posthumus Meyjes gave a fascinating account of his discovery of the *Meletius* in a *Festschrift* dedicated to his Leiden colleague J.J. Woltjer. When during the course of the year 1990 plans were developed to add appropriate lustre to Posthumus Meyjes' imminent retirement, it was an obvious choice to honour him as the discoverer of Grotius' earliest theological work and the zealous champion of the study of Grotius' theological œuvre by organizing a symposium dedicated to Hugo Grotius as a theologian.

Prominent Grotius specialists from home and abroad gladly participated in this colloquium, which was held on 3, 4 and 5 June 1992 in Leiden and Haarlem. It was decided to divide the colloquium into two parts: the first two days were styled as a closed workshop, while on the last day a wide audience of interested scholars and laymen heard lectures of a more general character. Posthumus Meyjes' valedictory lecture – not published here – was held on the afternoon of June 5 and constituted the pinnacle of these extremely fruitful days of συμφιλολογεῖν and συνθεολογεῖν, during which the *amicitia Grotianorum* also received new impulses.

In this volume, we have divided the final versions of the lectures into three categories, according to their subject: individual works; Grotius' theological activities against the background of his period; the influence of Grotius' theology on later centuries. For the greater part, this classification corresponds with the programme of the symposium. In the first section all Grotius' major theological works except *De satisfactione* are discussed: *Meletius*, *De imperio*, *De veritate*, and the *Annotationes* on the Old and New Testaments. The second category contains studies on Grotius' relationship with important spiritual movements and with some of their representatives set against the backdrop of the period. There are studies of Grotius' relationship with Erasmus, his polemics with the orthodox Calvinist Leiden professor and Hague court chaplain André Rivet, his views on scholarly and religious developments in contemporary France, and finally his opinions on Jews and Judaism. Four lectures on the reception of Grotius' theological thought in the 17th and 18th centuries in Great Britain, Switzerland and the Netherlands, constitute the third section. An appendix lists the titles of the most important contributions from the last 150 years on the theme 'Grotius as a theologian.'

The organization of the conference and the publication of this volume were made possible by grants from the Royal Netherlands Academy of Arts and Sciences, the Leiden University Trust (Leids Universiteitsfonds), which also made available the attractive ambiance of the Snouck Hurgronje House, the Faculty of Divinity of Leiden University, the M.A.O.C. Gravin van Bylandt Foundation, the Dr. C. Louise Thijssen-Schoute Foundation and the National Committee for the Commemoration of Grotius' Birth in 1983. The editors of the volume are likewise much indebted to the director of the "Constantijn Huygens Institute for text editions and intellectual history" of the Royal Netherlands Academy of Arts and Sciences, Professor H.T.M. van Vliet, to the past and present members of the supervising committee for the edition of Grotius' theological works, professors J. van den Berg, J.A.H. Bots, H.J. de Jonge, E.J. Kuiper and G.H.M. Posthumus Meyjes, as well as to Dr. Corry M. Ridderikhoff and Dr. Harm-Jan van Dam, staff members of the Grotius Department of the Constantijn Huygens Institute.

Last but not least, we extend our gratitude to Professor Heiko A. Oberman for his willingness to include this book in his prestigious series 'Studies in the History of Christian Thought'. We are extremely gratified that this volume has found a place in the same series in which Posthumus Meyjes' edition of the *Meletius* was published in 1988.

The Hague   Henk J.M. Nellen
June 14, 1993   Edwin Rabbie

ABBREVIATIONS

ASD	*Opera omnia Desiderii Erasmi Roterodami*, Amsterdam 1969–...
BG	JACOB TER MEULEN – P.J.J. DIERMANSE, *Bibliographie des écrits imprimés de Hugo Grotius*, La Haye 1950
BHR	*Bibliothèque d'Humanisme et Renaissance*
BsG	JACOB TER MEULEN – P.J.J. DIERMANSE, *Bibliographie des écrits sur Hugo Grotius imprimés au XVIIe siècle*, La Haye 1961
BW	*Briefwisseling van Hugo Grotius*, ed. P.C. MOLHUYSEN, B.L. MEULENBROEK, P.P. WITKAM, H.J.M. NELLEN, C.M. RIDDERIKHOFF, 14 vols. to date (1597–1643), 's-Gravenhage 1928–... [Rijks Geschiedkundige Publicatiën, Grote Serie] [*BG* no. 1212]
CWE	*Collected Works of Erasmus*, Toronto 1974–...
DNB	*The Dictionary of National Biography*, 63 vols., London 1885–1900
Ep.	*Opus epistolarum Des. Erasmi Roterodami*, ed. P.S. ALLEN, H.M. ALLEN, H.W. GARROD, 12 vols., Oxford 1906–58
EQ	*Hugonis Grotii ... Epistolae Quotquot reperiri potuerunt ...*, Amstelodami 1687 [*BG* no. 1210]
LB	*Desiderii Erasmi Roterodami Opera omnia*, ed. J. CLERICUS, 10 vols., Leiden 1703–06 (facsimile-reprint Hildesheim 1961–62)
NAKG	*Nederlands(ch) Archief voor Kerkgeschiedenis*
OTh	*Hugonis Grotii Opera omnia theologica, in tres tomos divisa ...*, Amstelædami 1679 [*BG* no. 919] (facsimile-reprint Stuttgart – Bad Cannstatt 1972)
TRE	*Theologische Realenzyklopädie*, ed. G. Müller [et al.], Berlin – New York 1977–...
TvG	*Tijdschrift voor Geschiedenis*
UL	University Library

PART ONE

INDIVIDUAL WORKS

SOME REMARKS ON GROTIUS' *EXCERPTA THEOLOGICA*, ESPECIALLY CONCERNING HIS *MELETIUS*[1]

GUILLAUME H.M. POSTHUMUS MEYJES
(Leiden)

INTRODUCTION

The purpose of this contribution is to convey something of my acquaintance and experience with the manuscripts of Grotius, thereby giving special attention to his so-called *excerpta theologica*. I would like to begin with some general observations on this subject and then I will attempt to answer the following question: What makes this material so special with regard to Grotius' earliest theological treatise, his *Meletius* of 1611?

However, before I begin I would like to stress the fact that my knowledge of the *excerpta* is modest and that I do not claim to have found the proper approach to it. I do not mean this to be regarded as a feeble excuse, as, in this particular case, it was not due to lack of diligence on my part. For in the course of many years I have spent hours and hours studying this material. Again and again I rushed in to conquer it, but to say I feel at all familiar, let alone at ease with its contents would be a gross overstatement.

EXCERPTA THEOLOGICA

All his life Grotius wrote books. To prepare himself for this, he kept in constant communication with learned friends of the Republic of Letters, with whom he had conversations or corresponded about learned subjects, thereby exchanging tips and useful material. Furthermore, he bought, borrowed and read books. In order to remember all he read he developed a habit, from quite an early age, of jotting down striking passages and pronouncements of the ancient philosophers, historians, church fathers, ecclesiastical councils, etc. This he did in the form of loose notes of which he made collections – usually written on folio sheets and then put in thematic order. In this way he built up a personal system of scholarly docu-

---

[1] This article is meant to redeem the promise I made at the end of the preface (p. XIII) of my edition of HUGO GROTIUS, *Meletius sive de iis quae inter christianos conveniunt epistola*. Critical edition with Translation, Commentary and Introduction, Leiden / New York / København / Köln 1988 [= Studies in the History of Christian Thought, 40] (= GROTIUS, *Meletius*).

mentation, which was exclusively meant for his own use, i.e. for the works he intended to write. The notes he made for this purpose, from time to time intermingled with personal annotations and remarks, were inserted into dossiers which he entitled *excerpta theologica*. These he used both for the composition of his treatises pertaining to some actual situation, such as the *Pietas Ordinum*, and for publications of a more systematic theological nature, such as *Meletius* and *De veritate*, for his famous *Annotationes ad Vetus et Novum Testamentum*, etc.

After his death, most of these dossiers came into the hands of members of his family, of professors of the Amsterdam Remonstrant Seminary, all great admirers of his, who kept these treasures very carefully. During Grotius' lifetime or at a later date the excerpts were often bound together in bulky volumes of hundreds of pages. All this material is still available to us. For the main part these papers can be found in the Municipal Library of Rotterdam and in the University Library of Amsterdam, where they were deposited by the Remonstrant Church in the last century.

It is impossible to give here a more precise survey of the character and extent of all this material. It is not necessary either, as for some years now there is a useful inventory at our disposal, compiled by Arthur Eyffinger, at the time working at the Grotius Institute in The Hague. It is entitled *The manuscript inheritance of Hugo Grotius*.[2] This is a provisional publication in typescript which, rightly so, was not brought on the market. It is marred by countless imperfections and was obviously done in a hurry. An untidy piece of work – the pages are not numbered and so on. However, even in its present very imperfect state, it provides invaluable service to those especially interested in the theological excerpts, as many of its pages are devoted to a survey of them. Besides this, the inventory offers a useful concise survey of what has happened to Grotius literary heritage throughout the centuries.

Eyffinger's primary aim in preparing this inventory was to obtain a survey of Grotius' theological documents bequeathed to us. He was induced to do so by the decision of the 'Grotius Commission' to re-publish Grotius' smaller theological works, now that the Correspondence (*Briefwisseling*) and the *Poemata* were nearing completion. A list of priorities was made, the first fruit of which we have

---

[2] A. EYFFINGER, *De handschriftelijke nalatenschap van Hugo de Groot. Inventaris van de papieren in Nederlandse openbare collecties*, Den Haag 1985. ("*The manuscript inheritance of Hugo Grotius. Inventory of the papers in Dutch Public Collections*").

already been handed some time ago: Edwin Rabbie's admirable and beautiful edition of Grotius' *De satisfactione*,[3] which will be followed in the near future by critical editions of the *Pietas Ordinum* and of *De imperio summarum potestatum circa sacra*.

Although for many years insiders knew that in the aforementioned libraries of Rotterdam and Amsterdam dossiers were available containing Grotius' theological excerpts, I know of no one who has paid special attention to them. No publications on the subject were ever written. Rogge, Molhuysen and other Grotius specialists have more than once handled the volumes, but they only did so for other purposes. They hoped to find letters in them or biographical data. They did not study the documents for their own sake. Thus the excerpts remain untrodden terrain.

Researchers planning to reconnoiter this terrain will encounter at least two obstacles, and at least one specific peculiarity inherent to Grotius. What then are these obstacles?

OBSTACLES

1. The excerpts may be considered as a sort of semimanufactured products, made by an extremely intelligent and diligent man, but a man who put his notes to paper in a notoriously difficult, hastily written, crabbed script. My experience is that about thirty to forty percent of his notes can be deciphered without too much difficulty, but many hours are needed – as well as the very necessary assistance of the kind specialists of the Grotius Institute! – to reach a more acceptable percentage and to discover precisely what was written. It is this difficult handwriting that makes one think twice before embarking on a transcription attempt, for what guarantee has one that the effort is worth the trouble? As a matter of fact this concerns what lawyers refer to as a 'buy by chance' – an enterprise with at least a fifty percent risk. It could produce something interesting, but may just as well leave you empty-handed. Obviously such a circumstance does not encourage one to commence this work with enthusiasm!

2. The fact that as a rule the excerpts are undated forms a considerable second obstacle for the researcher. In the case of an

---

[3] HUGO GROTIUS, *Defensio fidei catholicae de satisfactione Christi adversus Faustum Socinum Senensem*, edited, with an introduction and notes by EDWIN RABBIE, with an English translation by HOTZE MULDER, Assen – Maastricht 1990 [= HUGO GROTIUS, *Opera Theologica* edited by the Grotius Institute of the Royal Netherlands Academy of Arts and Sciences, vol. I], (= GROTIUS, *De satisfactione*).

excerpt of a book the year of its publication offers some indication
– at least if it appeared during Grotius' lifetime and not before. Yet
even such a date is of limited value, for how does one know whether he read the book immediately after its publication? He could also have done so many years later. If no supplementary evidence is
available, from his letters, for instance, or from his own works or
anywhere else, the only certainty one has is the *terminus post quem* of
the publication of the book concerned.

With older 16th-century editions consulted by him – and there
were a good many of them – another problem arises, due to the
fact that although he mostly indicated the pages or the chapters of
the work he consulted, he very often omitted to add which edition
he used. In this case too, one is in need of supplementary information.

PECULIARITY OF GROTIUS' EXCERPTA

One peculiarity, although not an obstacle, of Grotius' *excerpta* is that
he made them in quite a different way than most people nowadays
do. When we make an excerpt of a book we try to convert, in our
own words, as briefly and concisely as possible, the thoughts of the
author, as found in the chapters of the book he wrote. For us the
ideas of the author are of primary importance. This was not the
case with Grotius, for he was not so much interested in the train of
thought of the authors he read, but rather in the basis of their rea-
soning process, in other words in the arguments they used. His
attention was entirely focused on that. In other words: it is not primarily the ideas of the authors in question which his notes present,
but rather the testimonial evidence, i.e. statements and arguments,
no matter whether they are for or against. To put it more bluntly:
Grotius handled the intellectual products of others in a very selfish,
not to say egocentric, way. The authors he consulted were primarily regarded and used by him as deliverers of building stones for his
own works. This is exactly what the excerpts show us, time and
again.

Thus, I think, we come in touch here with a characteristic peculiarity of Grotius: in all his scholarly activities he was above all a
typical pleader and apologist. In another context I already stressed
this point[4] and did not fail to mention the excellent characterization
provided by the Geneva law-historian, our friend Haggenmacher,

---

[4] GROTIUS, *Meletius*, Introduction, p. 62.

who remarks: "... la démarche grotienne est avant tout celle d'un avocat... Avocat, il le reste en verité jusque dans ses exposés en apparence les plus théoriques, les plus détachés des questions concrètes: toujours il défend une cause, même si c'est celle du genre humain; toujours il plaide... Toutes ses oeuvres spéculatives, qu'elles soient du droit ou de la théologie, présentent une forte dimension pratique, apologétique."[5] I suspect that every Grotius specialist will agree with this excellent characterization.

How to explore the excerpta?

The two obstacles the researcher encounters while exploring the excerpts, i.e. the difficult script and the omission of dates, raise the question on how best to penetrate this jungle in order to pick the fruits in the end. In connection with this I should like to share with you one of my experiences.

When in September 1987 I had completed the manuscript of Grotius' *Meletius* and had taken it to Brill's in Leiden, I suggested to a student of mine, who at the time had just started to work on Grotius' *De veritate*,[6] to accompany me on a day trip to Amsterdam in order to have a look at the *Grotiana* deposited in the University Library. We asked for various Grotius' manuscripts including, amongst others, a bulky volume of the *excerpta*.[7] Leafing through it I was struck by a few Greek and Latin terms and citations, written down on a certain page, which we had opened haphazardly. The terms and citations in question were relatively easy to read for I knew them well, since Grotius had made use of them in his *Meletius*, with which at the time I was very familiar. My attention was alerted, and excitedly and hastily I tried to decipher what else he had written on the same page. To cut a long story short, this particular page and also a few others surrounding it, appeared to be entirely filled with notes pertaining to the *Meletius*. Serendipity had favoured us – we had found what was apparently a preliminary study of Grotius' first theological work.

Why do I mention this? Because I think that by this experience a strategy has been handed to us, as to how to delve into this dif-

---

[5] Peter Haggenmacher in a book-review in *Grotiana* NS 6 (1985), p. 49.

[6] In the meantime the work has been finished: Jan-Paul Heering, *Hugo de Groot als apologeet van de christelijke godsdienst*, diss. Leiden, 's-Gravenhage 1992. The book will be translated into English and appear in the series *Studies in the History of Christian Thought*, ed. by Heiko A. Oberman (Brill, Leiden).

[7] Amsterdam UL, *Remonstrant Collection*, shelf-mark III C 4.

ficult, almost inaccessible material. For the researcher who peruses the excerpts a thorough knowledge of one or more of Grotius' theological works is, it seems to me, an absolute necessity. He must know them by heart as it were, because only in that case he will be able to recognize related material in the excerpts, and so succeed in penetrating this jungle. In my opinion, therefore, the exploitation of this material must be done by those who are familiar with one or more parts of Grotius' oeuvre. I especially have in mind those scholars who prepare critical editions of his works – in which case Edwin Rabbie once more springs to mind. He was, as far as I know, the first scholar who, just because he had a solid knowledge of Grotius' *De satisfactione*, was able to recognize related material in the excerpts and so make use of it for his edition.[8] Those who lack such familiarity with Grotius' oeuvre would be ill advised to explore the dense jungle of the *excerpta*. They would almost immediately lose their way and close the volumes in utter bewilderment, to return home without booty but with a heavy load of frustration!

EXCERPTA CONCERNING MELETIUS

After these more general remarks on Grotius' theological excerpts I would like to conclude briefly with an estimation of the significance and value of this material as far as the *Meletius* is concerned. I will confine myself primarily to the most important issues and concentrate in particular on Grotius' notes on folio-pages 336r and 336v of the Amsterdam manuscript.[9] These pages contain, I think, what may be considered a sketch, a scheme, or a sort of scholastic skeleton, revealing to us what he had in his mind when he planned the book that we know now as his *Meletius*. In order to give an impression of the nature of this material I start by reproducing fol. 336r and 336v in facsimile and in transcription.

---

[8] GROTIUS, *De satisfactione*, pp. 51ff.
[9] Amsterdam UL, *Remonstrant Collection*, shelf-mark III C 4.

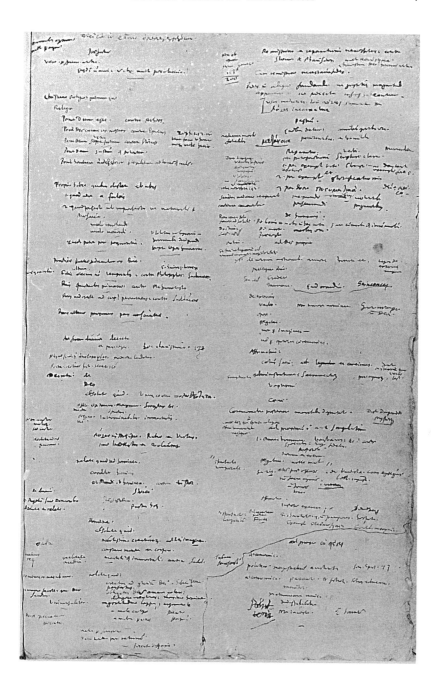

(facsimile of *Remonstrant Collection*, shelf-mark III C 4 fol. 336r)

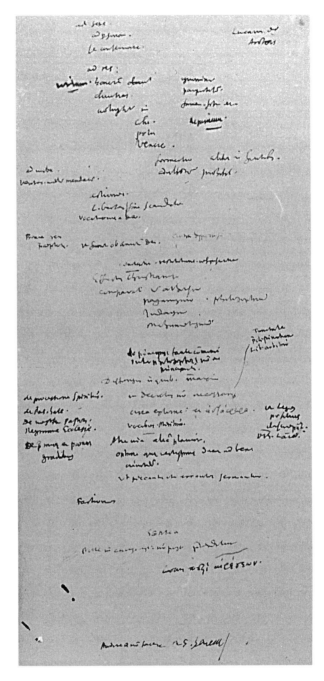

(facsimile of *Remonstrant Collection.* shelf-mark III C 4 fol. 336v)

As can be seen, it is rather a messy piece that cannot easily be deciphered. It is clearly visible that Grotius at first wrote down his notes in columns and that he added new notes afterwards, which he scribbled between the lines and in the margins. As these interlinear and marginal additions are often written in a still smaller spidery handwriting, they are very difficult to transcribe. This does not mean, however, that the rest is always totally clear. The opposite is true, and I must honestly confess that my attempts at transcription often ended in capitulation. One can spend hours looking at a given term, a reference, even a complete sentence, without finding any solution but the frustrating '*non liquet*,' or '*illegible.*'

In stead of burdening the transcription with '*non liquets*,' I simply left out, without further comment, the words or sentences I was not able to decipher. So it is not an integral transcription which is given. It shows only that of which I am more or less certain. Moreover, I added to the transcription, between brackets, Arabic and roman figures, by which I refer to the chapters and paragraphs of my edition of the *Meletius*.

(fol. 336r col. a)

περὶ τῶν ἐν χριστιανοῖς ὁμολογουμένων
Praefatio

[I]   Christiana religio: primum quae

       Religio

    [6]   Ponit Deum esse: contra atheos

    [8]   Ponit Deum curare res nostras: contra Epicurum

    [7]   Ponit Deum extra fatum: contra Stoicos

    [11]   Ponit Deum iustum et potentem

    [9]   Ponit hominem αὐτεξούσιον et flexibilem ad bonum
                                           et malum

[12] Propria habet quibus distat ab aliis

      1. quod abest a falsis

      2. quod perfecta ab imperfectis, ut naturalis
                                     et Mosaïca

vinculo recolendi

vinculo monendi   utilitas religionis

quod patet per sequentia   in hominibus dirigendis
                                                    super leges humanas

[II] ───

[13]   Practicae scientiae deducuntur ex fine

ultimus
[18] finis aeternus, non temporalis, contra philoso-
                                    phos ethnicos pluresque: Sadducaeos

[16] finis spiritualis: contra Mahumetistas

[18] finis indirecte ad corpus pertinens: contra
                                                            Sadducaeos

finis ulterior proximus pars conscientiae

[III] ───

[19] Ad finem ducunt decreta   haec clarissimae 172
             et praecepta
Aliquid scimus per ἀκαταληψίαν   modestia
                                                                  laudatur

[20]   Scita   Seneca 156

        Decreta: de
                Deo
                absolute quid. Unus: contra

[21] Affirmantia.   Optimus. Maximus. Simplex etc.
                                                        Spiritus

        Negantia.   Interminabilis. Immortalis

[23] Non auctor malorum sed rector

        [22]   λόγος καὶ πνεῦμα Ratio et virtus
                        sive Intellectus et Voluntas

                        relate quid ad hominem

        [28]   conditor hominum
                        et mundi ob hominem. contra Histor.
                                                Stoici

[26] De divinis
de Angelis sive Daemonibus
absolute et relate

   [29] Rectorem
                    iustus hominibus

   [30] Homine
          absolute quid
          nobilissima creaturarum. ad Dei imaginem
          constans mente et corpore
          mortali et immortali. contra Sadd.

   [31] πάθη
       dominus   qualitate
       rerum   media

   [33] colere quid

      creatus ad gloriam Dei

      perfectus

      diligere creaturas: maxime hominem

 [34] ingratitudine lapsus   argumenta

   [37] a mole culpae

   [38] a mole poenae

(fol. 336r col. b)

[42] Remissionis et reparationis necessitatem.
      contra Stoicos et Pharisaeos καύχημα
                     honestum Dei homine utitur
[43] cum remissione necessaria fides

[44] fides in aliquo fundando ut iustitiae magnitudo
      appareat et ne peccata (levia?) habeantur

[47] usus mediatoris τοῦ υἱοῦ   [54] sapientia Dei

   [51]   incarnatus

redimere   passus

   [50] μετάνοια   quibus detur   omnibus gentibus
                         paenitentibus et humilibus

reparatur   miracula

verbi
[54] Dion. Longinus   [51] per patefactionem Scripturae
    Veritas
    Antiquitas
    consensus
    Utilitas   [56]   1. per exemplum vitae Christi
    Simplicitas
    gratia necessaria   2. per exemplum eius glorificationis

        [57]   3. per dona πνευματικά   Θεία μοίρα

Sanitas remedium reciperet   incipiendi omnibus volentibus
                            perseverandi   pugnantibus

[IV] _____

Bona opera sola   [58]   De humanis
facere ad salutem

                  De bonis et malis in hac vita

Doctrina   de morte   morbus

     [59]   Praecepta

     [60]   Ad Deum proprie

               1. de internis actionibus animae   [61] leges de
                                          externae
                                          maxime
               praecipue duo

               Sen. 158 Credere
                     Invocare   quid orandum

     [63]   De externis

               verbo   non temere nominare   Gentes
                                        iurasse in deos

     [64]   non per operosas caeremonias

     Affirmative:

     [65]   coetus sacri: conciones   sunt
                                           mysteria sine
                                           verbo
                                         Lact.

        administrationes sacramentorum praecipuorum

Simplicitas
[65] baptismi
[66] caenae

[67] Caeremoniales posteriores mortalibus dignitate   Dist. Diogen.

de mysteriis

[68] ad proximos: aut singulatim

[69] 1. omnes homines.   barbaros: vid. contra Aristotelem

Interna et externa

spirituale   [70] negative. nolle malum
temporale

Sen. 219.   etiam post offensum – de vindicta   locus egregius

non facere iniuriam   nolle iniustitiam

affirmative

iustitiam exercere

et charitatem   pauperes   hospites

Exempla eleemosynes   Gentilibus incognita

ad proximos

[74] Tribuni   politeia   magistratuum auctoritas   Sen. ep. 73
sacrosancti

[71] oeconomica   [72] parentum et filiorum   filios educare
maritos

[73] matrimonium unicum
indissolubile
non iniuste   cf. Socr.

(fol. 336v)

[75]   ad sese

ad personam   Lucanus ad
Arctos

se conservare

[77]   ad res

[76]   vitam   honorem ignominiam

[78]   divitias   paupertatem

[79]   voluptates in   famem   sitim etc.

               cibo   [80]   ieiunium

               potu

               Venere

               fornicatio   aliter in gentibus

               [81] adulterium prohibetur

[83] ad verba

Veritas: nullum mendacium

      [82]   actiones

      Libertas sine scandalo

      Vocationes a Deo

[84]   servare rem
        praeceptam   et servant ob amorem Dei

      [88]   Effectus Christianismi
                  comparati cum Atheismo
                  paganismo philosophorum
                  Iudaismo
                  Mahumetismo

          [89]   De praeceptis

de processione Spiritus   Dissensus in quibus maxime   Trinitate
de Paschate   in decretis non necessariis   praedestinatione
de necessitate paparum in   circa externe et $\dot{\alpha}\delta\iota\dot{\alpha}\varphi o\rho\alpha$ libero arbitrio
Regimine Ecclesiae   vocibus   et legibus

                                       [90] vid. Laced.

de praemiorum et poenarum   Alia via alia planior
gradibus   optima quae rectissime ducit ad bene
                            vivendum
                     ut peccantes et errantes servantur

               Factiones

          Seneca

Nolle in causa est: non posse praetenditur [57]

[91] Locus περὶ αἱρέσεως

Audire et non facere. Seneca 25

What can be drawn from a comparison between the actual text of the *Meletius* and the notes in the excerpts referring to it?

1. The most striking discovery in such a comparison is that not only the overall plan of the *Meletius*, but also its argument are almost completely in accordance with the concept Grotius had in mind from the beginning. This becomes clear if one pays attention to the roman and Arabic figures in the transcription. These show that he stuck rigorously to the division of the chapters, and, to a great extent, to the division of the paragraphs.

This in itself is not a surprising or new discovery, for he who is but superficially acquainted with Grotius, knows that his knowledge of many fields was not only unparalleled, but that he was also a great master in classifying, arranging and ... manipulating this knowledge. Yes, perhaps one should even say that the greatest strength of his works lies in their very construction, composition and architecture. In this connection I would like to quote Huizinga, who, speaking about the difference between Erasmus and Grotius, observes: "Erasmus goes and sheds light; Grotius stands and produces order."[10] Well, this judgment is but confirmed when one compares the original plan of the *Meletius* with its final shape.

2. What one misses in the excerpts is any allusion to the person of the Greek Patriarch Meletios, to whom Grotius refers in the introduction as well as in the epilogue of the *Meletius*. The excerpts contain a few remarks on what he intended to write in his introduction (*praefatio*), but as far as these phrases are readable, they seem to contain nothing which was used in the final text of his book.

The crabbed notes in the excerpts concerning the epilogue seem to differ from the passage with which he actually ended his *Meletius*. One gets the impression from these notes that initially he had a more severe message in mind for his readers, instead of the impres-

---

[10] J. HUIZINGA, "Hugo de Groot en zijn eeuw," in *Verzamelde Werken* II, Haarlem 1948, pp. 389–403 (394): "Erasmus verspreidt, al gaande, licht; Grotius schept, al staande, orde."

sive irenical exhortation with which the *Meletius* actually ends. One can only guess what the reason of this change might have been. Maybe the Hague Conference (May 1611), which I suggested as a probable reason for the composition of his book,[11] can serve as an explanation for this change. This would imply, however, that he prepared his notes before that event took place. In that case he started working on the *Meletius* somewhat earlier than I suggested in the introduction to my edition.

3. More clearly than his letters, his poetry, and even his theological works, the excerpts show that to Grotius the dogma of Trinity as well as problems concerning free will and predestination were *adiaphora*, and as such could never be a serious reason for church-separation.[12] In the text of his *Meletius*, as well in his relevant correspondence with Walaeus in particular, Grotius expresses himself much less clearly.[13]

4. The folio-pages we discussed so far form part of a bundle of pages containing many other data which equally can be related to the *Meletius*.[14] These pages are fully packed with notes, 'Lesefrüchte,' taken mainly from older historical works, dating from what Grotius and his contemporaries considered to have been the Golden Age of Christianity: Augustine's *De civitate*,[15] Salvian's *De gubernatione Dei*, Ammianus Marcellinus, the *Historia Augusta*, as well as the history of the Roman Empire written by Zosimos,[16] a less well-known author who lived about 500 and whose work may be considered an anti-Christian counterpart of Augustine's *De civitate*.

From what Grotius wrote down in the excerpts it becomes clear that he was not so much interested in what these authors reported about Roman history as such, as well in their specific remarks about the Christian religion in general, and its unsurpassed ethical values in particular.[17] As a matter of fact he collected many citations from them – especially the positive ones –, which he afterwards inserted in his *Meletius*. In doing so his obvious intention was to show, firstly, how peacefully the adherents of early Christianity

---

[11] Grotius, *Meletius*, Introduction, p. 13.

[12] Cf. the transcription given above [89].

[13] Cf. Grotius, *Meletius*, pp. 53–55, 144–45 (23.40–43 *tria ... impartibilem*).

[14] In some way or another the following pages of the ms. in question (III C 4) contain material related to the *Meletius*: fol. 325r-v; 326v; 335r-v; 336r-v; 337r-v; 338r-v.

[15] III C 4 fol. 337r.

[16] III C 4 fol. 325r&v, 326v.

[17] III C 4 fol. 335r contains Grotius' annotations on the positive 'effectus christianismi' as compared to pagan religion. Cf. *Mel.* 88.

had lived together and, secondly, how deeply impressed even non-Christian authors had been by the values propagated and represented by this religion. Here again he reveals himself very clearly as a pleader and apologist above all.

Conclusion

1. It seems worthwhile to pay more attention to Grotius' theological excerpts than has been done until now, for this manuscript material may give us a better insight in his method, in the sources he consulted, in his principles of selection and – last but not least – in the way he made use of this material for his own works.

2. Because of the complicated nature of the excerpts – undated as they generally are and written in a very difficult handwriting, etc. – the study and exploitation of this material should be undertaken by specialists only, not by beginners.

3. The most promising way to penetrate and evaluate the excerpts seems to be by 'retroacting.' By this I mean that it is advisable to take the point of departure in one of Grotius' published works, to make oneself profoundly familiar with it and only after that to consult the volumes containing his excerpts. For fruitful discoveries in the jungle of Grotius' theological excerpts will happen only to those who have obtained a thorough knowledge of the work in question.

4. I would not plead for a separate publication of Grotius' excerpts. It seems preferable that future editors of his theological treatises include the results of their investigations of the excerpts into the editions they will prepare.

DE IMPERIO SUMMARUM POTESTATUM CIRCA SACRA*

HARM-JAN VAN DAM
(The Hague)

De Imperio Summarum Potestatum circa Sacra was the last work which Grotius completed before his arrest in August 1618.[1] Its subject, the relations between the religious and the secular authorities, can hardly be called original, but it was highly topical: Grotius had even cherished hopes that publication of this book would turn the tide and bring back peace to church and state. Eventually it was published in 1647, two years after his death; but for a correct assessment of it we must turn our eye to the last years of the Twelve Year Truce.[2]

In this paper I begin by giving some idea of the scope and aims of *De Imperio*. Then I shall go into its genesis, to end by touching on one specific problem, the changes which Grotius made in his text in the three months between December 1616 and April 1617. Since it has proved possible to pinpoint a number of modifications in the manuscript to a relatively short period of time, we may perhaps somewhat extend our knowledge of Grotius' way of composing, see which books he consulted at that exact time, and note the influence of contemporary politics. At the same time this may offer some more insight into the ideological background of the book.

---

* I wish to thank my colleagues Henk Nellen, Edwin Rabbie and Corry Ridderikhoff for critically reading an earlier version of this paper.

[1] The following abbreviation will be used throughout: *De Imperio*: H.GROTIUS *De Imperio Summarum Potestatum circa Sacra*, Lutetiae Parisiorum 1647 etc.: *BG* nos. 894–904. References to page, column and line are to *OTh* III.

[2] On *De Imperio* in general, see: G. SOLARI, *Il "jus circa sacra" nell'eta' e nella dottrina di Ugone Grozio*, Studi storici di filosofia del diritto, Torino 1949, pp. 25–71 [= Studi filosofico-giuridici dedicati a G. del Vecchio, Modena 1931, II pp. 369–433 = La filosofia politica, Bari 1974, I pp. 65 ff.], A.C.J. DE VRANKRIJKER, *De Staatsleer van Hugo de Groot en zijn Nederlandsche tijdgenoten*, Nijmegen/Utrecht 1937, pp. 107–09, D. NOBBS, *Theocracy and Toleration. A study of disputes in Dutch Calvinism from 1600 to 1650*, Cambridge 1938, esp. pp. 59–91, J. BOHATEC, "Das Territorial- und Kollegialsystem in der holländischen Publizistik," *Zeitschrift der Savigny-Stiftung für Rechtsgeschichte* 66, Kanon. Abt. 35 (1948), pp. 64–106, E. CONRING, *Kirche und Staat nach der Lehre der niederländischen Calvinisten in der ersten Hälfte des 17. Jahrhunderts*, Neukirchen-Vluyn 1965, esp. pp. 38–41, F. DE MICHELIS, *Le origini storiche e culturali del pensiero di Ugo Grozio*, Firenze 1967, Ch. 4 (offering a good analysis of the historical, philosophical and cultural background), esp. pp. 155–58, A. CASPANI, "Il De Imperio summarum potestatum circa sacra di Grozio," *Rivista di Filosofia Neo-scolastica* 79 (1987), pp. 218–49, 382–419. A summary in C. BRANDT – A. VAN CATTENBURGH *Historie van het leven des heeren Huig de Groot...*, Dordrecht – Amsterdam 1727, pp. 94–96. I am preparing a critical edition with commentary of *De Imperio*.

I

De Imperio was by no means Grotius' first work on ecclesiastical politics: he worked at it after finishing his *Ordinum Pietas*, published in October 1613 and the *Decretum pro pace ecclesiarum* composed in late 1613 and early 1614.[3] These three share many topics and especially quotations, but there are important differences. *Ordinum Pietas* is in fact – with all due reverence – a pamphlet: it is directed against an opponent, the Calvinist Franeker professor Lubbertus; it was ordered by Grotius' masters the States of Holland, and thus written for the occasion – though Grotius may already have had plans for such a book.[4] Of its twenty-seven pages in *OTh* only two thirds treat of church government and then mainly of two subjects: synods and offices. Its tone is polemical and acrimonious, even in the second impression where it is considerably watered down. The reactions, however, remained violent.[5] It might be said that all Grotius' next works until his arrest in 1618 form a vain attempt to repair the damage done by this book. The *Decretum*, on the other hand, is an official edict of the States, drawn up by Grotius, imposing moderation and toleration on the ministry – in vain, as it happened. It fills just one page in *OTh*, followed by thirty-one pages of quotations, mainly dealing with the Five Remonstrant Articles. It might be compared to a modern departmental memorandum, underpinned, not financially, as we would do, but verbally. Both these works (and a number of others of the years 1614–18[6]) were composed by Gro-

---

[3] *Ordinum Pietas*: *BG* nos. 817–24, in *OTh* III pp. 98–125. The *Decretum*: *BG* nos. 826–38, in *OTh* III p. 141. For the dates, cf. *BG* p. 391 Rem. 3, *BW* I p. 293 n. 2.

[4] See E. RABBIE on *Ordinum Pietas* in the *Acta of the International Neo-Latin Congress, held in Copenhagen 1991*. On this work also DE MICHELIS, *Le origini*, pp. 136 ff., C. VAN DER WOUDE, *Hugo Grotius en zijn "Pietas Ordinum Hollandiae ac Westfrisiae vindicata"*, Kampen 1961.

[5] E.g. Ubbo Emmius, see H. BRUGMANS (ed.), *Die Briefwechsel des Ubbo Emmius*, 2 vols, Aurich – 's-Gravenhage 1911–23, II pp. 166–67, 169, 171. See also note 9.

[6] Grotius drew up two advices for the magistrates of Goes on deposing two ministers, in his official capacity, in August 1613 (not in *BG*, published in *Archief. Vroegere en latere mededeelingen, voornamelijk in betrekking tot Zeeland* 7, 1869, pp. 222–26, cf. *ibid.* 5, 1863, pp. 97–100). In late 1614 he published his anonymous *Bona Fides Sibrandi Lubberti*, a pamphlet against Lubbertus' attack on *Ordinum Pietas*: *BG* nos. 839–43. Grotius had begun a Latin justification of the *Decretum* in 1614 or 1615, which was first published in *OTh* (pp. 195–200, *BG* nos. 910, 910A). In early December of 1615 he wrote a long letter on religious affairs to Gideon van Boetzelaer, the Dutch Ambassador in Paris, in reaction to a work by Pierre Dumoulin; its final part treats the role of the magistracy: *BW* I 438, esp. pp. 444–48, cf. *BG* no. 908. On April 23 of 1616 he officially addressed the Amsterdam magistrates to press them to obey the *Decretum*: *BG* nos. 844–54. In the same year he drew up a statute for the Rotterdam magistrates prohibiting the formation of new congrega-

tius in his official quality, first as Attorney General of Holland, then as a member of the Committee of Counsellors.

De Imperio, however, is a different matter. The first feature striking the reader (and especially the editor-to-be) is its size: it is Grotius' longest theological work after *De Veritate*, and, of course, the *Annotationes*, numbering 85 pages (without the index) in *OTh*. Whether it *is* a theological work is another question. Secondly, it is clearly meant to be a fairly comprehensive book on church government. The titles of its 12 chapters, given by Grotius himself, may give some impression:[7] I. That Authority about sacred things belongs to the highest powers. II. That this authority and the sacred function are distinct [that is to say that all functions are subsidiary to the highest power]. These two chapters form, as Grotius says, the *generalis tractatio*. III. Of the agreement of things sacred and secular as to the powers over them [that is to say that *summum imperium* concerns both matters sacred and profane, and why]. IV. Objections against the powers [that is against their power in sacred matters] answered. Of the judgment [*iudicium*] of the higher powers in sacred things. VI The manner of using this authority rightly. VII. Concerning synods, or councils. VIII Of legislation about sacred things. IX Of jurisdiction ecclesiastical. X. Of the election of pastors. XI. Concerning offices not always necessary [that is all except priests/ministers, whose sole task is preaching and administering the sacraments]. XII. Of substitution and delegation [that is the way in which minor authority may rest with the lower powers]. It is to be noted that there is hardly a word on dogma or belief in the book; in *Ordinum Pietas* and in most other works of the time by Grotius the two main issues of the religious troubles, that is to say predestination and ecclesiastical government, are treated together.

The text of *De Imperio* was finished in its final draft in 1617, but the book was not published during Grotius' lifetime. I will return to the reasons for that. It has no introduction, and Grotius probably never composed one. So his intentions must be reconstructed as

---

tions ("Schielandse keur": BRANDT-CATTENBURGH, *Historie van het leven*, p. 82). The so-called "scherpe resolutie" of the Holland Estates (August 4, 1617) and its Justification of 1618 have been drawn up by Grotius (*BG* no. 861). He also collaborated on the declaration of August 5, 1617, where the States of Holland defended their attitude in the religious troubles (*BG* nos. 855–60) and on a similar declaration of the Haarlem magistrates of January 1618 (*BG* no. 869). It looks as if Grotius also had a part in Barlaeus' *Epistola Ecclesiastarum, Quos in Belgio Remonstrantes vocant...*, Leiden 1617 (Knuttel no. 2434). Grotius himself mentions some more official works in his *Memorie van mijne intentien* (see note 8), pp. 1–6.

[7] The titles are quoted after the English translation by Clement Barksdale, London 1651, see *BG* no. 903 and note 78.

best we can from the letters and other documents, and from the text itself. Shortly after his arrival in Loevestein for life imprisonment, as it then seemed, Grotius prepared a written justification of his acts and opinions. In it he gives an admirable summary of *De Imperio* in one (long) sentence "as to my views on the power of the Christian authorities in ecclesiastical matters, I refer to my ... booklet *De Pietate Ordinum Hollandiae* and especially to an unpublished book *De Imperio summarum potestatum circa sacra*, where I have treated the matter in more detail ... I may summarize my feelings thus: that the authorities should scrutinize God's Word so thoroughly as to be certain to impose nothing which is against it; if they act in this way, they shall in good conscience have control of the public churches and public worship – but without persecuting those who err from the right way."[8] Since this deprives the ministry of all power, it is not surprising that some hard-boiled Calvinists qualified Grotius' inspiration as diabolical.[9]

Elsewhere Grotius mentions some of the qualities of *De Imperio*: it is, he says, detailed, methodical and theoretical; it brings something new and it is not written on commission. Methodical, *distinctus*, is what Grotius calls it in a letter to the Leiden professor Polyander.[10] In an interesting letter of September 3, 1617 to his friend Lingelsheim, councillor of the Elector Palatine, Grotius indicates that the book has a claim to being theoretical: for instance he stresses how carefully he has distinguished between *ius* and *usus iuris* in his work. This is true; he comes back to that point repeatedly in *De Imperio*, emphasizing for instance that abuse by the authorities does not rob

---

[8] R. FRUIN (ed.), *Verhooren en andere bescheiden betreffende het rechtsgeding van Hugo de Groot*, Utrecht 1871, p. 6 (Memorie van mijne intentien en notabele bejegeningen): "Aengaende mijn verstant over de AUTORITEIT eener Christelijcke Overheyt in kerckelike saecken referere mij tot het voorseyde boecxken *de Pietate Ordinum Hollandiae*, en vooral tot een ongedruckt boeck *de Imperio summarum Potestatum circa Sacra*, waerin ick dese materie wat nader heb verhandelt... Mijn meening is in 't cort, dat de Overheyt soo wel Godes woordt moet doorsoecken, dat sij verseeckert zij nyet te bevelen dat daerjegens strijdt, dat, doende dat, sij in goeder conscientie vermagh te disponeren over de publyque kercken en kerckendyenst, sonder te vervolgen deghene dye uyt een goede meninge souden mogen dwalen." Grotius repeats the gist of this in his *Verantwoordingh* of 1622, p. 173 (*BG* no. 875).

[9] "Diabolical": Althusius to Lubbertus, November 20, 1614, in JOH. ALTHUSIUS, *Politica methodice digesta* ed. C.J. FRIEDRICH, Cambridge Mass. 1932, p. CXXIX, cf. C. VAN DER WOUDE, *Sibrandus Lubbertus, Leven en werken, in het bijzonder naar zijn correspondentie*, Kampen 1963, p. 293.

[10] *BW* I 369, September 14, 1614: "scripto distinctiore." For its precision, see *ibid.*: "accuratius," also *BW* I 528, September 3, 1617 to Lingelsheim "(ut) accuratius totum hoc argumentum pertractarem"; *Verhooren*, p. 6 "wat nader." Cf. the judgment of Lingelsheim *BW* I 561, January 14, 1618 "omnia exacte, plane, perspicue, caute explicata et distincta."

them of *ius*.[11] In this same letter Grotius acknowledges a main reason for writing *De Imperio* (which we had already guessed), to take
away the bad impression which *Ordinum Pietas* had created – although Grotius himself chooses to say that that work is misrepre-
sented by his enemies.[12] *De Imperio*, he tells Lingelsheim, is meant as
a finished (*rotundus*) treatment of the subject, dealt with in all its aspects (*pertractatus*), as an implicit refutation of his critics. Lingelsheim
later acknowledges that it is learned, exact, methodical and in certain respects new.[13]

We know that Grotius wrote his *De Satisfactione*, for a similar reason, working more or less simultaneously on both books. Both take
their starting point from *Ordinum Pietas*. *De Satisfactione* picks up its
first, dogmatic part and aims at proving that the Arminians are far
from being Socinians.[14] *De Imperio* picks up and elaborates on the
second, larger part, on the power of the authorities in church matters. I want to suggest that *De Imperio* was meant by Grotius as a
kind of *De Iure Belli ac Pacis* in the field of ecclesiastical government:
Ordinum Pietas and other works can be considered as preliminary
studies to *De Imperio*,[15] just like *Meletius* to *De Veritate*, or *De Iure*

---

[11] See *De Imperio* p. 216 b 52–53 "cum ad modum recte utendi iuris pertineat,
de iure ipso nihil immutat"; p. 224 b 60 ff. "ut ratus sit actus pauciora requirantur
quam ut recta sit actio"; p. 227 b 53 ff. "Minime enim sequendi sunt nobis qui
iuris quaestionem cum hac quaestione de modo utendi iuris passim confundunt";
235 b 24 "ad modum utendi iuris, non ad ius ipsum"; p. 236 b 36–37 "agendi
modus pro temporum personarumque ratione diversus non facit ius novum"; p.
240 a 57–59 "ius universale asstruxerimus...sed an consultum sit"; p. 262 a 37 ff.
"videamus an ... summa potestas ipsa electionem facere possit; non quaeritur an ...
debeat neque an expediat..., sed an si faciat quicquam committat contra ius divi-
num"; p. 268 a 52 "quomodo non ... id ius duret (nam an uti expediat ... alia est
quaestio)" (uti *ms.*] et ubi *OTh*); p. 286 a 40–42 "Non satis ... ius suum nosse, nisi
... norit qua ratione suo iure optime utatur." The title of Ch. 6.1 is *Distinctio inter
ius et modum iuris recte exercendi.*

[12] *BW* I 528: Grotius was driven to composing *De Imperio* in order that nobody
"quae de iure potestatum antehac scripsi maligna interpretatione depravet" (p.
579); also *BW* I 543, October 30, 1617 to Overall "ne sententia mea sequius
quam se habet accipiatur." For its alleged disinterested character, that is not commissioned by the States: *BW* I 369, September 14, 1614 to Polyander "sententiam
meam quam nuper non nisi occasione a Sibrando data ... indicavi, nunc statui
scripto distinctiore persequi"; *BW* I 528 "antehac ex occasione scripsi."

[13] *BW* I 524 August 9, 1617 "multa noviter explicata magno iudicio" and note
10 above. Cf. Grotius' own claim *BW* 474, September 6, 1616 to Vossius "quaedam satis recte a nobis in hoc argumento ... observata, non satis visa hactenus."

[14] On the purpose and scope of *De Satisfactione* see RABBIE's edition (Assen/
Maastricht 1990), Introduction, especially 10 ff.

[15] Some twenty years later Grotius writes to his brother in law Reigersberch
(*BW* XI 3530, April 17, 1638) that *De Imperio* represents the same views as *Ordinum
Pietas*, the *Decretum*, the Amsterdam speech and the *Apologeticus* of 1622 ("dat hetsel-
ve wel met meer passagiën is verrijkt, maar in effecte deselve positiën inhout...").

Praedae in relation to *De Iure Belli ac Pacis*, or the *Antiquitates* to the
Annales. *De Imperio* is, in spite of its plethora of concrete examples
and quotations, the theoretical work of a lawyer.[16] It pretends to a
certain detachment; there is virtually no polemical word to be
found in it: other points of view are rarely attacked, and, if at all,
in a non-specific way. That is not to say that the tone of *De Imperio*
is a particularly conciliatory one. To argue that all Christians or all
believers were brothers, as Grotius had done in his *Meletius*,[17] had
proved ineffective. *Ordinum Pietas* had been polemical, and that had
proved counter-productive. *De Imperio* was, I think, intended as the
all-embracing study on the problems of church government by an
'impartial' 'elder statesman' and scholar, systematically proving by
reason and historical argument from Scripture and the early fathers
just what is right.[18] It may be remembered in this connection that
in the original plan for Grotius' *Opera Omnia* his *De Imperio* was to
appear in Book IV, dedicated to the 'Politica,' together with the
Amsterdam speech of 1616, the *Apologeticus* and *De Iure Belli ac
Pacis*.[19] The parallel with *De Iure* must not be pressed too far, of
course: for one thing, *De Imperio* arises much more from the situation of the moment than *De Iure*, but it may be instructive.[20]

---

[16] Cf. Solari, *Il "jus circa sacra"*, p. 47: "la soluzione giuridica dei problemi," followed by Caspani, "Il De imperio," pp. 394 ff. From *De Satisfactione* and *De Imperio*
Overall judges Grotius to be (note the order) "magnum iurisperitum et theologum
et politicum" (*BW* I 562, February 21, 1618).

[17] See G.H.M. POSTHUMUS MEYJES (ed.), *Hugo Grotius, Meletius...*, Leiden 1988,
pp. 22–25.

[18] DE MICHELIS, *Le origini*, pp. 154–55 draws attention to the "esigenza sistemati-
ca di universalità e completezza" of *De Imperio*. SOLARI, *Il "jus circa sacra"*, pp. 67–
71 confronts *De Imperio* with *De Iure Belli*, stressing the differences rather than the
similarities, however.

[19] See the Privilege for the *Opera Omnia* of October 2, 1653, printed a.o. in *OTh*
I p. ***2, cf. *BG* pp. XI, 337, 339, 453.

[20] Like *De Iure De Imperio* is systematically arranged, into 12 chapters and over
200 paragraphs; in its first chapters Grotius is mainly concerned with definitions
and distinctions (cf. note 11 above, also *De Iure prol.* 41, 56), some returning in a
similar way in *De Iure*: compare *De Imperio* III 3–4 (*OTh* pp. 211 b 58 – 212 b 12)
to *De Iure prol.* 30 and III 3 (*OTh* p. 212 b 14–23) to *De Iure* I.I.15.2. In *De Imperio*
and in *De Iure* Grotius starts with the *generalis tractatio* (*De Imperio* p. 211 a 55, *De
Iure prol.* 33). His way of distinguishing *ius* and *usus iuris* is similar, see note 11
above and *De Iure* I.III.24, also I.III.23, I.III.11,1. Compare also Lingelsheim's
"explicata et distincta" (note 10) to *De Iure prol.* 56 "(ut) definiendi rationes redde-
rem ... tractanda ... disponerem ... quae eadem ... videri poterant ... distinguerem."
Grotius claims that both works are new (albeit more emphatically, and more rightly, for *De Iure*), see note 13 above and *De Iure prol.* 1, 30, 36. In both works Grotius
shows himself more interested in the constitutional state as such than in its specific
constitutional form, see G. HOFFMANN-LOERTZER in H. MAIER a.o. (edd.), *Klassiker*

Grotius twice mentions the models for the views which he expressed in *De Imperio*: in his letter to Lingelsheim of September 3, 1617 he mentions five 'political' authors, the French theorists Bodin and Tolosanus (Pierre Grégoire) and three Germans: Keckermann, Althusius and Arnisaeus. In his justification drawn up at Loevestein Keckermann and Althusius return. There he adds four theologians: Musculus, Bucer, Rudolf Gwalther and Paraeus.[21] This is an ill-assorted company of authors who fundamentally disagreed both with each other and with Grotius on many points. It is impossible, for instance, that Grotius could share Althusius' views on the relationship between church and state: this staunch Calvinist kept inciting his great friend Lubbertus to take up the pen against Grotius, whose *Ordinum Pietas* he detested. And neither Grotius nor Althusius agreed with Bodin, that absolute monarchy is the best constitution.[22] One thing, however, which these authors can be said to

---

des politischen Denkens, vol. I, München 1986[6], pp. 229–44, esp. pp. 237–43, who also draws attention to the importance of *Romans* 13 in *De Iure* (important too, of course, in *De Imperio*). Themes and quotations occurring in *De Imperio* also recur in *De Iure*, e.g. the position of the *summa potestas* of *De Imperio* I.1 in *De Iure* I.III.7.1, a quotation from Horace *Carm.* III 1, 5–8 in *De Imperio* p. 217 b 42–43 and *De Iure* I.III.8,8. A careful comparison would yield more.

[21] *Locc. citt.* (notes 8, 10). In his *Verantwoordingh* p. 173 Grotius quotes as his authorities for the same views, without specifically naming *De Imperio*: the "politicians" Bodin, Tolosanus, Arnisaeus, Lipsius, Keckermann and Althusius and the "theologians" Marsilius Patavinus, Bucerus, Musculus and Paraeus. In *BW* I 514 of June 17, 1617 and 528 of September 3, 1617 (both to Lingelsheim) he insists that his views are the same as Paraeus', also in *BW* I 543 of October 30, 1617 to Overall. Much later, in a letter to Wtenbogaert of August 20, 1639 (*BW* XI 4262), Grotius compares his views and those of Wtenbogaert on the power of the authorities to the opinions of Marsilius of Padova, Musculus, Andrewes and most of the English authors, Casaubon, Goldast, Althusius and Arnisaeus.

[22] Modern authorities (Althusius' editor Friedrich [see note 9], de Vranckrijker) claim that Grotius never mentions Althusius, but this proves untrue. Althusius' *Politica* (ed. 1603, 1610, 1614) is not mentioned among Grotius' books. He must, however, have known both the man and the work, since Althusius was frequently in the Hague from 1604 onwards to negotiate for the city of Emden against the Frisian Count, a question in which Grotius was involved too. In a letter to his brother Willem (*BW* I 331, April 20, 1614) Grotius expresses the wish to buy Arnisaeus' *De Iure maiestatis libri III*, Frankfurt 1610; this was arranged, for in 1619 he possessed a copy: P.C. MOLHUYSEN, *De bibliotheek van Hugo de Groot in 1618*, Amsterdam 1943 [= Mededeelingen der Nederlandsche Akademie van Wetenschappen, Afd. Letterkunde, N.R. 6, 3], no. 243, cf. *De Satisfactione* ed. RABBIE p. 54 n. 4. Arnisaeus is mentioned in *De Imperio* III 8 (*OTh* p. 213 b 50) and it is evident that Grotius used his work in composing *De Imperio*. One supposes that Grotius possessed a copy of Bodin's *De Republica* (1586, French edition 1576); it is not mentioned among his books. Grotius mentions Bodin in *De Imperio* I 3 (*OTh* p. 204 a 58) and III 8, together with Arnisaeus. Of Pierre Grégoire (Gregorius Tolosanus, 1540–1597) Grotius probably refers to *Syntagma iuris universalis* (1582). Althusius, Keckermann and Tolosanus are not mentioned in *De Imperio*. For the theologians mentioned, see below pp. 37–38.

share is that they wrote systematic works. This is perhaps most
clear in the case of Keckermann, head of the Latin School at
Gdansk, obviously a very systematic person, who not only composed a *Systema doctrinae politicae*, but also *systemata* of logic, theology,
rhetoric and preaching, totalling some 4.000 pages in folio.[23] In
naming these authors Grotius would then once more refer to his
systematic approach in *De Imperio*.

Whatever Grotius exactly had in mind when naming these authors, I now wish to make use of these references as an illustration
of two final points about *De Imperio*: all the political authors treat of
the relationship between the monarch and the states, or between
higher and lesser magistrates, in the light of the power granted to
them by God – although their conclusions diverge. This draws our
attention to a permanent theme in *De Imperio*, that of sovereignty.
That is the absolute sovereignty of the States of Holland both in
relation to the king of Spain and to the States of the other provinces. In the first sentence of *De Imperio* it is already stated that *summum imperium* may be a person, but a group of persons as well. In
the important chapters about synods (VII) and the election of
priests (X) the conclusion is inevitable (though Grotius does not
make it explicit) that all decisions lie with the magistrates and States
of Holland.

The second point concerns the general, theoretical character of
De Imperio. We must not overlook that it is also an eclectic book.
Grotius writes expressly to his correspondent Lingelsheim that if a
Roman Catholic author makes a good point, one may use it without agreeing with the rest; and he very often puts together single
quotations from authors who fundamentally disagree both with
each other and with himself.[24] I suggest that we might not always
see this as wilful distortions. Behind it is the tradition of the com-
monplace-book, especially useful to the lawyer. And perhaps, in a
broader view, we may connect this with a more general tendency
of scholarship in Grotius' age to be interested in detail more than
in the whole, a different appreciation, or even perception, of unity

---

[23] First edition 1608. Grotius possessed the second edition of 1612, where he
made some marginal notes, cf. F.F. BLOK, *Contributions to the History of Isaac Vossius's
Library*, Amsterdam – London 1974 [= Verhandelingen der Koninklijke Nederlandse Akademie van Wetenschappen, Afd. Letterkunde, N.R. 83], no. 24. His
Opera Omnia were published in Geneva 1614.

[24] *BW* I 529, September 8, 1617. Even Calvin, who is mentioned six times in
De Imperio, is always quoted as a source of admiration and a support for Grotius'
views: *OTh* pp. 226 a 39, 271 b 43 and 55, 275 b 58, 277 b 63, 283 b 31.

– organic unity, as we would perhaps say, using a romantic metaphor.[25] Grotius is, if anything, less liable to it than his contemporaries, but he is not free from it. It is remarkable how often he picks on a parenthesis or digression in a writer whom he quotes as an authority to support an argument. The use which he makes of Balsamo's commentary on the early councils is a good illustration: almost invariably he takes out a parenthesis or digression to quote Balsamo as saying just that.[26]

Finally, as a transition to the second part of this paper, we may note that most of the authors whom Grotius names as his examples occur in a long letter of Vossius of February 10, 1616, to which I shall return.

II

The genesis of *De Imperio* can be followed to a certain extent in the correspondence; but it should be realized that there must have existed many more letters than we possess now. For example: between the end of October 1614 and mid April 1615, a period of 5 months, we have a mere 14 letters (to and from Grotius together), none of them autographs and practically all known only from 17th-century printed sources.

There are two main stages in the conception of the book: a first version was written in 1614, a second one in 1616. This second version, with some modifications made in early 1617, was sent as a final draft to England and the Palatinate in mid-1617.

At the end of August 1614 Grotius had finished *De Imperio*, but, as he says, it is as yet a provisional version.[27] A few weeks later he sends this to his friend Vossius and to the Leyden professor of Divinity Polyander, who is allowed to show it to his colleague Colonius and even to the fierce Calvinist preacher Hommius – in a later

---

[25] M.H. ABRAMS, *The Mirror and the Lamp: Romantic theory and the Critical tradition*, New York 1953, Chapter VIII.

[26] E.g. in *De Imperio* XII 4 (*OTh* p. 287 a 20), where Grotius quotes Balsamo as saying that senators and judges have as much right as the bishops to choose and depose bishops. In fact Balsamo explains the 29th canon of the Council of Chalcedon, which says that bishops can be deposed, but not degraded. As an illustration he tells the story of the bishops of Tyrus who were deposed by a colleague, but reinstated during the synod by the "fathers together with the civil authorities." Cf. also *De Imperio* X 10 and X 12 (*OTh* p. 216 a 24 and 63) compared with Balsamo's annotations on the 13th canon of Laodicea, the 13th canon of Carthage and the 4th canon of Nicaea.

[27] *BW* I 367, to Vossius: "Ego quod nuper coeperam conscribere de Iure magistratuum detexui, sed admodum subitario labore."

letter Grotius wisely omits Hommius' name.[28] Vossius' immediate
reaction to *De Imperio* is lost to us, and so are all comments by the
Leyden circle.[29] At the end of October of the same year Vossius expresses regret that the book has not been published together with
Grotius' latest, his *Bona Fides*, a pamphlet against Lubbertus. He ex-
horts him to publish it as soon as possible;[30] so we may infer that
Vossius thought well of it. However, in the next 16 months we hear
nothing more of *De Imperio*.

In the meantime the Middelburg professor Antonius Walaeus
published his *Het Ampt der Kerckendienaren*, itself a reaction to Wtenbogaert's *Tractaet van 't Ampt ende authoriteit eener hoogher Christelijcke
overheid in kerckelijkcke zaken* of 1610, both substantial (at least in size)
works on the relationship between ecclesiastical and secular government. Walaeus, a moderate counter-remonstrant and a friend of
Grotius, sent him his book as soon as it came from the press, on
November 29, 1615.[31] A few months later, on February 10 of 1616,
Vossius wrote an important letter to his friend. This *Dissertatio epistolica de Iure magistratus in rebus ecclesiasticis*, as it is called, occupies 36
pages in Grotius' correspondence. It was not published during Vossius' lifetime, because of its obvious Remonstrant views, but first
saw the light in 1669.[32] As it stands,[33] its first part consists of a general introduction on (in)tolerance, mainly on the subject of predestination and the sacrament. The second and much longer part is an
extensive, detailed and generally unfavourable review of Walaeus'
Ampt, stuffed with references to ancient and modern authorities. As
Grotius wrote back, he had asked for some notes, but received a

---

[28] *BW* I 369, September 14, 1614 to Polyander, *ibid.* 370, same date, to Vossius,
ibid. 373 September 28 to his brother Willem, where he says that Polyander should
not let "scriptum istud in ullius praeter suas aut Colonii manus venire."

[29] On October 11, 1614 (*BW* I 375) Grotius refers to a letter by Vossius touching upon *De Imperio*. This letter has not been transmitted.

[30] *BW* I 383, October 27, 1614.

[31] *BW* I 436. The Preface of the book is dated November 25. BOHATEC, "Das
Territorial- und Kollegialsystem," draws attention to Grotius' implicit criticism of
Walaeus in *De Imperio*, but not to the part played in it by Vossius. However, his
claim that Grotius is also engaged in a polemic with Voetius can not be upheld.

[32] *BW* I nr. 447, pp. 462–96. It was published separately by Blaeu in 1669 and
included in Vossius' Tractatus theologici (= *Opera* VI) of 1701, see MOLHUYSEN *ad
loc.*; C.S.M. RADEMAKER, *Life and Works of Gerardus Joannes Vossius (1577–1649)*, Assen 1981, "Checklist of Vossius' Works" (pp. 355ff.), no. 43. On the contents of
the treatise, see especially NOBBS, *Theocracy and Toleration*, pp. 49–58.

[33] It seems clear that there was some introduction or accompanying letter which
has been lost or omitted in print. The *dissertatio* starts without any explanation of
its reason for being; nor is there any mention in it of Vossius' notes on original sin,
to which Grotius refers in his answer of February 23.

treasure-house of ecclesiastical history.[34] Vossius had once again insisted on publication of De Imperio in this letter, the first thing we
hear about that book in 16 months; and it is clear that one of the
purposes of this letter is that of offering ammunition to Grotius,
who gratefully accepted it: in De Imperio many quotations recur,
sometimes with the page-number or the qualifying adjective which
had been given by Vossius.[35] I surmise that Grotius had put aside
De Imperio for a time because of criticism from his friends (or perhaps because on the contrary they were slow in rendering their
judgment), and that instead he had been working on his De Satisfactione, considering the religious side of the matters in hand more urgent than the political one. Now Vossius is exhorting him to work
on De Imperio again. Grotius cannot immediately begin to use Vossius' material when he receives the dissertatio, because he has other
work – there is much to do in the States of Holland and in April
1616 he is sent to Amsterdam in a vain attempt to persuade the
magistrates of that city to come over to the majority view in Holland on church politics. At the same time he is finishing De Satisfactione.[36]

At the end of May 1616, however, Grotius makes a fresh start
with De Imperio and after some three months he has finished: on
September 6 he sends the text to Vossius,[37] who had been appointed rector of the States College at Leyden University in the meantime – largely through Grotius' efforts. Some of Vossius' students
will make a copy of the manuscript, one for the English divines and
one for those from the Palatinate. This takes some time, but after

---

[34] "Ego schedas poposceram; tu mihi ingentem Ecclesiasticae antiquitatis thesaurum transmisisti": BW I 449, February 23, 1616.

[35] Grotius took over dozens of quotations from this letter; the most telling ones
are a quotation from Lancelot Andrewes' Tortura Torti (1609) in Vossius' letter BW
I p. 475 together with its page-number (364) in De Imperio VIII 2 (OTh p. 253 a
50–53; the page-number is in the ms., but not in the editions, see below) and an
edict by Justinian where Grotius includes Contius' favourable opinion of it as quoted by Vossius (BW I p. 473, OTh p. 224 b 3–6). On the collaboration between
Grotius and Vossius, see also C.W. ROLDANUS, "Vossius' verhouding tot Hugo de
Groot voor de synode van Dordt," TvG 57, 1942, pp. 241–53.

[36] On the genesis of De Satisfactione, see ed. RABBIE pp. 19–26. Vossius received
a first version of it (after Grotius had been working at it from time to time for two
years) on October 23, 1614, two months after Grotius had sent him the first draft
of De Imperio. Until June 1615, when De Satisfactione was sent to Walaeus for criticism, Grotius may have been mainly concerned with De Satisfactione; in early 1616
he was also working on it, for on May 29, 1616 Grotius had not yet found the
time to read Vossius' dissertatio thoroughly, but decides now to put away De Satisfactione for the time (BW I 456).

[37] BW I 474.

3½ months Grotius has received the results.[38] In the first days of the new year 1617 he re-reads *De Imperio*, and discovers a serious mistake: in both copies there is a large gap, of 6 to 7 pages, in the section *de episcopis et presbyteris*, that is chapter 11.[39] It takes Grotius three months to correct the work, not only because he has other things to do, but also because he borrows more books and adds to his work. He needs the manuscript of the Greek canonist Balsamo which Meursius possesses and asks the Leiden professor of Oriental languages Erpenius for information on Jewish history. On the first of April Grotius returns to Vossius his own original with additions and corrections and the two copies which must be corrected after it.[40]

Correction takes another two months, but in the first half of June 1617 the first corrected copy is sent to John Overall, Dean of St. Paul's, and shortly afterwards the other one goes to Lingelsheim in Heidelberg.[41] With their criticisms the book may at last be made ready for the printer. After Lingelsheim and Grotius have exchanged some letters about the book, the manuscript from the Palatinate returns in early 1618,[42] but in England things are not running smoothly: Overall was asked by Grotius to show *De Imperio* to Lancelot Andrewes, bishop of Ely and another old-time friend of Grotius, but this means delay: at first Andrewes is away for a time, then he does not want to read it without His Majesty's knowledge. It is now November 1617.[43] On October 6 the English Ambassador Carleton, speaking for his King, held a speech in the States General urging a National Synod, directed against the States of Holland. At almost the same moment Overall had implied that the English

---

[38] On December 10 Grotius had not yet received anything from Leiden, as appears from his letter to Lingelsheim of that day: *BW* I 489. On December 30 he announces to Vossius that he is going to re-read *De Imperio*; so the copies appear to have arrived shortly before: *BW* I 492 "Diatribam De Imperio nondum relegere coepi. Iam nunc incipiam."

[39] *BW* I 496, January 6, 1617 "mea relego invenioque in duobus apographis ingentem esse hiatum sex septem paginarum eo loco quo de Episcopis et Presbyteris agitur."

[40] Grotius asks Meursius and Vossius for books, awaits information from Erpenius and makes corrections and additions: *BW* I 493, 494, 496, 498, 501, 505. He sends it to Vossius: 508, April 1, 1617.

[41] On June 12 one copy has already been sent to Overall: *BW* I 513, to Vossius; the one to Lingelsheim is accompanied by a letter dated June 17: *BW* I 514.

[42] For some of these letters, see notes 10, 13, 24, 45. Lingelsheim sends it away shortly after January 14, 1618: *BW* I 561.

[43] *BW* I 516, from Overall, 519 to Overall, 526, 539 from Overall, 543 to Overall, 562 from Overall, 570 to Overall.

reaction on *De Imperio* could well be negative.[44] But Grotius remains optimistic. Between November 1617 and June 1618 we do not hear much of the book, but on June 30 of 1618 Grotius still writes to Lingelsheim that publication is delayed because he is waiting for the reactions from England.[45] Within two months he is arrested. I think there is no evidence that the turn of events made Grotius hesitate to publish *De Imperio*. We may well think that it would have been at the very least a useless undertaking, and probably a dangerous one. The so-called Sharp Resolution of the States of Holland is taken, provoking much unrest, and the National Synod is decided on by the States General,[46] while Grotius is busy corresponding with his foreign friends about technical details. But it may be argued that things did not really get on the move before July 1618, shortly after Grotius' last letter on *De Imperio*. However that may be, I have found no indication that Grotius decided to suppress the book.

In later years the subject of *De Imperio* crops up a few times in the correspondence, for the first time when the chaplain of Overall, who has died in the meantime, returns his copy of it to Grotius in Paris in June 1621.[47] The sum of it is that Grotius does not want to publish the book any more. The manuscript text, however, is copied. At the present time seven manuscripts of *De Imperio* remain, none of them autographs.

---

[44] Overall quotes Andrewes, who has said that the King is not in favour of secular authority in matters of belief. Overall himself thinks that the English will agree with Grotius except for some details, which turn out to concern the essence of *De Imperio*: *BW* I 539, of October 5, 1617.

[45] *BW* I 574.

[46] On the "scherpe resolutie" of August 4, 1617, see J. DEN TEX, *Oldenbarnevelt* III, Haarlem 1966, pp. 493 ff. The States General finally decided to call a National Synod on November 11 of that year, see J.G. SMIT (ed.), *Resolutiën der Staten Generaal* III, 's-Gravenhage 1975 [Rijks Geschiedkundige Publicatiën, Grote serie 152], pp. 264–66.

[47] *BW* II 660, June 30, 1621 (cf. 708, November 17); III 998, August 1, 1625 to Vossius: people are prepared to publish *De Imperio* if Grotius removes all references to Protestant authors, which he refuses; 1062, March 13, 1626; 1087, July 1, 1626; XI 3510 March 29, 1638; 3524 April 10, 1638 (both to his brother in law Reigersberch: Grotius is working on *De Imperio* from time to time); 3530, April 17, 1638; 4262, August 20, 1639, see note 21 (cf. 4389, November 15, 1639 and 4416, December 3, 1639).

III

One of these manuscripts is located in the Royal Library in The Hague.[48] It comes from the personal papers of Grotius himself.[49] And it has been possible to identify this manuscript as one of the copies written by a student in the States College for Grotius in the fall of 1616 and later corrected for him in the spring of 1617.[50] In later years Grotius has made notes on the pages preceding and following the text, but these do not concern us now. To know what Grotius added and corrected in the period from January to April 1617, we have to look at the additions and corrections in this manuscript, with two qualifications: they must be written in the hand of the scribe, to exclude the possibility that they were made later, by Grotius or someone else; and they must not be corrections of mistakes that the scribe could have made in copying and has redressed himself at once or directed by Grotius later. As it happens, we can use as a check a second manuscript, now in Paris, which proves to be the other copy taken at the States College.[51]

Now let us look at what Grotius has changed. We must realize that in fact the period in question, when he could be thinking, reading and taking notes, lies between September 6, 1616, when he sent the manuscript to Vossius, and April 1, 1617 when the corrected text went back. *De Imperio* is by no means the only one of his works which Grotius corrected; on the contrary, he kept meddling with his texts: his autograph copy of *De Iure Praedae* shows corrections and additions, that of the *Historiae* has several layers; the annotations in his printed copy of the *Inleidinge* form a well known case, not to mention the books which he revised for a second edition, such as *De satisfactione*, where Grotius started revision almost the moment it was published.[52]

---

[48] Shelf number 131 C 21.

[49] See my "Hugo Grotius' manuscript of *De Imperio Summarum Potestatum circa Sacra* identified," *Grotiana* N.S. 11 (1990), pp. 34–42.

[50] This is not the place for going into the proofs for the identification. Suffice it to say that the point where the scribe originally skipped 6 or 7 pages (see page 30 above) can be identified in this manuscript.

[51] BN Lat. 3234. I shall go into the textual tradition of *De Imperio* elsewhere

[52] On *De Iure Praedae* see R. Fruin, *Verspreide geschriften*, edd. P.J. Blok e.a., III, 's-Gravenhage 1901, p. 408, the reproduction of the manuscript in the series *The Classics of International Law*, Oxford – London 1950, and E.R. Molhuysen née Oppenheim in *Bibliotheca Visseriana* 5, Leiden 1925, pp. 75–100 with a list of the corrections made in the manuscript by Grotius between 1605 and 1608; this list, which ends at Ch. 11, 1, was found among the papers of Fruin. On *De Iure Belli ac Pacis*, see Molhuysen's edition pp. X–XII. The manuscript of the *Historiae* is in Leiden University Library, shelf number Pap. 9. On de *Inleidinge*, see the edition by

The general picture of the corrections in *De Imperio* is the following: Grotius' modifications consist mostly of additions; this is normal for him and, I daresay, for most authors. When he is not merely adding, but also changes, he clearly takes care when he changes a phrase to adapt the whole context, both grammatically and logically. The modifications are made all through the book, with a distinct emphasis on the chapters about synods and the election of priests (7 and 10). Since the greater part of chapter 11 was written anew by the scribe we do not know what Grotius changed there. Further there is a relative preponderance of minor changes in the first chapters. This is to be expected too in correcting a text. I estimate that altogether an extra 1 to 2 folio pages are added. The general tendency of *De Imperio* remains, of course, the same.

A first small group consists of minor stylistic changes, some 15 in all: thus *contra* becomes *adversus* or *hoc* changes into *id*, or a more precise wording is chosen. They show, if anything, that Grotius was not above such details. There is a second group, about as small, of mere additions. Thus Tacitus says that everything may best stay the way it is. Now Grotius adds two similar judgments by Saint Jerome and Saint Augustine (*OTh* 232 b 3 ff.). In *De Satisfactione* an important part of the changes made for the second edition consisted of adding and correcting Biblical references. This is something which did *not* have to be done for *De Imperio*. Either Grotius was more at home in the Bible on the subject of church government, or his sources were better; this could well be the case, for in the years preceding *De Imperio* several large books on the subject had been published by preachers and professors. What Grotius *has* apparently done is checking his references: in Tac. *Hist.* III 73, 1 he has correctly changed *imperat* into *exsequitur* (204 a 29), and in Anastasius bibliothecarius *eruditissimos* is corrected into *eruditos* (240 a 16).[53] He had seen that an original reference to Balsamo was incorrect: not on the 12th canon of Carthage, but of Antiochia (247 a 9). He now quotes Eusebius in the original Greek (254 b 5–6).[54] Elsewhere what was a mere reference is quoted in full.[55] There are a good deal of these corrections and they suggest that Grotius was not always so sloppy in quoting as it has sometimes been claimed.

DOVRING, FISCHER and MEIJERS, Leiden 1965[2], p. XII. On *De Satisfactione* the ed. RABBIE pp. 28–30.

[53] *Historia de vitis pontificum Romanorum* 275 = PL 128, 1154

[54] *HE* VI 34 = PG 20, 596 A.

[55] E.g. Johannes Pariensiensis and Victoria in I 14, Marsilius in VII 11.

It is interesting too that Grotius now takes eight or nine quotations from Vossius' *dissertatio epistolica*. He had already pillaged this letter in composing *De Imperio*, but as soon as he got back his copies he asked Vossius again for the loan of it. The same is true for Meursius' codex of Balsamo's commentary on the first councils: as he admits to Meursius, Grotius had already had it for a long time, but now he wants to see it again.[56] In the same way quotations are added from the *Codex* and the *Novellae*, books which Grotius already knew well, but leafed through once again. This, apparently, is how he worked: he consulted books and took arguments and (mainly) quotations from them; later he remembered other examples which could also come in handy; so, if the books were accessible and there was time, he went back to them. In this case this was done with care, for the extra borrowings from Vossius' *dissertatio* are sprinkled throughout *De Imperio*. This may prove a point of some use in future studies on the genesis of Grotius' texts, that corrections from a later date need not imply that Grotius had been reading a book for the first time.

The tone of the book as a whole was already superior rather than polemical, as I have said. Grotius wanted above all to avoid provoking the public – as he had done with *Ordinum Pietas*; in sending his last draft to Vossius he asks him to read the book critically once again before he hands it over to the correctors and to strike things which will unnecessarily irritate. He has already tried to omit such things, says Grotius, but he is aware that he is sometimes carried away in writing.[57] As far as I see, only two such remarks have been struck out. At one point Grotius criticizes those who permit the lower magistrates to take up the sword against the higher powers.[58] Here one remark has been erased in the manuscript: *ducem secuti hac in parte nimis Brutum*, "in this respect following Brutus too much." This refers to the French anti-royalist author Du Plessis Mornay, who wrote under the name Junius Brutus; and it looks as if Grotius did not want to irritate the ministry by comparing them to (would-be) regicides. But in fact this change contains a useful warning: in December 1617 Grotius, in discussing *De Imperio* with Lingelsheim, concedes a point: "if I have been too hard on Brutus, I shall soften it."[59] It seems impossible not to connect this with the

---

[56] *BW* I 493 to Vossius and 494 to Meursius, both of December 31, 1616.
[57] *BW* I 508, April 1, 1617.
[58] *OTh* p. 213 a 39–40.
[59] *BW* I 551, December 14, 1617 "Tamen de Bruto si quid dictum est durius, mitigabo."

removal of that particular phrase. But by then correction of the manuscript was long past: it had been finished and sent away! Nevertheless the same phrase is also crossed out in the other manuscript. This teaches us that mere erasions are very difficult to date and cannot be trusted as arguments.[60] Besides these two erasures a few remarks are added which are directed against the ministry, but in a more veiled manner. They occur closely together in the chapter about synods:[61] it is a well-known complaint, adds Grotius, that the main diseases of the church have been introduced by its priests; and a few lines below he adds a reference to a letter by Constantine complaining that the bishops provoke hatred and disorder – surely not without good reason. The other remarks are in a similar vein. We see that the changes in tone are minimal. Grotius protests his non-polemical intentions, but at the same time he is not above having a sly dig at the ministers. On the whole, however, the book retains its distanced character.

It is the same with the historical context: contemporary events were already in the background and there they remain. The majority of the additions (absolutely, and even more so relatively) occur in the chapter about synods and this fact appears to be the only indication of contemporary politics in the corrections in *De Imperio*: a national synod, already imminent when Grotius started his book in 1614, became more and more inevitable, and he reacts by proving more emphatically that it cannot be held without the consent of the States of Holland. We are well informed on the political situation of the time and the part Grotius played in it. We know, for instance, that in the first months of 1617 Grotius participated in the debates in the States of Holland about giving the counter-remonstrants the opportunity to preach in the Kloosterkerk in The Hague. He spent much time sitting in committees considering the desirability of restoring and opening this church – where Maurice later, on July 23, assisted at the counter-remonstrant service. Lawsuits by banned counter-remonstrant ministers multiplied and brought the States of Holland into conflict with its Court. Riots burst out in Amsterdam. Maurice, the States General and some of the cities of Holland clearly gained the upper hand against the States of Holland.[62] Nothing of all this penetrates into *De Imperio*. It is not as if Grotius is blind to these events: he participated in them as a politician.

---

[60] The other instance is in X 20, where three short polemical sentences were deleted.

[61] VII 7–8: *OTh* pp. 237 b 35 ff., 238 a 24 ff., b 34 ff.

[62] DEN TEX, *Oldenbarnevelt*, III, pp. 439–87.

When he had sent his book to Vossius six months ago he had already urged him to haste, for "the errors are turning into sedition."[63] But the only influence which the events have on the text of *De Imperio* is that Grotius heaps argument upon example, treating of ancient councils and those of Charlemagne and his sons to prove for the umpteenth time that the authorities must decide whether or not to call a synod, that they appoint the participants etcetera. The only practical consequence of the turn of events seems to be Grotius' choice of his critics, one in England and one in Germany, and as far as we know no Dutch friends. From the end of 1616 onwards he had set his hopes on a general (international) synod and especially on the beneficial influence of the foreigners attending.[64] He may have hoped against hope that Overall and Lingelsheim with their friends could be instrumental in this, persuaded by the irrefutable arguments of *De Imperio*.

Finally, a word on the books which Grotius consulted in the months in question. It is clear that he has had information on Jewish history, for in his additions he repeatedly quotes Maimonides, who had not been mentioned before. We remember that Grotius consulted Erpenius on Jewish history; and we know that Erpenius has written to his tutor in Amsterdam for an answer, the most learned of all Jews, as he is called.[65] Whoever this tutor was,[66] he or Erpenius appears to have directed Grotius to a recent book by Nic. Serrarius.[67] The re-reading of Balsamo and of Vossius' letter we

---

[63] "erroribus iam non longe a seditione recedentibus": *BW* I 474. On November 17 of 1616 (*BW* I 484), also to Vossius, Grotius is very dejected.

[64] FRUIN (ed.), *Memorie van mijne intentien*, pp. 16–17: proposes to the States (and to Maurice personally) to agree to a National Synod on condition that tolerance will be its aim, and that a General Synod will be called if that should prove impossible. Also *Deductie* (*ibid.*) pp. 260–61: "'t groot vertrouwen, dat ick hadde op de uytheemsche, onpartijdighe Theologanten" and the whole passage. *BW* I 527, August 31, 1617 to Lingelsheim: "Urgent multi synodum nationalem. Ego maiorem mallem et cuius pars magna ex exteris constaret." I think that Grotius already held that view in December 1616, when he announced to Lingelsheim that he would receive letters from both Calvinists and Remonstrants or "certe publico nomine": *BW* I 489, December 10, 1616.

[65] Above p. 30, *BW* I 493, December 31, 1616 and 496, January 6, 1617 both to Vossius (cf. also to Vossius 498, January 12, 1617 (p. 553) and 505, February 5); 497, January 9 (p. 547), from Vossius.

[66] About a Hebrew teacher of Erpenius nothing is known. Molhuysen (*BW* I p. 547 n. 8) tentatively identifies him as Josef (à) Pardo. On him, see *Jewish Encyclopaedia* IX, pp. 524–25, H.J. KOENEN, *Geschiedenis der Joden in Nederland*, Utrecht 1843, pp. 143, 428. I rather think of Isaak Uziel, a Jew from Fez, who died in Amsterdam on April 1, 1622. He was a poet, doctor and rabbi and taught Menasseh ben Israel. His Hebrew grammar was published by his pupils. See *Jewish Encyclopaedia* XII p. 393, KOENEN, *Geschiedenis*, pp. 144, 428.

[67] *Iosue ab utero ad ipsum usque tumulum ... explicatus*, Mainz 1609–10, a biography

have already seen. A number of new references to the confessions occur, most often to the Bohemian confession. This seems another case of reading his books again, for the confessions are quoted extensively already in the *Decretum* of 1614.[68] Some data about English synods and history may also come from books which Grotius had already used for earlier works. For in spite of his good intentions he does not seem to have used a brand-new book *Politia Anglicana* by Richard Mocket. This puritanic work was burnt as soon as it appeared in 1616, but not soon enough for Grotius, who wrote in November of that year to Vossius that he prepares himself to read it – with a distinct lack of enthusiasm.[69]

Grotius now also names and quotes a few times the German Lutheran reformer Jo. Brenz (Brentius). The book to which he refers is an appendix to the defence of the Württemberg confession of 1555, called *libellus aureus de officio principum saecularium in ecclesia*.[70] Brenz, "a conservative townsman," "a conservative on the issue of resistance ... a liberal on the issue of toleration,"[71] would seem to be a man after Grotius' heart. Vossius too may allude to this book when he urges Grotius to publish his *libellus aureus*, that is to say *De Imperio*.[72] It is not so much this particular work which I wish to emphasize, but what seems to be a general tendency of *De Imperio*: it makes us realize that most of the books and authors which Grotius mentions explicitly as his sources for it are German or Swiss. The political authors Althusius, Arnisaeus and Keckermann we have already met.[73] As theological sources he mentions Musculus, Bucer, Paraeus and Rudolf Gwalther.[74] Other books are lent to

---

of Joshua in two large volumes. It looks as if Grotius has found Maimonides' explications of Urim and Thummim, which he added to the manuscript, in this book.

[68] Grotius probably knew or possessed the book *Harmonia confessionum fidei orthodoxarum et reformatarum ecclesiarum...*, Genève 1581. It contains 11 confessions; Grotius would have been interested in section 19 *de magistratu politico*.

[69] *BW* I 484, November 17, 1616. RICHARD MOCKET, *Doctrina et politia Ecclesiae Anglicanae ... Quibus eiusdem Ecclesiae Apologia* [by John Jewel, Bishop of Salisbury] *praefigitur...*, London 1616. It was burnt in 1616 and immediately reprinted in 1617.

[70] I have as yet not been able to consult this book. See on it W. KÖHLER, *Bibliographia Brentiana*, Berlin 1904 (repr. Nieuwkoop 1963), nos. 324 and 325 (data on the location of Brentius' works have been rendered obsolete by two World wars), J.M. ESTES, *Christian Magistrate and State Church: The Reforming Career of Johannes Brenz*, Toronto etc. 1982, esp. Chapter 3, with note 87, and Chapter 6. The *libellus aureus* is in *Opera Omnia*, Tübingen 1576– 90, vol. VIII pp. 175–99.

[71] ESTES, *Christian Magistrate*, pp. 116, 123.

[72] *BW* I 447, the *dissertatio epistolica*, p. 497 "aureo hac de controversia libello tuo."

[73] Above pp. 25–26.

[74] MUSCULUS' *Loci communes*, in the same vein as Melanchthon and Bullinger, Basel 1599. Musculus is mentioned in *De Imperio* I 8, together with Paraeus, and X 27 (*OTh* pp. 205 b 41, 268 b 1). Bucer (not Swiss, as Walaeus states, but Alsatian,

him or recommended by Vossius: Hamelmann on synods, *loci communes* by Polanus.[75] And his lifelong hero in theological matters is Melanchthon, whom he used extensively.[76] Never before had Grotius emphasized that things are well in the Palatinate, where Lutherans and Calvinists can celebrate the Lord's Supper together.[77] I suggest that in the years 1614–1618 Grotius began to be somewhat less exclusively orientated upon England and the Anglican church in favour of Germany, the Lutherans and Zwinglians: his trip to England of 1613 and his contacts there had greatly impressed him. But on the one hand the behaviour of James I and especially his Ambassador must have diminished Grotius' hopes, although he put a brave face on it; on the other hand he had made friends in late 1613 with the learned Vossius, a man keenly interested in the English church, but also very well at home in the writings of the German reformers, a one time student in Heidelberg and in 1614 a

---

as Vossius points out to Grotius in *BW* I 447, the *dissertatio epistolica*, p. 497; but connected with Germany in many respects) composed many works, but we may perhaps think of his commentary on *Romans* and his *Constans defensio ... de Christiana reformatione, quam Hermannus archiepiscopus Coloniensis iam ante publicavit*, which is mentioned and quoted by Vossius in the *dissertatio*, *BW* I p. 475 (cf. MOLHUYSEN *ad loc.*). Bucer is mentioned in *De Imperio* X 14, XI 3 and 6 (*OTh* pp. 262 a 32, 271 b 55, 272 a 57). PARAEUS (see note 21) is best known for his *Irenicum* (1614); but his commentaries on Hosea (1605) and on Romans (1609) are also important for *De Imperio*. Gwalther was the son in law of Zwingli and Bullinger's successor in Zürich. He translated Zwingli's work into Latin.

[75] HERMANN HAMELMANN, *Quaestio an principes saeculares in synodis ... possint praesidere*, 1561, cf. *BW* I 360, August 11, 1614, from Vossius "Mitto ad te Hamelmanni libellum de iure principis in rebus Ecclesiasticis. Uteris eo quamdiu libet." Hamelmann is mentioned in *De Imperio* I 8 (*OTh* p. 205 b 39–41). AMAND POLANUS A POLANSDORF, *Syntagma theologiae christianae*, 1610, 1617, mentioned by Vossius in the *dissertatio epistolica* (*BW* I p. 497) as an example of German and Swiss *loci communes*.

[76] Although he mentions him only once in *De Imperio*. MELANCHTHON's *Loci communes* in *CR* XXI; on magistrates and church cols. 223–25, 542–57, 984–1015. Cf. also *CR* III cols. 271–86 *De potestate et primatu papae* and XVI cols. 85–105 *De officio principum, quod mandatum Dei praecipiat eis tollere abusus ecclesiasticos*. To give just one instance: according to BRANDT-CATTENBURGH, *Historie van het leven*, p. 234 Grotius often praised Melanchthon in his talks with Van Deventer, the commander of Loevestein.

[77] Sharing communion: *BW* I 514 to Lingelsheim, see note 21. Positive remarks about the situation in the Palatinate: *De Imperio* VI 9, X 27, XI 18, XII 4 (*OTh* pp. 231 a 52, 268 a 56, 284 b 35, 287 a 54). Grotius was especially impressed by the testament of Frederic III, which he mentions in *De Imperio* VI 9 (*OTh* p. 231 a 53) and in a letter to Lingelsheim of April 14, 1614 (*BW* I 327) "Mihi nullum unquam malis nostris remedium aptius visum est quam quod in extrema cera scriptum est testamentum illustrissimi Electoris Friderici." Grotius refers to the *Confessio fidei...* of Frederic III, part of his testament, published in German, French and Latin in February 1577, some four months after his death, printed a.o. in B.G. STRUVE, *Ausführlicher Bericht von der pfälzischen Kirchenhistorie*, Frankfurt 1721, pp. 175 ff. The complete testament in German in A. KLUCKHOHN in *Abhandlungen der bayerischen Akademie der Wissenschaften*, 3e *Kl.* 12 (1873), III pp. 41–104.

candidate for the chair of divinity in Steinfurt. The plan of the book and the methodical, legal approach are Grotius' own. But Vossius plays an important part in *De Imperio*.

IV

De Imperio was finally published in 1647. Although it went through four editions within five years, some of its actuality was lost and most of Grotius' one-time friends and enemies were dead or dying. France was being torn apart by the *Fronde* and at the same time the Peace of Westphalia was the centre of attention. The country where its theme was given most attention was England, on account of the execution of the king: a translation went through two editions in 1651 and 1655.[78] It is an ironic thought that, if the English had reacted more promptly in 1617–1618, they would, perhaps, have had less use for *De Imperio*.

---

[78] The 1651 translation: *BG* no. 903. The second edition of 1655 is not in *BG*, but see WING's *Short Title Catalogue*, 1982[2]. The Congregational Library in London and the Petyt library in Skipton, Yorkshire possess a copy. Thanks to the kindness of the curators of these libraries, I have seen photocopies of the title-pages.

HUGO GROTIUS' *DE VERITATE RELIGIONIS CHRISTIANAE*

JAN PAUL HEERING
(Leiden)

Of all the works written by Hugo Grotius, perhaps only the title of his opus magnum: *De iure belli ac pacis*, – the book that just cannot die, according to Van Vollenhoven – is still generally known.[1] However, even more popular in previous centuries, at least regarding its number of editions and translations, was his apologetic work *De veritate religionis christianae* (1640). Already in Grotius' lifetime, this work became famous and was accordingly called 'the golden booklet.' Huizinga rightly remarked that Grotius was to his century undoubtedly more the author of *De veritate* than of *De iure belli ac pacis*.[2]

Hugo Grotius' apologetic work has been the subject of five monographic studies already. The first study was made by the German scholar Johann Christoph Koecher and appeared in 1739,[3] the most recent study by Cornelia Roldanus appeared in 1944.[4] One can state without hesitation that these five studies are in all respects most deficient and have become obsolete. Moreover, in the past decades of our century much material has become available, providing a basis for a more elaborate evaluation and interpretation of Grotius' works. First of all we have at our disposal the monumental edition of the Correspondence of Hugo Grotius (*BW*), of which fourteen big volumes appeared. Second the *Meletius*, one of Grotius' earlier works, recently discovered by Posthumus Meyjes, should be mentioned here.[5] This work can be considered a predecessor of Grotius' *De veritate*. It offers a demonstration of the truth of Christian religion and elaborately deals with religion from a theoretical and practical point of view. A comparison of these two works could

---

[1] C. VAN VOLLENHOVEN, "Het boek van 1625," in *Verspreide Geschriften* I, Haarlem 1934, p. 225.

[2] J. HUIZINGA, "Grotius' plaats in de geschiedenis van den menschelijken geest," in *Tien Studiën*, Haarlem 1926, p. 118.

[3] J.C. KOECHER, *Historia libri Grotiani de Veritate Religionis Christianae*, in HUGO GROTIUS, *De veritate religionis christianae*. Variis dissertationibus illustratus, opera ac studio Io. CHR. KOECHERI, Halle 1739, pp. 1–192.

[4] C.W. ROLDANUS, *Hugo de Groot's Bewijs van den waren godsdienst*, Arnhem 1944. Cf. C. ROY, *Hugo Grotius considéré comme apologète*, Colmar 1855; T.C.L. WIJNMALEN, *Hugo de Groot als verdediger des Christendoms beschouwd. Eene litterarisch-apologetische proeve*, Utrecht 1869; C. LOOTEN, *De Grotio Christianae Religionis defensore*, Insulis 1889.

[5] *Hugo Grotius, Meletius sive de iis quae inter Christianos conveniunt epistola, Critical edition with translation, commentary and introduction by* GUILLAUME H.M. POSTHUMUS MEYJES, [= Studies in the History of Christian Thought, xl], Leiden etc. 1988.

result in a new insight into the continuity and development of Grotius' theological thought.

I have been occupied with a new study of Grotius' apologetic work, which is put into effect in a dissertation.[6] In this lecture I will focus on some results of this study, which might stimulate you to read my book, or perhaps on the contrary, cause you to leave it unread. Anyway, I will discuss five subjects now:

1) the genesis of Grotius' apologetic work
2) its content
3) the sources of the work
4) the author's intentions
5) the reception of the work during Grotius' lifetime.

GENESIS

In August 1618 the Dutch politicians Johan van Oldenbarnevelt, Rombout Hogerbeets and Hugo Grotius were arrested and sent to prison by order of the stadholder, Prince Maurice. Grotius was in fact dragged down in the political downfall of the Grand Pensionary Oldenbarnevelt. He was brought up for trial and condemned to life imprisonment. This sentence brought an abrupt end to his promising political career. Grotius submitted to his fate with a profound feeling of sadness; however, his daily prayers and his intensive reading of the bible gave him strength. In Loevestein castle he studied with remarkable discipline, using books sent by his learned friends Vossius and Erpenius. He developed great literary activities, resulting in translations, philological studies and theological and juridical treatises. He also wrote Dutch religious poetry, among which a rhymed catechism for his daughter.[7] This poem was printed and received very favourably in Holland. Gerard Vossius encouraged his friend Grotius to write more of this kind to enlist the sympathy of the Dutch. During the first months of the year 1620 Grotius composed a poetical work, which he initially presented to his friends and confidants as an introduction to the Christian belief. A manuscript of one of the first versions titled *Geloofs Voorberecht* has been preserved in the French national library in Paris.[8] A compari-

---

[6] J.P. HEERING, *Hugo de Groot als apologeet van de christelijke godsdienst. Een onderzoek van zijn geschrift De veritate religionis christianae (1640)*, diss. Leiden, 's-Gravenhage 1992.

[7] HUGO GROTIUS, *Vraghe en antwoordt over den doop. Ghestelt in zijn gevanckenisse voor zijn dochter Cornelia de Groot*, 1618 [= *BG* no. 59].

[8] HUGO GROTIUS, *Geloofs Voorberecht*. Cf. G. HUET, *Catalogue des manuscrits néerlandais de la Bibliothèque Nationale*, Paris 1886, no. 34: "Manuscrit non signé; copie con-

son of this manuscript with the printed version shows that Grotius took his friends' criticism – in particular of Episcopius and Vossius – seriously into account. The work was printed secretly in May 1622 under the title of *Bewijs van den waren godsdienst*.[9] Besides Grotius' text, the first edition contained a short poem by Willem de Groot and a contra–remonstrant preface, which had been added without the knowledge of Grotius. The anonymous author of this preface, titled: *Waerschouwinghe aen de eenvoudighe christenen* (Premonition to the ordinary Christians), was opposed to the irenic purport of Grotius' work and incited to combat the internal enemies of Christianity instead of the external adversaries, so to think of the Roman Catholics instead of the heathens, the Arians instead of the Jews and the Mennonites instead of the Moslems. The well-known Dutch historian Gerard Brandt supposed the author was the theologian Henricus Rosaeus, but Brandt had no evidence in support of this conjecture.[10] A second edition without the unwanted preface appeared in November 1622.[11] Grotius dedicated his *Bewijs* to the people of Holland, to whom he tried to prove his sincere patriotism. In the Introduction he addresses himself particularly to the Dutch seamen, whom he ordered to propagate Christianity all over the world.

After his escape from prison Grotius settled in Paris. There he translated his Dutch poem *Bewijs* into a Latin prose tract, which was published by Le Maire in Leiden in 1627, titled: *Sensus librorum sex quos pro veritate religionis christianae Batavice scripsit Hugo Grotius*.[12] This wordy title at least clearly indicates that the Latin tract is a translation or a paraphrase of the Dutch didactic poem. Grotius dedicated his tract to his friend Jerôme Bignon, who had become solicitor general at the French Parliament in 1626.

I will refrain from discussing the complicated history of the various editions of Grotius' apologetic work and will confine myself to a brief enumeration of the most important authorized editions. In 1629 Grotius presented a second enlarged and emendated edition, titled: *De veritate religionis christianae*.[13] The author maintained this

---

temporaine, avec des notes marginales et une partie des corrections de la main de l'auteur, 1620."

[9] *BG* no. 143.

[10] G. BRANDT, *Historie der Reformatie en andre kerkelyke geschiedenissen in en ontrent de Nederlanden*, vol. 4, Rotterdam 1704, p. 819.

[11] *BG* no. 144.

[12] *BG* no. 944.

[13] *BG* no. 946.

shortened title for the editions following. The third edition appeared in 1632 and was, like the second, published by Le Maire.[14] A
'new edition,' supplied with copious notes (*annotata*), was published
by Cramoisy in Paris in 1640.[15] This must be considered the final
authorized edition of Grotius' *De veritate*.

CONTENT

What is the content of Grotius' apologetic work? The work is organized in six books: the first three give evidence of the truth of the
Christian religion and the last three record the refutation of other
religions. The first book is a specimen of 'natural religion' and deals
with God and religion in general. Grotius gives a twofold proof of
the existence of God, deduces several properties of God and shows
that God is the cause of everything and that His providence gov-
erns all. He furthermore proves that the human soul lives on after
death and that man's destination is to be found in the felicity to be
expected of the next world. In order to acquire this bliss one should
aspire to the true religion. In the second book Grotius claims that
Christianity is the true religion. For this purpose he first shows the
factual truth of Christian belief: Jesus of Nazareth really lived and
was scandalously crucified. However, afterwards Jesus was honoured everywhere because of the miracles he had performed and,
above all, his resurrection from the dead. Grotius secondly argues
that Christianity surpasses all the other religions for its prospect of
reward, for its ethics and for its miraculous propagation. The third
book deals with the credibility of the bible. First Grotius elaborately
argues the credibility of the New Testament and proves the authenticity of the books included, the reliability of the authors of those
books, the veracity of the content and finally the purity of the New
Testament's texts. Then he briefly comments on the credibility of
the books of the Old Testament.

The fourth book is a refutation of paganism. Grotius is opposed
to pagan polytheism and the various forms of idolatry. He points
out the unreliability of pagan miracles and oracles and claims that
the rapid decline of paganism is an indication of its intrinsic weakness. Lastly, he proves that several important truths of Christian
faith were already evident in the doctrines of pagan philosophers

---

[14] *BG* no. 947.
[15] HUGO GROTIUS, *De veritate religionis christianae. Editio Nova, additis annotationibus in quibus testimonia*, Parisiis, Sumptibus Seb. Cramoisy, Typographi Regii, MDCXL. Cum privilegio regis [= *BG* no. 950].

like Plato. In the fifth book Grotius disputes Judaism. He argues
that the Jews should recognize the authenticity of Jesus' miracles,
that his doctrine is not in defiance of the law of Moses, and that Jesus is indeed the Messiah as announced in the prophecies of the
Old Testament. Jewish accusations implying that Christians recognize more than one God and worship a human being (Christ) are,
according to Grotius, without substantial foundation. Book six holds
a refutation of Islam. Grotius claims that the rise of Islam can be
considered God's punishment for serious sins committed in the early days of Christianity. He furthermore states that the Koran is not
reliable, because it is not open to investigation. A comparison between the religion of Jesus and that of Mohammed is in every respect to the advantage of Jesus. Grotius concludes his work with an
admonition for all Christians to live a simple, devout life in peace
and harmony.

SOURCES

Grotius did not mention the sources he used for the construction of
his apologetic work. The copious notes which he added later on
were meant to supply additional testimonies and do not provide
any insight into the sources of the text.[16] Fortunately the author
gave the reader at least one helpful clue. In the introduction of *De
veritate* Grotius expresses his admiration for the humanistic authors
Raimundus Sabundus, Juan–Luis Vives and Philippe Duplessis
Mornay.[17] Closer comparison shows that Grotius' work has quite a
few things in common with the apologetic writings of these authors,
with the exception of that of Sabundus. We may assume that the
works of Vives and Mornay have served as major sources to Grotius. Sabundus' work, *Theologia naturalis seu liber creaturarum*, has almost
nothing in common with Grotius' work and cannot possibly be considered a source.[18] There is reason to assume that Grotius used Sabundus' name as a cover for another name: that of the heretic
Faustus Socinus.

---

16 See HEERING, *Hugo de Groot als apologeet*, ch. 6, pp. 161–94.

17 HUGO GROTIUS, *De veritate religionis christianae* I 1, 1 (*OTh* III, p. 3 a 9–14):
"Non enim ignoras, ut qui omnia legi digna et quidem tanto cum judicio legeris,
quantum excoluerint istam materiam philosophica subtilitate Raemundus Sebun-
dus, dialogorum varietate Ludovicus Vives, maxima autem tum eruditione, tum facundia vestras Mornaeus."

18 RAIMUNDUS SABUNDUS, *Theologia naturalis seu liber creaturarum*, [Faksimi-
le–Neudruck der Ausgabe Sulzbach 1852, mit literargeschichtlicher Einführung
und kritischer Edition des Prologs und des Titulus I von FRIEDRICH STEGMÜLLER],
Stuttgart–Bad Cannstatt 1966.

Thus Grotius probably used three main sources: Mornay, Vives and – instead of Sabundus – Socinus. Every book of *De veritate* seems to be derived from one particular source: the first book from Mornay, the second and third books from Socinus, the fourth and fifth from Mornay again, and the sixth book from Vives. It seems that Grotius not only took separate arguments from these texts, but whole sequences or patterns of argumentation. This procedure of imitation (*imitatio*) was common in those days and can be defined as classicistic.[19] This does not imply an indiscriminate copying of arguments, but a free paraphrasing of the same material. Grotius found in the writings of his predecessors the patterns he used for his own argument. However, he felt free to deviate from these patterns at least once in every book of his work.

In the first book of Grotius' work one can recognize the pattern Mornay followed in his writing *De la verité de la religion chrétienne* (1581).[20] Grotius was more concise however, for he – unlike Mornay – deliberately omitted all dogmas of Christian theology. His elaborate explanation of God's providence based on the evidence of miracles and prophecies (§ 14–§ 16) – including an extensive account on the durability of the Jewish religion, the reliability of Moses' books and its affirmation by external testimonies – is only partially to be found in Mornay.

Up to recently it was assumed that Grotius' argumentation in the second and third book was new. Quite a similar line of argument, however, is to be found in Socinus' writing *De auctoritate Sacrae Scripturae* (1588).[21] Faustus Socinus composed this work around 1570, at a time he was working as a lawyer at the court of Isabella de Medici in Florence. The work was published probably for the first time in 1588 under the pseudonym Dominicus Lopez S.J.[22] Initially the work was appreciated by both Roman Catholics and Protestants,

---

[19] Cf. C.S. Baldwin, *Renaissance literary theory and practice. Classicism in the rhetoric and poetic of Italy, France, and England 1400–1600*, New York 1939; E.R. Curtius, *Europäische Literatur und Lateinisches Mittelalter*, Bern/München 1967[6], pp. 253–76; B. Völker–Hetzel, "Klassizismus," in *Handlexikon zur Literaturwissenschaft*, München 1974[2], pp. 226–30.

[20] Ph. Duplessis Mornay, *De la verité de la religion chrestienne contre les athées, epicuriens, païens, juifs, mahumédistes et autres infidèles*, Anvers 1581.

[21] Faustus Socinus, "De auctoritate Sacrae Scripturae," *Opera omnia in duos tomos distincta. Tomus primus continens eius opera exegetica et didactica [...]*, in *Bibliotheca fratrum Polonorum quos unitarios vocant*, vol. I, Irenopoli [= Amsterdam] 1656, pp. 265–80.

[22] Dominicus Lopez S.J. [= Faustus Socinus], *De auctoritate Sacrae Scripturae liber*, Hispali [= Sevilla] 1588.

however, after the real author was exposed, this appreciation evaporated like snow in summer.[23]

On comparing the second chapter of *De auctoritate* with the second book of Grotius' apologetic work one does not only find corresponding arguments, but complete patterns of corresponding argumentation. Moreover, the similarity in details is so striking that we cannot but assume that Grotius had Socinus' work at hand when composing his *Bewijs*.[24] There is no evidence on how Grotius got hold of Socinus' work in Loevestein. Possibly Gerard Vossius, who sent him a case of books almost every month, included his copy.[25] Vossius owned an anonymous edition of *De auctoritate* which was published in Steinfurt in 1611 and was provided with a preface of Conrad Vorstius.[26] Thus Grotius might have used this writing unaware of Socinus' authorship. This could explain why Grotius denied any influence of Socinus later on. However, considering that it was generally known that Socinus was indeed the author of this work, it is highly improbable that Grotius did not share this knowledge.

What is the line of argument in the second chapter of *De auctoritate*? Socinus aims to prove two things: first the fact that Christianity surpasses all other religions, and second that the truth of Christianity is based on convincing facts. Christianity exceeds other religions in three respects, namely in the nature of its promises, in its high standard ethics, and in its miraculous propagation. Second Socinus shows that the Christian truth is based on the facts that Jesus really lived, died a disgraceful death and was, nevertheless, posthumously

---

[23] Cf. C.C. SANDIUS, *Bibliotheca anti–trinitariorum*, Freistadt [= Amsterdam] 1684, pp. 66–67; E.M. WILBUR, *A History of Unitarianism, Socinianism and its Antecedents*, Cambridge Massachusetts 1945, pp. 390–91; D. CANTIMORI, *Italienische Haeretiker der Spätrenaissance*, Basel 1949, pp. 336–40; G. PIOLI, *Fausto Socino, Vita − Opere − Fortuna, Contributo alla storia del liberalismo religioso*, [Modena] 1952, pp. 98–106; G.H. WILLIAMS, *The Radical Reformation*, London [1962], pp. 750–51.

[24] Cf. H. BOTS − P. LEROY, *Correspondance intégrale d'André Rivet et de Claude Sarrau*, II, Amsterdam 1980, no. 273 (Rivet to Sarrau, 5 September 1644), p. 370: "Vous voyéz Monsieur, qu'il [= Th. Morton] ne le louë pas en ce qu'il a escrit pour accorder les Relig[ions] mais en ce qu'il [= Grotius] a escrit de *verit[ate] Relig[ionis] Christianae*, qui est un livre bien suivi, mais qui doibt beaucoup a celuy de Socin de *auctor[itate] S[acrae] Script[urae]* et qui a des maximes qui portent au mesme but que Socin."

[25] Cf. *Catalogus librorum Gerardi Vossii* [= Ms. University Library of Amsterdam III D 11a], fol. 244ʳ: "Socinus De auctoritate Sacrae Scripturae (in praef. Vorstii) Steinfurt 1611."

[26] *De auctoritate S. Scripturae. Opusculum his temporibus nostris utilissimum, quemadmodum intelligi potest ex praecipuis rerum, quae in ipso tractantur, capitibus. Ea vero proxime seqq pagellis notata sunt. In praefatione ad lectorem ratio huius editionis exponitur*, Steinfurti excudit Theoph. Caesar 1611.

honoured by many people for the miracles he had performed and, above all, his resurrection from the dead.[27]

In the second book of Grotius' *De veritate* one can discover the same two sequences of argumentation, be it in reverse order. First Grotius proves that Jesus really lived, subsequently died a scandalous death, but was honoured because of the miracles he had performed and his resurrection from the dead. He continues by arguing that Christianity surpasses all other religions by its promises, its ethics and its propagation. Grotius, however, shows his independence in his elaborate treatment of Christian ethics (§ 12–§ 17), which seems partly to be derived from his own work *Meletius*, as is already noted by Posthumus Meyjes.[28]

The third book of Grotius' work shows remarkable parallels with the first chapter of Socinus' *De auctoritate*. Both texts concern the authority and credibility of the Bible, especially the New Testament. Socinus used three criteria to establish that credibility: the authenticity of these books or their historical reliability, their veracity or plausibility, and their textual purity. The Italian heretic applied these criteria to the books of the New and the Old Testaments and concluded their credibility.[29] Grotius again argued in quite the same way, but deviated from Socinus on one point. In order to obtain a further affirmation of the reliability of the authors of the New Testament, Grotius referred to the miracles and prophecies they had performed – for convenience's sake identifying these authors with the apostles (§ 7–§ 8). Probably Hugo did not feel at ease with the argumentation of Socinus, that lacked any appeal to notions generally used in reformation theology like the inspiration and the internal testimony of the Holy Ghost.

We can be brief regarding the last three books of *De veritate*, because Grotius did not diverge from the usual lines of Christian apologetics. Apart from some arguments of his own, Grotius picked up Mornay's line of argument in the fourth book.[30] The fifth book can also be traced back to Mornay's work.[31] However, Grotius' argumentation of the abolition of certain commandments of the law of

---

[27] FAUSTUS SOCINUS, "De auctoritate Sacrae Scripturae," in *Bibliotheca fratrum Polonorum quos unitarios vocant*, vol. I, Irenopoli [= Amsterdam] 1656, pp. 271–75.

[28] POSTHUMUS MEYJES, *Hugo Grotius, Meletius*, pp. 154–60.

[29] FAUSTUS SOCINUS, "De auctoritate Sacrae Scripturae", in *Bibliotheca fratrum Polonorum quos unitarios vocant*, vol. I, Irenopoli [= Amsterdam] 1656, pp. 265–71.

[30] Cf. MORNAY, *De la verité*, ch. 21–23.

[31] Cf. MORNAY, *De la verité*, ch. 28–31.

Moses (§ 6–§ 12) seems to have been based primarily on a writing of the early Christian apologist Justin Martyr.[32] The material of Grotius' sixth book seems for the main part to have been derived from Vives' writing *De veritate fidei christianae* (1543).[33] Finally, one can remark that Grotius composed the concluding admonition probably on his own account.

THE AUTHOR'S INTENTIONS

Inspired by irenic motives Grotius wrote his apologetic work. Christianity's internal discord had been a major concern to Grotius for a long time. He considered this discord a disease like cancer, which was particularly caused by his contemporaries rigid dogmatism, the result of their longing for doctrinal certainty. In order to save them from too strong a fixation on dogmas, Grotius argued in earlier works like *Meletius* for a reduction of Christian dogmatics into a small number of necessary dogmas, which can all be found in the bible.[34] In the epilogue of his apologetic work he addresses himself to his Christian readers and strongly incites them to preserve mutual unity and peace. As a remedy for the discussions and disagreements on doctrinal issues he points out the relativity of all human knowledge. Grotius stated several times that he considered the truth of Christianity indissolubly connected with mutual peace and unity among the faithful. He was convinced of the fact that his contemporaries had lost sight of that truth, because of their fixation on doctrines.

In his apologetic work Grotius refrains from dealing with Christian dogmas, realizing that these would not appeal to outsiders. He thus dissociated apologetics from dogmatics, and this was really revolutionary. Willem de Groot realized this and asked his brother Hugo, right after the conception of the Dutch poem, why he had omitted generally acknowledged Christian doctrines, like the trinity and the divinity of Christ. Hugo answered thus: "It is evident that I do not treat Christian doctrines for Christian readers, but that I contrive to motivate atheists, heathens, Jews and Moslems to acknowledge that Christianity is the true religion, so that they could subsequently select those doctrines from the scripture themselves."[35]

---

[32] Iust. M. *Dial. Tryph.* I.

[33] Cf. J.L. VIVES, *De veritate fidei christianae*, "Liber Quartus contra sectam Mahumetis," in *Opera* II, Basel 1555, pp. 455–82.

[34] *Meletius*, 89–91.

[35] *BW* II no. 600 (Grotius to W. de Groot, 12 April 1620), pp. 30–31: "Res ipsa loquitur me non explicare dogmata christianae fidei christianis, sed hoc agere ut

In another letter Grotius claimed that Christian doctrines cannot be understood without divine revelation.[36] One can conclude that Grotius realized that Christian doctrines were not generally comprehensible and therefore not suitable to convert outsiders to Christianity. His apologetic strategy is based upon one of the fundamental rules of antique rhetoric, holding that to be convincing one should not rely on one's own presuppositions but on those of one's audience.

RECEPTION

I will likewise be brief on the reception of De veritate during the author's lifetime, so up to 1645. The criticism passed on Grotius' apologetic work remained notably limited. His earlier theological writings had raised considerable opposition and dispute. His De veritate, however, was widely praised. Criticism that did arise against it concentrated on the accusation of Socinianism. This accusation was expressed by Calvinist contra-remonstrants, who had made a habit of stigmatizing all remonstrants as Socinians. Grotius initially had no reason to be alarmed, as the accusation was a commonplace. He lost his imperturbability, however, when Gisbertus Voetius and Martinus Schoock took up arms against him.[37] Their major reproach was that Grotius had completely ignored the central doctrines of Christian theology, such as the trinity and the deity of Jesus Christ. Grotius did not address his opponents directly. He didn't appreciate theologians like Voetius, Schoock and Rivet. Moreover, he had an aversion to public polemics. Nevertheless, he

---

impii, ethnici, iudaei, mahometistae agnoscant veram esse religionem christianam, atque eius dogmata deinde petitum eant ex sacris nostris literis."

[36] BW X no. 3917 (Grotius to G.J. Vossius, 1 January 1639), p. 12: "Triados probationem in eo libro directe aggressus non sum memor ejus, quod a viro magno socero tuo [sc. Junio] audieram, peccasse Plessaeum et alios, quod rationibus a natura petitis et Platonicis saepe non valde appositis testimoniis astruere voluissent rem, non ponendam in illa cum atheis, paganis, judaeis, mahumetistis disputatione, qui omnes ad sacras literas ducendi sunt, ut inde talia hauriant, quae nisi Deo semet patefaciente cognosci nequeunt."

[37] G. VOETIUS, Thersites heautontimorumenos, hoc est remonstrantium hyperaspistes, catechesi, et liturgiae Germanicae, Gallicae, et Belgicae denuo insultans, retusus; idemque provocatus ad probationem mendaciorum, et calumniarum quae in illustr. dd. ordd. et ampliss. magistratus Belgii, religionem reformatam, ecclesias, synodos, pastores etc. sine ratione, sine modo effudit, Utrecht 1635.

M. SCHOOCKIUS, Claere en oprechte ontdeckinge der genaemder remonstranten leugenen en lasteringen, tegen de hooge en laage overigheden, gereformeerde kercken, en haere yeverighe voorstanders. Als oock een bondich vertooch van haere sociniaensche grouwelen, alles vergadert uyt drie naemloose boecxkens geintituleert: I. Proeve van de conscientieuse oprechtigheyt Gisberti Voetii. II. Academia Gisberti Voetii. III. Den rechten remonstrantsche theologant, Utrecht 1638.

felt the urge to answer to his friends and to defend himself in his letters against the accusations. He basically used four standard arguments:

1) He played off the successful reception of his work against the marginal criticism;

2) He appealed to his apologetic method which would consequently bring about a non-dogmatic treatment;

3) He did not deny possible similarities with Socinus, they were, as he claimed, absolutely accidental;

4) He referred to the early church as the only touchstone of religious truth.

During Grotius' life five translations of his apologetic work appeared: one English translation,[38] two German translations,[39] and two French translations.[40] Only one German translation was based on the Dutch poem *Bewijs*, but the translator was none other than the famous German poet Martin Opitz. The other translations were based upon one of the Latin versions of the text. Grotius mentioned in his letters also Greek and Persian translations, but these were in all probability never realized.[41]

The posthumous success of Grotius' apologetic work may be described as overwhelming. No less than 144 Latin and translated editions of the work have been published since 1645. Particularly remarkable is the large number of English editions and translations in the eighteenth and nineteenth century. In the twentieth century, however, the work has hardly been printed anymore.[42]

---

[38] *True Religion explained, and defended against the archenemies thereof in these times. In six bookes. Written in Latine by Hugo Grotius, and now done in English for the common good*, [by F. COVENTRY], London 1632 [= *BG* no. 1015].

[39] *Von der Warheit der Christlichen Religion. Auss Holländischer Sprache Hochdeutsch gegeben durch Martin Opitzen*, [Breslau] 1631 [= *BG* no.152]. *Die Meinung der Bücher Hugonis Grotii Von der Warheit der Christlichen Religion. Von ihm selbst auss dem Holländischen inn Latein, und auss diesem inn das Deutsche gezogen durch Christoph Colerum*. In Vorlegung David Müllers 1631 [= *BG* no. 1008].

[40] *Traicté de la verité de la religion chrestienne*, Traduit du Latin de l'auteur [par E. DE COURCELLES], Amsterdam 1636 [= *BG* no. 1060]. *La vérité de la religion chrestienne*, [par F.E. DE MÉZERAY], Paris [1644] [= *BG* no. 1061].

[41] *BW* X no. 3917 (Grotius to G. J. Vossius, 1 January 1639), p. 12: "Vertit eum [= De veritate] Graece pastor legati hic Anglicani." *BW* IX no. 3874 (Grotius to W. de Groot, 4 December 1638), p. 730: "Liber meus de Veritate religionis christianae, mi frater, qui socinianus est Voetianis, adeo hic pro tali non habetur, ut studio religiosorum pontificorum vertatur in sermonem Persicum ad convertendos, si Deus coepto annuat, ejus imperii mahumetistas." Cf. H.C. MILLIES, "Over de Oostersche vertalingen van het beroemde geschrift van Hugo Grotius, *De veritate religionis christianae*," in *Verslagen en Mededeelingen der Koninklijke Akademie van Wetenschappen*, Afd. Letterkunde, vol. 7, Amsterdam 1863, pp. 108–34.

[42] H. GROTIUS, *True Religion*, London 1632, [= The English Experience, its record in early printed books published in facsimile, no. 318], Amsterdam/New York

Some concluding remarks. Grotius' *De veritate* must be considered a rather traditional work, because the author derived almost all, if not all his arguments from existing apologetic literature. He showed his originality by presenting the material of his predecessors in a new order. Only the reduction he applied was pioneering and innovative: he refrained from discussing Christian dogmas and thus dissociated apologetics from dogmatics. This reduction is characteristic of his predominantly ethical view of the Christian religion. Philosophers of the early enlightenment followed Grotius in that respect.

The so called 'golden book' of Grotius is a typical product of late humanistic classicism. This classicism lost its appeal as early as in the seventeenth century, due to the appearance of great innovators on the fields of science and philosophy like Bacon, Hobbes, Descartes, Pascal, and Spinoza. To the modern reader Grotius' apologetic work has lost most of its charm. Nowadays there will not be many readers who would be convinced by its typical humanistic rhetorical argumentation. This consideration does not diminish the historical significance of Grotius' work as a link between late humanism and early enlightenment.

1971. H. GROTIUS, *Della vera religione cristiana*. A cura di FIORELLA PINTACUDA DE MICHELIS, [= Piccola biblioteca filosofica Laterza, 86] Milano 1973.

GROTIUS ET LES RELIGIONS DU PAGANISME DANS LES *ANNOTATIONES IN VETUS TESTAMENTUM*

François Laplanche
(Angers)

Cette communication sera centrée sur les *Annotationes in Vetus Testamentum* publiées par Grotius à Paris en 1644. Mais j'ai utilisé aussi l'*Explicatio Decalogi ut in Graece exstat*, écrit anonyme de 1640 inséré dans le commentaire du chapitre 20 de l'Exode dans l'édition des *Opera omnia theologica* de 1679. C'est sur cette édition qu'est basé mon travail, qui puisera aussi des renseignements dans les *Annotationes in Novum Testamentum*, publiées de 1641 à 1650, parce qu'elles offrent quelques textes majeurs relatifs à l'idolâtrie. L'idolâtrie, c'est ainsi qu'au XVIIe siècle, la théologie chrétienne désigne les religions du paganisme. Dans la *Somme Théologique* de Saint Thomas d'Aquin, devenue le manuel de l'enseignement à partir du XVIe siècle, l'idolâtrie est étudiée au chapitre des péchés contre la vertu de religion. Elle constitue une variante de la superstition, c'est-à-dire d'un péché qui verse du côté de l'excès et qui consiste à rendre un culte indû à une créature[1] (culte nécessairement indû puisque le culte ne doit être rendu qu'à Dieu).

Grotius observe, au commentaire de Exode 20, que le mot grec εἰδωλολατρεία traduit l'hebreu *abôdah zarah, cultus a lege alienus,* non parce que εἴδωλον, l'image, signifierait par soi quelque chose de mauvais, mais parce que la Loi en interdit l'usage: "C'est pourquoi le sens n'est pas rendu mot à mot, mais se trouve assez clairement exprimé."[2] Nous aurons lieu de voir que cette remarque philologique va loin et engage déjà l'interprétation théologique de Grotius. Il ajoute, au commentaire de la première épître aux Corinthiens, 5.9, après avoir repris cet éclaircissement sémantique, que les chrétiens ont continué d'employer le terme d'idolâtrie, quoique non soumis, eux, à l'interdiction des images. Le rapprochement des deux textes est donc très intéressant.[3] Mais, avant de venir à la question de l'interprétation, nous allons observer la manière dont Grotius considère les rites des religions païennes. C'est en effet sur les rites des peuples contemporains des Hébreux, de la période égyptienne à la période romaine, que portent la plupart des indications de Grotius sur les religions païennes dans les *Annotationes* (à la

---

[1] S. Thomas d'Aquin, *Somme théologique*, qu. 94, art. 1.
[2] *OTh* I, p. 39 b 10.
[3] *OTh* II/2, p. 782 b 34.

différence du *De Veritate*). Bien entendu, il rappelle l'existence de
convergences ou même de similitudes soit entre la Bible et les doctrines des philosophes anciens, soit entre le Décalogue et les législa-
tions antiques sur le serment, le meurtre, l'adultère. Ceci est notable dans le commentaire du premier chapitre de la Genèse et du
chapitre 20 de l'Exode pour l'Ancien Testament; dans le commentaire du chapitre 17 des Actes et du chapitre premier de l'épître
aux Romains pour le Nouveau. Mais il s'agit là de thèmes familiers
à l'apologétique humaniste, développés dans le *De Veritate Religionis
Christianae*. Ces rapprochements portent rarement sur le culte et
c'est avant tout à partir des observations et réflexions grotiennes sur
les rites du paganisme que je voudrais suggérer la présence d'interprétations théologiques.

A. Observations et réflexions sur les rites païens dans les
"Annotationes in Vetus Testamentum"

A première lecture, Grotius ne semble guère original, puisque sa
description et sa réflexion s'inspirent de celles de Maïmonide et de
Vossius. Les textes importants du premier sur le problème de l'idolâtrie se trouvent dans le commentaire du traité *Abodah Zarah*, qui
fait partie de la Mishnah; dans la section IV du *Livre de la connaissance*, premier livre du *Mishneh Torah*; enfin dans le *Guide des égarés*,
3e partie, à partir du chapitre 29. Grotius ne donne pas de référence précise. Je pense, par le rapprochement des contenus, qu'il a
surtout utilisé le *Guide des égarés*. Johann Buxtorf en avait publié une
édition latine en 1627 à Bâle. Par ailleurs, nous savons que l'édition
hébréo-latine de la section IV du *Livre de la connaissance* ne parut
qu'en 1641 mais que le traducteur Denys Vossius avait achevé le
manuscrit dès 1636.[4] Et même si le grand ouvrage du père de
celui-ci, G.J. Vossius, sur l'idolâtrie, le *De theologia gentili ac physiologia
christiana* ne fut connu de Grotius qu'après l'impression des *Annotationes in Vetus Testamentum* sur le Pentateuque,[5] pour l'*Explicatio Decalogi*
(1640), Grotius a bénéficié des conseils de G.J. Vossius et de Menasseh ben Israël, selon Ter Meulen et Diermanse.[6] Sa vision des
paganismes se ressent donc de la fréquentation des textes de Maï-

---

[4] *BW* VII 2860 p. 542, de G.J. Vossius à Grotius, 30 novembre 1636.
[5] C'est ce qui ressort du rapprochement de la lettre 5367 (14 septembre 1641)
BW XII, p. 510 et de la lettre 5712 (10 mai 1642) *BW* XIII, p. 218. Ces deux lettres sont adressées par Grotius à G.J. Vossius et leur rapprochement montre que
les annotations sur le Pentateuque étaient presque toutes imprimées quand Grotius
reçut le *De theologia gentili* et le *De idololatria*.
[6] *BG* p. 548.

monide et de son amitié avec les Vossius. Cependant, nous allons voir comment Grotius garde beaucoup d'initiative dans le traitement du problème.

Nous trouvons dans le *Guide des égarés* des indications sur les sources de Maïmonide relatives à l'histoire de l'idolâtrie et surtout une comparaison entre rites juifs et rites païens, très éclairante sur ceux-ci. Le philosophe juif distingue en effet une double finalité des lois rituelles imposées à son peuple par le Seigneur. Ce qui contredit les usages païens n'est pas interdit à cause d'un caractère intrinsèquement mauvais, mais à cause de son emploi dans les rites des nations. Ce qui s'accorde au contraire avec ces usages est autorisé en vertu de la pédagogie de Dieu, qui ne veut pas arracher brutalement les juifs aux coutumes religieuses de leur environnement. De plus, ajoute Maïmonide, l'ensemble du rituel juif est beaucoup moins onéreux que les systèmes d'interdit des idolâtres.[7] Les lois rituelles des juifs permettent donc une triple entrée dans les religions du paganisme. Mais Grotius ne s'intéresse qu'aux deux premières.

1 En ce qui concerne les rites interdits pour cause d'usage idolâtrique, Maïmonide se bornait à évoquer les rites des populations arabes ou chaldéennes qu'avaient critiqués avant lui les auteurs musulmans. Maïmonide ayant donné des indications sur ses sources au chapitre 29 de la 3e partie du *Guide des égarés,* Munk a composé pour son édition des notes très érudites sur ces divers traités, en particulier sur *L'Agriculture nabatéenne* de Ibn Wa'hschiyya (Xe siècle).[8] Grotius à cause de sa connaissance étendue de la littérature grecque et latine enrichit beaucoup l'observation. Il utilise les poètes grecs et latins, leurs commentateurs (surtout Servius, commentateur de Virgile à la fin du IVe siècle), les historiens (Hérodote, Josèphe, Tacite, Diodore de Sicile), les interprètes des religions antiques, soit chrétiens (Origène, Eusèbe, Augustin, Lactance), soit païens (néoplatoniciens comme Jamblique, Proclus et surtout Porphyre; ou stoïciens comme Cicéron; ou l'éclectique et religieux Plutarque). Il recourt aussi aux naturalistes: Pline, Strabon.

Sur cette large base d'information, il se trouve en mesure d'enrichir la première considération de Maïmonide, que les interdits de la Loi ont pour fin d'empêcher l'idolâtrie. Nous nous arrêterons pour

---

[7] MAIMONIDE, *Guide des égarés,* 3e partie, chap. 30–32 et 47, trad. MUNK, Paris 1960, 3 vol., t. III, pp. 243ss.
[8] *Guide des égarés,* trad. MUNK, t. III, pp. 231ss.

commencer à l'interdit des images développé dans le commentaire
du Décalogue. Ce commandement est précédé de l'interdiction des
dieux étrangers. Quels furent ceux-ci? Ici Grotius esquisse une généalogie de l'apparition des dieux qui combine les renseignements
de Maïmonide et ceux qui viennent des chapitres 14 de la Sagesse
et 1 de l'épître aux Romains. Cette généalogie se rapproche beaucoup de celle que décrit Vossius dans le *De theologia gentili* et de celle
qu'offrent les *De dis Syris Syntagmata II,* de Selden (encore plus anciens, puisque la première édition est de 1617).

Selon cette généalogie, les premiers dieux furent les *ignes coelestes,*
les astres. Ce sont des faux dieux, non qu'ils ne soient pas bienfai-
sants, mais parce qu'ils n'ont ni intelligence ni liberté. Puis les rois
furent adorés *simul cum astris et in astris.* Coutume plutôt phénicienne
qu'égyptienne en ses origines, opine Grotius. Car les Phéniciens
adoraient leur roi dans l'astre appelé Chronos par les Grecs, Satur-
ne par les Latins et par eux-mêmes, Moloch (où l'on retrouve la ra-
cine MLK qui signifie roi). Ensuite comme les hommes ont donné
des noms d'animaux aux constellations, soit à cause de leur forme,
soit en vertu d'une communication particulière d'une espèce vivante
avec un astre, les animaux furent à leur tout mis au rang des dieux.
Par extension, leurs propriétés spécifiques servirent aussi à les divi-
niser. Enfin, on crut que les démons investissaient les corps d'animaux.[9]

Après cette généalogie des dieux, Grotius passe au commentaire
de l'interdiction des images, deux fois reprise dans le chapitre 20 de
l'Exode, v. 4.[10] Il insiste beaucoup sur l'emploi magique des statues.
Il explique qu'il s'agit bien de statues car, si les LXX ont employé
εἴδωλον, le mot hébreu *pêsêl,* formé sur le verbe *pâsal* – tailler –
évoque la statue de bois ou de pierre, ainsi que le γλυπτόν des autres interprètes grecs. La précision n'est pas sans importance, car ce
sont les creux des statues qui permettaient aux païens de croire
qu'elles contenaient des esprits dont on pouvait capter les influences. Le caractère absolu de l'interdit a pour fin d'empêcher ces
usages magiques. Grotius situe encore un certain nombre d'interdits
du chapitre 19 du Lévitique comme relatifs à des pratiques magiques: l'interdiction de l'hybridation (19.19), des incisions et tatou-
ages (19.26); la sévérité des sanctions contre ceux qui se tournent

---

[9] *OTh* I, p. 36 a 7 à p. 37 a 45.
[10] Grotius ne pense pas que le redoublement du commandement ("Tu ne feras
pas d'idole, ni aucune image...") signifie qu'il y aurait là deux commandements
distincts. *OTh* I, p. 39 a 17–47.

vers les nécromanciens et les oracles (20.6 et 20.27).[11] Sur le chapitre de la nécromancie, Grotius se montre très informé. Au commentaire de I Samuel 28.4–20, il explique que la divination par le
moyen des morts est la forme la plus antique de cet art. Elle té-
moigne de la croyance à la permanence des âmes. Elle est attestée
chez Eschyle et Hérodote. Et les Hébreux ont été souillés par cette
pratique, comme nous le savons par les rapports de Saül avec la
sorcière d'En-Dor.[12]

A propos d'autres pratiques, la prostitution sacrée, les sacrifices
humains, Grotius charge son commentaire de références à la littérature antique. Pour la prostitution, il utilise Hérodote qui attribue
cette coutume aux Babyloniens et à toutes les nations voisines. Il
affirme que les Phéniciens la transportèrent à Chypre.[13] Il consacre
un grand soin à la question des sacrifices humains, parce que
l'expression de Deutéronome 18.10 lui semble trop faible: "Il ne se
trouvera chez toi personne pour faire passer par le feu son fils ou sa
fille." Utilisant d'autres textes bibliques (Ez. 20.26; 23.37–39), Grotius démontre que le passage du Deutéronome qu'il commente (18.
10) évoque sans ambiguïté les sacrifices humains. De la Bible à Philon de Byblos, la coutume est bien attestée. Porphyre offre, dit-il,
une bonne récapitulation du sujet: elle se trouve effectivement dans
le *De Abstinentia*, livre II, 53–56. Nous savons de plus par Plutarque,
Lactance, Tertullien, Augustin que les Phéniciens et les Carthagi-
nois s'adonnaient particulièrement à cette pratique, qui fut progressivement remplacée soit par les sacrifices animaux, soit par le passage de la victime à travers le feu. A cause des navigations des Phéniciens, l'on retrouve encore cette pratique dans les îles de l'Atlanti-
que proches du continent africain et dans celles de l'Océan In-
dien.[14]

En résumé, Grotius enrichit beaucoup les indications de Maïmonide sur la fonction des interdits de la Loi. Ils lui apparaissent comme des mesures pratiques destinées à écarter Israël des cultes idolâ-
triques, parce que les poètes et les historiens les présentent effectivement comme magiques et immoraux. Toutefois, il souligne qu'en

---

[11] *OTh* I, p. 66 b 36 à p. 68 b 14.
[12] Il s'agit dans ce passage, selon Grotius, non de l'évocation de l'âme de Samuel, mais de l'apparition d'un esprit de mensonge. Cette interprétation était celle
des Pères de l'Eglise mais elle avait été abandonnée au temps de la Réforme catholique, de façon à justifier la croyance au purgatoire et l'intervention des âmes
du purgatoire en faveur des vivants. *OTh* I, p. 129 b 9–49.
[13] *OTh* I, p. 68 a 38–45 sur Lév. 19.29. Les textes d'Hérodote se trouvent dans
L'Enquête, I 93; II 64.
[14] *OTh* I, p. 92 a 8 à p. 93 b 56.

des temps très lointains, les cultes du paganisme avaient des formes plus pures: ils n'admettaient pas le culte des images et, à l'époque de la migration du clan de Jacob en Egypte, il n'y avait pas encore d'idolâtrie en cette contrée.[15]

2 La participation des Hébreux à la culture religieuse de l'Antiquité

L'autre thèse de Maïmonide est que la concordance entre rituels juifs et païens provient de la pédagogie divine. Chez le penseur juif, cette thèse s'accompagne d'une forte insistance sur le caractère non-miraculeux de l'action divine: Dieu n'accomplit pas de miracle pour transformer les hommes soudainement.[16] Il utilise donc le rituel païen pour amener progressivement les Hébreux à la vraie foi. Grotius semble plutôt procéder ici en pur historien, car il accumule les rapprochements érudits, mais sans y joindre de réflexion théologique.

Il montre d'abord que les Hébreux ont usé de coutumes générales aux peuples antiques: l'offrande des prémices (Ex. 23.10), les ablutions avec l'offrande des sacrifices (Ex. 30.39), les impuretés contractées au contact des cadavres (Nb. 19.19) ou provoquées par les pertes de sang, de sperme et les rapports sexuels (Lév. 15.16), l'effroi causé par l'écoulement du sang, dû à la conviction que l'âme réside en celui-ci (Lév. 17.1), l'examen du soupçon d'adultère par une ordalie spécifique (Nb 5.17), les propriétés requises des animaux à sacrifier (Ex. 12).[17]

A propos de la classification identique des sacrifices chez les peuples antiques, Grotius livre un peu plus sa pensée. C'est en particulier sur le commentaire du chant III de l'Enéide par Servius qu'il s'appuie, faisant remarquer que le poète latin distingue quatre sortes de sacrifices dans lesquelles lui, Grotius, reconnaît le sacrifice pacifique (shelêm), le sacrifice pour le péché (hata'ah ou asham), le sacrifice de louange (zébah tôdâh), l'holocauste (olah). Ce commentaire

---

[15] OTh I, p. 40 b 26–39 et p. 84 a 20 à p. 84 b 18.

[16] "Ce n'est pas que nous croyions que le changement de la nature d'un individu quelconque soit difficile pour Dieu. Cependant, selon les principes contenus dans la loi du Pentateuque, Dieu n'a jamais voulu le faire et ne le fera jamais; car si c'était sa volonté de changer chaque fois la nature de l'individu humain, à cause de ce qu'il veut obtenir de cet individu, la mission des prophètes et toute la législation seraient inutiles" (MAÏMONIDE, Guide des Égarés, 3e partie, chap. 32, éd. MUNK, t. III, pp. 256–57).

[17] OTh I, p. 54 b 7–15 (prémices); p. 56 b 61 à p. 57 a 5 (ablutions); p. 77 a 43–56 (cadavres); p. 64 b 20–44 (pertes, rapports sexuels); p. 65 b 40 à p. 66 a 5 (âme dans le sang); p. 73 a 1–57 (eau de jalousie); p. 30 b 22–30 (les victimes).

se trouve dans les *Annotationes* sur le Lévitique 1.19.[18] Grotius livre ici deux observations très précieuses: 1° La similitude des rites pourrait venir de leur transmission des Hébreux aux autres nations, ou, *quod credibilius est*, s'expliquer par des emprunts faits aux Syriens et aux Egyptiens, mais avec des corrections chez les Hébreux, sans correction chez les autres nations. 2° La deuxième observation se lit un peu plus loin, toujours dans le commentaire du même verset: *mirum est quam vetustissima sacra inter se congruant*. Remarque sur la concordance des rites qui semble innocente, mais l'est-elle vraiment? Il est parfois possible de donner la raison de cette surprenante similitude: par exemple, les Hébreux ont accepté les interdits alimentaires des Egyptiens pour des motifs d'hygiène déjà signalés par Maïmonide.[19] Pour la couleur de la vache du sacrifice (Nb 19.2), qui selon la Loi, doit être rousse, Grotius avoue qu'il n'a pas d'explication. Même Salomon, en toute sa sagesse, n'est pas parvenu à deviner cette énigme.[20]

L'abondance des références à la littérature antique dans les *Annotationes in Vetus Testamentum* a agacé Richard Simon.[21] En fait, ne cacheraient-elles pas des intentions théologiques? C'est ce que nous devons examiner maintenant, en interrogeant Grotius lui-même.

B Les intentions théologiques de Grotius

1 En insistant sur la finalité pratique de l'interdiction des images, Grotius entend montrer le caractère temporaire de ce commandement, entièrement relatif aux conditions de promiscuité où vivait le peuple hébreu. A lire seulement le commentaire du Décalogue, l'on pourrait croire que Grotius ne dépasse pas Maïmonide:

> Ces interdits relatifs aux statues et aux images d'êtres vivants semblent appartenir au genre de choses qui ne sont pas illicites par nature, mais qui sont défendues pour éviter un mal. Mais il en est ainsi de la plupart des préceptes de la Loi de Moïse. Il s'agit d'ἀδιάφορα, directement opposés aux institutions égyptiennes, phéniciennes et arabes pour éloigner plus efficacement les Hébreux du polythéisme. C'est ce qu'a sagement noté Maïmonide.[22]

---

[18] *OTh* I, p. 60 a 36 à p. 60 b 38.
[19] *OTh* I, p. 63 a 34–37.
[20] *OTh* I, p. 77 a 18–29.
[21] Richard Simon, *Histoire critique du Vieux Testament*, Rotterdam 1685, l. III, chap. XV, pp. 443b–444a.
[22] *OTh* I, p. 40 a 52–60.

Mais, dans les *Annotationes ad Consultationem Cassandri,* qui datent de
la même époque,[23] Grotius est clair: l'interdiction des images ne
vise pas les chrétiens. Elle est si bien un commandement positif que
Dieu y a lui-même fait des exceptions (le serpent d'airain, l'image
des chérubins dans le saint des saints). Voici les propres termes de
Grotius:

> Or, ces commandements positifs de l'ancienne loi – qui ne touchent
> en rien les mœurs, mais avaient pour fin de séparer les juifs des gen-
> tils – n'obligent en rien les chrétiens, pas plus que la loi du Sabbat
> qui se trouve aussi dans le Décalogue. C'est pourquoi le Christ,
> quand il reprend les commandements du Décalogue destinés à durer,
> ne fait aucune mention de ceux-ci.[24]

Dans les *Animadversiones in Animadversiones Riveti,* Grotius assure
qu'aucune concorde avec les catholiques ne sera possible si les protestants continuent à les traiter d'idolâtres.[25] Dans la *Rivetiani Apolo-
getici discussio,* il revient encore sur le problème en ajoutant un argument supplémentaire. Les interdictions portées au temps d'Adam et
de Noé visent l'humanité entière, la Loi de Moïse n'était adressée
qu'au peuple juif, comme le montre bien la préface du Décalogue,
qui fait allusion à la sortie d'Egypte.[26] Puis Grotius répète une fois
de plus que la vénération des images n'était pas interdite parce que
mauvaise, mais mauvaise parce qu'interdite.[27]

Il ressort de cette insistance et de ces répétitions que le regard de
Grotius sur les rituels païens est original par rapport à celui des
érudits protestants de son temps. Moins préoccupés d'irénisme, ils
partagent ou du moins alimentent cette forme de controverse, qui
consiste à identifier le paganisme et le catholicisme, puisque tout
autant que les catholiques, les païens entendaient vénérer non
l'image, la stèle ou la statue, mais le dieu dont ceux-ci n'étaient que
les symboles. Amorcé dans le *De dis Syris* de Selden, le thème de la

---

[23] Voir *BG* nos. 1165–1201: les volumes contenant la controverse avec Rivet pa-
rurent de 1642 à 1645.

[24] "Positiva autem illa quae fuere in lege veteri, nihil obligant christianos, non
magis quam lex Sabbathi, quae et ipsa in Decalogo est posita. Propterea Christus
cum perpetuo mansura Decalogi praecepta repetit, horum nullam facit mentio-
nem." *OTh* III, p. 624 b 16–22.

[25] *OTh* III, p. 644 b 29–35.

[26] *OTh* III, p. 707 b 34–35.

[27] "Quis non vidit haec, quae explicavimus, mala fuisse Judaeis, quia erant vetita, non autem vetita quod per se essent mala? Quid enim naturaliter in eo illicitum est, si quis exstantem habeat aut hominis aut animalis imaginem? Quid etiam
in eo per se illicitum erat, si quis Deo supplicaret in eo loco ubi erant tales imagi-
nes, praesertim quo tempore omnis locus Deo sacrari poterat, ut ante legem?" *OTh*
III, p. 708 a 6–14. Sur l'utilisation de la théologie symbolique par J. Basnage, voir
l'article de F. LAPLANCHE, "Basnage historien des paganismes antiques ou la crise
de l'apologétique chrétienne à l'aube des Lumières", *Lias* 15 (1988), pp. 171–90.

théologie symbolique occupera tout le livre IX du *De theologia gentili* de Vossius, non sans que l'auteur, dès le livre I (chap. V) ait souligné l'importance de la distinction culte propre/culte symbolique, assez méconnue avant lui, affirme-t-il.[28] En insistant sur le caractère magique des rites païens, Grotius au contraire les éloigne le plus possible du culte du vrai Dieu. Le rôle qu'y jouent les esprits mauvais est bien plus accentué que chez Maïmonide, puisque, pour le philosophe juif, les démons n'ont pas de réalité.[29] La condamnation des sacrifices humains est plus sévère aussi que chez Maïmonide, Grotius ayant prouvé qu'il ne s'agissait pas seulement d'une lustration par le feu, rite dérivé, qui fut substitué à l'immolation cruelle de l'être humain.[30] Ces noires descriptions du paganisme empêchent toute confusion entre le catholicisme et lui. On voit ici une première application de l'irénisme de Grotius.

2 Chez Maïmonide, comme l'ont observé ses commentateurs les plus récents, existe une tension entre la critique des anthropomorphismes bibliques ou des rites et la prise au sérieux de la Loi de Moïse, qui, devant tout à l'intellect et non à l'imagination de ce grand prophète, ne peut être dépassée. Maïmonide refuse en conséquence de distinguer absolument entre les commandements que la raison peut comprendre et ceux qui relèvent de la seule volonté divine. Il dit seulement que tous les commandements ont une raison, mais qu'elle est connue ou inconnue des hommes. Les commandements de la première espèce sont les *mishpathim* et ceux dont l'utilité reste énigmatique, les *huqqim*. Grotius utilise la distinction dans le commentaire de Nombres 19.2 en renvoyant à un passage du *De iure belli ac pacis* (l. I, chap. I, no. IX).[31] Mais il n'embrouille pas comme Maïmonide les rapports de la raison et de la Loi, car, chez le penseur juif, cette obscurité est voulue. Grotius au contraire accentue la distinction entre ce qui est bon ou mauvais par nature et ce qui est tel seulement en vertu de la Loi. La conséquence de cette distinction tranchée est la séparation entre l'extérieur et l'intérieur de la religion. Les mêmes rites de sacrifice ou de purification ont pu servir aux juifs et aux païens, ce que Grotius démontre am-

---

[28] G.J. Vossius, *De theologia gentili ac physiologia christiana*, Amsterdam 1668, p. 15a et b.

[29] Voir *Le livre de la connaissance*. Traduit de l'hébreu et annoté par Valentin Nikiprowetzky et André Zaoui, Paris 1961, section IV, chapitre XI, no. XVI, pp. 337–38.

[30] Voir *Guide des Égarés*, 3e partie, chap. 37, éd. Munk, t. III, pp. 288–89.

[31] *OTh* I, p. 77 a 18–29.

plement grâce à son érudition classique. Mais cela n'a aucune importance puisque le corps matériel du rite n'est pas l'essentiel de la religion. Maïmonide était d'autant plus attaché à la Loi qu'elle offrait pour lui la seule garantie de survie de la communauté juive. La réflexion de Grotius sur les rites ne poursuit pas les mêmes fins. Il ne fait aucune mention de la condescendance divine, comme nous l'avons vu, et considère la similitude des rites comme un phénomène historique. Ainsi le monothéisme n'est pas lié de soi à l'interdiction des images. Ce qui semble le plus important pour Grotius, c'est la croyance en un Dieu unique, car elle a une fonction politique qu'il souligne à la fin du commentaire du premier commandement, en assurant, à la suite de Philon, que le monothéisme maintient la cohésion de la société plus fermement que toute autre religion.[32] Nous retrouvons d'ailleurs l'affirmation de cette fonction pratique du monothéisme dans le commentaire du premier chapitre de l'épître aux Romains où le τὸ γνωστὸν τοῦ θεοῦ se rapporte, selon Grotius, uniquement à la toute puissance et à l'universelle juridiction du Très-Haut, les autres attributs de celui-ci "étant moins nécessaires à la conduite de la vie et partant plus obscurs."[33] L'on sait que ces aperçus sur la fonction politique et éthique de la religion sont développés ailleurs dans l'œuvre de Grotius, en particulier dans le *De iure belli ac pacis* (l. II, chap. XX, nos. XLIV-XLV).

En définitive, la manière dont Grotius considère les religions du paganisme met en lumière le caractère pratique de sa théologie. Il s'agit, selon les interprétations proposées, d'éviter tout amalgame entre catholicisme et paganisme, d'une part, et, d'autre part, de souligner l'insignifiance religieuse d'une grande partie des rites, bien commun de toutes les religions antiques. Toutes ces réflexions ont certainement ouvert la voie à une meilleure insertion de la Bible en son temps, mais c'est là un gain pour l'histoire plutôt que pour la théologie. En ce qui concerne celle-ci, pour des raisons de paix religieuse, nationale et même internationale, Grotius évite, à la différence de Maïmonide, de s'affronter au paradoxe d'une Révélation divine exprimée dans le cercle d'une communauté particulière et soumise aux aléas de l'histoire. Pendant près de deux siècles, la pensée européenne, se détournant de la violence justement imputée aux orthodoxies, laissera en friche ces grandes questions, qu'avaient fort bien vues les médiévaux, qu'ils fussent musulmans, juifs ou chrétiens. Il

---

[32] *OTh* I, p. 39 a 7–15.
[33] "minus ad vitam dirigendam necessaria eoque obscuriora." *OTh* II/2, p. 676 a 48 à p. 676 b 2.

fallait peut-être soulever cette question dans un colloque spécifiquement consacré à la personnalité théologique de Grotius. Si Grotius
est un théologien, de quelle théologie s'agit-il? Ou quel est le Dieu
dont il parle?

GROTIUS' VIEW OF THE GOSPELS AND THE EVANGELISTS

HENK JAN DE JONGE
(Leiden)

A. THE PLACE AND FUNCTION OF THE GOSPELS IN GROTIUS' THEOLOGY[1]

It would not be entirely correct to state that Grotius' theology is founded on the Gospels.[2] In his own view, the basis of Christian theology was not the written Gospels, but 'the' gospel, in the singular, that is, the Truth revealed by Christ during his earthly ministry and subsequently preached by the apostles.[3]

This gospel of Christ, which underlies the written Gospels, was defined by Grotius as "a new doctrine demanding a radical change of mind and conduct, and promising the remission of sins and eternal life."[4] The content of the Gospel revealed by Christ, according

---

[1] This contribution is partly based on research done by Ms. M.H. DE LANG, research-assistant in the Faculty of theology of Leiden University. She kindly allowed me to use the excursus she devoted to Grotius in her doctoral dissertation *De opkomst van de historische en literaire kritiek in de synoptische beschouwing van de evangeliën van Calvijn (1555) tot Griesbach (1774)* (diss. Leiden), Leiden 1993, pp. 125–35. That the late 18th and 19th-century literary criticism of the Gospels originated as an apologetic reaction to the radical, almost a-historical hypercriticism leveled against the Gospels by the Deists, is an idea I owe to Ms. De Lang. This idea plays a crucial role in my assessment of Grotius as an exegete in section C below.

[2] Recent studies of Grotius' biblical exegesis include H. GRAF REVENTLOW, "L'exégèse humaniste de Hugo Grotius", in J.-R. ARMOGATHE (ed.), *Bible de tous les temps*, Vol. 6, *Le Grand Siècle et la Bible*, Paris 1989, pp. 141–54; H. GRAF REVENTLOW, "Humanistic Exegesis: The Famous Hugo Grotius", in B. UFFENHEIMER – H. GRAF REVENTLOW (edd.), *Creative Biblical Exegesis* (Journal for the Study of the Old Testament, Supplement Series 59), Sheffield 1988, pp. 175–91; H.J. DE JONGE, "Hugo Grotius: exégète du Nouveau Testament," in *The World of Hugo Grotius (1583–1645)*, Amsterdam/Maarssen 1984, pp. 97–115; H.J. DE JONGE, "Grotius as an Interpreter of the Bible, particularly the New Testament," in *Hugo Grotius: A Great European, 1583–1645*, Delft 1983, pp. 59–65. Earlier literature on the subject is mentioned in the footnotes to the studies just mentioned.

[3] HUGO GROTIUS, *De veritate religionis christianae* II,7, in *OTh* III, col. 36b: " ... Christus, ut et sui et alieni fatentur, novum protulit dogma"; *De veritate* VI,11, in *OTh* III, col. 94a: "Monentur deinde sanctum illud dogma Christi, ut pretiosissimum thesaurum sollicite custodire; atque eam ob rem saepe legere Sacra scripta." *BW* II, no. 640 (Grotius to P. Dupuy, [May 1621?]), p. 73: "Evangelium, id est dogma novum ... perfecte a Christo revelatum, et per Apostolos per orbem totum iussum praedicari."

[4] *BW* II, no. 640 (Grotius to P. Dupuy [May 1621?]), p. 73: "Evangelium, id est dogma novum resipiscentiam exactam deposcens, et promittens remissionem peccatorum et vitam aeternam, quod praeparationis modo a Baptista annuntiatum est, perfecte vero a Christo revelatum, et per Apostolos per orbem totum iussum prae-

to this definition, was, first, the necessity of a radical change of life
(*resipiscentia*), and second, the promise of eternal salvation. It is no
accident that Grotius mentions the necessary change of life in the
first place. The main thing in the message of Christ, according to
Grotius, was the commandment of love.[5] In the teaching of Christ,
as viewed by Grotius and other Christian humanists, the *praxis pietatis* was of prime importance.[6] This is not to say that Grotius limited
the role of Christ to that of a teacher or Revealer. Christ was certainly also the one who through his expiatory death had brought
about forgiveness of sins and the Atonement.[7] But one could not
know Christ as Saviour unless through the gospel that he himself
had been the first to preach.

The primary function of the Gospels, then, is that in preserving
the message of Jesus in a written form, they disclose the truth
which God wanted to communicate to mankind.

In Grotius' theology, however, the Gospels have also another
function. They have also to warrant the unique divine authority of
the message brought by Jesus. For how can one know for certain
that the gospel preached by Jesus is the exclusive Truth coming
from God? To answer this question Grotius does not resort to the
doctrine of the inspiration of Scripture. Many protestant theologians of the 16th and 17th centuries, both Lutherans and Calvinists, held that the divine authority of the content of Scripture was

---

dicari, ..." In what follows I shall have to mention Grotius' letter to Pierre Dupuy,
BW II, no. 640, still more than once. The autograph of this extremely important
letter is kept in Paris, Bibliothèque Nationale, Fonds Dupuy 16, no. 101. The letter bears no date; see L. DOREZ, *Catalogue de la Collection Dupuy*, I (nos. 1–500), Paris
1899, under nr. 16, p. 20: "s(ans) d(ate), autographe (101)." Molhuysen dated it to
[May 1621] because it follows a letter of 8 May 1621 in *Epistolae* (now no. 639 in
BW). MOLHUYSEN, *BW* II, p. 73, n. 1, rightly observed that no. 640 offers no clue
for dating it more precisely.

[5] HUGO GROTIUS, *Annotationes in Novum Testamentum*, ad Rom. 15.7: "quum in
evangelio praecipuum sit dilectio"; *ad* Eph. 1.4: "... dilectionis, in qua est evangelii
τὸ πᾶν."

[6] For the dominant place of ethics in Grotius' theology, see, e.g., W.C. VAN UN-
NIK, "Hugo Grotius als uitlegger van het Nieuwe Testament", first published in
NAKG N.S. 25 (1932), pp. 1–48; reprinted in W.C. VAN UNNIK, *Woorden gaan leven*,
Kampen 1979, pp. 172–214, especially pp. 182–83; G.H.M. POSTHUMUS MEYJES,
Hugo Grotius: Meletius sive De iis quae inter Christianos conveniunt Epistola, pp. 33–35;
G.H.M. POSTHUMUS MEYJES, "Hugo de Groot's 'Meletius' (1611), His Earliest The-
ological Work, Rediscovered," *Lias* 11 (1984), pp. 147–50, especially p. 150: "(Gro-
tius) repeatedly made it clear that for him ethics was by far the most important
(...)", *i.e.*, more important than dogmatics.

[7] This becomes of course perfectly clear from Grotius' work *De satisfactione*,
Leiden 1617[1]. See E. RABBIE, *Hugo Grotius. Defensio fidei catholicae De satisfactione
Christi adversus Faustum Socinum Senensem* (Opera Theologica edited by the Grotius
Institute of the Royal Netherlands Academy of Arts and Sciences I), Assen –
Maastricht 1990.

secured by its being divinely inspired. In this theory the validity of the teaching of Christ and his apostles was guaranteed by the inspiration of Scripture. But Grotius preferred not to appeal to the doctrine of the inspiration, because this doctrine could not be supposed to be valid for non-Christians.[8] In order to prove the exclusive truth of the teaching of Christ, Grotius used another argumentation, which he considered to be cogent for Christians and non-Christians alike. This argumentation consists of four steps, each of which derives its validity from the following step. Grotius argued as follows.

(1) The teaching of Christ must be of divine authority because he himself was a divine person[9] or at least someone who spoke by God's order.[10]

(2) The divine nature of Christ's mission is proven by the miracles he worked and by his resurrection.[11]

(3) The historicity of the miracles Jesus worked and of his resurrection is beyond doubt because they are recorded by trustworthy writers. These writers include Matthew and John, direct pupils of Jesus and eyewitnesses of his ministry, and Mark and Luke who were equally well informed, Mark because he was a pupil of Peter and Luke because he collected solid information on Jesus' activity from eyewitnesses in Palestine.[12]

---

[8] In his *De veritate religionis christianae*, III,5 (*OTh* III, col. 51), Grotius maintains the doctrine of the inspiration of Scripture only in a few cases in which the biblical authors appear to have had knowledge which they could not have derived from experience or from tradition. This applies to (1) the visions in the book of Revelation, and (2) some passages in the Epistle to the Hebrews in which the author himself appeals to the inspiration of the Holy Ghost. That Grotius had not yet familiarized himself entirely with the rejection of the inspiration appears from his epilogue to *De veritate*, where he speaks of the "scriptores sacrae scripturae" as "afflatus divini pleniores." This traditional phrase is inconsistent with Grotius' rejection of the inspiration in the rest of *De veritate*. Grotius did not reject the inspiration only in *De veritate* for apologetic reasons. The same view is presupposed in his letter nr. 640 of [May 1621?] to P. Dupuy, *BW* II, p. 73, and in the controversy with Rivet. See, e.g., *Votum pro pace ecclesiastica*, *OTh* III, cols. 672b–673a, "De canonicis Scripturis," where Grotius states *inter alia*: "A Spiritu Sancto dictari historias nihil fuit opus: satis fuit scriptorem memoria valere circa res spectatas, aut diligentia in describendis veterum commentariis."

[9] See GROTIUS, Ep. 640 (to P. Dupuy [May 1621?]), *BW* II, p. 73: "per quae omnia [sc. through his resurrection and ascension to heaven] apertissime filius Dei declaratus est." And some lines further down: "eius [sc. Christ's] personam a qua Evangelium suam habet auctoritatem."

[10] GROTIUS, *De veritate* II,7 (*OTh* III, col. 36b): "Christus ... novum protulit dogma tamquam mandato divino."

[11] GROTIUS, *De veritate* II,7 (*OTh* III, col. 36b).

[12] GROTIUS, *De veritate* III,5 (*OTh* III, col. 51 a-b).

As P.T. van Rooden has observed and J.P. Heering has demonstrated, Grotius owed the three step argumentation just mentioned for the most part to Faustus Socinus' work *De auctoritate Sacrae Scripturae* (Amsterdam 1588[1]; Steinfurt 1611[2]; Grotius probably used G.J. Vossius' copy of the latter edition).[13] Grotius himself added a fourth step:

(4) The authority of the disciples and evangelists is proven by the miracles they worked and by the miracles that took place near their graves.[14]

From this train of thought it becomes clear that in Grotius' view the Gospels were not only important because they preserve the content of Jesus' teaching, on which faith and theology have to be based. The Gospels have a second function. Through their stories about Jesus' miracles and bodily resurrection, the Gospels guarantee the divine authority of Jesus' message. In this manner Grotius believed he could prove the unique and divine nature of the teaching of Christ on purely historical, 'objective' grounds, without appealing to the doctrine of the inspiration of Scripture.

Summarizing the first part of this contribution, I submit that in Grotius' theology the Gospels have a twofold function. Firstly, in those passages which present the words of Jesus, they give access to the truth God had decided to make known to man. Secondly, in their narrative parts, especially in the miracle stories, they give firm evidence that this truth is of divine authority.

---

[13] P.T. VAN ROODEN – J.W. WESSELIUS, "The Early Enlightenment and Judaism: The 'Civil Dispute' between Philippus van Limborch and Isaac Orobio de Castro (1687)," *Studia Rosenthaliana* 21 (1987), pp. 140–53, especially pp. 151–52 with n. 39, argue that Grotius' "source" was the Socinian Catechism of Rakov (1609) and that the argumentation referred to above, and used in the Catechism of Rakov, was in its turn "a logical development of Faustus Socinus' conception of the authority of the Bible. Cf. his 'De auctoritate Sacrae Scripturae' and 'Lectiones sacrae' in the *Opera Omnia* (Irenopoli [= Amstelodami], 1656)." J.P. HEERING, *Hugo de Groot als apologeet van de christelijke godsdienst. Een onderzoek van zijn geschrift De veritate religionis christianae (1640)*, diss. Leiden, The Hague 1992, pp. 118–19, argues that Grotius' *De Veritate* II-III is directly dependent on Socinus' *De auctoritate* in the Steinfurt 1611 edition. The first step of Grotius' argumentation mentioned above is discernible as a distinct step only in Ep. 640.

[14] GROTIUS, *De veritate* III,7 (*OTh* III, cols. 51b–52a). This fourth step added by Grotius himself cannot be described as fortunate. For it provokes inevitably the question how one can be sure that the miracles that are said to have been performed by the apostles and to have occurred near their graves, really took place. This question does not seem to have worried Grotius. That he based his rationalistic plea for the historicity of the events narrated in the Gospels and, ultimately, for the truth of the Christian religion on the more than dubious traditions about miracles on the graves of the apostles, is a surprising weakness in his apologetic work. This lack of critical sense, too, shows that Grotius belonged to the latter days of humanism, not to the dawning era of Descartes.

B. Grotius' View of the Relationship between the Gospels and the Historical Jesus

From what precedes one might infer that according to Grotius the ministry and teaching of Jesus could reliably be reconstructed. This conclusion is correct, but it needs some qualifications.

Firstly, Grotius held that in recording Jesus' ministry none of the evangelists had retained the correct chronological order. Each of them had composed his Gospel with considerable freedom as regards order. Thus, each evangelist had arranged his material in the sequence which he himself had deemed most fit for creating a convincing and coherent narrative. Now Grotius believed that in a historical reconstruction of Jesus' career most of the narratives contained in the Gospels could be assigned their chronologically correct place. Occasionally, however, Grotius observes that the context in which a given saying of Jesus occurs in one or another Gospel cannot have been that saying's primitive setting in the life of the historical Jesus. For some of these sayings it was impossible, Grotius believed, to indicate at which point in Jesus' biography they had to be inserted. Here we find a slight touch of historical scepticism in regard to the question whether the Gospels allow a reliable historical reconstruction of Jesus' ministry.

Sayings of Jesus of which, according to Grotius, the original place in the history of Jesus' activity could not be determined any more include the following.

(a) Luke 6.39: "Can one blind man be guide to another? Will they not both fall into the ditch?" Luke combined this saying with other words of Jesus, "although," as Grotius says, "it was perhaps spoken at another time and another occasion."

(b) The dialogues recorded in Luke 9.57–58, 59–60, and 61–62. It is Luke who joined these dialogues because of their affinity in content. In reality they took place on different occasions. When precisely in Jesus' ministry each of these dialogues must be placed, cannot be ascertained.

(c) Luke 13.32: "Go and tell that fox (i.e., Herod Antipas), 'Listen: today and tomorrow I shall be casting out devils and working cures; on the third day I reach my goal'", and what follows in v. 33. Grotius took the days mentioned here to mean years. Consequently, Jesus must have spoken these words about three years before his death, not some months or weeks before he died, as Luke's Gospel suggests. But when precisely Jesus spoke the words in question cannot be ascertained any more.

A second reservation Grotius made in regard to the reliability of a historical reconstruction of Jesus' ministry was that the evangelists as narrators were not unerring. Grotius believed that the evangelists could err in historical and geographical details.[15] For in composing their Gospels they were not guided by the Holy Ghost. They simply related what they remembered as eyewitnesses or what they had heard from their informants. Grotius points out the following error in Matthew and Mark. They mention as the cause of the violent death of John the Baptist that John had criticized Herod's marriage with the former wife of his brother.[16] Grotius observes that Josephus mentions a different cause for John's death, namely Herod's fear of a popular revolt that might have been elicited by John's teaching.[17] In Grotius' opinion, then, Josephus' authority as an historian cannot be ignored. Consequently, the evangelists must be in error here.

Thirdly, it was perfectly clear to Grotius that the material contained in the four Gospels does not suffice to compose a more or less adequate biography of Jesus. Their content is only a selection of such material as portrays him as the Son of God. They give the divine message he brought, his teaching, and the stories about the miracles that give evidence of his authority. But they omit everything that does not contribute to present Jesus as God's unique Messenger. Apart from the birth-stories, the Gospels tell us nothing about Jesus' life until he was baptized, at the age of about thirty. The Gospels focus on the last two and a half years of Jesus' career. The reason of this, as Grotius correctly understood and pointed out, is that the evangelists did not intend to write history, but Gospels, which through their account of his teaching and miracles had to demonstrate that Jesus was God's Son.[18]

Thus, in Grotius' opinion the Gospels could be used for a historical reconstruction of Jesus' ministry except with three reservations: (1) for some sayings of Jesus it was impossible to determine at which moment they had been pronounced; (2) in a few historical and geographical details the evangelists have made a mistake; (3) the Gospels contain only a selection of material about Jesus, that is, only such material as depicts him as the authoritative Messenger of God. These three reservations, however, sum up about all the rela-

---

[15] GROTIUS, *Annotationes in Acta Apostolorum, ad* Acts 7.3.
[16] Mark 6.17–19; Matthew 14.3–4.
[17] JOSEPHUS, *Antiquitates* XVIII, v, 2, 118.
[18] This is what Grotius argues in his letter 640 of [May 1621?] to P. Dupuy, *BW* II, p. 73.

tivism that one can discern in Grotius' view of the historicity of the Gospels. True, it must be conceded that this relativism goes further than in the exegetical works of most of his contemporaries and predecessors, the more favourable exceptions being Sebastian Castellio and John Calvin.[19] Nevertheless, Grotius' contribution to the development of New Testament scholarship cannot be said to consist in his historical criticism of the Gospels. On the whole, Grotius had great confidence in the possibility of reconstructing the ministry of Jesus. He assumed that in such a reconstruction the texts of the Gospels could be integrated as they stood. He consistently reasoned away discrepancies between the Gospels by means of a variety of traditional harmonizations.

In short, Grotius' view of the relationship between the Gospels and the historical reality of Jesus' ministry was still rather naive. In Grotius' treatment of the Gospels historical criticism does not yet play a role of great significance.

C. An Assessment of Grotius' View of the Gospels and the Evangelists

There can be no doubt that Grotius' exegesis of the Gospels is in several respects an impressive improvement on that of his contemporaries. His main merit lies in his constant effort to explain the language and thoughts of the evangelists in light of the usage and ideas of ancient authors: Hellenistic, Greek, Hebrew, Roman, Jewish. Grotius tried to recover the meaning the Gospels had had for their original readers in antiquity, and not to utilize them for underpinning a denominational theology of the seventeenth century. In other words, Grotius tried to understand the Gospels as documents of the first century C.E., not as ammunition for defending a seventeenth-century theological position. The choice of illustrative material Grotius adduced to elucidate the biblical texts is often so felicitous that his *Annotationes* on the Gospels remain a useful commentary up to the present day.

Really innovative was Grotius' view of the evangelists as authors who were free to arrange their material in accordance with their own narrative intentions.[20] This insight enabled him to explain

---

[19] For the relativism of Castellio and Calvin in regard to the possibility of reconstructing the history behind the Gospels, see M.H. DE LANG, *De opkomst van de historische en literaire kritiek* (see n. 1), pp. 23–32; 43–46.

[20] H.J. DE JONGE, "Hugo Grotius: exégète du Nouveau Testament" (see n. 2 above), pp. 106–07. See also GROTIUS' *Annotationes in Novum Testamentum*, ad Mt. 26.6, 26.64, Lk. 22.63, John 6.15, Apoc. 9.1, and Lk. 3.16, 6.39, 4.21, 13.32.

many a passage in terms of the specific intentions each individual evangelist had had in composing his Gospel. Equally innovative is Grotius' view of the evangelists as ordinary writers who composed their works without divine inspiration. By rejecting both verbal and direct inspiration, Grotius 'secularized' the image of the evangelists. The importance of this is that the understanding of the evangelists as independent authors made the Gospels a more attractive object for the application of the methods of philological, literary and historical research.

It testifies to Grotius' keen insight into the nature of the Gospels that he characterized them as a kind of Christological manifestos, rather than as historiography. Thus, he explained with success why they record Jesus' teaching and miracles while omitting almost all biographical material up to the moment he assumed his public ministry.[21]

Grotius' 'secularization' of the evangelists was beneficial to the rise of sound exegesis, but it also held a danger. It had no doubt an apologetic intention. Grotius intended to place the unique authority of the message preached by Christ on the 'objective' footing of the verifiable historicity of his miracles and resurrection, instead of on the inspiration of Scripture. Eventually, the secularization of the evangelists aimed at the reinforcement of the objective validity of the Christian religion. The danger of this apologetic search for objectivity was soon to become clear. Strikingly, it was a danger Grotius had not foreseen. Philosophical criticism of the possibility of miracles and bodily resurrection, as expressed by Spinoza and the Deists, could not but entail the rejection of the truth of the Christian religion in so far as it was based on those supernatural events.

We have mentioned several elements in Grotius' view of the Gospels that have contributed to a more historical understanding of these documents. It need not be concealed that the way Grotius viewed the Gospels also shows that he was a child of his time. Grotius remained traditional in that he did not make an issue of the historical reliability of the Gospels' report of Jesus' words and deeds. Grotius believed that the reconstruction of Jesus' teaching

---

[21] GROTIUS, Ep. 640, *BW* II, p. 73. Grotius' view on the Gospels as a kind of "Christological manifestos," which because of that specific character offered only such material as could serve to present Jesus as the Son of God, did not remain unnoticed in the eighteenth century. Grotius' letter on the subject, now no. 640 in *BW* II, pp. 73–74, is quoted in extenso by J.A. FABRICIUS, *Codex Apocryphus Novi Testamenti*, Pars III, Hamburg 1719, pp. 412–15, as an excursus under the heading "Quare Evangelistae nihil fere de Christo commemorent ante annum a nativitate eius tricesimum. Hugo Grotius Epist. CXLIII ad Petrum Pateannum [*sic*]."

and activity that he thought could be made on the basis of a harmonization of the four Gospels, was a faithful description of what Jesus taught and did. Grotius did not yet realize that the Gospels might include ideas and material that originated in the circle of Jesus' followers, in the Jesus movement after his death, and in early Christian communities. Grotius was also very traditional in the way he consistently tried to reconcile the different versions of corresponding stories in two or more Gospels by arguing away the discrepancies.

Moreover, Grotius naively assumed that his reconstruction of Jesus' teaching could serve immediately as theology of the seventeenth century. For that is the supposition of the *Annotationes* on the New Testament. In this work Grotius wanted to clarify the meaning the message of Christ and the apostles had had for the original audience in the first centuries C.E. But Grotius supposed this historical meaning also to be valid for his seventeenth-century audience.

Finally, for a correct assessment of Grotius as an interpreter of the Gospels, it is of vital importance to take due note of the fact that Grotius kept a firm belief in the possibility of a historical reconstruction of Jesus' ministry and in the historical reliability of such a reconstruction. This is important, since the course which the critical study of the Gospels as a scholarly discipline was to take was via the radical rejection of the Gospels' historicity by the Deists (ca. 1670 – ca. 1750)[22] to the valuable literary criticism of the late eighteenth century.[23] Obviously, the loss of faith in the historicity of the Gospels was necessary for the sound literary-critical theories concerning the interrelationships of the Gospels to emerge. I am referring here to the Proto-Gospel Hypothesis of Lessing and the Two Gospel Hypothesis of Griesbach.[24] These theories tried to ex-

---

[22] H. GRAF REVENTLOW, *Bibelautorität und Geist der Moderne*, Göttingen 1980; H.J. DE JONGE, *Van Erasmus tot Reimarus*, Leiden 1991; idem, "The Loss of Faith in the Historicity of the Gospels: H.S. Reimarus (ca. 1750) on John and the Synoptics," in A. DENAUX (ed.), *John and the Synoptics* [Bibliotheca Ephemeridum Theologicarum Lovaniensium 101], Louvain 1992, pp. 409–22.

[23] M.H. DE LANG, "Literary and Historical Criticism as Apologetics. Biblical Scholarship at the End of the Eighteenth Century," *NAKG/Dutch Review of Church History* N.S. 72 (1992), pp. 149–65; M.H. DE LANG, "Gospel Synopses from the 16th to the 18th Centuries and the Rise of Literary Criticism of the Gospels," in C. FOCANT (ed.), *The Synoptic Gospels. Source Criticism and the New Literary Criticism* [Bibliotheca Ephemeridum Theologicarum Lovaniensium 110], Louvain 1993, pp. 599–607.

[24] On these theories, see, e.g., W.G. KÜMMEL, *Einleitung in das Neue Testament*, Heidelberg 1978[19], pp. 19 (on Lessing's Proto-Gospel Hypothesis, "Urevangeliumshypothese") and 21–22 (on Griesbach's Two Gospel Hypothesis).

plain the form of the Gospels by assuming that they are literarily
dependent on earlier sources or on each other. The rise of a sound
literary criticism of the Gospels obviously needed the stimulus of a
radical historical scepticism. For all his merits for biblical exegesis,
then, Grotius hardly contributed to the development of the historical criticism of the Gospels. Grotius' work on the Gospels is the cli-
max of the era of humanistic exegesis, it is not the beginning of a
new era.

PART TWO

GROTIUS' THEOLOGY AND CONTEMPORARY
THOUGHT

GROTIUS AND ERASMUS*

JOHANNES TRAPMAN
(The Hague)

The relationship between Grotius and Erasmus may be approached in several ways. To begin with, one could try to make a comparison between their work, pointing out similarities and differences. If we are familiar with what Erasmus wrote, and then turn to Grotius, we will be struck by the absence of anything like the *Praise of Folly* or the *Colloquies*. On the other hand, in Erasmus' works one would look in vain for anything comparable to the powerful systematic structure of *De iure belli ac pacis*. The Dutch historian, Johan Huizinga, quite appropriately compared the latter work to a building, referring instead to the "effusion," the "flowing stream" of Erasmus' *Enchiridion*; whereas Erasmus has a "coordinating" method of working, Grotius "subordinates."[1] Both Erasmus and Grotius left us annotations on the Bible. Unlike Grotius, Erasmus did not deal with the Old Testament. Indeed, his knowledge of Hebrew was rudimentary. Erasmus' annotations on the New Testament are full of polemical observations concerning contemporary religious matters. For this reason, Richard Simon claimed that there was sometimes more about him of a "declamateur" than an "interprète," more of a "theologien" than a "critique exact."[2] Grotius, however, usually managed to keep within the bounds of philology.[3]

In the past the names of Erasmus and Grotius were often bracketed together. In many cases they have had the same admirers and they have a biographer, Burigny, in common.[4] They are however

---

* I wish to thank Mr Scott Mandelbrote (Oxford) for correcting the English text.

[1] *Verzamelde Werken* II, Haarlem 1948, pp. 389–403 (written in 1925).

[2] RICHARD SIMON, *Histoire critique des principaux commentateurs du Nouveau Testament, depuis le commencement du Christianisme jusques à nôtre tems*, Rotterdam 1693, pp. 504, 509.

[3] Cf. H.J. DE JONGE, "Hugo Grotius: exégète du Nouveau Testament," in *The World of Hugo Grotius (1583-1645). Proceedings of the International Colloquium ... Rotterdam 6-9 April 1983*, Amsterdam-Maarssen 1984, pp. 97-115.

[4] J. LEVESQUE DE BURIGNY, *Vie de Grotius*, Paris 1752; id., *Vie d'Erasme*, Paris 1757. Cf. BRUCE MANSFIELD, *Phoenix of His Age. Interpretations of Erasmus c 1550-1750*, Toronto 1979, pp. 285–95. With regard to "Grotius and Erasmus" see ibid., pp. 137–44; G.J. DE VOOGD, *Erasmus en Grotius. Twee grote Nederlanders en hun boodschap aan onze tijd*, Leiden [1947], pp. 128–34; H.J. DE J(ONGE), "De waardering voor Erasmus in het Leidse universitaire milieu tot circa 1650," in R. BREUGELMANS et al. (edd.), *Erasmus en Leiden. Catalogus van de tentoonstelling gehouden in het Academisch Historisch Museum te Leiden van 23 oktober tot 19 december 1986*, Leiden 1986, pp. 30–41, at pp. 30–31 and 40–41.

usually combined in a rather superficial way, as two great scholars, both born in Holland. In the seventeenth-century, the author of the *Polyhistor*, Daniel Morhof, had already observed that both Dutchmen, Erasmus and Grotius, would scarcely find their equals in the ages to come.[5] Similarly, in a well-known note, which he inserted in the second volume of his edition of the Collected Works of Erasmus, Jean le Clerc asked the rhetorical question: "… is there any country that can boast of scholars equally great as Erasmus and Grotius and having deserved so well of the Respublica Christiana?"[6] To give another example, the eighteenth-century Dutch poet Joan de Haas – a minor poet indeed – sang the praise of the "wise heroes of letters" whose portraits he had in his library.[7]

However, in view of the theme 'Grotius as a theologian,' the observations made by, for instance, Werner Kaegi may be more relevant. He has shown that in the Age of Enlightenment Erasmus was not only seen as a sceptic; instead he had a profound influence on Swiss theologians of the period, who admired him as a biblical scholar and as a moderate theologian. When these theologians mentioned Erasmus as a favourite author, he was not infrequently in the company of Grotius, whose *Opera theologica* were reprinted at Basle in 1732.[8]

I intend to concentrate here on how Erasmus was seen by Grotius himself. In order to address this question I will discuss four successive passages from Grotius' works, in which we can detect a shift in his emphases. I will also take a look at Grotius' correspondence and at some miscellaneous statements of his. His *Annotationes* will be left aside; they require to be dealt with separately. The four texts with which I will begin are to be found in the *Parallela*, the *Historiae*, the *Pietas* and the *Verantwoordingh*, drawn from the years 1601 to 1622.

---

[5] DANIEL GEORGIUS MORHOF, *Polyhistor sive de notitia auctorum et rerum commentarii...* Lübeck 1688 (*BsG* no. 46), pp. 294–95.

[6] *Desiderii Erasmi Opera omnia* II, Leiden 1703 (hereafter *LB*), col. 1084 F (note to adagium 3535 "Auris Batava"). Cf. C. REEDIJK, *Tandem bona causa triumphat. Zur Geschichte des Gesamtwerkes des Erasmus von Rotterdam* (Vorträge der Aeneas-Silvius-Stiftung an der Universität Basel, XVI), Basel – Stuttgart 1980, p. 40.

[7] JOAN DE HAES, *Alle de gedichten*, Delft 1724, pp. 400–01.

[8] WERNER KAEGI, "Erasmus im achtzehnten Jahrhundert," in *Gedenkschrift zum 400. Todestage des Erasmus von Rotterdam*, Basel 1936, pp. 205–27, on pp. 214–15, 223–25, 227.

PARALLELA

As a young man, Grotius wrote a book on the parallels between the Dutch and the ancient Greek and Roman republics. This book, written in 1601–2, when the author had not yet reached his twentieth birthday, was only published two centuries later, in 1801–3 by Johan Meerman, in the days of the Batavian republic.[9]

Nowhere else did Grotius write more enthusiastically about Erasmus. So, what did Erasmus represent to the young Grotius? In the first place, Erasmus was the glory of Holland. Secondly, he was an incomparable scholar, who had brought learning and letters into the light in a world which had been filled with darkness for eight centuries, that is ever since Charlemagne; Grotius calls Erasmus the Christian Varro,[10] thus comparing him to proverbially the greatest scholar of Antiquity. In his enthusiasm, Grotius bends the historical truth, for he suggests that Erasmus appeared as a shining sun in an age when in Italy or France "there were scarcely one or two who had the boldness to think," ignoring completely Italian humanists such as Petrarch, Poliziano, Pico, Ficino and others. However, 'patriotism' is not the only theme of this eulogy, for Grotius says that he is afraid that he was not quite correct in calling Erasmus a Batavian since Erasmus belonged to the whole world.[11]

So, we have Erasmus the outstanding Dutchman, the great scholar and conqueror of barbarism. In the heart of this paragraph, Grotius also points out what Erasmus had done for theology. Here I must quote, for the way in which Grotius characterizes Erasmus is very Erasmian in itself.

> You cleansed again holy theology, more polluted than the Augean stable, from disgusting quibblings and cavillings and, with liberating hand, set it free from the cruel tyranny of the sophists [...] You dared to condemn as errors, opinions long accepted and to pierce with stings the lazy herd of drones.[12]

---

[9] *Hugonis Grotii, Batavi, Parallelon rerumpublicarum liber tertius...*, ed. JOHAN MEERMAN, 4 vols, Haarlem 1801–03 (*BG* no. 750), vol. 3, pp. 33–35. For a comparison of Grotius and Erasmus, see MEERMAN's note, pp. 315–19.

[10] Cf. Guillaume Budé to Erasmus, <26.11.1516>, Ep. 493, l. 415: "... qui te Varronem esse memoriae nostrae autumnant, nisi quod plus eloquentiam amplecteris."

[11] *Parallelon*, vol. 3, p. 35: "Nam et hoc vereor, ut satis recte Batavum dixerim. Erasmus totius orbis possessio est." Cf. Budé to Erasmus, 1.5.<1516>, Ep. 403, ll. 7–11: "'Ego vero nec dicere,' inquam, 'nec eloqui ac ne proloqui quidem possim, O noster Erasme' (maior enim esse mihi videre quam ut meum te appellem, cum omnibus nostris unus satis esse possis; quin et usque adeo publicus scriptis tuis factus es ut nemo sibi privatim vindicare te possit)."

[12] Translation follows MANSFIELD, *Phoenix* (see n. 4), p. 140, with an alteration after "to pierce" (Mansfield: "to pierce deceptions with stinging thrusts" for "et fu-

This is how Erasmus was seen in his own lifetime, and this is also how he saw himself, struggling to purify theology from the hair-splitting quibbles of the scholastic theologians. This picture of Erasmus as a theologian is completed by a short remark:

> You opened the way of truth to us and taught with such prudence, such moderation and strength of character that the supreme pontiff, then the master of sacred things, feared you, but you were not afraid of him.[13]

Thus, on the one hand, Erasmus is the teacher of the truth, that is to say the evangelical truth; on the other hand, this teaching is presented in a moderate but still powerful way. One should realize that this passage on Erasmus forms part of the chapter on learning (ch. 24) and not of chapter 26, in which Grotius is concerned with religion.

In the latter, though, Erasmus is not missing. As the light of Holland, both he and Luther – the light of Germany – sharpened their pens and denounced abuses, albeit in different ways, according to Grotius. Luther, seeing the persistence of the disease, also took stronger action.[14] In other respects, the two men are on the same level, in the view of Grotius; many people turned to divine truth thanks to their learning and eloquence (eruditione et facundia).[15] Grotius was later to become more critical of the 'stronger action' of Luther, because it had resulted in schism.

Annales et Historiae

At about the time Grotius wrote the eulogy of Erasmus, he was asked by the States of Holland and West Friesland to write a history of the Revolt. Grotius did so. He finished this work about ten years later, in 1612. These Annales et Historiae, were published only after his death, in 1657.[16] The work ends with the start of the Twelve-Years Truce and the beginning of the controversy between Arminius and Gomarus. In dealing with this, Grotius intended to show that Arminius and his fellow Remonstrants were not innovators, but rather that they had every right to be considered as full members of the Reformed Church, in fact that they even had the prior claim. In his Historiae, Grotius evoked an image of the events

---

cos, ignavum pecus, aculeis pungere" [cf. Virgil, Aen.. I, 435]).

[13] Translation follows MANSFIELD, Phoenix, p. 140.

[14] Cf. Erasmus to John Fisher, 4.9.1524, Ep. 1489, ll. 28–30: "Optarim ex hoc tumulto quem Lutherus excitavit velut ex amaro violentoque pharmaco nasci bonam aliquam sanitatem Ecclesiae."

[15] Parallelon, vol. 3, pp. 89–90.

[16] BG no. 741.

leading up to the bitter controversy between Arminius and Gomarus, with which he kept faith until the end of his life.

Grotius tries to suggest that belief in absolute predestination is
rather an exceptional phenomenon in the history of the Church.
The first person to hold this belief was Augustine, in the later stages
of his life, after his disputes with Pelagius. The Greek Church however held on to "the old and less complicated opinion" as Grotius
says. Because of his great reputation, the Western Church followed
Augustine, or, as Grotius puts it, with a certain innuendo, many
people were persuaded into agreement ("magnum Augustini nomen
multos traxit in consensum").[17] Grotius does not refrain from adding here that there have been discussions within the Catholic
Church regarding the right interpretation of Augustine's opinions.
This is not said without reason; for the fact that such discussions on
predestination have been possible is one of Grotius' favourite arguments, by which he can implicitly criticize the strictly orthodox Calvinists, who were not willing to tolerate dissenting voices. Grotius
goes on to say that Luther went further still in destroying what Augustine had left of free will. Grotius argues that Erasmus, although
he agreed with Luther in some things, or passed them over without
comment, strongly opposed Luther's belief in absolute predestination and his denial of free will. It was thanks to Erasmus that Melanchthon changed his original position. In this respect, he was followed perhaps by Luther himself, and certainly by later Lutherans.
This remark on an alleged change of mind in Luther himself is just
a suggestion which Grotius makes to strengthen his argument. Grotius does not produce any evidence for it; he only vaguely refers to
"many holding this opinion." Nevertheless it is not open to question
that Melanchthon changed his mind in the revised editions of his
famous *Loci communes*.

Grotius views the development of the doctrine of predestination
in the period after Luther in the following manner: Calvin sided
with Luther (Grotius says actually with Luther's original statements
– prima dicta); Calvin introduced the idea that one could not fall
away from true belief, an idea that had been unknown even to Augustine. The later Calvinists, such as Calvin's successor Beza, became increasingly extremist and rigid in this matter. But what happened in Holland? Grotius does not elaborate on the first decades
of the Reformation in Holland. All he says is that there was no

---

[17] *Annales et Historiae*, Amsterdam 1658, pp. 551–52. According to Bossuet the
way Augustine is dealt with here testifies to Grotius' semi-Pelagianism, cf. J.A.G.
TANS, *Bossuet en Hollande*, Maastricht 1949, p. 24.

room for quarrel at the time, so that people with dissenting opinions were able to treat one another with fairness. The religious
troubles started only after an increasing number of young preachers, who had been educated at foreign academies, began to contradict the dissidents. Grotius continues that this explains why many
complaints were made to the authorities, in which it was argued
that theologians such as Anastasius Veluanus had always openly
preached their doctrines without ever being previously hindered. Finally, came the conflict between the two Leyden professors, which
spread rapidly.

In general, the opinion of Gomarus was accepted by the clergy,
whereas the civil authorities were on the side of Arminius. Grotius
specifies that Gomarus' opinion was "more received" (*receptior*), but
Arminius' was more in favour with the people (*popularior* – in this
context the word has no negative connotation). When Grotius describes the extreme Calvinist opinion as "*receptior*," he can only have
had in mind those theologians for whom absolute predestination
was already a received idea.

To summarize, Grotius wants to give the impression that intolerance in religious matters was imported by theologians who owed
their ideas to foreign masters, teaching in the Reformed Academies
at Geneva (founded 1559), Heidelberg (Reformed since 1563) and
Herborn (founded 1584). The Calvinist ministers gained the upper
hand, although the regents, and a considerable part of the population, did not sympathize with strict Calvinism. In order to substantiate his claim that, before the invasion of Calvinists who had been
trained abroad, dissenters were left alone, Grotius mentions several
names. In addition to Anastasius Veluanus, whom we have already
met, he mentions Gellius Snecanus, Hubertus Duifhuys, Holmannus, Clemens Martens and Herman Herberts. Grotius only gives
these men's names, he does not refer to any of their works. For that
we have to turn to the *Pietas* which Grotius wrote and published in
1613.

Ordinum Pietas

The *Pietas*,[18] the famous apologia for the way in which the States of
Holland and West Friesland had acted in the religious controversy,
has a short paragraph on the development of the Reformation in

---

[18] *BG* no. 817. Dutch translation by Johannes Uyttenbogaert, The Hague
1613, *BG* no. 823. For the Latin text see also *OTh* III, pp. 97–125, esp. pp.
106–09, 111.

the Low Countries. The picture which Grotius delineates there was especially appreciated by the Remonstrant historian Gerard Brandt and, through the medium of his well known *History of the Reformation*,[19] by all his liberal Protestant successors.[20]

Compared with the *Historiae*, the *Pietas* contains several new elements, particularly with regard to Calvin and Erasmus. It is only in the *Pietas* that Erasmus begins his career as the main Dutch Reformer, a career which is to reach its culmination in the nineteenth century with the nationalistic church history of Ypey and Dermout.[21] Let us begin with Calvin. In the *Historiae* Grotius had given a rough outline of the conflict on predestination and free will. He had named Augustine (that is the older Augustine), Luther, Calvin, Beza and other Reformed theologians of the second generation as opponents of free will. They were increasingly rigorous and, therefore, increasingly unsympathetic for Grotius. Melanchthon had sided with Luther only for a time, but had eventually become a sensible Erasmian. In the *Pietas* Calvin is treated differently. Grotius' main concern was not − and, for that matter, had never been − to show that Calvin and his fellow believers were wrong, but rather to make a plea for a church that would tolerate dissenting opinions. That is why Grotius, as a skilful apologist, appealed to the authority of Calvin himself, who despite his disagreement with Melanchthon had still considered the German theologian as a brother in Christ.

Very appropriately, Grotius reminds his reader here of the preface which Calvin had written for the French translation of Melanchthon's *Loci* (1546 and 1551). Calvin observed there that Melanchthon only treated of what was necessary and edifying, refraining from "disputes subtiles" or "disputes perplexes et confuses."[22]

---

[19] GEERAERT BRANDT, *Historie der Reformatie*, 4 vols, Amsterdam 1671–74 (vol. 1–2), Rotterdam 1704 (vol. 3–4); *BG* no. 893; *BsG* no. 287. See esp. I, pp. 550–51. English translation by JOHN CHAMBERLAYNE, *The History of the Reformation*, 4 vols, London 1720–23, see esp. I, pp. 308–09; cf. MANSFIELD, *Phoenix*, pp. 144–47 and P. BURKE, "The Politics of Reformation History: Burnet and Brandt," in A.C. DUKE − C.A. TAMSE (edd.), *Clio's Mirror. Historiography in Britain and the Netherlands*, Zutphen 1985, pp. 73–85.

[20] E.g. F. Pijper (1859–1926) and J. Lindeboom (1882–1958), cf. J.C.H. BLOM − C.J. MISSET, "'Een onvervalschte Nederlandsche geest.' Enkele historiografische kanttekeningen bij het concept van een nationaal-gereformeerde richting," in *Geschiedenis godsdienst letterkunde. Opstellen aangeboden aan dr. S.B.J. Zilverberg...*, Roden 1989, pp. 221–32; BRUCE MANSFIELD, *Man On His Own. Interpretations of Erasmus c 1750–1920*, Toronto 1992, pp. 306–09.

[21] A. YPEIJ − I.J. DERMOUT, *Geschiedenis der Nederlandsche Hervormde Kerk*, 4 vols, Breda 1819–27, vol. I, pp. 23, 37.

[22] CALVIN, *Opera* IX = *Corpus Reformatorum* 37, cols. 847–49.

The implication of Grotius' remarks is obvious: the Remonstrants shared certain ideas with Melanchthon; Calvin had accepted him in spite of these ideas; so why should the Dutch Calvinists be less tolerant than Calvin himself?

Grotius gives a central part to Erasmus here, pointing out that very many (*plurimi*) of his own Dutch ancestors did not agree with Luther's doctrine on predestination and free will. Grotius has in mind the period from the origin of the Reformation (which he calls "the morning twilight of truth") until the coming of those ministers who had been educated in Geneva and the other Reformed Academies. Elsewhere he refers back only to the beginning of the Revolt. According to Grotius, a large part of the population (*plebis pars magna*) had been spontaneously in favour of Erasmus' work. Anastasius Veluanus and Coornhert were popular primarily because their ideas on predestination were considered to be in line with those of Erasmus. Erasmus is also mentioned in another context: discussing the question of fundamental and non-fundamental articles, Grotius quotes Erasmus as advocating accommodation and concord[23] and as pointing out elsewhere that these can only be achieved if as few matters as possible are defined.[24]

So far, I have not spoken about the other conflict that divided Remonstrants from Counter-Remonstrants, namely the part played by the secular authorities in religious matters. In his *Pietas*, Grotius had shown himself not to have a very high opinion of synods. Princes had often taken decisions without convening a synod. With irony, Grotius continues "Why should anybody give credence to a hundred ministers, many of them new from university, rather than to many distinguished authors of the Western and all authors of the Eastern Church? But, it might be objected a synod could decide that both opinions are to be tolerated. In that case, what do we need a synod for, anyway?"[25]

Grotius gave more attention to this second subject of controversy – the differing views on the relationship between Church and State

---

[23] *Ordinum Pietas*, *OTh* III, pp. 107, 111. For "concord" cf. Erasmus, *De sarcienda ecclesiae concordia* (R. Stupperich, ed.) in *ASD* V,3, p. 304, ll. 617–18: "Accedat illa συγκατάβασις, ut utraque pars alteri sese nonnihil accommodet, sine qua nulla constat concordia," cf. p. 311, ll. 884–86.

[24] Cf. Erasmus to John Carondelet, 5.1.1523. Ep. 1334 (= the preface to Erasmus' edition of Hilary), ll. 217–19: "Summa nostrae religionis est pax et unanimitas. Ea vix constare poterit, nisi de [quam potest *added in 1535*] paucissimis definiamus, et in multis liberum relinquamus suum cuique iudicium...". This passage was among those censured by the Faculty of Theology at Paris in 1526, see *LB* IX, col. 926 B-D (censura) and Erasmus' reply cols. 926 D – 927 A.

[25] *Ordinum Pietas*, *OTh* III, p. 109.

– in another apologia, written almost ten years after the *Pietas*, the *Verantwoordingh*.

VERANTWOORDINGH (APOLOGETICUS)

During those ten years, things had changed radically, both for the country and for Grotius personally. The Remonstrants had been expelled from the Reformed Church by the Synod of Dordrecht, Oldenbarnevelt had been executed, Grotius had at first been imprisoned, then he had escaped and had been living in exile in Paris since 1621. In his *Verantwoordingh* of 1622 – a Latin version of which, the *Apologeticus*, appeared in the same year[26] – Grotius looks back. Reviewing past quarrels, he clearly distinguishes two conflicting concepts of reforming the Church: a broader concept involving the abolition of abuses and restoration of the original purity of the Church, and a more restricted concept implying a decision as to what was right doctrine and its definition. The first concept had found favour with the regents, whose primary responsibility was to maintain peace and concord within the Republic; they therefore preferred tolerance and accommodation, rather than closer definitions which were bound to lead to disruption.[27] In this respect, many regents owed their ideas to the writings of Erasmus, "who had always been highly inclined to peace and accommodation."[28]

Grotius and the regents did not particularly like the expression 'Reformed Religion,' which was however music to the ears of the orthodox ministers. Grotius *cum suis* preferred to employ the designation 'Christian' or 'evangelical religion.' In this context, Grotius cited various official documents which made mention of the 'true Christian religion,' the 'Christian evangelical religion' or the 'reformed evangelical religion.' These terms reflected his broader concept of reformation.

Since Grotius focuses here on the role of the secular authorities, it is not surprising that he points out that Veluanus had dedicated his book *Der leeken wechwijzer*[29] (*The Layman's Guide*) to the States of

---

[26] *Verantwoordingh van de wettelijcke regieringh van Hollandt ende West-Vrieslandt...,* Hoorn 1622, *BG* no. 872. Grotius himself translated this into Latin: *Apologeticus eorum qui Hollandiae VVestfrisiaeque et vicinis quibusdam nationibus ex legibus praefuerunt...,* Paris 1622, *BG* no. 880.

[27] *Verantwoordingh,* p. 35.

[28] *Verantwoordingh,* p. 29.

[29] Text in F. PIJPER (ed.), *Bibliotheca Reformatoria Neerlandica,* vol. IV, 's-Gravenhage 1906, pp. 123–376. Cf. G. MORSINK, *Joannes Anastasius Veluanus, Jan Gerritsz. Versteghe. Levensloop en ontwikkelingsgang* (diss. Vrije Universiteit Amsterdam), Kampen 1986.

his province (Gelderland) and that Gellius Snecanus – one of the other names to whom Grotius frequently refers – had done likewise in Friesland. The opinions of these men had always been tolerated. However, the magistrates had not always tolerated all dissenting opinions. For instance, the case of Coornhert, one of Grotius' witnesses, had been cited as proof against Grotius. In 1578, the States of Holland had forbidden Coornhert to publish anything concerning religion without their permission.[30] Grotius has no difficulty in finding a way out of this argument; he claims that the charges brought against Coornhert concerned a variety of matters, and not specifically predestination. So the case of Coornhert did not apply to the question at issue. The same holds true for other cases as well. Whatever the States may have done, they never wished to define the Reformed Religion so strictly as to exclude those who accepted only conditional predestination, that is 'some' ministers, 'many' magistrates, and 'countless' church members. The idea of conditional predestination was not an innovation introduced by Arminius, but was to be found in the works of Melanchthon and the 'sweet explanation' of Bullinger.[31]

In referring to Calvinist preachers, Grotius usually shows a condescending irony. They are apparently not capable of independent thinking, but merely repeat what they have been taught by their masters, and then force their opinions upon the people of the Low Countries. Grotius also reveals a certain dislike of foreigners, especially in the *Verantwoordingh*. Since the beginning of the Revolt, a certain group of people had been aspiring to a change in government: zealots such as the preachers (who, we have seen, owed their intolerance to their foreign education), and, secondly, people who had been trying to participate in the government, without success, either because they were foreigners, or because they did not belong

---

[30] Cf. H. BONGER, *Leven en werk van D.V. Coornhert*, Amsterdam 1978, pp. 90–91.

[31] *Verantwoordingh*, pp. 32–33. Cf. WALTER HOLLWEG, *Heinrich Bullingers Hausbuch. Eine Untersuchung über die Anfänge der reformierten Predigtliteratur*, Neukirchen 1956, pp. 117–18. In the memoranda Grotius wrote during his trial in 1618–1619, he also appealed to Melanchthon and Bullinger. Erasmus is mentioned only in a passage on the eight months of his imprisonment in The Hague, during which Grotius used to read The New Testament with the *Paraphrases* and the *Annotationes* of Erasmus, and the annotations of Beza, Drusius and Casaubon; sometimes he would also read Calvin's commentary on the Harmony of the Gospels, see R. FRUIN (ed.), *Verhooren en andere bescheiden betreffende het rechtsgeding van Hugo de Groot* (Werken uitgegeven door het Historisch Genootschap gevestigd te Utrecht, Nieuwe Reeks, no. 14), Utrecht 1871, pp. 5, 70, 260. In the "Kort verhael" which he wrote at Loevestein (i.e. between 6.6. 1619 and 22.3.1621), Grotius speaks of "those of the opinion of Melanchthon called Remonstrants" (*ibid.*, pp. 356–57); for Melanchthon cf. *ibid.*, pp. 355, 361 and 363; for Melanchthon and Bullinger, *ibid.*, p. 355.

to the old governing families.[32] This is the very voice of the regents, seeing both the secular and the religious establishment being menaced by upstarts and newcomers. One is reminded here of two works written by kindred spirits to Grotius, the satirical *Sardi venales* by Peter Cunaeus (1612)[33] and *Bogermannus* ἐλεγχόμενος by Caspar Barlaeus (1615).[34] In the former, there is a complaint about the increasing number of lower class scholars, a 'proletaria turba,' among whom it is suggested that many are theologians.[35] Three years later, Barlaeus explicitly criticized the "proletaria theologorum turba."[36]

I will now try to summarize this section. What did Erasmus represent to Grotius in the four works which I have been discussing? In his early work, the *Parallela*, Grotius praised Erasmus as the great scholar, the glory of Holland, and the moderate theologian who had liberated religion from scholasticism. Both he and Luther were considered to be the founders of the Reformation. The *Parallela* was written before the outbreak of the Arminian controversy. By the time of the *Historiae* , the situation had changed, and Erasmus and Luther no longer walked side by side. Henceforth, there was a dividing line between, on the one hand, Augustine, Luther, Calvin and Beza, and, on the other hand, the Greek Fathers, Erasmus and (thanks to Erasmus) Melanchthon, and native Dutch theologians such as Anastasius Veluanus. The next important step was taken in the *Pietas*, where Grotius asserted for the first time that Erasmus was widely read in the Low Countries and that, as a consequence, the majority of the population had adopted Erasmus' views on free will; and finally, that the opinions of Veluanus and Coornhert were appreciated because they were in this respect Erasmian.

Lastly, in the *Verantwoordingh* Grotius again emphasized the popularity of Erasmus' writings, without however focusing on the issue of free will and predestination in connection with this. This time, the alleged impact of Erasmus' work was of a more general nature. It made people in the Low Countries familiar with the idea of reformation in the broader sense of the abolition of abuses and of a return to the original purity and simplicity of the Church.

---

[32] *Verantwoordingh*, pp. 94–95. Cf. J.G.C.A. BRIELS, *De Zuidnederlandse immigratie in Amsterdam en Haarlem omstreeks 1572–1630* (diss. Universiteit Utrecht), s.l. 1976, pp. 32–37, 134–35.

[33] C. MATHEEUSSEN – C.L. HEESAKKERS (edd.), *Two Neo-Latin Menippean Satires, Justus Lipsius: Somnium. Petrus Cunaeus: Sardi Venales*, Leiden 1980.

[34] CASPAR BARLAEUS, *Bogermannus* ἐλεγχόμενος, Leiden 1615; *BsG* no. 242; cf. MANSFIELD, *Phoenix*, pp. 136–37.

[35] *Sardi venales*, p. 112, cf. p. 12.

[36] *Bogermannus*, p. 5.

Now, I would like to consider whether there is any historical evidence for all of these statements of Grotius. Discussing the *Pietas*, Posthumus Meyjes has said that Grotius' argument is not primarily historical, but rather apologetic; it is the argument of an advocate seeking to persuade his audience.[37] This is certainly true. Therefore, it is only to be expected that Grotius withholds information that does not suit his argument. For instance, the Academy of Geneva could not really have been as dangerous as Grotius makes out, because it appears that it had not done any harm to the future leaders of the Remonstrants, Arminius and Uyttenbogaert, in their own student days. As I have already mentioned, Grotius called upon Calvin in order to confirm the authority of Melanchthon. But he must have suppressed all thought of Calvin when introducing Coornhert, whom Calvin detested.[38] There are many other inconsistencies like this in Grotius' work. Nevertheless, Grotius' claims must have corresponded in part to reality to have been convincing. This also holds true for a remark such as that to be found in the *Verantwoordingh* that "many witnesses could confirm his (Grotius') words."[39]

Now I shall return to the *Pietas*: Is it true, for instance, that many of Grotius' ancestors preferred Erasmus' views on predestination to those of Luther? The early dissidents in the Low Countries were in fact more interested in other subjects, such as the value of ecclesiastical law, the Eucharist, the veneration of the Virgin Mary and of the Saints, or the relationship between faith and good works.[40] The first Dutch translation of Erasmus' *De libero arbitrio* did not appear until 1612, only one year before the publication of Grotius' *Pietas*. This translation was published at Rotterdam by Matthys Bastiaensz, who sympathized with the Remonstrant cause and who al-

---

[37] G.H.M. POSTHUMUS MEYJES, "De doorwerking van de Moderne Devotie met name bij de Remonstranten," in P. BANGE et al. (edd.), *De doorwerking van de Moderne Devotie. Windesheim 1387–1987. Voordrachten gehouden tijdens het Windesheim Symposium Zwolle/Windesheim 15–17 oktober 1987*, Hilversum 1988, pp. 81–94, esp. pp. 90–91.

[38] Calvin considered Coornhert ("un certain Hollandais" – he did not know his name) as a "peste mortelle," Bonger, *Coornhert*, p. 28. Discussing the way Calvin treated his opponents, Grotius relates that Coornhert was branded a "nebulo" and a "canis," *Votum pro pace ecclesiastica* (1642 *BG* nos. 1183–84) in *OTh*. III, p. 655.

[39] *Verantwoordingh*, p. 33.

[40] Cf. ALASTAIR DUKE, *Reformation and Revolt in the Low Countries*, London – Ronceverte 1990, pp. 29–59. With reference to the County of Flanders J. DECAVELE observes, that in the hundreds of trials he studied, he did not come across any clear statement about predestination before 1566, cf. his "Vroege reformatorische bedrijvigheid in de grote Nederlandse steden: Claes van der Elst te Brussel, Antwerpen, Amsterdam en Leiden (1524–1528)," *NAKG* 70 (1990), p. 29, n. 46. A disputation on predestination at Anderlecht in 1526 was a rather exceptional case, *ibid*. p. 18.

so published works by Melanchthon and by Bullinger.[41] Grotius was confronted with the popularity of this kind of theological literature among his Remonstrant contemporaries. Therefore, what he wrote about Erasmus with respect to the decades preceding the rise of Calvinism was certainly anachronistic.

But was Grotius wittingly or unwittingly anachronistic? The latter alternative can certainly not be excluded, since Grotius had rather vague notions about the first decades of the Reformation in the Low Countries. When Grotius discusses Dutch Reformation history, his starting point is usually the Revolt. To him, books such as Veluanus' *Layman's Guide* and Bullinger's *Decades* belonged to the early period of the Reformation. The *Guide* however appeared only in 1554, the Dutch translation of the *Decades* only in 1563.[42]

Aside from this, it must however be admitted that Grotius was right in looking upon Anastasius Veluanus as a forerunner of the Remonstrants. Anastasius had criticized Augustine as the first 'predestinator,' and had upheld the 'little free will,' a concept he had unquestionably borrowed from Erasmus.[43] But since Anastasius refers in this context to Melanchthon, not to Erasmus, the average reader of the *Guide* would not have realized who Anastasius' true source was. The popularity of the *Guide* was thus not brought about by the fact that its teaching was felt to be Erasmian, as Grotius seems to suggest; it neither proves nor disproves Grotius' claim that Erasmus' comments on free will were widely known in the Netherlands at an early stage of the Reformation. In this context, attention should be drawn to the fact that Johannes Uyttenbogaert, when he defended the Remonstrant cause in his *Kerckelicke Historie* (1646)[44] did not call upon the authority of Erasmus either.[45]

---

[41] S.W. Bijl, *Erasmus in het Nederlands tot 1617*, Nieuwkoop 1978, pp. 309–18. In 1612, Bastiaensz published a treatise by the Rotterdam minister Franciscus Lansbergius, who pointed out that what the Remonstrants said had already been said before by Melanchthon and Bullinger, see *Kort ende Christelijck examen over de leerpoincten die ten huydighen daghe in gheschil ghetrocken werden ofse het fondament der saligheyt raken ofte niet?* (Knuttel no. 1979), fol. A4ᵛ, cf. C2ʳ, G1ᵛ. Among others, Anastasius Veluanus and Gellius Snecanus are mentioned, but not Erasmus. Franciscus' son Samuel Lansbergius tried to prove that, although his ideas corresponded to those of the Remonstrants, Bullinger had always been accepted as a teacher of the Reformed Church: *Christelijcke aenleydinghe tot vrede ende onderlinge verdraechsaemheyt...*, Rotterdam 1612, also printed by Bastiaensz (Knuttel no. 1980; cf. Hollweg, *Bullingers Hausbuch* (n. 31 above), pp. 121–24). Here Erasmus is quoted once (fol. H 2ʳ), sc. the sentence "The sum of our religion is peace and concord...," cf. note 24 above.

[42] Cf. Hollweg, *Bullingers Hausbuch*, p. 91.

[43] Cf. Morsink, *Anastasius Veluanus* (n. 29 above), pp. 82–83.

[44] *BG* no. 892; *BsG* no. 282. A Calvinist reply was written by Jacob Trigland, *Kerckelycke Geschiedenissen...*, Leiden 1650; *BsG* no. 284.

[45] Cf. Posthumus Meyjes, "De doorwerking..." (n. 37 above), pp. 93–94. The

However, it is beyond doubt that Erasmus' works, and in particular the *Enchiridion*, were much in favour. As early as 1523 the *Enchiridion* could be read in a Dutch translation, which was often reprinted.[46] The reading of the *Enchiridion* was enough in itself to disseminate the broader concept of Church reform which Grotius would discuss, particularly in the *Verantwoordingh*. So here there is a case for taking Grotius' claims seriously. But the question still remains to what extent Erasmus really exerted his influence on the Dutch. Grotius suggests more than once that a majority was kindly disposed to Erasmus, but how could he know? It is possible that Grotius was inspired by a vague recollection of a passage which he had read in one of the letters appended to the *Vita Erasmi* of 1607, which had once been in his library.[47] In it, Erasmus quoted the Franciscan Nicholas of Herborn, who had written: "Luther has won over a great part of the Church, Zwingli and Oecolampadius some part, Erasmus the greatest part."[48] Nicholas had not meant this to be a compliment, and he was not referring particularly to the Netherlands, but his words might have stuck in Grotius' mind in any case.

When we think of statements such those as made by Bruce Mansfield or Henri Meylan, about Grotius' thoughts returning again and again to Erasmus,[49] or about the many times that the name of Erasmus is spontaneously evoked in his works,[50] we may be disappointed when we turn to Grotius' correspondence. Among the thirteen impressive volumes of the *Briefwisseling* that have been published to date, which concern the years up to and including 1642, three volumes contain no mention of Erasmus' name at all.[51]

---

conspicuous absence of Erasmus in Uyttenbogaert's work has also been noted by C.M. VAN DER KEMP, the judicious critic of Ypeij and Dermout (in his view "crypto-Remonstrants"), see *De eere der Nederlandsche Hervormde Kerk gehandhaafd tegen Ypey en Dermout*, 3 vols, Rotterdam 1830–33, I, p. 22. With reference to Anastasius Veluanus, the favourite precursor of the Remonstrants, Van der Kemp observed that his views were not entirely correct, and indeed that Trigland had already shown that Veluanus had never been a *reformed* minister, *ibid.*, pp. 174–75.

[46] Cf. BIJL, *Erasmus in het Nederlands*, pp. 57–79.

[47] Cf. P.C. MOLHUYSEN, *De bibliotheek van Hugo de Groot in 1618. Mededeelingen der Nederlandsche Akademie van Wetenschappen, Afd. Letterkunde*, N.R., dl. 6, no. 3, Amsterdam 1943, p. 16.

[48] Erasmus to John Choler, 19.2.1534, Ep. 2906, ll. 60–61: "Lutherus magnam Ecclesiae partem ad se traxit; nonnullam Zwinglius et Oecolampadius, maximam Erasmus"; *Vita Erasmi*, Leiden 1607, p. 117.

[49] MANSFIELD, *Phoenix*, p. 144: "It is not to be wondered at that Grotius' mind returned again and again to Erasmus."

[50] H. MEYLAN, "Grotius théologien," in *Hommage à Grotius*, Lausanne 1946, p. 40: "Combien de fois le nom d'Erasme, le grand Hollandais, le grand compatriote dont il est si fier, ne vient-il pas tout naturellement sous sa plume!"

[51] *BW*, vols. III, VI, VIII.

In the other volumes, Erasmus does appear, but only rarely. In four volumes, he is referred to only once by Grotius himself.[52] A single substantial paragraph on Erasmus is to be found in a letter from G.J. Vossius written 16 September 1614 and concerned with the fierce attack made by Matthew Slade on the reputation of Erasmus.[53] Grotius' correspondence for the years 1643–1645, still to be published in the new edition, does not yield much on Erasmus either. Nevertheless, Erasmus did play a role in Grotius' correspondence, however limited it may have been. Excluding some citations of classical proverbs, which Grotius may have taken from the *Adagia*, we can divide the references to Erasmus into three groups which sometimes overlap.

Firstly, there are a couple of references to works by Erasmus which Grotius may have had in his library. Secondly, Grotius drew attention to Erasmus in relation to Holland and especially to Rotterdam; finally, there is Grotius' consideration of Erasmus the theologian.

The first group of references is hardly worth mentioning. In quoting a passage on the Eucharist from Erasmus' correspondence, Grotius refers to the third volume of the *Opera*, (i.e. the Basel edition of 1540).[54] Then in 1636, Grotius returned some books which did not belong to him; among these was a copy of the *Colloquies*.[55] A couple of years later, he mentions a Latin translation made by Erasmus of the Liturgy of Chrysostom.[56] Grotius does not say that he owned any of these books. However, in one case we can be sure that he did have a book by Erasmus in his library. In 1638, Grotius wrote to his brother[57] to complain that the chaplains who were preaching in his residence were unsatisfactory; however, he says that he made up for this by reading the New Testament, Thomas à Kempis, Poppius (a Remonstrant who wrote a popular work of piety) and Erasmus. No title is given, but Grotius might have been reading Erasmus' *Paraphrases*. This information is not very impressive. We know something about the state of Grotius' library in 1618, thanks to the list published by Molhuysen. It is interesting to

---

[52] *BW*, vols. V, VII, IX, X.
[53] G.J. Vossius to H. Grotius, 16.9.1614, *BW* I, no. 372, pp. 354–59.
[54] H. Grotius to C. Salmasius, 23.6.1630; *BW* IV, no. 1521, pp. 234–35.
[55] H. Grotius to W. de Groot, 14.5.1636, *BW* VII, no. 2591, p. 147.
[56] H. Grotius to W. de Groot, 5.7.1642, *BW* XIII, no. 5775, p. 298 with n. 9. On this edition, see PIERRE FRAENKEL, "Une lettre oubliée de Beatus Rhenanus: sa préface à la liturgie de S. Jean Chrysostome dédiée à Johannes Hoffmeister 24 janvier 1540," *BHR* 48 (1986), pp. 387–404.
[57] H. Grotius to W. de Groot, 27.2.1638, *BW* IX no. 3473, p. 117.

note that only one of the 337 entries concerns Erasmus, that is a reference to his *Vita*, published in 1607. This edition also contained 84 letters of Erasmus.[58]

Among the second group of references, we need not dwell on Rotterdam being called the city of Erasmus.[59] However, who could omit here the famous visit which Grotius made to the statue of Erasmus in 1631? By then, Grotius had left Paris and was seeking to be rehabilitated in his own country. The way in which he described his visit in a letter to Uyttenbogaert[60] will lead us at last to Erasmus the theologian. But first, we must consider Grotius' disappointment when, having identified himself with Erasmus, he wrote eight years after his visit to the statue: Erasmus now has his admirers in Holland, but in his lifetime he was nowhere less appreciated than by his own people.[61] This picture of Erasmus does not agree with the earlier one given in the *Pietas*, where the people of Holland welcome Erasmus' book on free will.

The third group of references concerns Erasmus the theologian. What these passages mostly emphasize is Erasmus' irenical and moderate character and behaviour. Grotius is never very specific here. Replying to a letter in which Vossius had discussed Slade's attack on Erasmus' alleged atheism in detail, Grotius wrote that it would be advisable to ignore the slandering of the great Erasmus by such a little man, Slade.[62] In other letters Vossius again has something to say about Erasmus; whereas Grotius' reactions are short and do not reveal anything of importance. There is one instance, in 1630, where Grotius refers with approval to a letter in which Erasmus seems to identify the early Christian 'agape'-meal with the Eucharist.[63] The same reference is to be found in a short tract which Grotius wrote at the time on the question of whether the Eucharist may be administered without the presence of a pas-

---

[58] Cf. n. 47.

[59] Cf. e.g. H. Grotius to I. Casaubonus, 22.6.1613, on his moving from The Hague (the birthplace of Janus Secundus) to Rotterdam: "ex Secundi patria in Erasmi civitatem migro," *BW* I, no. 272, p. 248.

[60] See below p. 16 and n. 65.

[61] H. Grotius to J.F. Gronovius, 7.5.1639, *BW* X, no. 4096, p. 308: "Ipse etiam Erasmus habet nunc ibi suarum virtutum admiratores; at certe, dum vixit, nullis minus quam suis fuit cognitus. Quare et ubivis potius locorum quam ibi potissimam aetatis suae partem voluit agere."

[62] H. Grotius to G.J. Vossius, 11.10.1614, *BW* I, no. 375, p. 361; cf. W. Nijenhuis (ed.), *Matthew Slade 1569–1628. Letters to the English Ambassador*, Leiden 1986, p. 20.

[63] H. Grotius to C. Salmasius, 23.6.1630, *BW* IV, no. 1521, pp. 234–35; cf. Erasmus to Cuthbert Tunstall, 3.1.1530, Ep. 2263, ll. 72–88; cf. id., *Annot.* ad 1 Cor. 10.16, *LB* VI, 711 E.

tor.[64] On the basis of historical evidence, Grotius was inclined to take the affirmative view. Given a circumstance 'where there are no pastors' this had hardly any practical significance, but Grotius' viewpoint left room for questioning the necessity of priestly ordination in the Roman Catholic sense. The blurring of the boundary between agape and the Eucharist, however, involved a certain erosion of the sacramental aspect of the latter, and could not fail to annoy Protestants and Catholics alike. Thus, one of Grotius' Protestant critics, the theologian Johannes Cloppenburg, blamed him for "indocte" confusing the Lord's Supper with the agape-meal, the latter being little more than an "adiaphorum civile."[65]

Some years later, the same Cloppenburg censured Grotius in one of his disputations for having used the appellation 'fabulae' to denote the parables in the New Testament.[66] On 18th March 1645, Grotius wrote to Isaac Vossius,[67] who had informed him about Cloppenburg's attack,[68] that Erasmus in his own time had been criticized for the same reason.[69] What Grotius was suggesting was that philologists, such as Erasmus and himself, knew exactly when and how to use words like 'fabula,' whereas he implicitly compared Cloppenburg to the ever-suspicious scholastic theologians, who used to challenge Erasmus.

Grotius' famous words written to Uyttenbogaert after his visit to Erasmus' statue at least represent a clear statement of his views. According to Grotius, the people of Holland cannot be grateful enough to Erasmus, because he has shown "the way to a legitimate reformation not committing himself to disputable questions or ceremonies on one side or the other."[70] Needless to say, in putting it

---

64 *Dissertatio de coenae administratione ubi pastores non sunt. Item an semper communicandum per symbola*, Amsterdam 1638, *BG* no. 1091; *OTh.* III, pp. 507–09; 510–12. Erasmus is quoted at p. 509, where he is introduced as the man "qui nihil prope non vidit." For the background of *De coena* see H.J.M. Nellen's contribution in this volume.

65 JOHANNES CLOPPENBURG, *Theologica Opera omnia*, 2 vols, Amsterdam 1684, *BsG* no. 312, I, pp. 595–96.

66 CLOPPENBURG, *Opera*, I, p. 703 and II, pp. 7–8, referring to *De iure belli ac pacis* l. II, c. XX, 48 and c. XXIV, 4 and to l. III, c. I, 10.

67 *EQ* no. 1742, p. 746.

68 I. Vossius to H. Grotius, 6.3.1645, MS. UB Amsterdam, coll. RK VI F 30, p. 69: "Cloppenburgius habuit disputationem, qua ostendere voluit Exc. V. non male tantum, sed et impie parabolam appellasse fabulam."

69 Cf. Erasmus, *Supputatio errorum in censuris Beddae*, *LB* IX, 563 E – 565 D; 653 F – 654 C, cf. *Responsio ad Albertum Pium*, *LB* IX, 1109 C.

70 H. Grotius to J. Uyttenbogaert, 26.1.1632, *BW* V, no. 1735, p. 15; cf. MANSFIELD, *Phoenix*, p. 143. Mansfield's translation "measured reformation" for "rechtmaetige reformatie" is not impossible though "rechtmatig" in this sense occurs only in 16th-century dictionaries, cf. *Woordenboek der Nederlandse Taal*, XII, iii, 's-

this way, Grotius played down the reformation carried out by Luther and Calvin. If he had not done so, a mediating, irenic position would have been untenable anyway. For Grotius, the originator and founder of irenicism was without any doubt Erasmus. That is why he often puts Erasmus' name at the beginning of a series, such as: Erasmus, Cassander, Witzel, Casaubon, Brachet de la Milletière (1640)[71] or, as in his epigram *Qui gaudes* (1642): Erasmus, Cassander, Cordesius, Melanchthon, Witzel, Modrevius, De Dominis, James I, Casaubon (see Appendix). These men had fought the good fight, or were still fighting it.

As the founding father of irenicism, Erasmus came to symbolize it for Grotius. Significantly, it is Erasmus' *statue* that first comes to Grotius' mind in the epigram under discussion. Having idealized Erasmus in this way, there was no need to quote him in detail, or to refer frequently to his works. The Erasmian inspiration was common ground for all irenicists,[72] and was, as such, taken for granted. For practical purposes, Grotius could benefit more from the works of theologians of later generations. In contrast to Erasmus, they had been confronted with the already established Reformed and Lutheran churches, with an independent Church of England, and with the Roman Catholic Church after the Council of Trent.

Since the death of Erasmus, the religious and political situation had changed completely, and a variety of efforts had been made to restore unity to the Churches. As a consequence, there had been an increase in the quantity and the quality of 'irenic' literature. In his *Via ad pacem ecclesiasticam* of 1642[73] – an Erasmian sounding title, Grotius referred especially to Cassander, who had tried to show that the Roman Catholic and Lutheran confessions shared the same 'fundamental articles'. Thus, in the *Via*, Grotius published the Confession of Trent, the Confessio Augustana, Cassander's *Consultatio*, and four other documents. But nothing was taken from the works of Erasmus, not even from his book "On restoring the unity of the Church."[74]

Gravenhage – Leiden 1972, col. 604. CHAMBERLAYNE, *The History* (see n. 19 above) I, p. 29, has "a true Reformation."

[71] H. Grotius to W. de Groot, 14.4.1640, *BW* XI, no. 4599, p. 203.

[72] Cf. G.H.M. POSTHUMUS MEYJES, "Hugo Grotius as an irenicist," in *The World of Hugo Grotius* (see n. 3 above), pp. 43–62, esp. pp. 44, 50, 55–56.

[73] *BG* no. 1166.

[74] *De sarcienda ecclesiae concordia* (or: *De amabili ecclesiae concordia*) Basel 1533, ed. by R. STUPPERICH in *ASD* V,3, pp. 245–313. This treatise was condemned by the Sorbonne in 1551 and put on the Index in 1554, *ibid.*, p. 253. The title of *De sarcienda* is listed in the *Syllabus auctorum qui de conciliatione controversiarum in religione scripserunt* which is incorporated in the Amsterdam edition of the *Via ad pacem ecclesiasticam* (1642, *BG* no. 1167), p. 82 ("De amicabili ecclesiae concordia"). On the complicat-

If it is true that Grotius did not see the need for frequently referring to Erasmus, may we also go a step further and suggest that several of Erasmus' works were only vaguely known to him? The following quotation from *De iure belli ac pacis* (1625) may serve as an illustration. Apart from an insignificant note in book III,[75] this is the only time that Grotius feels obliged to introduce Erasmus in *De iure*. After having criticized the Christian world for its "lack of restraint in relation to war," Grotius goes on to say:

> Confronted with such utter ruthlessness many men, who are the very furthest from being bad men, have come to the point of forbidding all use of arms to the Christian, whose rule of conduct above everything else comprises the duty of loving all men. To this opinion sometimes John Ferus and my fellow-countryman Erasmus seem to incline, men who have the utmost devotion to peace in both Church and State; but their purpose, as I take it, is, when things have gone in one direction, to force them in the opposite direction, as we are accustomed to do, that they may come back to a true middle ground. But the very effort of pressing too hard in the opposite direction is often so far from being helpful that it does harm, because in such arguments the detection of what is extreme is easy, and results in weakening the influence of other statements which are well within the bounds of truth. For both extremes therefore a remedy must be found, that men may not believe either that nothing is allowable, or that everything is.[76]

Despite a certain circumspection ("sometimes ... seem to incline"), Grotius seems to be arguing that Erasmus spoke out for the pacifist case. It is true that Grotius puts forward in Erasmus' defense that he may have exaggerated with the best of intentions, but nevertheless, his remained a case of 'pressing too hard in the opposite [pacifist] direction.' Here two things should be noted: First, the way Grotius tries to excuse Erasmus' exaggeration echoes what Erasmus himself had said, with respect to Tertullian's pacifism, in his letter to Nicolaas Broeckhoven (Buscoducensis) of 31st August 1521:

> This sort of exaggeration is almost allowable even in the orthodox, whenever they either seek to deter us from different faults or encourage us to actions far removed from those which they wish to avoid. They act like those who, given a curved stick, do not bend it until it is straight but curve it right back in the opposite direction, that it may end up by returning to the straight.[77]

---

ed history of the *Syllabus* and its compiler Jean Hotman, see G.H.M. Posthumus Meyjes, "Jean Hotman and Hugo Grotius," *Grotiana* N.S. 2 (1981), pp. 3–29, on pp. 22–29.

[75] L. III, c. I, 16, n. 2 ad "splendide mendax": "... vide si vacat et Moriae Encomio Erasmum..." (= *De iure*, ed. 1646, p. 442).

[76] *Prolegomena* c. 29. Translation taken from *De iure belli ac pacis libri tres*, vol. 2: *The translation*, by Francis W. Kelsey, Oxford – London 1925, p. 20.

[77] Erasmus Ep. 1232, ll. 50–57. Transl. *CWE* 8, p. 291, l. 58 – p. 292, l. 64; cf.

Secondly, it is worth asking why Grotius should feel obliged to ex-
onerate Erasmus in the way in which he did; it would have been
more convincing to point out that Erasmus, despite his devotion to
peace, had never forbidden absolutely all use of arms. In the well-
known letter to Volz (1518), preceding the *Enchiridion*, Erasmus
complains that, in discouraging wars fought for worthless objects,
he is "blackened with false accusations of sympathy with those who
say that Christians must never go to war."[78] Even in the 'pacifist'
Institutio principis christiani (1516), Erasmus had written that "The
good prince will never start a war at all unless, after everything has
been tried, it cannot by any means be avoided."[79] And in *De bello
Turcico* (1530) Erasmus called the opinion that a Christian should
never fight in war "too absurd to refute."[80]

In all probability, therefore, Grotius shared the contemporary
view of Erasmus as a pacifist.[81] The reason why he did not qualify
this, by referring to the writings quoted above, may simply have
been that he was less familiar with them than he was with Erasmus'
correspondence.

APPENDIX

Introductory note

In his 'Grotiana,' Guy Patin records his having reproached Grotius for not
mentioning his compatriot Erasmus, "to whose immense erudition we owe
the renaissance of *bonae litterae*," in any of his poems. Grotius had replied
that he could not explain why he had overlooked Erasmus; he would
atone for this by making something specially in honour of this great
man.[82] This conversation would have taken place about June 1643, and

---

R. REGOUT s.j., "Erasmus en de theorie van den rechtvaardigen oorlog," in *Voordrachten gehouden ter herdenking van den sterfdag van Erasmus op 10 en 11 Juli 1936 te Rotterdam*, 's-Gravenhage 1936, pp. 155–71, esp. 160–61, 165, 169–70.

[78] Erasmus Ep. 858, ll. 378–80. Transl. *CWE* 6, p. 84, ll. 402–04.

[79] Cf. *ASD* IV,1 (ed. O. HERDING), p. 213, l. 463 – p. 214 l. 464. Transl. *CWE*
27, p. 282.

[80] Cf. *ASD* V, 3 (ed. A.G. WEILER), p. 54, l. 415–20 and the commentary ad
loc.

[81] Cf. Peter HAGGENMACHER, *Grotius et la doctrine de la guerre juste*, Paris 1983, pp.
43–44.

[82] RENÉ PINTARD, *La Mothe le Vayer – Gassendi – Guy Patin. Etudes de bibliographie et
de critique suivies de textes inédits de Guy Patin*, Paris [1943], pp. 77–78: "Comme je luy
eusse dit que i'avois quelque droit de me plaindre de luy parce qu'il n'avoit en
tous ses Poëmes où il a loué tant de monde fait aucune mention du bon Erasme
qui estoit Hollandais comme luy et cujus infinitae eruditioni debemus παλιν-
γενεσίαν bonarum litterarum, il me respondit: Vous avez raison, ie ne scay comment ie l'ay oublié, mais ie veux reparer la faute: ie veux faire exprès quelque
chose en l'honneur de ce grand homme, qui a esté veritablement incomparable,"
quidquid contra effutiant Monachi et Loyolitae, impurum hominum genus." Cf.

there is no reason why Patin should have invented the story. However this may be, no poem in honour of Erasmus has been handed down to us. The epigram *Qui gaudes* does not meet the requirements, but it does deserve some attention since in it Grotius shows Erasmus as the first link in an irenicist chain.

The epigram (*BG* no. 295) was first printed in the *Annotata ad consultationem Cassandri* (Paris, 1641, (*BG* no. 1165) and afterwards in the *Via ad pacem ecclesiasticam* (Paris, 1642, *BG* no. 1166; Amsterdam, 1642, *BG* nos. 1167–68), and in *OTh* III, p. 636. It is also to be found in Andreas Rivetus' refutation of the *Annotata*: *Hugonis Grotii in consultationem G. Cassandri annotata cum necessariis animadversionibus Andreae Riveti* (Leiden, 1642, *BG* no 1172), p. 255, followed by a highly critical "exegesis epigrammatis" (pp. 255–63). With reference to Erasmus, Rivetus observes that the humanist tried in vain to mediate between the religious parties, since he was much more inclined to one of them (i.e. the Catholic party). Likewise, Erasmus' imitators could not expect to be any more successful. Witzel e.g. is disapprovingly characterized as "totus Erasmianus" (p. 258), seeking a "third or intermediate religion" (*tertiam religionem vel mediam*, pp. 259–60). Rivetus' refutation contained also an anonymous epigram against the irenic – and consequently, in the poet's view, pro-catholic – tendency of *Qui gaudes* (text in *BW* XIII, p. 171, n. 4; cf. p. 278). The author turned out to be Constantijn Huygens. This publication led to a controversy and lasting coolness between Grotius and Huygens.[83]

The text of *Qui gaudes* printed below is taken from the *Via ad pacem*, Amsterdam, 1642, p. 56. Spelling and punctuation have been adapted to modern usage. The text of the English version by Clement Barksdale[84] (*BG* no 308) is from his translation of Grotius' *De iure belli ac pacis*: *Of the law of warre and peace*, London, 1654 (*BG* no 627), last part ("Memorials of the life and death of H. Grotius"), p. [63]; here the orthography and punctuation of the original have been maintained.

> Qui gaudes Batavis quod aheneus adstat Erasmus,
>   Praemia sed meritis ista minora putas;
> Qui quod Cassandri veracia scripta teruntur
>   Cordesio[85] grates haec bona propter agis;
> Quem praedulce iuvat stillante Melanchthone nectar,
>   Qui Wiceli chartas Modreviique legis;

---

also J.-Cl. MARGOLIN, "Guy Patin, lecteur d'Erasme," in *Colloquia Erasmiana Turonensia. Douzième stage international d'études humanistes, Tours 1969*, ed. J.-Cl. MARGOLIN, I, Paris 1972, p. 334; Margolin supposes that the thrust at monks and Jesuits is rather "du style patinien."

[83] Cf. H.J.M. NELLEN, "Een Haags dichter over 'de Delftse Cicero.' Hugo Grotius in de brieven en gedichten van Constantijn Huygens," *De zeventiende eeuw* 3 (1987), pp. 125–37.

[84] Clement Barksdale (1609–1687), clergyman, prolific writer and translator, i.a. of works by Grotius, *DNB* III (1885), pp. 215–16.

[85] Jean de Cordes (1570–1642), priest and bibliophile, who had edited CASSANDER's *Opera* in 1616, *BW* XII, p. 299, n. 11. Rivetus writes in his "exegesis epigrammatis" (p. 257) that Cordesius will not be pleased with the revelation that this edition of Cassander was his work.

Qui pia vota probas Spalatinis[86] insita libris,
    Deque decem velles non periisse duos;
Quique putas Regem multum sapuisse Britannum,
    Cum sua mandavit sensa Casaubonidae:
Accipe, sed placidus, quae si non optima, certe
    Expressit nobis non mala pacis amor.
Et tibi dic: nostro labor hic si displicet aevo
    A grata pretium posteritate feret.

That Roterdam Erasmus stands in Brass;
(Yet this Reward to 's worth inferiour was:)
That mild Cassander's Works are published,
(Thanks to Cordesius) and by thee are read:
That Nectar drops from sweet Melancthon's vein;
Wicel and Modreve write in the same strein:
That in Spalato's Books good Votes are seen
For Unity: (ill lost are Two of Ten:)
That Great Great-Britains King hath wisely done,
In signifying his mind by Casaubon:
Who joy'st in all this, view with gentle look
Our way of Reconcilement in this Book,
Good, if not best: 'Twill please thou mayst presage,
Though not the Present, yet the Future Age.

---

[86] This does not refer to the German humanist and reformer Georg Spalatin (1484–1545), but to Marco Antonio de Dominis (1566–1624), Archbishop of Spalato.

HUGO GROTIUS AND JUDAISM

Edwin Rabbie
(The Hague)

Whoever announces a lecture on the subject 'Hugo Grotius and Judaism' should first make clear what exactly he is going to speak about. For there is a multitude of possible subjects which present themselves. Will it be about Grotius as a Hebraist, as an expert on post-biblical Jewish literature, as a judge of the Jewish religion as a historical phenomenon, as a lawyer vis-à-vis the legal position of his Jewish contemporaries, as a scholar in contact with rabbis, or as an exegete of the Old (and New) Testaments? What you may count on here is a pinch of everything, with here and there a somewhat more in-depth discussion. I will concentrate on the way Grotius portrays Jewish religion and his attitude towards post-biblical Jewish literature, viz. the Mishnah and the Talmud and the Jewish exegetical literature. Before this, however, I will present a short overview of the sources of our knowledge of Grotius' opinions on Jews and Judaism and a survey of the *Stand der Forschung*, inasmuch as we can speak about that.

About Grotius and Judaism there is a wide variety of reports. Rumor has it (in this case circulated by Jerôme Bignon and recorded in the *Patiniana*) that if he had given up his Christian faith, he would have considered converting to Judaism;[1] on the other hand he has more recently been depicted as having been not very fond of Jews.[2] In between these two extreme positions there are various accusations of philo-Semitism, 'iudaizare,' by more orthodox Calvinistic and Lutheran contemporaries,[3] and various present-day

---

[1] *Naudaeana et Patiniana*, Amsterdam 1703 II, p. 118, quoted by H.J.M. Nellen, "'Geene vredemaeckers zijn zonder tegenspreeckers,' Hugo Grotius' buitenkerkelijke positie," *De Zeventiende Eeuw* 5 (1989) 1, pp. 103–12 on p. 109.
[2] Thus especially Jozeph Michman, "Historiography of the Jews in the Netherlands," in Jozeph Michman – Tirtsah Levie (edd.), *Dutch Jewish History, Proceedings of the Symposium on the History of the Jews in the Netherlands November 28 – December 3, 1982 Tel-Aviv – Jerusalem*, Jerusalem 1984, pp. 7–29, on pp. 16–22.
[3] André Rivet described Grotius' *Annotationes* on the Old Testament as "Iudaico-Socinianae" (*Operum theologicorum ... tomus alter*, Roterodami 1652, p. 814); the Lutheran theologian Abraham Calovius opposed Grotius' commentaries on the Bible by means of a commentary of his own (1672; 1719²), in which the accusation of "iudaizare" is rife. It should, however, not be forgotten that accusations of "papizare" against Grotius were even more frequent. On Calovius' accusations cf. A. Kuenen, "Hugo de Groot als uitlegger van het Oude Verbond," *Verslagen en mededeelingen der Koninklijke Akademie van Wetenschappen. Afdeeling letterkunde. Tweede reeks. Twaalfde Deel*, Amsterdam 1883, pp. 301–32, on pp. 324–26; on the often gratui-

assessments of his attitude towards his Jewish contemporaries, including the accusation that Grotius' attitude in this respect was "out of touch with reality."[4]

The sources. Let me begin by saying that there is, as far as I know, no passage in Grotius' oeuvre in which he expresses himself exhaustively and in a more or less systematic way on the Jewish religion. Time and again his point of view is determined by and his argumentation is subordinate to the goal which he had in mind in a particular work or passage. Therefore, his remarks should always be considered in their respective contexts, and in particular the aims of the work in which they are found as a whole must be taken into account.

Without providing a philosophical or theological survey of Judaism,[5] Grotius' longest continuous and at the same time earliest text on the subject of Jews and Judaism is a memorandum, drawn up by him in 1615 in his capacity of Pensionary of the city of Rotterdam, by order of the States of Holland and Westfriesland, which bears the sonorous title: *Remonstrantie nopende de ordre dije in de landen van Hollandt ende Westvrieslandt dijent gestelt op de Joden* ("Remonstration concerning the order which in the countries of Holland and Westfriesland should be imposed upon the Jews"). The manuscript[6] (which is no autograph, but certainly was in Grotius' possession and according to reports is provided with autographic notes) was part of the famous collection of Grotiana which until shortly before the year 1864 was still in the possession of Grotius' descendants and which was auctioned in December of that year at Martinus Nijhoff's in The Hague.[7] It was bought by D. Henriques de Castro Mzn.[8] and after the latter's death the manuscript was sold again in

---

tously uttered accusations of "iudaizare" in the 16th century cf. JEROME FRIEDMAN, *The Most Ancient Testimony: Sixteenth-century Christian Hebraica in the Age of Renaissance Nostalgia*, Athens, Ohio 1983, pp. 182–94; esp. p. 182: "This term was often used as a catchall epithet to describe the religious views of all opponents no matter how incongruous the charge."

[4] Thus DANIEL SWETSCHINSKI, *The Portuguese Jewish Merchants of Seventeenth-Century Amsterdam: A Social Profile*, diss. Brandeis University 1979 (microfilm), p. 47.

[5] Thus likewise SWETSCHINSKI, *The Portuguese Jewish Merchants*, p. 46 on the *Remonstrantie*: "The most striking characteristic of Grotius' argument is the relative absence of a consistent ideological commitment."

[6] Cf. L. FUKS – R.G. FUKS-MANSFELD, *Hebrew and Judaic manuscripts in Amsterdam public collections, II: Catalogue of the manuscripts of Ets Haim, Livraria Montezinos – Sephardic community of Amsterdam*, Leiden 1975, no. 341.

[7] W.J.M. VAN EYSINGA – L.J. NOORDHOFF, *Catalogue de manuscrits autographes de Hugo Grotius, dont la vente aura lieu à La Haye le 15 Novembre 1864 sous la direction et au domicile de Martinus Nijhoff, deuxième édition avec annotations*, La Haye 1952, p. 25 no. 73.

[8] On De Castro cf. E. SLIJPER, in *Nieuw Nederlandsch Biographisch Woordenboek* I (1911), col. 589.

1899, when it was bought by David Montezinos for the amount of ƒ 60.00. The last-mentioned collector donated it, together with his complete library, to the Portuguese-Jewish community in Amsterdam, where the work remained for fifty years, during which it was studied but remained unpublished; only in 1949 did the librarian of the Livraria Montezinos, J. Meijer, publish it (together with some other papers relating to the same subject, also originating from the Nijhoff-auction, which are not products of Grotius' pen[9]); until now, this is still the only edition.[10]

The purpose behind the *Remonstrantie* becomes sufficiently clear from the title: the immigration of so-called Portuguese, i.e., Sephardic Jews and of Marranos revealing themselves as Jews in Amsterdam and other cities, which started after the fall of Antwerp in 1585, prompted the States of Holland to formulate a fundamental position with respect to this phenomenon. After the expulsion of the Jews from the Netherlands in the late Middle Ages plus the bans on their stay from the period of Charles V, the renewed Jewish immigration under the altered political circumstances at the end of the 16th century constituted a problem for the central government. On the one hand these Jews were political refugees who had suffered the same Spanish violence as the Dutch Protestants; on the other it was hard to swallow for some that a government which refused freedom of religion to Roman Catholics, and even discriminated between various Protestant denominations (as e.g. between Remonstrants and Counter-remonstrants) did permit free exercise of a non-Christian religion. The Pensionaries of the cities of Amsterdam and Rotterdam, Adriaen Pauw and Hugo Grotius, were commissioned to draw up a concept for regulations on the legal status of the Jews.[11] However, a decision was only reached in December 1619, i.e., more than one year after Grotius' arrest; then it was decided that each city was allowed to make its own rules for the admission of Jews; there have never been national regulations.

---

[9] Van Eysinga – Noordhoff, *Catalogue*, pp. 25–26 nos. 74–75.

[10] *BG* no. 816: Hugo de Groot, *Remonstrantie nopende de ordre dije in de landen van Hollandt ende Westvrieslandt dijent gestelt op de Joden, naar het manuscript in de Livraria D. Montezinos* uitgegeven en ingeleid door J. Meijer, Amsterdam 1949 – 5709.

[11] Against Meijer's opinion, *Remonstrantie*, pp. 9; 95-98 W.J.M. van Eysinga, *De Groots Jodenreglement*, Amsterdam 1950 [= Mededelingen der Koninklijke Nederlandse Akademie van Wetenschappen, afd. Letterkunde, Nieuwe reeks, deel 13, no. 1] = *Sparsa Collecta, een aantal der verspreide geschriften van Jonkheer Mr. W.J.M. van Eysinga* edd. F.M. van Asbeck, E.N. van Kleffens, K.P. van der Mandele en J.R. Stellinga, Leiden 1958, pp. 423–29, on p. 425 n.1.

During his imprisonment at Loevestein, Grotius wrote his Dutch poem *Bewijs van den waren Godsdienst*[12] ("Proof of the True Religion"), which was published in a Latin translation in 1627 and as such became known as *De veritate religionis Christianae*;[13] in 1640 this version was re-edited with an additional apparatus of notes.[14] It is self-evident that the truth of Christian religion cannot be 'proved' without at least in passing paying attention to Judaism. Grotius acted accordingly, and, to be sure, in two respects: on the one hand the Old Testament constitutes for him evidence for the truth of Christianity, on the other post-Christian Judaism is to be considered a superseded stage; accordingly, it is elaborately refuted in the fifth book of this work.

Towards the end of his life Grotius set out to write a commentary on the whole of the Bible with enormous energy. The thousands of pages which constitute his *Annotationes* are replete with countless references to Jewish customs, early and late Jewish authors and facts from Jewish history. This makes these works the third important source for our knowledge of Grotius' opinions on Judaism.

Last but not least, the most important source for our knowledge of Grotius' life and works is the correspondence. One is easily inclined to overlook those impressive green volumes, and for this reason I have explicitly referred to them.

The study of Judaism in its religious and historical aspects requires the knowledge of Hebrew. Even more so than today, this held true during Grotius' youth (before ca. 1620), when even the most important works of post-biblical literature had not been translated, apart from rare exceptions, as e.g. the Mishnaic tractate *Pirke avoth* and Maimonides' *More Nevukhim*, the "Guide of the Perplex," of which there was an inadequate Latin translation. How exactly this situation was changed during Grotius' life and what kind of consequences this had we shall see later on. Even in those days nobody would have considered making statements about classical antiquity without a consummate knowledge of Greek and Latin. But when, just to give an example, the Leiden professor Petrus Cunaeus in 1617 published his *De republica Hebraeorum*, by virtue of his knowledge of post-Biblical Hebrew sources alone, he was able to outclass his two immediate predecessors who had written on this subject; the result of

---

[12] *BG* no. 143.
[13] *BG* no. 944.
[14] *BG* no. 950.

this was that Cunaeus' book remained a standard manual for several generations.

And Grotius? Did he know Hebrew? The question has been asked several times and has been answered in different ways. The attack on Grotius' competence in the field of post-biblical Hebrew was opened by the before-mentioned editor of the *Remonstrantie*, J. Meijer, who reached the conclusion that "at least rabbinical literature was for Grotius 'terra incognita'."[15] This judgment lets the possibility open that he had perhaps a certain degree of knowledge of biblical Hebrew. Meijer's judgment encountered vehement opposition by some and has been supported by others, but after all is said and done[16] Van Rooden in his impressive study on Constantijn L'Empereur concluded the matter in one single footnote; the conclusion supports Meijer's judgment in principle: Grotius' knowledge of rabbinical literature left a lot to be desired; his competence in the field of post-biblical Hebrew has to be assessed as slight, if not minimal.

In this respect the following fact should be considered. Learning post-biblical Hebrew, especially learning to read the Talmud, is a very complicated business, which according to the rules of Jewish tradition but also for practical reasons should not be practiced without a teacher. The great Christian Hebraists of the Renaissance had clearly understood this, and thus we know, for instance, that Johannes Reuchlin, and, to take an example closer to home, Josephus Scaliger, Franciscus Gomarus and Johannes Drusius, to mention some birds of different feathers, each had a Jewish teacher, whether he was baptized or not. Even at the beginning of the 17th century there were no other teachers available than (baptized) Jews; only towards the end of the century it actually turned out to be possible that Christians were taught post-biblical Hebrew by other Christians. A figure like Erasmus, on the other hand, never had a

---

[15] MEIJER, *Remonstrantie*, p. 67.

[16] Cf. SALO W. BARON, *A Social and Religious History of the Jews* XV, New York – London – Philadelphia 1973², pp. 26; 390 n. 31; PHYLLIS S. LACHS, "Hugo Grotius' Use of Jewish Sources in 'On the Law of War and Peace'," *Renaissance Quarterly* 30 (1977), pp. 181–200; A.W. ROSENBERG, "Hugo Grotius as a Hebraist," *Studia Rosenthaliana* 12 (1978), pp. 62–90; A.L. KATCHEN, *Christian Hebraists and Dutch Rabbis, Seventeenth Century Apologetics and the Study of Maimonides' Mishneh Torah*, Cambridge, Massachusetts – London 1984 [= Harvard Judaic Texts and Studies, 3], pp. 55-65. See most recently PETER T. VAN ROODEN, *Theology, Biblical Scholarship and Rabbinical Studies in the Seventeenth Century, Constantijn L'Empereur (1591–1648), Professor of Hebrew and Theology at Leiden*, Leiden etc. 1989 [= Studies in the History of Leiden University, vol. 6], p. 144 with n. 86, whose conclusion is in agreement with Meijer's opinion.

Jewish teacher; consequently, there are no signs of his having had more than a rudimentary knowledge of Hebrew.

The fact that Grotius was well aware of the usefulness of Jewish teachers becomes clear from a passage in the *Remonstrantie*: "the scholars among them can be of use to us to learn the Hebrew language."[17] But just like Erasmus he is not known to have had a Jewish teacher. Indeed, as far as his Dutch period is concerned, this seems unlikely, if we take into consideration some remarks in letters which were exchanged between Grotius and Gerardus Vossius in December 1616 and January 1617.[18] Grotius had asked the Leiden orientalist and professor of Arabic, Thomas Erpenius', advice concerning some questions relating to Jewish history. Vossius informed him that Erpenius had sent a list with questions to his teacher in Amsterdam, "the most learned of the Jews alive nowadays."[19] If Grotius himself would have known a person like that, he would not have had to address Erpenius.[20] Nevertheless a certain knowledge of Hebrew cannot be denied to Grotius. Where, then, did he get that? There seems to be a consensus that Grotius learned Hebrew from Franciscus Junius, professor of theology at Leiden university from 1592 until his death in 1602.[21] Junius himself had had a long-time cooperation with Immanuel Tremellius (1510–1580), a baptized Jew; together they had edited a famous Bible-edition, part of which was, among other things, a Latin translation of the Syriac text by Tremellius. And it is well known that Grotius as a student had lived in Junius' house. Now, opinions are divided as to Junius' expertise. The devastating judgment on him in the *Scaligerana* is as follows: "Junius had read nothing, and wanted to be considered learned in several languages. Only his pupils take that seriously; ig-

---

17 *Remonstrantie* ed. MEIJER p. 113: "de geleerden onder hemluijden connen ons dijenstich zijn tot kennisse van de Hebreusche tale."
18 *BW* I,493 p. 543 of 31.12.1616 to G.J. Vossius; I,496 p. 545 of 6.1.1617 to G.J. Vossius; I,497 p. 547 of 9.1.1617 from G.J. Vossius.
19 "Iudaeorum quotquot hodie vivunt eruditissimu[s]." According to MOLHUYSEN ad loc. (p. 547 n. 8) perhaps Joseph Pardo is meant, the first Amsterdam chief rabbi of the Sephardic community (1597–1619), on whom cf. J. ZWARTS, in *Nieuw Nederlandsch Biographisch Woordenboek* VI (1924), cols. 1097–98. Cf., however, MEIJER, *Remonstrantie*, pp. 68-69 and H.-J. VAN DAM's remarks in this volume.
20 VAN ROODEN, *Theology, Biblical Scholarship and Rabbinical Studies*, p. 163 n. 271 refers to *BW* V, p. 151 for contacts of Grotius with rabbis in Amsterdam before 1619. However, the reference is erroneous; I have been unable to trace it.
21 Thus KATCHEN, *Christian Hebraists and Dutch Rabbis*, pp. 64–65, apparently after MEIJER, *Remonstrantie*, p. 58, who, however, rightly points to Raphelengius. Katchen's reference to *De verit.* 1.16 n. 62, *OTh* III, p. 22 a 36-38 does not prove much. RALPH A. MELNICK, *From Polemics to Apologetics, Jewish-Christian Rapprochement in 17th Century Amsterdam*, Assen 1981, p. 13 just like that calls Junius Grotius' "first Hebrew instructor."

noramuses who do not know what scholars are."[22] When we look at Grotius' own statements on Junius, it is striking that he mentions him time and again as the person from whom he learned his ideals on the unification of Christendom, without ever mentioning him as a Hebraist.[23]

A more likely candidate for Grotius' teacher of Hebrew may possibly be Franciscus Raphelengius (1539–1597), professor of Hebrew at Leiden University from 1586 until his death.[24] It becomes clear from a letter which was most likely written in the year 1605 that Grotius attended Raphelengius' lectures in Arabic.[25] And finally, the greatest orientalist at Leiden during the period Grotius studied there was of course Joseph Scaliger – but whether this scholar occupied himself with teaching elementary Hebrew is of course very unlikely.

However, the success of a study becomes clear primarily from its results in later scholarly publications. Now, in Grotius' first publications there are almost no signs of great familiarity with the Hebrew language. Under the poem which he wrote around the year 1596, at the age of ca. 13, in the album amicorum of his future brother-in-law Jonas van Reigersberch, he quotes a psalm-verse in Hebrew. In the appendix to the edition of the *Adamus Exsul* of the year 1600 he mentions a project, entitled *Philarchaeus*, containing among other things a substantiation of the truth of the books of Moses from pagan authors,[26] but although a book such as this can, in fact, also

---

[22] "Junius n'avoit rien leu, et vouloit estre estimé sçavant en plusieurs langues [...]; il n'y a que ses disciples qui en font estat; des ignorans qui ne sçavent ce que c'est des hommes doctes." *Scaligerana ou bons mots, rencontres agreables, et remarques judicieuses et sçavantes de J. Scaliger.* Avec des notes de Mr. LE FEVRE, et de Mr. DE COLOMIES, Cologne 1695, p. 221 s.v. Junius. There also the harsh statement that Junius, as soon as he deviates from his teacher Tremellius in their Bible-edition, immediately slips up.

[23] Cf. *BW* I,181 p. 158 of 24.12.1609 to F. Gomarus; I,215 p. 185 of 11.11. 1611 to A. Walaeus; II,705 p. 152 of 20.11.1621 to G.J. Vossius. Cf. also *BW* I, 498 p. 556 of 12.1.1617 to G.J. Vossius: "[Junius], cuius ego iudicium semper soleo plurimum facere" and especially the elaborate and as it seems well-balanced judgment of Vossius on his father-in-law, *BW* II,691 pp. 138–39 ca. 12.9.1621, where i.a. the following words are found: "Quem theologum Romana, quem reformatae ecclesiae dabunt in quo vasta adeo tum linguarum, tum philologiae, historiae externae philosophiaeque cognitio fuerit?"

[24] On Raphelengius as teacher of Hebrew at Leiden cf. J.C.H. LEBRAM, "Hebräische Studien zwischen Ideal und Wirklichkeit an der Universität Leiden in den Jahren 1575–1619," *NAKG* N.S. 56 (1975/76), pp. 317–57, on pp. 342–46.

[25] Cf. *BW* I,64 p. 54 of 23.3.[1605] to F. Raphelengius [jr.].

[26] Cf. on this writing also CASPAR BRANDT – ADRIAAN VAN CATTENBURGH, *Historie van het leven des heeren Huig de Groot...*, Dordrecht-Amsterdam 1727, I, p. 19; ARTHUR C. EYFFINGER, "A note on Grotius's early pursuits," in J.L.M. ELDERS et al.,

be compiled without knowledge of Hebrew, it is unknown whether Grotius ever realized his intention to write this work at all. At any rate, it has left no traces. In the correspondence during the Dutch years a Hebrew word is found only sporadically; single passages in the poetry of those years might testify to his knowledge of Hebrew.[27] The inventory of Grotius' library, compiled in 1620,[28] confirms this image: under no. 108 a "Grammatica Hebrea" is found (according to a later discovery[29] this must have been the grammar of Elias Levita, Basle 1532); no. 166 is "een Hebreeus boeck," perhaps a Hebrew Old Testament. That is all there is.

When examining Grotius' opinions on Jews and Judaism, it is convenient to distinguish between three phases: his Dutch period, before his apprehension in 1618; an intermediate period, from 1618 until ca. 1630, and the later years, from ca. 1630 onwards. I hope to make clear the usefulness of this distinction.

For more than one reason it is appropriate to start our survey with Grotius' earliest theological work, the *Meletius sive de iis quae inter Christianos conveniunt epistola* of the year 1611. Here we find Grotius' first statements on Jews and Judaism. It is important to keep in mind that the work is dedicated to the Zeeland jurist, theologian (albeit not a professional one) and orientalist Johannes Boreel. We happen to know that the Boreel family in Middelburg was in touch with the local Jewish community (which was no doubt very small);[30] Johannes Boreel, who at an earlier stage perhaps had lived in the same house as Grotius and with whom he was on good terms during all of his years in Holland, had even visited the Holy Land.[31] In the preface to the *Meletius* Grotius mentions the Jews, "who now settle amongst us."[32] A summary statement, but at any rate one of the first testimonies to the settlement of Jews in the Northern Netherlands.

Hugo Grotius: 1583–1983, Maastricht Hugo Grotius Colloquium March 31, 1983, Assen 1984, pp. 55–62, on p. 58.

[27] Cf. the *Epithalamium Ioannis Borelii et Agnetis Haymannae* of the year 1608, *Dichtwerken van Hugo Grotius* I 2 A/B 4, pp. 192–95 with note on v. 49 (p. 203).

[28] P.C. MOLHUYSEN, *De bibliotheek van Hugo de Groot in 1618*, Amsterdam 1943 [= Mededeelingen der Nederlandsche Akademie van Wetenschappen, afd. letterkunde, N.R. 6 no. 3].

[29] FOLKE DOVRING, *Nouvelles recherches sur la bibliothèque de Grotius en Suède et en Italie*, Amsterdam 1951 [= Mededeelingen der Koninklijke Nederlandsche Akademie van Wetenschappen, afd. letterkunde, N.R. 14 no. 10], no. 9.

[30] Cf. MEIJER, *Remonstrantie*, pp. 69–70.

[31] This becomes clear from the text of the before-mentioned epithalamium (n. 27), vv. 56–61.

[32] "qui nunc se nobis inserunt"; § 2.

As a matter of fact, in the *Meletius* Jews and Judaism are only mentioned in passing, always in contrast to the superior Christian religion; for instance, the erroneous Jewish view of the hereafter as a luxurious house of eating and drinking, grace which was only granted to Jews, in contrast to universal Christian grace, the predicted violence of the Jewish messiah, the cumbrous ceremonies Judaism is full of, Jewish charity which is restricted to fellow-Jews, as opposed to Christian charity which encompasses all of humankind, and the superfluous dietary laws.[33] All these opinions can already be found in older authors,[34] and, as far as they are based on sources like the Talmud, there is no reason to assume that Grotius consulted any of these. It should also be noted that in this work Grotius puts Judaism on one line with natural religion as "true, but nevertheless less perfect" than Christianity, a remark which provoked criticism from his correspondent Antonius Walaeus, much more a Calvinist than Grotius. In accordance with Calvin's opinion Walaeus maintains that Mosaic religion was "in its kind" perfect.[35] Nothing in the *Meletius* testifies to a closer acquaintance of the author with Judaism. The attitude is that of a more or less orthodox Christian, who can consider Judaism as nothing but an outdated transitional stage. While one cannot call this anti-Semitism, neither is there reason to call the author a philo-Semite. Judaism is only important in as far as it offers arguments for the superior truth of Christianity.

The *Remonstrantie*, written four years after the *Meletius*, betrays the same attitude. This is his only work which as a whole is concerned with a Jewish subject, as has been said, the question of the admission of the Jews to Holland. This *Remonstrantie* is a curious document, thus much has become clear by now as a result of the studies of Meijer and others, down to the last detail typical of Grotius' attitude. In order to bring out the highly peculiar character of this text it is perhaps best to read it backwards, starting at the conclusion, leaving out the rules proper (which contain 49 points) as well as the so-called "reasons for the principal articles," which do not concern

---

[33] §§ 16; 50; 56; 64; 69; 79.

[34] As to the opinion on the hereafter: earliest non-Hebrew source Sebastian Münster's note on Gen. 1.21 after Rashi ad loc.; other references in VAN ROODEN, *Theology, Biblical Scholarship and Rabbinical Studies*, p. 91 with n. 133; violent messiah: PHILIPPE DE MORNAY, SIEUR DU PLESSIS MARLY, *De la verité de la religion chrestienne: Contre les Athées, Epicuriens, Payens, Juifs, Mahumedistes, et autres Infideles*, Anvers 1581, pp. 769–70. For the remaining remarks no knowledge of Jewish literature is required.

[35] "suo genere"; § 12 with POSTHUMUS MEYJES' note ad loc.

the real issue at stake, viz. whether the Jews should be admitted and, if so, whether they are to be granted freedom of religion. The conclusion is as follows: "the Jews are to be admitted to Holland; they are to be granted freedom of religion, provided that certain rules are laid down, in order not to endanger Christian religion and public order."[36] Therefore, this conclusion seems very positive for the Jews. But if you read the preceding parts, it is remarkable how the author has reached this conclusion. In these parts he has enumerated all kinds of reasons which argue against admission. The arguments against admission are: 1) no two religions should be tolerated in one state; 2) Jews hate Christians; 3) Jews have murdered Christians both in the remote and in the near past and most importantly, 4) they have slaughtered children in order to ridicule Christianity (here follows a long list of places where ritual murders are said to have taken place). The arguments against freedom of religion are simple: no idolatry is to be tolerated; it would after all be unfitting to allow the Jews what is refused to the Catholics.

Of course, all these counter-arguments are successively refuted, but in order to be able to evaluate this half-hearted document, especially the first part, a "magisterial memorandum," one indeed has to dispose of a blind Grotius-worship of the kind Van Eysinga[37] had. For one should not forget that the question to which Grotius devoted more than two thirds of his introduction, viz. whether Jews should be admitted to the country, was not under discussion at all; the Jews were already there, and the only question was which status they were to be assigned: the resolution of the States of March 4, 1615, mentions rules "which the Jews who are living in these countries ... will have to observe."[38]

Especially the part on the blood libel stings in an unpleasant way. Did Grotius really believe these stories? Some scholars have

---

[36] ed. MEIJER p. 115: "Presupponerende dan, dat men de Joden in t' landt zal toelaeten ende oock hemluijden gunnen exercitie van haere religie, treft te letten op de ordre, dije men in haer regard zall hebben te stellen. Waer in generaelijck moeten gehouden werden twee oogemercken, te weten: de welstant van de Christelijcke religie, ende de welstandt van de Politije. All wat hijer nijet jegens en strijt, behoort men de Joden te gunnen zoowel als de Christenen, om hemluyden metter daet te doen proeven de Christelijcke goedaerdicheijt."

[37] VAN EYSINGA, *Sparsa collecta*, p. 424.

[38] "... waernaer de Joden (in dese landen hen onthoudende) ... hen sullen hebben te reguleren." Therefore incorrect ARTHUR K. KUHN, "Hugo Grotius and the Emancipation of the Jews in Holland," *Publications of the American Jewish Historical Society* 31 (1928), pp. 173–80, on p. 175: "... the states of Holland were induced to appoint a commission ... to advise the states whether the Jews should be permitted to settle and upon what conditions."

made the assumption that with these remarks Grotius only tried to placate the orthodox reformed party, which was more opposed to freedom for the Jews than the Remonstrants.[39] This is wishful thinking, and it can be proved with near-mathematical certainty. Notwithstanding the fact that Grotius remarks "that certain facts, which historians have imputed to the Jews have not been judicially investigated," the main accusation remains intact: until recently Jews have killed Christian children for the sake of religion. So let's look at a case which has been "judicially investigated." In 1636 a number of Jews in the Polish city of Lublin were accused of murdering a Christian child. In court, they persisted in their denial, but in second instance they were sentenced to death on obscure grounds. A young Polish nobleman, Jerzy Slupecki, who as an adolescent had taken lessons from Grotius in Paris, asked his former teacher what he should think of this kind of accusations. Slupecki's letter and Grotius' answer have both been preserved.[40] The young man is unable to reach a conclusion, although he is strongly inclined to believe that the (frequent) accusations of ritual murder are lies.[41] What he wishes to know from Grotius is the following: whether similar accusations against Jews have been voiced in Western Europe; whether clear evidence of Jewish guilt has been found, and finally whether something about this question is to be found in the Talmud.

The questions, therefore, are sufficiently clear, but Grotius' answer is of a shameful equivocality. On the one hand he praises Slupecki's impartiality, on the other he repeats almost literally the accusations which he had also expressed in the *Remonstrantie*: Jews hate Christians, because thus it is written in the Talmud;[42] they also have often actually murdered dissidents. The blood of children is considered a remedy against leprosy (this view turns up here for the

---

[39] Thus MEIJER, *Remonstrantie*, p. 74 ("misschien ook om daarmede de Calvinisten wat gras voor de voeten weg te maaien") and VAN EYSINGA, *Sparsa collecta*, pp. 426–27. MICHMAN, "Historiography," p. 17, rightly questions the assumption that the Remonstrants were more kindly disposed towards the Jews than the Counterremonstrants.

[40] Printed in STANISLAW KOT, "Hugo Grotius a Polska," *Reformacja w Polsce* 4 (1926), pp. 100–20; 198–206, on pp. 202–03, in MAJER BALABAN, "Hugo Grotius und die Ritualmordprozesse in Lublin (1636)," in ISMAR ELBOGEN – JOSEF MEISL – MARK WISCHNITZER (edd.), *Festschrift zu Simon Dubnows siebzigsten Geburtstag (2. Tischri 5691)*, Berlin 1930, pp. 87–112, on pp. 110–12 and (with an excellent commentary) in F.F. BLOK, *Seventy-seven Neo-Latin Letters*, Groningen 1985, pp. 204–09; only Grotius' letter in *BW* VII,2884 pp. 576–80.

[41] "... conficta esse potius quam ex vero deprompta..."

[42] "... ut ex Thalmudicis aliisque libris apparet." Note especially the word "aliisque."

first time, i.e., it is not found in the *Remonstrantie*, but the elder Pliny already mentions it[43]), and since Jews hate Christians, it is possible that they have resorted to this remedy more easily. Grotius concludes these reasonings with the following sample of dialectics: "one should not believe everything of this, but neither nothing of it"[44] – followed by a classical quotation, of course (from Hesiod). The remainder of the letter is not much better. Evidence which has been given under duress is of dubious quality, our jurist teaches. In Holland there are no blood-libels against Jews; perhaps the Jews themselves have improved as a result of their kind treatment, or perhaps they lie low because they have only been living in Holland for a short time. But it will not have been without reason that they have been expelled from Holland and France in earlier times.

Ironically – and this only makes it much more painful for Grotius – Jerzi's brother Krzystof Slupecki, who between 1627 and 1629 had lodged with Gerardus Vossius in Leiden for one and a half year, consulted his former teacher about the same question. His letter and Vossius' answer have likewise been preserved.[45] Much more so than his brother, Krzystof is inclined to attach credence to accusations against Jews. Still, he wishes to learn Vossius' opinion on the whole matter. The latter's answer is of a heartwarming unambiguity: according to him, such libels against Jews are blatant lies. The blame lies with the Christians, who rather than persuading the Jews of the truth of Christianity persecute them by fire and the sword.

So, Grotius has never been able to convince himself of the falsehood of the accusations of ritual murder. Something like that speaks volumes. In this respect it is amazing how many positive things he is able to say about Jews and Judaism.

A first stage in this respect is the apologetic work which Grotius first wrote at Loevestein as a Dutch poem, subsequently translated

---

[43] *Nat. hist.* 26.5. Cf. on this kind of accusations HERMANN L. STRACK, *The Jew and Human Sacrifice, Human Blood and Jewish Ritual, An Historical and Sociological Inquiry,* London [1909], pp. 62–65.

[44] "... neque omnibus neque nulli credendum est," which of course does *not* mean: "not a single one of them is to be believed," as KATCHEN, *Christian Hebraists and Dutch Rabbis,* p. 57 thinks. Incidentally, it is noteworthy that STRACK, *The Jew and Human Sacrifice,* p. 169 n. * quotes almost the same words from EISENMENGER's infamous anti-Semitic book, *Entdecktes Judenthum* II, p. 227. In the preceding sentence all editions (*EQ,* Kot, Balaban, *BW,* Blok) have "Utrum apud nos sit." The ms. Rotterdam R.K. Cat. van hss. no. 674 fo. 5r (a copy) has "Utrum apud *vos* sit," which is certainly the correct reading.

[45] Lastly printed in BLOK, *Seventy-seven Neo-Latin Letters,* pp. 210–14.

into Latin prose and twenty years after the writing provided with copious notes, the *Bewijs van den waren godsdienst* or in Latin *De veritate religionis christianae*. A refutation of Judaism is a standard element of apologetic works in the tradition of which *De veritate* is a part.[46] The two most important predecessors which are mentioned by Grotius, Juan Luiz Vives,[47] author of *De veritate fidei christianae* (1542) and Philippe Duplessis-Mornay,[48] author of *De la verité de la religion chrestienne* (1581) both have a corresponding chapter. Especially Duplessis-Mornay in his refutation testifies to his intimate knowledge of post-Biblical Hebrew literature. Compared to these two authors Grotius does not have much new to offer; the arguments he puts forward are for the greater part already found in his two predecessors. On the other hand, especially in the second book the Jewish religious writings, including the Talmud, constitute evidence for the earliest history and therewith for the truth of Christianity, as we have seen on a somewhat smaller scale in the *Meletius*.

Nevertheless the exordium of the fifth book of *De veritate*, which proposes to refute Judaism, is of an extraordinary kindness towards the Jews as people (not so much towards Jewish religion, which is called an intermediate stage between the darkness of Paganism and the light of truth, that is Christianity). Grotius, basing his views on St. Paul's words in *Romans 11*, requests the Jews to "listen to us benevolently. It is known to us that they are the offspring of holy men, whom God used to visit through his prophets and angels; that from the same line the Messiah and the first Christian teachers were born; that they are the guardians of God's oracles, which we revere as much as they do"; he expresses the hope that the day may not be far away that the Jews may also behold the fulfillment of the Law, so that together united in piety they may worship the only God, the God of Abraham, Isaac and Jacob. Incidentally, this passage has been taken almost without change from the *Remonstrantie*, which was written six years earlier.[49] Compared to the vicious

---

[46] Cf. FRANÇOIS LAPLANCHE, *L'évidence du Dieu chrétien. Religion, culture et société dans l'apologie protestante de la France classique (1576–1670)*, [Strasbourg]1983, pp. 177–81.

[47] JUAN LUIZ VIVES, *Opera omnia* VIII, Valentiae Edetanorum 1790 [= London 1964], pp. 247–364: *De veritate fidei christianae liber tertius, qui est contra Iudaeos quod Iesus est messias*.

[48] DUPLESSIS MORNAY, *De la verité de la religion chrestienne*, chap. XXXI: "Solution des obiections que les Iuifs alleguent contre Iesus pour ne le receuoir pour le vray Christ ou Messie."

[49] ed. MEIJER p. 111: "Sij zijn de kinderen Abrahams, Isaacs ende Jacobs, de Israeliten, der welcker is de aenneminge tot kinderen, de heerlickheijt, de verbonden, de wetgevinge, de Goodsdijenst ende beloften; der welcker zijn de voorvaderen ende vuijt de welcken Christus selffs is, nae den vleesche, de rechte bloetver-

language with which Vives addresses the Jews, both passages in Grotius can certainly be called philo-Semitic.

The argumentation of the remainder of the fifth book is again typically Grotian, i.e., it is based on rational arguments, and therefore cuts no ice. The miracles performed by Jesus have been sufficiently proved; the prophecies of the Old Testament have been fulfilled, etc. Meanwhile, some harsh words are bandied on post-Biblical Jewish literature, of course mainly on the Talmud. This book is full of infamous tall stories and ridiculous doctrines; they simply go too far, and Grotius thinks it is useless to refute such nonsense. The Jews dare to call it the oral doctrine and to compare it with Moses' law, nay even prefer it to this. As to this passage, which apparently is taken almost verbatim from one of his predecessors[50] it should in the first place be said that the distinction and the difference in status between the aggadic and halakhic, i.e., the narrative and legal parts of the Talmud was apparently unknown to Grotius. Otherwise he would not have lumped together both elements, which have a completely different force. The fact that Grotius bases his arguments on second-hand knowledge (in his note on this passage he refers to the rather infamous and at any rate very tendentious work of the baptized Jew Gerson on the Talmud) and nevertheless passes so severe a judgment on a book of which he cannot have seen more than 5 % in translation, is of course to be explained from the objectives he had in mind at least originally when writing *De veritate*: he did not want to give a scholarly treatment, but a purposely partial refutation of a false religion. The fact that the notes, which were added twenty years later, nevertheless give the impression of a learned apparatus, makes the work a hybrid whole.[51]

Furthermore, the lack of understanding strikes with which Grotius looks at Judaism as a religion. Apparently he was quite unaware of the fact that it is the very Talmud and oral doctrine which he abhors so much (albeit according to contemporary habit) which make possible a correct understanding of Jewish religious practice. Therefore, any refutation of Judaism should first be a refutation of the Talmud, and the remark that the stories found therein are too

---

wanten van de Apostelen en eerste leeraers van onse religie: Jae de genen aen de welcken Godts Oraculen zijn vertrouwt."

[50] Cf. DUPLESSIS MORNAY, *De la verité de la religion chrestienne*, pp. 766–67; VIVES, *Opera omnia* VIII, pp. 252–54.

[51] MEIJER, *Remonstrantie*, pp. 63–64 already points to the remarkable discrepancy between the notes and the text of *De veritate*. For the former, Grotius was able to make use of the first translations of Jewish sources, published in the late '20s and '30s; at the time he wrote the text this had hardly been possible.

ridiculous for refutation does not suffice. In his refutation of Judaism Grotius does not concern himself with contemporary Judaism, but relies completely on what he considers the only authoritative source, the Old Testament. Evidently such a refutation is without much foundation.

To what extent the apologetic character of *De veritate* determines the character of Grotius' assessment of Judaism and Jewish literature becomes clear from a comparison with a work written only a few years later, the famous *De iure belli ac pacis libri tres* of 1625. In the prolegomena to this work Grotius enumerates his predecessors and sources. After mentioning the Old and New Testaments he refers (§ 49) to the Hebrew commentators on Scripture, who according to him have made important contributions to the understanding of these books, mainly insofar as they had an excellent knowledge of Hebrew idiom and Jewish antiquities. In the notes on the same work the Mediaeval Jewish commentators and especially Maimonides are mentioned with honor. Incidentally, it is to Grotius' credit that he was impressed by the brilliant Maimonides.

It was the references to Jewish sources in *De iure belli* which occasioned the major controversy in recent literature on Grotius as a Hebraist. The manner in which this issue was discussed is in my view not very fruitful; most authors have mistakenly assumed that the mention of a source by Grotius presupposes first-hand knowledge of the author concerned.[52] Now that it has been made clear by others[53] how Grotius handles his sources, we will have to look mainly for what I will conveniently call 'intermediate' sources, as has already been shown by Meijer for the references to Jewish sources in *De veritate*.

In this connection I should point to the fact that the number of Grotius' references to rabbinical sources increases exponentially from the thirties onwards. This phenomenon can be observed, e.g., in the reprint 1640 of *De veritate*, the first to have a corpus of notes,

---

[52] Exceptions mainly MEIJER, *Remonstrantie*, pp. 64–67 and VAN ROODEN, *Theology, Biblical Scholarship and Rabbinical Studies*, p. 144 n. 186; see also LACHS, "Hugo Grotius Use of Jewish Sources."

[53] Viz. in research into the sources of the legal tracts, on which cf. mainly R. FEENSTRA, "Quelques remarques sur les sources utilisées par Grotius dans ses travaux de droit naturel," in *The World of Hugo Grotius (1583–1645), Proceedings of the International Colloquium organized by the Grotius Committee of the Royal Netherlands Academy of Arts and Sciences, Rotterdam 6–9 April 1983*, Amsterdam – Maarssen 1984, pp. 65–81. A similar attempt concerning the theological work *Defensio fidei catholicae de satisfactione Christi* of 1617 in the introduction to my edition, Assen 1990 [= Hugo Grotius Opera theologica, I]

and the reprint 1642 of *De iure belli ac pacis*,[54] in which the number of references to Jewish authors has grown considerably. This is no coincidence. It was in the thirties that the first Latin translations of rabbinical texts had come on the market:[55] first, still in 1629 Johannes Cocceius' edition of the Mishnaic tractates *Sanhedrin* and *Makkoth*, followed one year later by Constantijn L'Empereur van Oppijck's edition of the tractate *Middoth*; in 1637 the same scholar edited the tractate *Bava Kamma* ("De legibus Ebraeorum forensibus"), which was very useful for Grotius' purposes. Other editions followed, but these were to remain the only ones until Grotius' death, apart from an edition with a Latin translation of the Mishnaic tractate *Pirke Avoth* (which is unique in its sort as being ethical rather than legal) by Paulus Fagius of the year 1541, which was also read by Grotius.[56]

Grotius has made much use of these editions, as well as of editions of Jewish commentators on the Old Testament edited by L'Empereur and others[57] and of several partial translations of Maimonides' code.[58] The full breadth of Grotius' newly acquired knowledge of rabbinical literature, albeit in translation, is evident from what in bulk may be called his principal work, the *Annotationes in Novum Testamentum*. This impressive commentary appeared partly posthumously in the years 1641-50,[59] but had already been in preparation since 1619.[60] In view of the above, we may assume that the manifold references to rabbinical sources were added later and are based on editions with Latin translation only.

The results of this increased knowledge can best be shown by means of a not quite random sample from Grotius' commentary, viz. his notes on the 26th chapter of Matthew, the description of

---

[54] *BG* no. 571.

[55] Cf. for this development VAN ROODEN, *Theology, Biblical Scholarship and Rabbinical Studies*, pp. 110–32.

[56] On Fagius cf. FRIEDMAN, *The Most Ancient Testimony*, pp. 99–118. An excerpt from Fagius' edition in ms. Amsterdam UL R.K. III C 4 fo. 67r-v.

[57] E.g., *D. Isaaci Abrabanielis et R. Mosis Alschechi Commentarii in Esaiae prophetiam 30*, Lugduni Batavorum 1631; *Paraphrasis Iosephi Iachiadae in Danielem*, Amstelodami 1633, both by L'EMPEREUR.

[58] E.g., *R. Mosis Maimonidae de idolatria liber*, Amsterdami 1642 by DIONYSIUS VOSSIUS; *Constitutiones de fundamentis legis Rabbi Mosis F. Maiiemon*, Amstelodami 1638 by G.H. VORSTIUS; *Canones ethici R. Moseh Meimonidis*, Amstelodami 1640 by GEORGIUS GENTIUS.

[59] *BG* nos. 1135; 1138; 1141.

[60] On the genesis and scope of the *Annotationes* cf. W.C. VAN UNNIK, "Hugo Grotius als uitlegger van het Nieuwe Testament," *NAKG* N.S. 25 (1932), pp. 1–48, and H.J. DE JONGE, "Hugo Grotius: exégète du Nouveau Testament," in *The World of Hugo Grotius*, pp. 97–115.

the Last Supper. If anywhere, it is here that he had the possibility of pointing to parallels with early and contemporary Jewish customs concerning the celebration of the Passover meal, the so-called 'seder.' In his note on verse 2 Grotius disputes the opinion of those who think that the Passover lamb was slaughtered on the eve of 14 Nissan, and supports his own opinion that this was done on the afternoon of this day with a reference to "the age-old custom of the Jews, which provides the best explanation of the Law."[61] On verse 17 he refers to the practice of searching the home for leftovers of leaven on the eve of 14 Nissan, "when they even collect crumbs"; the Jews "still have that habit today."[62] A bit further, in the midst of a complicated discussion of the exact date of the Last Supper, he mentions the fact that "cooking on the Sabbath was not allowed, but was permitted on a holiday."[63] This last remark in particular testifies to a much more profound knowledge of Judaism than could be found before in Grotius, for this correct observation cannot be easily deduced from the literal text of the Old Testament. Grotius refers to Exod. 12.16, and therefore apparently aims at the difference in phrasing between *melekhet 'avodah* and *melakhah*, 'labor of duty' (with reference to the holidays) and mere 'labor' (with reference to the Sabbath). Now, the fact that this difference in phrasing entails a practical difference concerning the prohibition of labor, which allows cooking food and carrying objects outdoors on holidays but forbids it on Sabbath, is completely based on the oral doctrine as we find it in the Mishna and Talmud. Likewise, Grotius' explanation of drinking wine after the supper with reference to the saying of grace after the meal over a cup of wine is excellent.[64]

This is not meant to say that Grotius' opinions on Judaism as they appear in his notes on this chapter are completely above criticism. For example, in Grotius' – if I see right impossible – view Jesus celebrated the πάσχα one day early, on the eve of 14 Nissan. In order to refute the – correct – objection that therewith he would have broken the Law, Grotius distinguishes between the πάσχα θύσιμον and the πάσχα μνημονευτικόν. The former involves the sacrifice of a lamb and could consequently only be celebrated during the temple and in Jerusalem, the latter is merely a reminder of this sacrifice and the exodus, and according to our commentator is "rather voluntary than based on a legal injunction."[65] This explanation

---

[61] *Annot. in Matth.* 26.2, *OTh* II, p. 241 b 9–10.
[62] *Annot. in Matth.* 26.17, *OTh* II, p. 245 b 35–45.
[63] ibid., *OTh* II, p. 246 a 1–2.
[64] *Annot. in Matth.* 26.26, *OTh* II, p. 248 b 31–39.
[65] *Annot. in Matth.* 26.18, *OTh* II, p. 246 b 39–59; cf. p. 247 a 31.

does no justice whatsoever to the discussion in the Talmud about the question of which of the commandments of the Passover celebration nowadays, without the possibility of making the prescribed sacrifice, are to be considered so-called *mitsvoth mideoraita* ('Scriptural commandments') and which are *mitsvoth miderabbanan* ('rabbinical commandments'). For your information: the eating of the first helping of unleavened bread is a Scriptural injunction (cf. Exod. 12. 18), irrespective of the question whether the Pesakh is eaten or not;[66] the eating of the bitter herbs and the second helping of unleavened bread without the lamb is nowadays, after the destruction of the temple, a rabbinical injunction (cf. Exod. 12.46).[67] Grotius' description of the Passover meal,[68] which follows next, indicates that the author is unaware of the fact that the lamb was eaten last,[69] something which is even today evident from Jewish practice.

So, it can hardly be disputed that even in his later years and notwithstanding his increased knowledge of rabbinical literature Grotius was insufficiently familiar with Jewish practice and lacked adequate background information concerning Judaism. In this context it is worthwhile to pay some attention to his much less elaborate and less important commentary on the Old Testament, which was published in 1644.[70] In the preface to this work the author remarks: "in the Law [i.e., the five books of Moses] I have added the intent and raison d'être of the commandments and the customs relating to them, basing myself mainly on ancient Jewish scholars."

In practice not much has come of this, apart from an elaborate commentary on the ten commandments which had already been published earlier; one example taken from another passage.

The note on Deut. 17.18, the commandment to the king of Israel to write for himself a scroll of the Law, is certainly noteworthy. Grotius states: "he had to copy the complete Pentateuch, first as any Jew, then again as a king."[71] This explanation is in accordance with post-Biblical Jewish sources, and is of necessity taken from a

---

66 MAIMONIDES, *The Commandments, Sefer Ha-Mitzvoth of Maimonides in two volumes ...* translated from the Hebrew with foreword, notes, glossary, appendices and indices by CHARLES B. CHAVEL, London – New York [1967] I, no. 158 pp. 168–69 with reference to Talmud Bavli *Pesakhim* 120a.

67 MAIMONIDES, *The Commandments* I, no. 56 p. 67 with reference to Talmud Bavli *Pesakhim* loc. cit.

68 *Annot. in Matth.* 26.18, *OTh* II, pp. 246 b 59–247 a 9.

69 MAIMONIDES, *The Commandments* I, no. 56 pp. 66–67 with reference to *Mekhilta* on Exod. 12.8.

70 *BG* no. 1137.

71 *Annot. in Deut.* 17.18, *OTh* I, p. 91 b 45–47.

Jewish author.[72] For the obligation for every Jew to write or acquire a scroll of the Law is based on a halakhic explanation of a verse in Deut. 31.19: "Now therefore write ye this song for you," and only through the knowledge of the fact that it is not allowed to write a partial scroll of the Law is it possible to deduce that these words contain the commandment mentioned before. It is even more noteworthy, for that matter, that Grotius does not comment upon the latter passage.

In any event, it has been mainly his explanations of passages in the Old Testament which were traditionally interpreted in a Christological sense, as, e.g., the 53rd chapter of Isaiah, which have brought Grotius in disrepute as being a Judaizer.[73] However, these accusations are not well founded. He is not concerned with the exposition of the Old Testament in a rabbinical sense, much less with the removal of the foundations of Christianity by postulating the invalidity of the Christological explanations. Rather, he has consistently tried to explain the Old Testament as writings by Jews for Jews.

To sum up. In Grotius' attitude towards Judaism an evolution can be discerned, while on the other hand there are certain constants. First the areas in which he has undergone a development. This is mainly his knowledge of post-Biblical Jewish authors, which had grown considerably through the years: whereas his remarks on Jews and Judaism in his earliest works are exclusively based on secondary, in part even anti-Semitic literature, sometimes products of spiteful baptized Jews, from the thirties onwards he is able, mainly thanks to the publications of Constantijn L'Empereur and others to consult the original sources in Latin translation (incidentally, these translations were not written to promote the knowledge of Jewish heritage, either). His admiration for Maimonides is beyond dispute; in a letter to his friend Gerardus Vossius of the year 1636 he calls him "almost the only Jew with a sound judgment."[74] He also appreciated Ibn Ezra, as many Christians did. On the other hand,

---

[72] Indirectly, that is. Cf. PAULUS FAGIUS ad loc., a passage Grotius may also have known from JOHANNES WTENBOGAERT, *Tractaet Van t'Ampt ende Authoriteyt eener Hoogher Christelicker Overheydt In Kerckelicke Saecken*, s'Graven-Haghe 1610[2], p. 74. Cf. MAIMONIDES, *The Commandments* I, p. 25 with reference to Talmud Bavli *Sanhedrin* 21b.

[73] Cf. KUENEN, "Hugo de Groot als uitlegger van het Oude Verbond," pp. 318–26; 331–32; VAN ROODEN, *Theology, Biblical Scholarship and Rabbinical Studies*, pp. 145–48.

[74] *BW* VII,2885 p. 581 of 12.12.1636 to G.J. Vossius: "... Maimonides, Iudaeorum prope solus sani iudicii."

there is a very noticeable constant factor in Grotius' attitude towards Jewish literature: it contains almost exclusively absurdities and ridicule. As far as we can see, this verdict has remained unchanged from our earliest testimony, the *Meletius* of 1611, until the forties. In a letter to the Englishman Samson Johnson of the year 1638 Grotius passes judgment on the works of the Amsterdam rabbi Menasseh ben Israel: "there are some things in them which are praiseworthy, but also some rabbinical, i.e., absurd and ridiculous stuff."[75] Jewish philosophy contains no ancient elements; it is completely derived from Greek sources via the Arabs, he says in a letter to the French Hebraist Joseph de Voisin of 1636; the Cabbala consists largely of concoctions. The only thing that can be learned from the Jews is the interpretation of the Law of Moses as hallmarked by practice; much is to be discovered in this field.[76]

Grotius hardly seems to have maintained personal relations with Jews. He corresponded with the Amsterdam rabbi Menasseh ben Israel,[77] but there are no signs of an affectionate relationship. Elsewhere there is a reference to contacts with baptized Jews.[78]

In his study *Barocke Juden – Christen – Judenchristen* Hans-Joachim Schoeps distinguishes five different types of philo-Semitism: "1) The Christian-missionary type, for which Judaism within certain margins is subject to positive assessment and, as a result, an object of advance; 2) often not sharply to be distinguished from 1, the Biblical-Chiliastic type, which concerns itself with Jews because they will play a role in the last act of the world-drama; 3) the utilitarian type, which supports the settlement of Jews in a country because it expects tangible advantages from this; 4) the liberal-humanitarian type, which wants to demonstrate by means of the Jews its principles of tolerance and emancipation of all those who are human; 5)

---

[75] *BW* IX,3781 p. 597 of 30.9.1638: "Manasses ... ben Israel tum in Conciliatore suo tum in libro de Creatione et Resurrectione ... ut nonnulla habet laude digna, ita quaedam etiam rabbinica, id est absurda atque ridicula."

[76] *BW* VII,2495 p. 92 of 14.4.1636: "Philosophica quae sunt Hebraeorum nihil habent antiqui. Ad eos venere per Arabum rivos ex Graeciae fontibus, unde haurire est limpidiora. Cavalae pleraque somnia otiosorum. Vnum quod a Iudaeis petendum est, interpretatio est legis per Mosem datae usu approbata. Multae autem sunt partes dignae nosci et intactae hactenus."

[77] Cf. CECIL ROTH, *A Life of Menasseh Ben Israel, Rabbi, Printer, and Diplomat*, Philadelphia 1934, pp. 146–48; A.K. OFFENBERG, "Some Remarks regarding Six Autograph Letters by Menasseh ben Israel in the Amsterdam University Library," in YOSEF KAPLAN – HENRY MÉCHOULAN – RICHARD H. POPKIN (edd.), *Menasseh Ben Israel and his world*, Leiden – New York 1989 [= Brill's studies in intellectual history, v. 15], pp. 191–98.

[78] *BW* V,1826 p. 109 of 23.3.1633 to G.J. Vossius on a certain Michael Gellingius.

the religious type, which from a decision of faith accomplishes the advance and even the move to Judaism."[79] When applying these distinctions to Grotius, it is remarkably difficult to capture him in this scheme. I take it for granted that one should not call him an anti-Semite. But a philo-Semite? Indeed we find positive remarks by him on Judaism (type 1); as an example I remind you of the introduction of the fifth book of *De veritate*. At any rate, I have not found anywhere the Calvinistic view that Judaism after the arrival of Jesus is to be considered idolatry. In the *Remonstrantie* again, the utilitarian aspects hold a prominent place: Jewish scholars can be useful for acquiring knowledge of Hebrew. With a touch of wishful thinking several earlier scholars have tried to portray him as belonging to the fourth type, the tolerant liberal.[80] I have my doubts about that. And finally, if we are to believe Jerôme Bignon and Guy Patin (but after what has been said I am inclined to say that we are not), he would even have belonged to the fifth type, because he would have considered converting to Judaism.

Perhaps Grotius' attitude can best be summarized as follows: he has never had any real interest in Jews as individuals nor in Judaism as a religious practice. For that he has met too few Jews, and Judaism was too remote from him. He, who emphasized so much practical devotion and the dangers of dogmas, has been either unable or unwilling to perceive the unchristian, but nevertheless truly existing, devotion in the Talmud and the lack of dogmas in rabbinical literature. His point of view was and remained that of a philologist: he took an interest in the explanations of Jewish commentators on Scripture, preferably of the oldest, and in early Judaism as a preliminary stage of Christianity and thereby evidence of its truth.

---

[79] HANS-JOACHIM SCHOEPS, *Barocke Juden, Christen, Judenchristen*, Bern - München [1965], pp. 7–8: "1. Der christlich-missionarische Typus, dem das Judentum in einem gewissen Spielraum der Wertungen ein Gegenstand positiver Schätzung und demzufolge Ziel der Annäherung ist, 2. oft nicht scharf von 1 zu unterscheiden, der biblisch-chiliastische Typus, der sich um die Juden bemüht, weil sie im letzten Akt des Weltdramas eine Rolle spielen werden, 3. der utilitaristische Typus, der die Niederlassung der Juden in einem Lande verficht, weil er sich greifbare Vorteile davon verspricht; 4. der liberal-humanitäre Typus, der an den Juden seine Prinzipien der Toleranz und der Gleichberechtigung alles dessen, was Menschenantlitz trägt, beweisen will; 5. der religiöse Typus, der aus einer Glaubensentscheidung heraus die Annäherung und sogar den Übertritt zum Judentum vollzieht."
[80] Thus, e.g., ARTHUR LÖWENSTAMM, "Hugo Grotius' Stellung zum Judentum," in *Festschrift zum 75 jährigen Bestehen des jüdisch-theologischen Seminars Fraenkelscher Stiftung* II, Breslau 1929, pp. 295–302.

This is perhaps less than might have been expected on the basis of his reputation.[81]

---

[81] I am grateful to professor Johan P. Snapper, Queen Beatrix professor of Dutch Language and Literature at the University of California, Berkeley, and to Ms. Nicolette Vanderhoeven for correcting my English.

DISPUTANDO INCLARESCET VERITAS[1]
GROTIUS AS A PUBLICIST IN FRANCE (1621–1645)

HENK J.M. NELLEN
(The Hague)

I

The French man of letters Gilles Ménage tells us that after meals Hugo Grotius had the habit of presenting his visitors with butter that he had summoned by shouting "hop" to his servants.[2] Unfortunately, such peculiar family customs only rarely emerge from Grotius' correspondence. Although a relatively large number of the letters sent and received by this famous Dutchman – over 7600 of them – are still extant, it never ceases to amaze us how little they reveal about his private life. All we have is the occasional reference in the correspondence with his wife, Maria van Reigersberch, or with his brother Willem or brother-in-law Nicolaes van Reigersberch to shed a little light on day-to-day life in the Grotius home. But it is then that the cardboard figure of Grotius comes to life. In the correspondence we read, for example, that in 1643 Grotius split his sides with laughter on at least two occasions. The first happened in May while he was reading a letter from his brother Willem relating that the preachers in Holland were spreading the rumour that, to pave the way for his elevation to the cardinalate, Grotius had asked the Pope for dispensation for his marriage.[3] Six months later he could not help laughing at the idea of the theologian Conradus Vorstius being described as a Calvinist in a book by the Jesuit Denis Petau.[4] In this second case his laugh will have had a scornful ring, since in reality Vorstius was an extremely liberal, not to say heterodox thinker, whose appointment in 1610 to a chair at the

---

[1] This Latin phrase is taken from a letter from Grotius to W. de Groot, *BW* IX, no. 3874, 4 December 1638.

[2] *Menagiana, ou les bons mots, les pensées critiques, historiques, morales et d'erudition de M. Ménage ...*, Paris 1694, p. 378: "Après le repas il faisoit ordinairement apporter du beurre, et il falloit boire. Il n'appelloit jamais ses gens par leur nom, mais lors qu'il vouloit leur parler, il crioit: Hop. Au reste c'étoit le plus honnête homme du monde." Presumably Grotius served a sort of buttered ale (bière beurrée), a drink consisting of spiced and sugared strong beer, supplemented with yolk of egg and butter.

[3] *BW* XIV, no. 6216, to Willem de Groot, 16 May 1643, in reply to a letter of 4 May 1643 (*BW* XIV, no. 6202).

[4] *BW* XIV, no. 6532, to Willem de Groot, 14 November 1643. Cf. D. PETAU, *Theologicorum dogmatum tomus primus*, Paris 1644, Book II, Ch. II,1 (p. 110) and Book III, Ch. VII,4 (p. 216).

University of Leiden had set off a heated political struggle that ultimately precipitated the Republic of the United Provinces into unprecedented administrative chaos. Grotius himself was unable to
avoid getting embroiled in this controversy and was sentenced to
life imprisonment. After a miraculous escape from Loevestein Castle he was forced to seek asylum in France in the hope that there
would come a day when he could return to Holland without loss of
face.

The only way Grotius could maintain contact with Holland was
to write letter after letter, and because this epistolary contact has
left so many traces it is now possible to follow him in exile. Although Grotius' correspondence does not reveal many domestic se-
crets, a number of other topics are regularly touched upon – so
regularly, indeed, and with such dedication and frankness that they
can be seen as basic themes that deserve closer study, particularly
since his official writings mention them either not at all or only in a
mitigated form. I should like to elaborate here on one such theme:
Grotius' view of his host country, France.[5] In doing this I shall concentrate on the political and religious controversies of the day. In
this way we can establish the stance adopted by Grotius after his
débâcle in Holland and the way in which he slowly allowed himself
to be inveigled into a commitment reminiscent of his militance
during the Truce controversies. We are helped in this by the writings he published while living in France. For practical reasons I
must, however, restrict myself here to a very global overview and
will only be able to deal in somewhat greater detail with a limited
number of writings, primarily *De coena*, *De antichristo* and his *Appendix
de antichristo*.

II

The correspondence between 1621 and 1645 shows how negative
Grotius generally was about France. He could not get used to the
French: he considered them capricious,[6] unreliable,[7] insolent and

---

[5] The first phase of Grotius' exile has been described by H.C. ROGGE, "Hugo
de Groot te Parijs van 1621 tot 1625," *De Gids* 57, 4th series, 11 (1893), pp. 249–
73 and 450–77.

[6] *BW* VII, no. 2893, to A. Oxenstierna, 18 December 1636: "... gentis ingenium per se mutabile..." See also *BW* VIII, no. 3088, to A. Oxenstierna, 22 May
1637: "... mutabile gentis Gallicae ingenium..."

[7] *BW* V, no. 2013, to P. Schmalz, 15 March 1635: "Quid agas de ea gente,
quae altera manu fert lapidem, panem ostentat altera [Plautus, *Aul.* 195; cf. A.
OTTO, *Die Sprichwörter und sprichwörtlichen Redensarten der Römer*, Leipzig 1890, p. 186]".

frivolous,[8] noisy,[9] bombastic[10], selfish and opportunistic.[11] Although he asserted in 1624 that he had a soft spot for the country and that he did not wish to leave France until he had convinced the outside world that he had had no choice,[12] he never intended to settle there permanently. Refugee Remonstrants were not permitted to practice freedom of religion and their most illustrious representative, Hugo Grotius, was under continual pressure to convert to Roman Catholicism.[13] In a despondent mood he concluded that yes-men ruled the roost in his new surroundings.[14] He, on the other hand, adhered to his religious convictions and refused to be taken in by the leaders of the French government. He had no desire to create ties with a country that was so politically unstable and where deception had taken such deep root.[15] Reliability – particularly at court – was a rare virtue.[16] He also saw much irreligion, supersti-

---

Mihi adversus aulica taedia magnum est solatium in virorum literatissimorum colloquiis, quibus libenter id largior temporis, quod a negotiis decidi potest." See also *BW* VI, no. 2255, to A. Oxenstierna, 27 August 1635: "... illos [homines] novi promos vocum, rerum condos."

[8] *BW* VIII, no. 3183, to L. Camerarius, 31 July 1637: "... gens est oris liberi..." See also *BW* IX, no. 3881, to A. Oxenstierna, 10 December 1638, where, after a description of the intrigues at the French court, Grotius concludes: "Haec significari haud multum forte interest, nisi ut cognoscatur quam saepe hic levia praevertantur maximis, tum vero quantae quamque repentinae mutationes rerum consiliis huius regiae et aliis ab ea non parum pendentibus intervenire possint."

[9] *BW* VII, no. 2577, to J. Skytte, 1 May 1636: "... gens adeo strepera et tumultuosa..."

[10] *BW* VIII, no. 3211, to A. Oxenstierna, 16 August 1637: "... Galli suorum prosperorum minime parci praedicatores..."; *BW* IX, no. 3783, to L. Camerarius, 2 October 1638: "... Galli sermonum largi..."

[11] *BW* VII, no. 2623, to A. Oxenstierna, 6 June 1636; *BW* VIII, no. 3184, to N. van Reigersberch, 31 July 1637; *BW* X, no. 4035, to L. Camerarius, 26 March 1639: "... non sunt autem Galli faciles de suo largiri, ut aliis commodent."

[12] *BW* II, no. 933, to B. Aubéry du Maurier, 29 November 1624: "... mihi constitutum est Galliam, cuius amicitiam plurimi feci semper, non deserere, nisi prius ita deserar, ut et mihi et aliis omnibus constare possit consilii mei ratio."

[13] *BW* III, no. 1297, to N. van Reigersberch, 13 August 1628: "Te leven in een landt, daer men geen exec. en heeft van religie ende daerover altijd quelling subject is, is swaer... Hyer en wil men niet ten halve gedyent zijn, gelijck ick uE. voor desen meermael heb geadviseert."

[14] Cf. *BW* VII, no. 2721, to A. Oxenstierna, 22 August 1636, where Grotius writes about his strained relationship with the French authorities: "Nec solent hi homines cuique fidere nisi quem sibi obnoxium habent." See also *BW* VII, no. 2745, to N. van Reigersberch, 5 September 1636. In this letter Grotius refers to an attempt of the French to bring him over to their side with a tempting donation: "Vellent habere sibi obnoxios. Andere luiden soecken sij niet."

[15] *BW* III, no. 1134, to N. van Reigersberch, 20 February 1627: "... in een rijck sooveel veranderingh subject ende daer men ommegaet met sooveel bedryegerije."

[16] Cf. *BW* IV, no. 1482, to W. de Groot, 1 March 1630: "Frater regius in urbe fuit, vidit matrem reginam, principes foeminas, etiam virginem Mantuanam, cui

tion and immorality around him, none of which were being dealt with effectively by the government of the day.[17] When the king issued an edict against luxury and excess, Grotius observed: we already have excellent laws; all I miss is one law that makes people respect all the other ones.[18]

Grotius agreed that a powerful monarchy was necessary, but repeatedly pointed out that there was none in France. Unlike his father, Louis XIII was a weak, indecisive and capricious person, allowing himself to be flattered by favourites, who used him to their own ends.[19] Although Grotius recognized that Richelieu was a great statesman, he held that the cardinal was a ruthless exponent of a kind of power politics that often violated Christian ethics.[20] Grotius'

---

rem promisit in Gallo raram τὸ πιστὸν καὶ τὸ βέβαιον." See also *BW* V, no. 1828, to J. de Cordes, 2 April 1633; in this letter Grotius condoles Antoine des Hayes, whose son had been decapitated because of his complicity in a conspiracy led by Gaston of Orleans. "Quod si ex hoc infortunio," Grotius then continues, "id sibi ipse felicitatis fabricavit, ut aulae spes mendaces et personatas amicitias totus effugerit, ne id quidem parum est. Sic enim oportet in vita non minus quam in alea minus recte quod ceciderit arte corrigere." See also *BW* VIII, no. 3072, to A. Oxenstierna, 15 May 1637: "... solet haec aula ... saepe aliud simulare, aliud agere, saepe consilia sumere extemporalia."

[17] *BW* IV, no. 1416, to J. Wtenbogaert, 6 August 1629: "Van de atheisterie seyt uE. de waerheyt: deselve regneert hyer dapper, Godt betert; 't welck de eenige oorsaecke is dye mij de compaignie van veele personen allerley stands, dyen ick sulcx bevinde, doet mijden." See also *BW* VI, no. 2155, to A. Oxenstierna, 22 June 1635: "Ad haec mala [among other things rebellions against high taxes] et aliud malum, non repente quidem sed sensim noxium, superstitio gliscit..."

[18] *BW* V, no. 2020, to P. Schmalz, 22 March 1635: "Luxui in dies gliscenti quae remedia rex admoverit, ex edicto, quod transmitto, dabitur conspicere. Optimae sunt in Gallia leges; deest una, quae ceteras observari efficiat."

[19] See, for example, *BW* IV, no. 1581, to N. van Reigersberch, 6 February 1631; in this letter Grotius refers to the lack of funds the French authorities had to cope with. A change for the better was too much to be expected under a weak king, "qui velut semper pupillus est." Cf. R. PINTARD, *La Mothe le Vayer, Gassendi – Guy Patin...*, *Appendice: Textes inédits de Guy Patin; II Grotiana* [= Publications de l'Université de Poitiers, Série des sciences de l'homme, 5], Paris [1943] (hereafter cited as *Grotiana*), p. 83: "Henry IV estoit un grand capitaine et un bon prince ... Il avoit en son conseil de braves gens, habiles et bons..., desquels il estoit tousiours le maistre et ne s'en laissoit gourmander ny gouverner, comme depuis Louys XIII son fils s'est laissé mener par le nez à ses favoris."

[20] Shortly after the death of cardinal Richelieu Grotius confided to his brother-in-law Nicolaes van Reigersberch: "Mijn credyt is bij den cardinael noit groot geweest, alzoo hij niemant en conde lijden die zoude dencken: *hoc non licet.*" (*BW* XIII, no. 6015, to N. van Reigersberch, 26 December 1642). In many letters Grotius gave vent to his aversion to the cardinal's practices. His negative attitude can be traced back to a conversation they once had, when he visited the French court as a poor exile. After discussing his role in the troubles of the Truce, Richelieu remarked that in matters of state the weak always were in the wrong. Grotius refused to agree with this cynical statement, but, dumbfounded as he was, he could only reply that God and time would bring the truth to light. (*BW* II, no. 974, to N. van Reigersberch, 1 May 1625). When, in the last years of his embassy,

negative view of France and her leaders[21] seems only to have increased as he gained more experience there as Sweden's ambassador from 1635. It was his job to promote Swedish interests in a country that was fighting side by side with Sweden against the Hapsburg hegemony in Europe. His reports are coloured even more intensely than before by anti-French sentiments; his dispatches from Paris bristle with fulminations against French short-sightedness, selfishness and merciless expansionism.[22] When it suited him, Grotius wrote, Richelieu would ignore the obligations imposed by the terms of the Swedish alliance. Under the cardinal there was an army of men in important positions lining their own pockets. The war was being prolonged even though it meant gargantuan taxes and was bringing the country to the verge of ruin. Sweden was well advised to stand up for her interests.[23]

In many letters Grotius emphasized that it was the Pope who effectively ran France. Ultramontane clergy, notably the Jesuits, were instrumental in perpetuating the influence of Rome not only on French politics, but also the country's spiritual life. The Parliament in Paris, with its strongly Gallican ties, was rabidly anti-Jesuit, but the Jesuits did not allow this to affect them. They claimed that all they needed to have was patience, secure in the knowledge that their opponents would perish one by one, while the order would never die. And indeed Grotius had to admit that there was more than a grain of truth in that assertion, "car les gens de bien meu-

---

Grotius refers to the government of Richelieu, he always stresses his tyranny and immorality. The execution of François-Auguste de Thou (1642) could be considered particular proof of the misuse of power during the cardinal's administration.

[21] Grotius made an exception for Henri II de Bourbon, third prince of Condé, whom he had already met in 1598, during his first stay in France. Throughout the correspondence, several reports of conversations have been preserved that Grotius had had with Condé. Grotius considered Condé a congenial spirit, who took great interest in, even partly subscribed to his ideas regarding the relationship between church and state and the unification of Christian churches. Cf. *BW* VIII, no. 2957, to A. Oxenstierna, 12 February 1637; *BW* X, no. 3951, to A. Oxenstierna, 29 January 1639; and *Rikskansleren Axel Oxenstiernas skrifter och brefvexling...*, II,4, *Hugo Grotii bref 1640–1645*, Stockholm 1891, pp. 437–39, no. 537, to A. Oxenstierna, 18 June 1644.

[22] See, for instance, a letter Grotius wrote to A. Oxenstierna (*BW* V, no. 1994, 5 March 1635) shortly after arriving in Paris as Swedish ambassador; a description of the delicate internal situation is concluded with the remark: "Et talia regna tamen manent, vigent, florent mira Dei in homines lenitate."

[23] *BW* IV, no. 1581, to N. van Reigersberch, 6 February 1631. See also *BW* VI, no. 2365, to A. Oxenstierna, 25 November 1635; *BW* VII, no. 2800, to L. Camerarius, 17 October 1636: "Galli in spe danda liberales sunt, dum ne federibus se obstringant; etiam federibus adstricti saepe elabuntur"; *BW* VIII, no. 3043, to L. Camerarius, 24 April 1637.

rent tous les jours et les meschans ne meurent jamais."[24] Grotius
subscribed to the aims of Gallicanism. His correspondence contains
such frequent criticisms of the influence of Rome on French politics
and spiritual life that one is justified in accusing him of riding a
hobby-horse.

As long as Richelieu was dancing to the Pope's tune, said Grotius, there was no question of the Hapsburgs being challenged.[25] He
showed little appreciation of the precarious position in which Richelieu found himself, despite the fact that he knew that devout
Romanist circles continually joined a monstrous alliance with the
particularist nobility against the cardinal's anti-Hapsburg policies.
He continued to believe that Richelieu conceded too much to the
Romanists; in May 1636 he even writes to chancellor Oxenstierna
that the Pope's power in France had increased more in a few years
than in the previous couple of centuries.[26] Venerable institutions
like the Paris Parliament and the Sorbonne, which had always tak-
en up cudgels to protect France's freedoms, proved not to be able
to resist the dominance of the monks.[27] It was this kind of instabili-
ty, said Grotius, that allowed all kinds of tendencies inimical to
state, monarchy and church free rein.

To counterbalance Rome's influence there was, on the other
side of the politico-religious force field, Calvinism. Although Richelieu had made sure after the fall of La Rochelle in 1628 that Calvinism was a spent political force, nevertheless it continued to rear
its head in occasional rebellion in the province. Grotius was always
very dismissive about militant Calvinists. In his view, history had
taught that rebellion often turned against the legitimate authorities
under the guise of religious zeal. The Calvinist preachers played a
very dubious role in this: in their recalcitrance they were the cause
of a great deal of agitation not only in France but also in Scotland,
England and the Republic. This is why they encountered animosity
and it was hardly surprising that the French authorities curbed

---

[24] *Grotiana*, p. 71. According to Grotius, Jacques-Auguste de Thou (1553–1617),
Louis Servin († 1626) and Achille de Harlay (1536–1619) distinguished themselves
among the "gens de bien", who challenged the overwhelming influence of the
order. Cf. *BW* V, nos. 1844, 1845, 1846 and 1866. In *BW* V, no. 1845, to J. Dupuy, 1 June 1633, Grotius states: "Ita est saeculum, ut nulli meliorem animum ha-
beant quam quorum mala est causa."

[25] Cf. *BW* VI, no. 2235, to L. Camerarius, 17 August 1635.

[26] *BW* VII, no. 2593, to A. Oxenstierna, 15 May 1636: "Pontificis potestas plus
intra paucos annos in Gallia profecit quam duobus ante seculis."

[27] *BW* VI, no. 2389, to L. Camerarius, 13 December 1635; *BW* VII, no. 2893,
to A. Oxenstierna, 18 December 1636; *BW* IX, no. 3663, to L. Camerarius, 10
July 1638.

their freedom of action more and more.[28] Although they indignant-
ly protested against this, they were being hypocritical: wherever
they had gained the upper hand they had themselves been guilty of
an intolerance they had vociferously reproached their adversaries
for. Grotius had no time for the fanaticism and rebelliousness of the
Calvinists, because they were just as dangerous to the state as the
intrigues of the ultramontane clergy. He was also aware of the dogmatic gulf dividing him from the French Calvinists. It is therefore
not surprising that negotiations with a view to his admission to the
community of Charenton were doomed to fail from the start.[29]

While distancing himself from Calvinism, Grotius was also of the
opinion that the influence of Rome was not adequately resisted. As
a fugitive representative of a religious community banned in Holland, in his new surroundings he found himself between two poles,
both of which repelled him. From this one cannot but conclude
that he felt isolated and cut off from his roots. Later, during his period as ambassador, this situation will not have changed very much,
particularly since the French were aware of his negative reports and
insisted on his recall right from the start.[30] It would, however, be
incorrect to imagine that this isolation was complete. Grotius established ties with religiously like-minded men who often stood outside
organized congregations, Arminians in exile, moderate Catholics,
Protestants rejected by the French church, and Polish Socinians.
Furthermore he had connections with the Parisian intellectual elite,
whose principal meeting place was the Cabinet Dupuy. This motley
collection of erudite men, mostly of respectable bourgeois stock and
closely associated with the classes that ruled Paris, the university
and parliament, contained representatives of all kinds of disciplines
and professions: not only philologists, historians, lawyers and civic
administrators, but also church dignitaries and diplomats. What
united them was their interest in classical and early Christian litera-

---

[28] Cf. *BW* VIII, no. 3072, to A. Oxenstierna, 15 May 1637, where the letter-
writer announces that the French Calvinists were seriously concerned about their
position. Thereupon he concludes rather laconically: "Sed vana est sine viribus
ira." See also *BW* IX, no. 3585, to L. Camerarius, 21 May 1638: "Protestantibus
... ubique acriter iniungitur aulaea ut oppedant [= oppandant] foribus suis, quo
die circumferetur Sacramentum, quod antehac facere coacti non sunt. In aliis quoque rebus libertas eorum multum circumciditur et omnis edictorum interpretatio
contra eos cadit."

[29] Cf. H.J.M. NELLEN, "Grotius' Relations with the Huguenot Community of
Charenton (1621–1635)," *Lias* 12 (1985), pp. 147–77.

[30] *BW* VII, no. 2745, to N. van Reigersberch, 5 September 1636. Cf. JOHANN
ARCKENHOLTZ, *Mémoires concernant Christine, reine de Suede...*, Amsterdam – Leipzig
1751–1760, I, pp. 73–77, III, p. 148 and IV, pp. 310–11 and 316–17.

ture, a moderate and undogmatic stance in church matters, fervent
Gallicanism, and a preference for a strong monarchy.[31] Grotius' letters show that his ties with this group were extremely strong, with
particular importance attached to the contacts with Pierre and Jacques Dupuy, Jean de Cordes, Gabriel Naudé, Marin Mersenne, Is-
mael Boulliau, Claude Saumaise and Guy Patin. When Grotius
writes that the embassy allows him enough time for study, writing
letters and conversation, he is certainly also referring to the Cabinet.[32]

Grotius closely followed events in the French state, church and
scholarship and automatically passed judgment on the controversies
of the day. One example of his commitment was the cause célèbre
surrounding Edmond Richer, syndic of the Sorbonne. In 1612 he
had been sacked for publishing a pamphlet emphasizing the sovereignty and independence of the French state and church against the
Church of Rome. His arguments were of such a Gallicanist nature
that they were promptly condemned by the French clergy.[33] Many
years later Richer was forced to recant by the French authorities.
Old and demoralized, Richer allowed Richelieu, who had personally intervened in the affair, to prevail upon him to sign a document
to this effect.[34] Grotius was told by the French nuncio Bagni that
this recantation was regarded in Rome as a greater victory than the
fall of the Huguenot bastion of La Rochelle in 1628.[35] Grotius
knew Richer well and subscribed to his ideas, but he was unable to
excuse his complaisance with the authorities, accusing him of repu-
diating his innermost convictions. As other Frenchmen did the

---

[31] Cf. R. Pintard, *Le libertinage érudit dans la première moitié du dix-septième siècle*,
Paris 1943. See also, for a description of the Parisian intellectual circle led by the
Dupuy brothers, K. Garber, "A propos de la politisation de l'humanisme tardif
européen: Jacques Auguste de Thou et le 'Cabinet Dupuy' à Paris," in C. Lau-
vergnat-Gagnière – B. Yon (edd.), *Le juste et l'injuste à la Renaissance et à l'âge classique. Actes du colloque international tenu à Saint-Etienne du 21 au 23 avril 1983*, Saint-
Étienne 1986, pp. 157–77.

[32] *BW* IX, no. 3705, to M. Opitz, 6 August 1638: "Legatio quae mihi obtigit, id
habet commodi, quod aliquantum mihi temporis relinquit ad legendum, si quid
prodit novi, aut etiam si quid antiqui in lucem protrahitur; deinde ad colenda cum
viris eruditis aut sermonis aut literarum commercia; inter multorum literas tuae
mihi semper erunt suavissimae."

[33] *De ecclesiastica et politica potestate libellus*, Paris 1611.

[34] On Edmond Richer (1559–1631) see *Dictionnaire de Théologie catholique* XIII
(Paris 1936), cols. 2698–2702. Cf. E. Préclin, "Edmond Richer (1559–1631), sa
vie, son œuvre, le richérisme," *Revue d'Histoire moderne* 5 (1930), pp. 241–69 and pp.
321–36.

[35] Cf. *Grotiana*, p. 75: "Le nonce qui lors estoit icy me dit à moy: Nous faisons
bien estat de la prise de La Rochelle, mais encore plus de la retractation de Richer." See also *BW* V, no. 1736, to [N. van Reigersberch], 30 January [1632].

same, it seemed to be becoming a custom to adapt doctrine to personal advantage. This had not been the attitude of the first Christians.[36] He reserved his main criticism, however, for the role Richelieu had played in the affair: he had made it perfectly plain that he was pursuing his own ambitions to the detriment of the interests of the state and the church.[37]

Grotius frequently noted that Gallicanist books were forbidden in France, and he devoted many letters to the publication and subsequent condemnation of Pierre Dupuy's *Traictez des droits et libertez de l'Eglise gallicane* (1639). These documents, collected by Dupuy, defended the absolute autonomy of the French king and of the French church against Rome; their condemnation demonstrated how the rights of the king were disregarded while the Pope's power perceptibly increased.[38]

The condemnation of Dupuy's book was for Grotius yet another proof of Richelieu's design to fall in as much as possible with the Vatican's wishes. In his letters Grotius noted how movements meant to deepen religious experience were sometimes suppressed by the government. The trend of religious thought that was later to play such an important part in French religious and political life under the name of Jansenism originally enjoyed Grotius' support because it seemed to be aiming at reinforcing practical devotion. In

---

[36] *BW* IV, no. 1464, to W. de Groot, 28 December 1629: "... Ita mos fit ex usu vertere dogmata. At non tales illi a quibus nos christianum nomen accepimus." In order to add force to his argumentation Grotius also recalled the case of François de Harlay (1585–1653), archbishop of Rouen, who shortly before had published his *Ecclesiasticae historiae liber primus* (Paris 1629), which provoked a storm of protests in ultramontane circles. A meeting of French clergymen, presided over by cardinal François de La Rochefoucauld, pressed the author to retract his book. Cf. TALLEMANT DES RÉAUX, *Historiettes*, ed. A. ADAM, II, Paris 1961, pp. 40 and 946.

[37] *Grotiana*, p. 75: "... tout cela est venu du cardinal de Richelieu, qui ne se soucioit que de son ambition aux despens de qui que ce pust estre, ou de l'Estat ou de la Religion. Il n'avoit autre soin que de se conserver et regner, comme il a malheureusement fait pour le bien de toute l'Europe. Cet homme estoit aveuglé d'ambition, et sur ce seul pivot rouloit son esprit qui remuoit toute la terre."

[38] *BW* X, nos. 3937, 3941, 3951, 3968, 3971, 3972 and 3991. Pierre Dupuy's book was censured in a meeting of French clergymen presided over by cardinal La Rochefoucauld (9 February 1639). Some months before, an "arrêt du Conseil" had been issued that prohibited the distribution of the publication. Cf. G. DEMANTE, "Histoire de la publication des livres de Pierre Dupuy sur les libertés de l'Eglise gallicane," *Bibliothèque de l'Ecole des Chartes* 5 (1843–44), pp. 585–606 and P. BLET (ed.), *Correspondance du nonce en France Ranuccio Scotti (1639–1641)* [Acta nuntiaturae Gallicae, 5], Rome – Paris 1965, p. 240. In a letter to chancellor Axel Oxenstierna, dated 12 February 1639 (no. 3972), Grotius protested most sharply against the ultramontane clergy that had banned Dupuy's book: "Homines ecclesiastici, qui pacis auctores esse debuerant, sicut in Scotia validissimi sunt turbarum concitores, ita in Gallia regia iura proculcant..."

1638 the Oratorian Claude Seguenot was arrested and thrown into
the Bastille. He had published a translation of a tract by Augustine
and had included a commentary showing a strict rigorism reminiscent of that of Jean Duvergier de Hauranne, abbot of Saint-Cyran.
This leading Jansenist was shortly afterwards imprisoned in the
dungeons of Vincennes. Grotius considered both arrests reprehensi-
ble; in his view they were the result of the machinations of monks
and an unmistakable sign of the excessive influence the Vatican had
in France.[39] Later on Grotius was to take up a more critical stance
towards Jansenism when it became clear that the Jansenist doctrine
of grace closely resembled that of the Calvinists.[40] He refused to
make this view public, however, because Jansenism enjoyed a good
deal of support at the Sorbonne. He admitted to having great
respect for the Sorbonne and little affinity with the Jansenists'
fiercest opponents, the Jesuits.[41]

III

This description of the French political and spiritual climate as formulated in his correspondence prompts us to take a closer look at
Grotius' place in this environment as a scholar and writer. It is
important to note that during these years in Paris Grotius under-
went considerable development. He became a more pronounced
advocate of church unity, a cause he had supported, he says, since
his youth.[42] Initially he had been unwilling to show his true colours
in this respect.[43] The dedication to *De iure belli ac pacis* and the end

---

[39] *BW* IX, nos. 3575, 3576, 3580 and 3585, Grotius to L. Camerarius, 15 May
1638, to W. de Groot, 15 May 1638, to A. Oxenstierna, 16 May 1638 and to L.
Camerarius, 21 May 1638. In his answer to Grotius' letter (*BW* IX, no. 3591, 24
May 1638) W. de Groot gave to understand that in Holland Seguenot's arrest had
caused much surprise: "De presbytero oratorii in carcerem misso mirantur omnes:
nulla enim nova placita, sed veteris ecclesiae scita defendit." On the incarceration
of Seguenot and Saint-Cyran, see JEAN ORCIBAL, *Jean Duvergier de Hauranne, abbé de
Saint-Cyran, et son temps (1581–1638)*, Louvain – Paris 1947 [= Bibliothèque de la
Revue d'Histoire ecclésiastique, 26; Les origines du Jansénisme, 2], pp. 553–94.
[40] *BW* XIV, no. 6403, to W. de Groot, 5 September 1643; *EQ*, pp. 965–66,
App. no. 699, and p. 969, App. no. 712, to W. de Groot, 9 April and 2 July 1644.
[41] *Grotiana*, pp. 84–85: "Cette nouvelle theologie de Jansenius, evesque d'Ipres,
touchant la grace, m'est suspecte. Il me semble qu'elle approche trop de la doctrine de Calvin. Si telle est l'opinion de S. Augustin, comme on dit que c'est, crederem divum Augustinum idem sensisse cum Calvino. Les jesuites se sont declarez
ennemis de ce Jansenius qu'on dit avoir esté fort homme de bien, et duquel la
doctrine est fort approuvée en Sorbonne: ce qui fait que je me retiens, car j'honore toute la Sorbonne, et la prefere de tout en tout aux jesuites."
[42] Cf. H. GROTIUS, *Votum pro pace ecclesiastica* in *OTh* III, p. 653.
[43] See, for instance, *BW* VIII, no. 3248, to A. Oxenstierna, 12 September 1637.

of *De veritate* do contain references to the need for church unity, but these were cautious, indirect attempts at sounding out opinion.[44] He kept back a treatise supporting France's right to conclude treaties with Protestant powers for fear that his unpartisan approach would not appease either Catholics or Protestants.[45] Furthermore, freedom of expression in France was not yet such that he felt free to publish his annotations to the New Testament, which he had been working on ever since his imprisonment in Loevestein.[46] This need for caution was confirmed when it appeared that his dedication to Louis XIII in *De iure* did not elicit a fee. He assumed that the French authorities had ignored him because he had expressed views on sacred affairs as a non-Catholic.[47]

While normally shying away from controversial themes in his writings, in *De veritate*, which he sent to press with no little reluctance,[48] he reveals himself as an advocate of an undogmatic religion aimed at practical devotion, a vision he also expressed in many let-

---

[44] Before Grotius decided to stand up openly for the cause of the unity of the churches, he had to overcome many qualms. Cf. H.J.M. NELLEN, "Grotius et les Luthériens parisiens. Contribution à l'histoire des premières années de la communauté luthérienne à Paris," *NAKG* 67 (1987), pp. 175ff.

[45] Within a few days Grotius wrote an *Epistola* against *G.G.R. theologi ad Ludovicum decimum tertium ... admonitio ... qua ... demonstratur Galliam foede et turpiter impium foedus iniisse et iniustum bellum hoc tempore contra catholicos movisse salvaque religione prosequi non posse* (1625). Cf. *BW* III, no. 1060, to N. van Reigersberch, 27 [February 1626]; *BW* III, no. 1067, to W. de Groot, 3 April 1626, where Grotius states: "... vero ita scriptus est liber noster, ut nec catholicis hic nec apud vos reformatis sim satisfacturus. Talia scribere eorum est, qui sua ope stant nec quemquam habent, quem respiciant." See also *BW* III, no. 1068, to N. van Reigersberch, [3 April 1626] and P. Blet, *Le clergé de France et la monarchie. Etude sur les assemblées générales du clergé de 1615 à 1666* [= Analecta Gregoriana, 106 A 8,9], Rome 1959, I, pp. 335–69.

[46] *BW* II, no. 931, to W. de Groot, 15 November 1624. Referring to his exegetical studies Grotius states: "Mihi id incommodissimum accidit quod cuncta interpretans ex primae antiquitatis sententia, sine ullo partium studio, locum non invenio ubi nostra excudi possint; et si possint, vereor ne hic me viliorem faciat insumta opera in explicandis locis, quibus dogmata quaedam superstruuntur, quae nunc hic publice probata vetustati placuisse mihi persuadere non possum." See also *BW* III, no. 1189, to G.J. Vossius, 16 October 1627; *BW* V, no. 2004, to Cl. Saumaise, 9 March 1635.

[47] *BW* IV, no. 1464, to W. de Groot, 28 December 1629: "Nolunt a segregibus quicquam tractari quod ad sacra ullatenus accedat. Ergo quiescendum erit, aut honos sperandus a Deo et paucis bonis."

[48] *BW* III, no. 1088, to W. de Groot, 10 July 1626. Eventually Grotius preferred to publish the book in Holland: "Mitto ... ad te versionem Latinam sex librorum de Veritate christiana, quam a me hic amici impetrarunt et urgent, ut edam. Sed pauca quaedam hic theologis non satis probantur." Shortly before he received a copy of *De veritate*, Grotius wrote to G.J. Vossius (*BW* III, no. 1189, 16 October 1627): "Videbimus quae futura sint fastidiosi satis saeculi iudicia. Certe adversus impietatem remediis Gallia non parum indiget; ipse nisi expertus vix crederem."

ters.[49] The book, which was dedicated to the Catholic Parisian magistrate Jérôme Bignon, led orthodox Calvinists to promptly accuse him of Socinian sympathies.[50] The unfavourable reception by this circle will have confirmed his conviction that he had to be careful. Nevertheless, Grotius adjusted his views gradually in the course of the 1630's. This began with a controversy that was remarkably similar to those surrounding Richer and Dupuy, since here too, the authorities, in this case Rome-oriented governing circles of the church, tried to impose shackles on free scholarship.

It is especially in his correspondence with Claude Saumaise that Grotius showed great interest when, during 1629, the curator of the Bibliothèque du roi, Nicolas Rigault, became involved in a conflict with Gabriel de l'Aubespine, Bishop of Orleans. This was sparked off by the commentary Rigault had written to accompany his edition of a work by Tertullian, *De exhortatione castitatis*. The bishop said that Rigault had wrongly interpreted a passage[51] in this work dealing with priesthood and laity: it was not true, the churchman asserted, that in the early Christian church the Eucharist might be administered by laymen in the absence of priests. A fierce polemic blew up between the two scholars, in which Rigault had a rather rough time, and when even his orthodoxy and faith in the Roman Catholic church were called into question he felt obliged to alter his stand. Jérôme Bignon prevailed upon Grotius to intercede between the combatants,[52] but ultimately his services were not needed, probably because he announced that his position outside the church gave him the freedom to judge both sides harshly. De l'Aubespine's position was untenable, and Rigault had not only defended a correct interpretation of Tertullian ineptly, but had also deviated from his standpoint against his own better judgment.

In Claude Saumaise Grotius had found a kindred spirit, who was equally convinced that Rigault's interpretation was the right one. In a long, somewhat unclear argumentation Saumaise explained to Grotius that De l'Aubespine had crossed swords with Rigault to defend the orthodox Roman Catholic conception of the

---

[49] See, for example, *BW* IV, no. 1502, to N. van Reigersberch, 16 May 1630, a very informative letter, which quite rightly bears the remark: "epistola notabilis" on its back; *BW* IV, no. 1554, to J. Wtenbogaert, 25 October 1630; *BW* VI, no. 2207, to P. Holing, 1 August 1635; and *BW* XIII, no. 5657, to N. van Reigersberch, 29 March 1642.

[50] *BW* III, no. 1325, to W. de Groot, 28 October 1628.

[51] *De exhortatione castitatis* 7, 13–35 [ed. A. KROYMANN, Corpus scriptorum ecclesiasticorum Latinorum, LXX, 2, Vienna – Leipzig 1942, pp. 138–39].

[52] *BW* IV, no. 1501, to Cl. Saumaise, 13 May 1630.

Eucharist. The bishop blamed the Protestant ministers for not being in the possession of 'character', a supernatural quality, imprinted by ordination, which authorized them to administer the Eucharist. In catholic theology, 'character' was essential, since it underpinned the view of the Eucharist as a mystery in which transubstantiation took place. In this way the polemic was, according to Saumaise, of the greatest importance, not only for the knowledge of the rites of the early Christian church, but also for the administration of the sacraments in the present-day church.[53]

Although Grotius did not arbitrate in this dispute, he still felt called upon to commit his view of the issue to paper. In defence of Rigault's point of view he quickly wrote a tract in 1630 entitled *De coena*, which he shortly afterwards sent to his brother Willem for perusal.[54] For the moment there was no question of publishing it, for Grotius was not the stuff heroes are made of and he preferred not to go public. He wished to avoid having to go back on strongly held convictions and then regretting his actions later, as so many others had done.[55] He compared Rigault with Richer and noted in a letter to Claude Saumaise:[56] "When you see how these scholars

---

[53] *BW* IV, no. 1526, Saumaise to Grotius, 13 July 1630. In a letter to André Rivet, Saumaise claimed that he himself had got the quarrel going by confronting De l'Aubespine with the passage in Tertullian. See P. LEROY – H. BOTS (edd.), *Claude Saumaise et André Rivet, correspondance échangée entre 1632 et 1648*, Amsterdam – Maarssen 1987, pp. 58–59, Saumaise to Rivet, 23 January [1634]. Further information on the origin of the polemics is to be found in CASPAR BRANDT – ADRIAAN VAN CATTENBURGH, *Historie van het leven des heeren Huig de Groot*, Dordrecht – Amsterdam 1727, II, pp. 191–93, and Amsterdam UL, Coll. Rem. Kerk, III E 8[7–12], letters from Cl. Saumaise to Isaac Vossius, esp. III E 8[8], Cl. Saumaise to I. Vossius, 8 August 1638. For a general survey of the controversy on the Eucharist, see REMI SNOEKS, *L'argument de tradition dans la controverse eucharistique entre catholiques et réformés français au XVIIe siècle*, Louvain – Gembloux 1951 [= Universitas Catholica Lovaniensis, Dissertationes ad gradum magistri in Facultate Theologica II, 44], esp. p. 164. See also *BG* no. 1095 rem. 1.

[54] *BW* IV, nos. 1516 and 1520, to W. de Groot, 14 and 21 June 1630. Apparently Grotius was tempted to commit his ideas to paper after reading SIMON EPISCOPIUS' *Apologia pro confessione sive declaratio sententiae eorum qui in foederato Belgio vocantur Remonstrantes* (1629). See also H.C. Rogge (ed.), *Brieven en onuitgegeven stukken van Johannes Wtenbogaert* III,3 (1630) [= Werken uitgegeven door het Historisch Genootschap gevestigd te Utrecht, nieuwe reeks 20], Utrecht 1874, pp. 158–59, W. de Groot to J. Wtenbogaert, 1 May [= 1 July] 1630.

[55] *BW* IV, no. 1495, to Cl. Saumaise, 27 April 1630: "Ego vero quid agam, nisi ut dulcibus musis pascam animum, mihi intus canens cum Aspendio, quando aliis adeo prodesse non licet, ut odia scribendo vitari vix queant. Et satius est tacere quam bene dicta in iugulum revocare, quod scis iam plurimis accidisse, quibus quid restat aliud nisi ut paenitentiae suae paenitentiam agant, ille praesertim cui cum Aurelianensi nova iam proelia..." The expression "intus canere cum Aspendio" applies to a person who prefers a secure, profitable silence to honour; cf. A. OTTO, *Die Sprichwörter*, p. 43.

[56] *BW* IV, no. 1546, to Cl. Saumaise, 5 October 1630: "Quis dubitat haec vi-

make concessions under pressure from the authorities, there seems
to be no doubt that France is doomed to godlessness." In a rather
pathetic strain he continues: "Every day I observe so many symp-
toms of this deterioration that life is almost too much to bear, especially life here." Grotius was a little prone to exaggeration: although
he left France not long after this, he returned in 1635, in spite of
his aversion, to serve there as an ambassador. Publishing controversial works did not enter his mind until he decided in 1637–38 to
champion the cause of church union.

Grotius was aware that his actions would encounter resistance
that would seriously weaken his already precarious position as a
diplomat. This explains why he set about the task hesitantly and
with the greatest of caution. From early 1638 he worked on an
exposition of passages in the Bible dealing with Antichrist.[57] In the
hope of reducing the chasm between Roman Catholicism and the
Reformation it was his aim to refute the commonly held Protestant
view that Antichrist was the Roman Pope. It was also in this period
that he decided to send his tract prompted by the controversy
between Rigault and De l'Aubespine to Holland for publication.
Finally, Grotius, assisted by his brother, started looking for a printer
for his *Annotationes* to the New Testament,[58] which he intended to
publish as soon as he had had a chance to see the annotations of
his rival Daniel Heinsius.[59] While there were indications that there
was absolutely no chance of church union in Sweden,[60] and France
did not yet seem to be ripe for such an ideal, Grotius nevertheless
decided to make his move. There were various reasons for this
apparently sudden change of mind: Grotius had given up all hope
of an honourable return to Holland and had come to the conclusion that his career in the foreign service of the Swedish crown was
– not least thanks to French opposition – going nowhere.[61] He con-

---

dens quin aperte in impietatem ruat Gallia, cuius ego pestis tam multa quotidie
παθογνωμονικά video ut vivere me paene taedeat, inter tales vivere taedeat omnino.
Etiam libri plurimi prodeunt nihil credere docentes. Et haec vident feruntque οἱ
ἀναμάρτητοι, per quos quae Tertullianei loci fuerit sententia dicere non licet."

[57] *BW* IX, no. 3405, to W. de Groot, 2 January 1638: "Diebus Dominicis scribo
quaedam ad loca Novi Testamenti de Antichristo loquentia aut quae de eo solent
intelligi, multum diversa ab iis quae multis nunc probantur."

[58] *BW* IX, no. 3874, to W. de Groot, 4 December 1638; *BW* X, no. 3917, to
G.J. Vossius, 1 January 1639, etc.

[59] *BW* X, no. 4119, to W. de Groot, 21 May 1639. See also many other letters,
written at the time, for instance nos. 4157, 4196, 4255, 4262, 4288, 4301, 4306,
4314, 4395, etc. The *Sacrarum exercitationum ad Novum Testamentum libri XX* of Daniel
Heinsius were published by Elzevier in Leiden in 1639.

[60] *BW* IX, no. 3556, to W. de Groot, 1 May 1638.

[61] Cf. H.J.M. Nellen, *Hugo de Groot (1583–1645). De loopbaan van een geleerd staats-*

tinued to throw himself into his diplomatic duties but, in the knowledge that he too was mortal,[62] he began attaching more and more importance to publicizing the need for unity among the Christian religions. He was quite convinced that this was a god-given task; as time went on he even assumed that his diplomatic post was a means towards this conciliatory end, his embassy furnishing him with a refuge from which he could propound his ideas without hindrance.[63] Since experience had taught him that there was little hope of overtures from rabid Calvinists, he abandoned his original strategy of first winning the Protestant denominations over to his ideal. Now his plan was to effect a rapprochement between moderate Protestants and Roman Catholics.

In the course of 1638 Grotius prepared his tract *De coena* for the press together with another treatise entitled *An semper communicandum* and had them published in Amsterdam in all secrecy.[64] Even such confidants as his brother Willem and his son Pieter were not privy to this plan. In August 1638 the book must already have been on sale, judging by the fact that Grotius asked Willem in passing how the publication was being received. At the same time he professed that everybody in Paris assumed Claude Saumaise to be the author.[65] Furthermore, in a letter to the English diplomat John Scudamore he deliberately feigned no knowledge of the author. He wrote that the book had been sent to him from Amsterdam, and that he had read the first tract, which had originated in the circle of Rigault's friends, years ago before it was in print. The ideas it contained had found acceptance among the Parisian intellectuals not-

---

man, Weesp 1985, pp. 59–78.

[62] That Grotius took into account the possibility of a premature death, already comes to light in his correspondence of 1638; cf. *BW* IX, nos. 3603 and 3635, to G.J. Vossius, 28 May 1638 ("Incerta vita est"), and to A. Oxenstierna, 19 June 1638 ("... mihi, cuius aetas iam praecipitat...").

[63] *BW* XI, nos. 4599, 4663, and *BW* XII, no. 5061, letters to W. de Groot, 14 April, 26 May 1640 and 16 February 1641; in the last letter Grotius says: "Deus hanc legationem mihi dedit, ut libere loquar; quod, etiamsi legatio absit, alicubi facturus sum."

[64] *Dissertatio de coenae administratione ubi pastores non sunt. Item an semper communicandum per symbola*, Amstelodami, Apud I. Columnam Anno Domini 1638 (*BG* no. 1091). The second edition of these two tracts ([Amsterdam?] 1639; *BG* no. 1092) does not contain any important textual differences. The autograph of the first tract, *Dissertatio de coenae administratione*, is in Amsterdam UL, Coll. Rem. Kerk, L 2.

[65] *BW* IX, no. 3725, to W. de Groot, 14 August 1638. Cf. *BW* IX, nos. 3718 and 3743, from Pieter de Groot, 8 and 24 August 1638. According to Pieter it was surprizing that the printer, J. Columna (Jacob Aertsz. Colom, 1624–1667), should have been willing to publish the work, since he was known for his Calvinist sympathies. Columna's list of books in print, however, includes works by Erasmus, Coornhert, Poppius and Socinus; Grotius' *De coena* was not out of place in this list.

withstanding the views of De l'Aubespine and the Jesuit Petau, who
had published a refutation in the meantime.[66]

De coena is important because it shows that Grotius was also prepared to defend the religious heritage of the early Christian church
if it was clear that such a standpoint was inimical to representatives
of the Roman Catholic church.[67] He was convinced that the early
Christian church offered a blueprint for a religious community that
could accept all Christians. He therefore regarded it as of the essence that scholars should clarify the early church's dogmas and
rites on the basis of meticulously prepared published sources.[68] In
the second tract that appeared with *De coena*, *An semper communicandum*, he included a short passage in which he reacted against the
advanced fragmentation of the Christian church. As sects flourished, so faith declined;[69] whoever stood outside the community
and was not accepted anywhere as a member, should bear his fate
with equanimity until such time as intolerance had passed over.

Although Grotius had taken great pains to maintain the anonymity of the booklet, it soon became known who the real author
was. An interested reader of the calibre of Saumaise knew at once
who had written the book after he had read the second tract, *An*

---

[66] *BW* X, no. 4074, to J. Scudamore, 16 April 1639. Grotius replies to a (as yet
unpublished) letter, in which Scudamore at the instance of an unnamed informant,
possibly archbishop William Laud, pointed out the danger of the book: "Order
hee gave mee to speak with you of it, and added that the thesis may bee right but
in some cases, and that in the times where wee are, men might serve themselves of
it to put all in disorder." Cf. London, British Museum, Scudamore Papers, vol. IV,
f. 96, from J. Scudamore, 21 March 1638 o.s. Petau refuted *De coena* in his *De potestate consecrandi et sacrificandi ... diatriba*, Paris 1639. Cf. H. TREVOR-ROPER, *From
Counter-Reformation to Glorious Revolution*, London 1992, pp. 65–72.

[67] Cf. KONRAD REPGEN, "Grotius 'papizans'", in ERWIN ISERLOH – KONRAD
REPGEN (edd.), *Reformata reformanda. Festgabe für Hubert Jedin...*, Münster [1965], II,
pp. 373, 385–86 and 398. Later on, however, in the fierce polemics with André
Rivet, Grotius repudiated the publication, claiming that the text had been enlarged
with interpolations he could not approve of. Furthermore, the book was only
meant to elicit the opinions of other scholars. Cf. *BG* no. 1091, rem. 4 and *OTh*
III, pp. 658 a 49–52, 694 a 3–11 and 715 a 51–55.

[68] *BW* V, no. 1747, to P. Dupuy, 23 February 1632; *BW* V, no. 1844, to J. de
Cordes, 1 June 1633: "Quaerenda sunt per omnes recessus ista primi saeculi multum de apostolico auro retinentis fragmenta nec abiicienda statim, si quid forte al-
levit adultera manus, sed, quod in metallis fieri solet, periti artificis manu separan-
da scoria a materia puriore."

[69] *OTh* III, p. 511 b 7ff. Cf. *BW* VIII, no. 3310, to W. de Groot, 22 October
1637. In this letter Grotius defends himself against opponents who reproached him
for sympathizing with Socinianism. He was no Socinian and if he adhered to ideas
that also had been ventilated by Socinus, this did not mean that they were, therefore, heretical. He then continues: "Videant illi qui in ecclesia scissuras aut faciunt
aut alunt, ne occasionem multis dent longius abeundi a christianismo quam abiit
Socinus." See also *BW* XIII, no. 5808, to W. de Groot, 26 July 1642, and *BW*
XIV, no. 6475, to H. Appelboom, 10 October 1643.

semper communicandum. Evidently, he had forgotten that he had in his possession a letter from Grotius in which the latter expounded ideas about the Eucharist in words that are echoed in *De coena.*[70]

In the meantime, again in all secrecy, the final manuscript of *De antichristo* had been dispatched to Amsterdam. In this case, too, Grotius preferred to remain anonymous. Anonymity could best be preserved in Holland; moreover the printer, Johan Blaeu, was a kindred spirit who would not obstruct Grotius in the pursuit of his aims. The fact that communication took place via intermediaries was a drawback Grotius was prepared to accept. Evidently Paris was out of the question as far as publishing the work was concerned, and it must have been quite a disappointment when problems arose with Blaeu in Amsterdam. On 7 February 1639[71] an unsuspecting Willem de Groot reported to his brother that the publication was being prepared in Amsterdam of a pamphlet on Antichrist that everybody assumed had been written by Hugo Grotius. A close friend, Gerardus Joannes Vossius had, according to Willem, read the document and had so many objections to the contents that he had been able to delay publication. Willem was promptly instructed to feign ignorance.[72] The correspondence does not tell us exactly how it was that the pamphlet was eventually published.[73] Some weeks later Blaeu reports that he was on the point of printing,[74] but it would take until the end of the year before the plan was finalized. *De antichristo* was not to appear until March 1640. Together with two other short exegetic studies it constitutes the first of an impressive series of biblical annotations published by Grotius in the last few years of his life.[75]

---

[70] Cf. Amsterdam UL, Coll. Rem. Kerk, III 8[9,12], Cl. Saumaise to I. Vossius, 21 and 26 August 1638; D.J.H. TER HORST, *Isaac Vossius en Salmasius, een episode uit de 17de-eeuwsche geleerdengeschiedenis,* The Hague 1938, pp. 35–36, and *BW* IV, no. 1521, to Cl. Saumaise, 23 June 1630.

[71] *BW* X, no. 3965.

[72] *BW* X, no. 3980, to W. de Groot, 19 February 1639: "De libro de quo scribis dic omnibus nihil te eius scire."

[73] The Remonstrant Etienne de Courcelles acted as intermediary between Grotius and the Amsterdam printing house of Blaeu. Cf. *BW* X, no. 4006, from J. Blaeu, 7 March 1639; *BW* XI, nos. 4453 and 4552, from W. de Groot, 2 January 1640; to W. de Groot, 10 March 1640.

[74] *BW* X, no. 4006, from J. Blaeu, 7 March 1639. Blaeu announces here that at the very moment one of the treatises ("een van uwe tractaten") was being set. He does not mention this treatise by name, but the editor of *BW* takes it for granted that the printer refers to *De antichristo.*

[75] *BG* nos. 1100 (*De antichristo*), 1109 (*De fide et operibus*) and 1117 (*Explicatio Decalogi*). Cf. *BW* XI, nos. 4523 and 4552, to W. de Groot, 25 February and 10 March 1640, where Grotius complains that the publication of the tract had been delayed for more than a year.

IV

The correspondence shows that Grotius expected immediate success for his undertaking in France. He had, he said, perceived during those years a stronger inclination on the part of Richelieu to take an independent stance vis-à-vis Rome. In a letter dated 19 June 1638 he wrote to Oxenstierna that the chance of a schism in France was not very great because supporters of Gallicanist philosophy were thrown into prison there and the monks had their informers everywhere.[76] This scepticism comes to the surface in other letters of that same period,[77] but it is noteworthy that he gradually began to see more indicators of a change of opinion. Until then Rome had managed to block drastic reform in France by cunningly taking advantage of the self-interest of the authorities.[78] But it was certain that once hostilities in Europe had been brought to an end with a lasting political peace, it would be possible to convene a council at which the western Christian churches could reach agreement.[79] Against this background it was important that Richelieu should appear to be bent on an unprecedented increase in power for himself in the French church: he wanted to become legate of the Holy See and primate of the French church. He was also angling for the title of Patriarch,[80] and in this capacity particularly he could embark on reforms that would be impossible under the patronage of Rome. Here Grotius was thinking of such measures as

---

[76] *BW* IX, no. 3635, to A. Oxenstierna, 19 June 1638. Cf. *BW* IX, no. 3619, to A. Oxenstierna, 5 June 1638 and *BW* IX, no. 3697, to L. Camerarius, 31 July 1638.

[77] Initially Grotius supposed that there was no chance of church unity being realized in France, as becomes clear in his decided rejection of the efforts of Théophile Brachet de La Milletière. Cf. *BW* VII, no. 2757, to A. Oxenstierna, 11 September 1636, where Grotius refers to La Milletière in a very negative sense: "... Neque videt cardinalem aliosque pontificis ministros sub pacis vocabulo nihil aliud agere quam ut speciosum obtentum subministrent iis qui ob metum aut spem a parte afflicta ad valentiorem cupiunt transgredi." This letter proves that Grotius remained very sceptical when it came to evaluating the chances of church unity in France and the willingness of cardinal Richelieu to support this cause. More than a year afterwards Grotius still did not approve of the ideals of La Milletière. He was convinced that this conciliator was too indulgent towards Rome: "Quid opus est nos liberales esse in eos qui omnia rapiunt?" Cf. *BW* IX, no. 3473, to W. de Groot, 27 February 1638.

[78] *BW* X, nos. 4430, 4432, 4433, 4438.

[79] *BW* X, no. 4446, to W. de Groot, 31 December 1639; *BW* XI, no. 4568, to W. de Groot, 24 March 1640.

[80] *BW* XI, no. 4491, to L. Camerarius, 28 January 1640. On the position of Richelieu, see also J. ORCIBAL, "Appendice IV: Le patriarcat de Richelieu devant l'opinion," in J. ORCIBAL, *Jean Duvergier de Hauranne...*, *Appendices, bibliographie et tables* [= Les origines du Jansénisme, 3], Paris 1948, pp. 108–46, and P. BLET, "Le plan de Richelieu pour la réunion des protestants," *Gregorianum* 48 (1967), pp. 100–29.

the abolition of simony and superstition and the improvement of Christian morals, aims that had to be achieved under the auspices of a reformed episcopate.[81]

Grotius set great store by the publication of his exegetical studies, convinced as he was that they furthered his unionist cause. At first he was not sure where to publish his *Annotationes in Novum Testamentum*. He even toyed with the idea of having it typeset and printed at his home and then collaborating with a bookseller in the Republic to assist in the distribution.[82] This plan fell through after difficult negotiations ended in a joint venture with the Amsterdam publishing house of Blaeu. Wherever the annotations appeared, Grotius was afraid of the criticism his exegetical work would incur from Protestants and Catholics alike.[83] He refused to keep silent, however, and will therefore have been very relieved towards the end of 1639 when he realized that if necessary he could publish his works in France. This change of heart occurred when he heard that Richelieu had given him permission to publish whatever he wanted, without having to deal with the censor.[84] Another reason for Grotius to believe that the French government would not be ill-disposed to his publishing programme was the granting of a royal privilege for a reprint of *De veritate*.[85]

Grotius felt that the time had come to make his move. He had read Heinsius' Bible annotations,[86] and he discovered that a conciliator like Théophile Brachet de La Milletière was receiving help from Richelieu.[87] Support from such a man was an important fac-

---

[81] *BW* XIV, no. 6096, to W. de Groot, [21/22] February 1643; *Grotiana*, p. 80.

[82] *BW* X, no. 4196, to W. de Groot, 9–16 July 1639.

[83] *BW* X, no. 4332, to G.J. Vossius, 10 October 1639: "... de nostris in Novum Testamentum quid potissimum constituere debeam, haereo incertus. Facile hic typographum inveniam, sed metuo turbas a theologis, qui nihil volunt tale edi nisi a se probatum. Ego autem neutri parti aptare me per omnia possum; ac ne silentii quidem in rebus utilibus legem pati. Cogitabo, qua ratione huic malo medear."

[84] *BW* X, no. 4437, to W. de Groot, 24 December 1639: "Iamnunc nuntium accipio, posse me in Gallia edere quae velim sine censore; cardinalem id velle. Id tamen dicas nemini."

[85] *BW* XI, nos. 4561 and 4599, to W. de Groot, 17 March and 14 April 1640. In other letters, too, Grotius' optimism comes to the surface. See for instance *BW* XII, no. 5230, to W. de Groot, 15 June 1641 and *BW* XII, no. 5425, to W. de Groot, 19 October 1641. In the latter letter he writes: "Ego aequitatis vias me institisse confido speroque fore, ut in Gallia sarciatur haec ruptura ad illas ferme quas dixi leges." On the edition of *De veritate religionis christianae*, printed by Sébastien Cramoisy (*BG* no. 950), see J.P. HEERING, *Hugo de Groot als apologeet van de christelijke godsdienst*, diss. Leiden, The Hague 1992, pp. 39–40.

[86] *BW* X, no. 4416, to J. Wtenbogaert, 3 December 1639.

[87] *BW* XII, no. 5005, to W. de Groot, 12 January 1641: "Cardinalis Riceliacus reconciliationem ecclesiarum plane putat fieri posse et strenue in eo laborat Mileterius."

tor, Grotius thought, because the cardinal had the good fortune
never to touch an undertaking without it succeeding.[88] Without delay, Grotius set about consciously pursuing the path he had started
on with such trepidation. He had not bothered about keeping his
authorship of *De antichristo* secret for a long time.[89] The fact that in
spite of his precautions there were rumours that he was the author
no longer filled him with dread: it would help to sell the book.[90] He
assumed that opposition to his tract would soon fade away.[91] In
August 1640 Blaeu received Grotius' *Annotationes in Novum Testamentum* for printing. Shortly afterwards the latter decided to publish under his own name an *Appendix de antichristo* to answer the critics of
De antichristo and to express his opinions freely and without equivo-
cation. In this new tract, after carefully explaining once again that
it was mistaken to think that the New Testament references to
Antichrist had anything at all to do with the Pope, he argued that
the papal standpoints on a variety of religious controversies were
not as objectionable as Protestants tended to think.[92] Strikingly
enough, Grotius did not repudiate his sympathy for Gallicanism,
but recalled the independent position the French king and church
once had in its relations with Rome.[93] The *Appendix* also triggered
off much criticism, but Grotius professed not to let this worry him.
In Holland in the past he had been branded as a heretic because of
his writings, and now he was going to be hated again.[94] He intended his defence of the papacy against unjustified Calvinist attacks as

---

[88] *BW* XI, no. 4599, to W. de Groot, 14 April 1640: "Ipse cardinalis profitetur
se eius negotii tutorem, homo ita felix, ut nihil unquam susceperit, quod non
effecerit." See also *BW* XII, no. 5018, to W. de Groot, 19 January 1641. In this
letter Grotius confides to his brother that church unity was easier to realize than
the Calvinists thought: "Nam in quibus praecipue Reformatio posita creditur, ea
manere poterunt bona pontificis pace, modo ne iniuriis exasperetur. Nihil ea de re
dixi temere et cardinalis Riceliacus rem successuram putat. Ita certe loquitur multis."

[89] *BW* X, no. 4437, to W. de Groot, 24 December 1639. The recent publication of *De antichristo* (*BG* no. 1100), as well as the preparation of a second tract in
the same tenor, *De fide et operibus*, (*BG* no. 1109) induced Grotius to write: "Si qui
coniectent me esse auctorem, non multum id curo; si tamen mutare vis quae mea
manu sunt addita, ita ut mea manus non ita appareat, non intercedo."

[90] *BW* XI, no. 4589, to W. de Groot, 7 April 1640: "Quod me auctorem fama
destinat, eo non moveor. Erit tanto liber vendibilior."

[91] Cf. *BW* XI, no. 4581, to W. de Groot, 31 March 1640.

[92] *Appendix ad interpretationem locorum N. Testamenti quae de Antichristo agunt, aut agere
putantur. In qua via sternitur ad Christianorum concordiam*, Amsterdami, Apud Joh. et
Cornelium Blaeu, 1641 (*BG* no. 1128).

[93] *Appendix* in *OTh* III, pp. 483 b 57 – 484 a 14; 486 a 30–50; 501 b 60 – 502 a
5; 503 a 3–9.

[94] *BW* XII, no. 5284, to W. de Groot, 20 July 1641: "Non dubito, quin inter
pontificios, lutheranos et anabaptistas futuri sint qui longo partium studio fascinati

a toning down of earlier writings produced in a mood of excessive patriotism.[95] With his *Annotata ad Consultationem Cassandri*, which appeared in autumn 1641 and was reprinted shortly afterwards in *Via ad pacem ecclesiasticam*, Grotius threw all caution to the winds: it was to be made clear to the whole world how he thought unity might be achieved.[96] Since both works appeared in Paris, Grotius seems to have been living in the assumption that the air there had cleared sufficiently to give church unity a real chance of success.

Grotius quickly realized that he had badly misjudged the situation. First of all, he did not receive the support he had expected from Richelieu. As Grotius was later to admit, he had never discussed his ideals in this respect with the cardinal, either directly or even through intermediaries,[97] but in the course of 1642 it became clear to him that there was no point in expecting revolutionary church politics from the French government. The breaking point came in spring 1642, when the rumour got about that Richelieu had publicly distanced himself from unionists like François Véron and La Milletière.[98] After Richelieu's death Grotius asserted that the cardinal's plans had never progressed beyond the stage of awarding grants for individual conversions to the Catholic church.[99] Furthermore, the positive reactions, even from close friends, to Grotius' conciliatory writings were lukewarm, while the opposition from orthodox Calvinists and Lutherans remained grim. Grotius

---

pro miris habituri sunt quae dixi. Nam calvinistas et puritanos quin habiturus sim infestissimos, mi frater, minime mirum... Quid si invidiam haec mihi concitent, ut multa antea quae pro patria feci? Deus iudicabit."

[95] *BW* XII, no. 5039, to W. de Groot, 2 February 1641: "Scripsi antehac non pauca abreptus amore patriae, quibus remedium aut lenimentum aliquod adhibendum etiam conscientiae meae exonerandae causa necessarium iudico. Id fiet per istam Appendicem." When Grotius referred to the writings of his Dutch period, he presumably meant particularly those of his poems in which he had criticized the papacy. Cf. A. EYFFINGER, *Grotius Poeta, Aspecten van Grotius' dichterschap*, diss. Amsterdam 1981, pp. 204–05. On Grotius' position see also *BW* XII, no. 5425, to W. de Groot, 19 October 1641, where he defends himself against the objections his brother Willem had raised against another work, the *Annotata ad Consultationem Cassandri* (*BG* no. 1165).

[96] After the provisional, limited edition of the *Annotata ad Consultationem Cassandri* ([Paris] 1641, *BG* no. 1165), the *Via ad pacem ecclesiasticam* (Paris 1642, *BG* no. 1166) was published without any restrictions in a normal edition. Evidently Grotius considered his unionist ideals fit for realization.

[97] Cf. *BW* XIV, no. 6023, to N. van Reigersberch, 3 January 1643.

[98] See H. BOTS – P. LEROY, "La mort de Richelieu vue par des protestants. André Rivet et ses correspondants," *Lias* 4 (1977), pp. 90–93. Cf. *BW* XIII, nos. 5647 and 5675, to W. de Groot, [22/24] March and 12 April 1642, and R.J.M. VAN DE SCHOOR, *De irenische theologie van Théophile Brachet de La Milletière (1588–1665)*, diss. Nijmegen 1991, pp. 111 and 148–54.

[99] *BW* XIII, no. 6015, to N. van Reigersberch, 26 December 1642.

must also have been shocked by the avalanche of poisonous pamphlets that engulfed him.

Highly dissatisfied with the way Blaeu had seen the *Annotationes in Novum Testamentum* through the press, Grotius decided to publish his exegetical work on the Old Testament in Paris. His choice fell on Sébastien Cramoisy, who started printing the book in 1642.[100] Although Denis Petau and other Parisian theologians read the proofs and did not come across any ideas contrary to Roman Catholicism,[101] Cramoisy could not obtain a royal privilege for the work. The chancellor, Pierre Séguier, refused to comply with the printer's request, since he was unwilling to honour books, however respectable they might be, that were written by non-Catholics. *De veritate* was therefore the only theological work of Grotius that was granted a royal privilege.[102]

V

This description of Grotius as a publicist in France brings us to a number of important conclusions. Although Grotius never explicitly compares the French cultural climate with that of the Republic, it appears that he did not expect his theological studies to be given a particularly rapturous welcome at first, neither in France, nor in Holland. Initially he chose to publish anonymously in Holland, but when it looked as if Richelieu's anti-papal policies were heralding a change, he also published his conciliatory works in Paris. Contrary to expectations, the loosening of ties or break with Rome did not take place and Grotius had to go without support for his ideas from the French government leaders. He gave the impression that he abominated Richelieu for his inconsistent policy towards Rome. In the summer of 1643, that is six months after the cardinal's death, he analyzed the latter's policies and expressed his deep aversion to

---

[100] *Annotata ad Vetus Testamentum*, Paris 1644; *BG* no. 1137, rem. 1 and 2. On Cramoisy, see H.-J. MARTIN, "Renouvellements et concurrences," in *Histoire de l'édition française*, I: *Le livre conquérant; Du Moyen Âge au milieu du XVIIe siècle*, Paris 1982, pp. 381–83.

[101] *BW* XII, no. 5408, to D. Petau, 8 October 1641; *BW* XIII, nos. 5657 and 5727, to N. van Reigersberch, 29 March and 24 May 1642. Cf. *BW* XIII, no. 5943, to [D. Petau], 8 November 1642 and *BW* XIV, no. 6244, to W. de Groot, 6 June 1643.

[102] *EQ*, pp. 970–71, App. no. 720, to W. de Groot, 27 August 1644. Eventually a 'permission verbale' or a tacit agreement with the authorities enabled the printers to sell Grotius' exegetical works. Cf. H. BOTS – P. LEROY, *Correspondance intégrale d'André Rivet et de Claude Sarrau*, vol. III, Amsterdam – Maarssen 1982, pp. 320–21, Claude Sarrau to André Rivet, 2 February 1646.

the man. Gallicanism was smothered, the power of Rome had grown and the country was exhausted. The sad end of Richelieu, racked as he was by disease, reflected the decline that France had undergone during his term of office.[103]

Clearly, Grotius' judgment of the French statesman was too negative. He did not realize that Richelieu had very little room for manoeuvre in the Catholic France of the time. He worked for independence from Rome, but in the struggle with the Hapsburgs he could not afford an open breach because of the repercussions this might have on the delicate domestic political situation. Unlike Grotius, Richelieu believed that plans for breaking away from Rome and drastic ecclesiastical reform were subservient to the struggle against the Hapsburgs, for it was only this struggle that offered guarantees for the maintenance of France's might and greatness.[104]

Furthermore, the development in Grotius' thought described above is of importance for the way in which, as a publicist, he slowly graduated from a passive, opportunistic[105] attitude to an uncompromising struggle for the realization of his church ideals. He recorded what moved him in a letter addressed to the Swede Harald Appelboom, in which he hints at the friction that existed between his diplomatic duties and the battle he had fought in the cause of church reunion. Man had two roles to play in this life, said Grotius: the first, in the service of the greatest public good, was imposed by God, while the second was individual and was determined by one's office, one's family or by choice.[106] Although Grotius asserted that he wanted to carry out both tasks as well as possible, everything points to the fact that after 1638 he gave priority to the first task. How the country of his Swedish masters or that of his hosts reacted to his writings thus became matters of secondary importance. Whatever the case may be, Grotius gave little thought to the French. He had never felt at home in France, and for this reason he will in the end have disapproved of an unknown French nobleman who compared him in a Latin epigram with the great Scaliger:

---

[103] *Grotiana*, pp. 51 and 75–76: "C'estoit un miserable homme qui a tout troublé et tout ruiné, et apres avoir rongé jusqu'aux os la pauvre France, Dieu a permis qu'il soit mort luy mesme tout maigre et tout sec."

[104] Cf. J. ORCIBAL, *Appendice IV: Le patriarcat de Richelieu*, pp. 140–46.

[105] Cf. H.J.M. NELLEN, "'Geene vredemaeckers zijn zonder tegenspreeckers': Hugo Grotius' buitenkerkelijke positie," *De Zeventiende Eeuw* 5 (1989), pp. 106–07.

[106] Cf. *BW* XIV, no. 6112, to H. Appelboom, 28 February 1643: "Didici ... a sapientibus plerisque nostrum duas impositas esse personas, alteram communem a Deo, alteram peculiarem a principibus, parentibus, aut dilectu proprio. Velim utranque bene implere."

Gallia, Scaligerum dederas male sana Batavis,
    Grotiaden reddit terra Batava tibi.
Ingratam expertus patriam venerandus uterque est,
    Felix mutato erit uterque solo.

Spurned by their own countries of origin, the two scholars had
sought refuge in each other's country. Like Scaliger in the Republic, Grotius would, according to the poet, eventually find good fortune in France.[107] In reality, however, happiness constantly eluded
him there.

---

[107] The epigram is cited in *BW* VIII, no. 3114, to W. de Groot, 12 June 1637.
Cf. BRANDT – VAN CATTENBURGH, *Historie van het leven*, II, p. 108–09, where, besides a Dutch translation, a slightly different version of the poem is given; the
fourth line, for instance, reads: "Felix mutato crevit uterque solo."

HUGO GROTIUS ET ANDRÉ RIVET: DEUX LUMIÈRES OPPOSÉES, DEUX VOCATIONS CONTRADICTOIRES

Hans Bots
(Nijmegen)

Au bas d'une lettre datée du 24 août 1643 André Rivet écrit en post-scriptum: "jour mémorable et funeste, l'an 1572, auquel j'avois deux mois."[1] Par cette formule touchante et suggestive on sent bien qu'à l'âge de 71 ans André Rivet ne peut toujours pas s'empêcher dans une lettre à son ami, le parlementaire parisien Claude Sarrau, d'évoquer avec émotion cette date du 24 août 1572, jour de la Saint Barthélemy. L'illustre théologien mêlait ainsi, après trois quarts de siècle, son année de naissance avec le souvenir d'une des pages les plus sanglantes de l'histoire de la Réforme en France. Ces souvenirs presque involontaires d'une page cruelle du martyrologe huguenot s'accompagnent d'autres images dramatiques que Rivet gardait toujours dans sa mémoire: le long cortège des drames de sa propre province natale, le Poitou, depuis la fin du XVIe siècle. A cette profondeur de souvenirs s'ajoutent des éléments liés à son appartenance sociale. Il sort en effet de cette 'gentry',[2] classe qui est au cœur des transformations de la société française et dont une notable partie rallia très tôt comme la famille Rivet, la Réforme. Nul doute donc que la première partie de sa vie ait été profondément marquée par les événements tragiques que la France a subis en cette fin de XVIe siècle et par cet enracinement familial.

L'enfance et la jeunesse de Hugo Grotius sont bien éloignées d'aussi funestes souvenirs. Né à Delft dans une famille patricienne – son père était jurisconsulte et depuis 1594 curateur de la toute jeune université de Leyde –, le jeune Grotius a dû ressentir très tôt l'élan de la République des Provinces-Unies car ce jeune état puisait justement sa légitimité dans la conquête de la liberté religieuse et politique. Elan qui était donné et nourri par l'humanisme érasmien auquel sa classe sociale était tant attachée. On comprend mieux que dans un tel milieu des qualités intellectuelles hors du

---

[1] H. Bots – P. Leroy (éds.), *Correspondance intégrale d'André Rivet et de Claude Sarrau 1641-1650*, Amsterdam – Maarssen 1978–82, 3 vols., II, p. 82; André Rivet naquit le 22 juin 1572.

[2] Cf. George Huppert, *Bourgeois et Gentilhommes. La Réussite sociale en France au XVIe siècle*, Paris 1983. Notons que chez Rivet la famille au sens large du terme tiendra une place importante pendant toute sa vie; on en trouve dans sa correspondance de multiples traces.

commun de ce jeune enfant aient pu trouver un épanouissement si remarquable.[3]

Retournons en Poitou: après ses années d'études la première partie de la carrière de Rivet jusqu'en 1620 se déroule dans sa province natale où il sera pasteur d'une paroisse et en même temps chapelain et conseiller d'une grande famille de seigneurs réformés les La Trémouille.[4] Vingt-cinq années s'écoulèrent alors; elles furent à la fois heureuses et pleines d'incertitudes, car l'édit de Nantes permettait à partir de 1598 la cohabitation relativement pacifique des deux confessions; Rivet semble lui-même y avoir été très attaché: 20 ans plus tard n'évoque-t-il pas ce temps où il a "vescu civilement avec les Catholiques Romains..., notamment à Thouars, où [il] a esté autant regretté d'eux que des nostres." Oui, ajoute-t-il, il avait "aimé et cheri cette paix civile" qu'il avait entretenue de tout son pouvoir. Mais dès cette période son caractère et sa réflexion étaient marqués par deux lignes directrices: d'une part il voulait éviter les troubles en maîtrisant les esprits remuants qui pourraient "porter nos églises dans le malheur qui nous a osté nostre liberté" et d'autre part il s'attachait fermement à "la doctrine" et "au zele contre la superstition." Dans ce domaine il avait "tousiours esté entier graces à Dieu."[5]

Dans la première partie de la carrière brillante du juriste Grotius, on discerne aussi deux grandes préoccupations, mais de nature bien différente: des travaux de grande érudition sur l'histoire nationale et le droit international, mais aussi une première esquisse, conçue dans le *Meletius*, de ce qui allait devenir le grand dessein de sa vie: élaborer une doctrine chrétienne plutôt éthique que dogmatique, véritable fondement pour une religion utopique qui permettrait à tous les hommes d'honorer Dieu non pas en se battant sur des dogmes, mais en suivant un mode de vie, "sine bellis, sine litibus, sine egestate, in summa pace atque concordia": sans guerre, sans querelles, sans pauvreté, dans la plus grande paix et concorde.[6]

La première partie que nous venons d'évoquer, de la vie de ces deux hommes laisse déjà deviner qu'il s'agit de deux destins voués à

---

[3] Voir notamment S. DRESDEN, *Beeld van een verbannen intellectueel: Hugo de Groot*, Amsterdam – Oxford – New York 1983 et H. J. M. NELLEN, *Hugo de Groot 1583–1645. De loopbaan van een geleerd staatsman*, Weesp 1985.

[4] Pour la biographie d'André Rivet, voir toujours H. J. HONDERS, *Andreas Rivetus als invloedrijk theoloog in Holland's Bloeitijd*, 's-Gravenhage 1930.

[5] BOTS – LEROY, *Correspondance Rivet-Sarrau*, I, p. 171.

[6] Cf. H. GROTIUS, *Meletius sive de iis quae inter Christianos conveniunt epistola, Critical Edition with translation, commentary and introduction by* GUILLAUME H.M. POSTHUMUS MEYJES, Leiden [etc.] 1988, pp. 40 et 101. NELLEN, *Hugo de Groot*, p. 18.

des itinéraires opposés. Entre 1619 et 1621 l'orientation de la vie de Grotius et de Rivet allait changer radicalement. Emporté dans le flot arminien, Grotius allait être arrêté et condamné à la prison à vie. Ce n'est qu'à la suite d'une fuite rocambolesque qu'il retrouvera en 1621 la liberté: il doit alors quitter son pays et gagner la France. Parallèlement Rivet, auquel son roi avait interdit d'assister au synode de Dordrecht qui avait condamné les arminiens, quittait lui aussi son pays, en 1620, pour occuper une chaire de théologie à l'Académie de Leyde devenue vacante par l'épuration anti-arminienne; il prit possession de sa charge en prononçant le 12 octobre de cette année un discours inaugural dont le titre semble paradoxal après une telle crise dans la société politique et religieuse de la jeune République: *De bono pacis et Concordiae in Ecclesia*. On peut cependant s'expliquer facilement un tel sujet, si l'on se rappelle les préoccupations de Rivet, évoquées ci-dessus: la paix et l'orthodoxie de la doctrine.[7]

Ainsi à peu de temps d'intervalle venaient de se croiser de France aux Provinces-Unies et des Provinces-Unies en France deux personnalités qui avaient donné jusqu'alors assez de preuves de leur génie; Rivet venait de connaître une promotion, Grotius de son côté avait vu s'évanouir l'espoir d'une brillante carrière. Comment l'un et l'autre allaient-ils relever ces défis contraires?

Pour le théologien français les étapes suivantes de sa vie devaient se dérouler avec éclat: après un enseignement fructueux qui devait marquer une génération de pasteurs, il fut appelé en 1632 définitivement à la cour du stathouder pour être précepteur du jeune prince d'Orange, le futur Guillaume II.[8] Une fonction d'un tel prestige lui était confiée, parce que Frédéric-Henri avait apprécié sans nul doute ses qualités de pédagogue, sa fermeté doctrinale et en même temps son refus de vaines controverses, "les poinctilles." Cette faveur princière allait faire de cet homme d'expérience une célébrité dans la République des Lettres et une éminence grise – les envieux l'ont même surnommé le pape – pour l'Eglise réformée, particulièrement en France. C'est ce qui explique le vaste développement de son réseau de correspondants à partir des années 30. En 1646, à soixante-quatorze ans, Rivet se vit encore confier une dernière mis-

---

[7] Voir ce discours dans: *Opera Theologica, partim exegetica, partim didactica, partim polemica*, III tomi, Rotterdam 1651–60, t. II, pp. 1243–50; il finit ce discours par citer une exhortation de St Augustin: "Si velimus vivere de Spiritu Sancto, teneamus charitatem, amemus veritatem, desideremus unitatem, ut perveniamus ad aeternitatem."

[8] Voir pour cette période de sa vie, A.G. VAN OPSTAL, *André Rivet. Een invloedrijk theoloog aan het Hof van Frederik Hendrik*, Harderwijk 1937.

sion pédagogique, celle de curateur de la nouvelle Ecole Illustre de
Breda, où il mourut le 7 janvier 1651. A cette date Grotius avait
déjà rendu sa belle âme à Dieu depuis plus de cinq ans dans des
circonstances dramatiques loin des siens et de son pays.

Depuis sa fuite des Provinces-Unies Grotius avait vécu, pendant
plus de dix ans encore, à Paris, dans la gêne et l'inquiétude finan-
cière, tout en espérant retrouver un jour le sol natal; ce n'est qu'en
1634, on le sait, qu'en entrant au service de la Suède il devait trouver une activité plus rémunératrice et adaptée à son génie. L'exil et
surtout ses fonctions diplomatiques lui permettaient, à l'instar de
Rivet, d'étendre un vaste réseau épistolaire. Cependant jusqu'en
1636 il garda sur le sujet qui constituait une préoccupation si importante pour lui, la réunion des églises, une attitude de réserve qui
s'explique assez bien par ses origines, son lieu de résidence, ses positions antérieures, sa fonction diplomatique et ses rapports délicats
avec la communauté réformée de Charenton.[9]

Désormais Grotius allait jeter le masque qu'il s'était volontaire-
ment imposé; l'âge avançait et le temps pressait.[10]

C'est à partir de cette période que nos deux protagonistes al-
laient directement croiser l'épée. Le débat théologique sur la réunion des églises entre Grotius et Rivet a été étudié de diverses ma-
nières et sera sans doute repris encore à l'avenir.[11] Quant à nous,
plus modestement, nous voudrions dans le cadre de cette communication attirer seulement l'attention sur un aspect particulier dans ce
débat; nous l'avons directement dégagé du contact avec les sources
épistolaires, notamment avec la correspondance d'André Rivet et
de Claude Sarrau. Il s'agit là de l'image que les deux antagonistes
ont voulu donner d'eux-mêmes: Rivet sous sa propre plume, Grotius dans le reflet d'un ami presque trop dévoué, le parlementaire parisien Claude Sarrau et quelques autres membres de l'illustre Académie putéane, fréquentée par l'ambassadeur de Suède.

Cette ample polémique, qui a été nourrie par huit ouvrages,
quatre de chacun des auteurs, entre 1641 et 1646, est marquée par
un caractère de bonne tenue; certes, c'est une polémique vive, mais
la qualité des combattants semble leur avoir évité les bassesses que
l'on trouve parfois dans des querelles contemporaines. Remarquons

---

[9] Voir pour ces réserves et le changement dans son attitude, NELLEN, *Hugo de
Groot*, pp. 68–78.
[10] *BW* XI, p. 276, lettre du 19 mai 1640: "Incertus ego, quantum mihi vitae
supersit, omnino exstare volo testimonia sententiarum mearum super iis, quae
Christianum orbem tam graviter concutiunt."
[11] Voir HONDERS, *Andreas Rivetus*, chap. IV, pp. 88–106; DIETER WOLF, *Die Irenik
des Hugo Grotius*, Marburg 1969.

tout de suite que la position des deux hommes était toute différente. Grotius sort de l'ombre avec un recueil de textes controversés tiré à un nombre restreint et dans l'intention avoué de recueillir seulement le sentiment de personnes compétentes; Rivet avec sa lucidité coutumière décide aussitôt de porter le fer contre un adversaire dont il estime l'érudition, mais dont il ne peut que condamner la démarche dangereuse à ses yeux.[12] C'est le théologien de La Haye qui va révéler au grand jour le dessein profond de Grotius qui s'en plaint aussitôt à ses amis: Rivet ne faisait-il pas "plus de bruict en Hollande contre ses escrits que tous les autres ministres du pais ensemble"?[13] En effet Rivet se sent mû par des sentiments très profonds dans sa démarche de publicité qu'il va bientôt prolonger par la plume: en se taisant, il n'aurait pas seulement fait preuve "d'imprudence, mais aussi de lascheté et de prevarication." Fidèle à ce qu'il considère comme sa vocation, c'est-à-dire défendre la paix civile par une croyance ferme, il dénonce chez son adversaire le laxisme religieux, lui qui n'avait choisi aucune communion, "a monstré sa haine particuliere contre Calvin et Beze, et nous a voulu rendre odieux aux puissances superieures par des interpretations calomnieuses." Rivet ne s'était vraiment pas attendu à de telles malices chez "un homme de sa qualité."[14]

C'est pourquoi Rivet dès son premier ouvrage va droit au but et ne manque pas de souligner le caractère ambigu et contradictoire de la démarche de Grotius. Car, si ce dernier ménageait les idées des catholiques romains sur l'infaillibilité pontificale et refusait la doctrine calviniste sur la supériorité des écritures sur la tradition, sur l'imputation et la justification...,[15] il n'allait certainement pas assez loin pour se faire catholique. Aussi finirait-il, selon Rivet, par être rejeté par les deux confessions. Sarrau avait bien compris l'argumentation quasi imparable de Rivet: "quelque mine que face l'Adversaire, il est percé à iour et faut qu'il rende les armes."[16] En effet Grotius descendait aussitôt dans l'arène et seule une mort subite devait la lui faire quitter. Ce n'est pas toutefois de gaîté de cœur,

---

[12] Dans la préface aux *Animadversiones* de Rivet (*Opera Theologica*, t. III) on lit à la page 926: "H. Grotius, Vir Clarissimus, et inter Doctos hoc tempore primi nominis, qui, si se continuisset intra limites, quos ei videbatur praefixisse vitae genus quod ab initio elegerat, melius fortasse sibi et aliis consuluisset. Sed cum vir ingenii sit tam ampli et capacis, ut nullis coarctari possit terminis, ubique jurisdictionem exercet, in literatura omnis generis, in linguarum cognitione, in legum et juris peritia: ac tandem in Theologia dictaturam sibi voluit attribuere..."

[13] BOTS – LEROY, *Correspondance Rivet-Sarrau*, I, p. 32, lettre du 3 janvier 1642.

[14] BOTS – LEROY, *Correspondance Rivet-Sarrau*, I, p. 42, le 13 janvier 1642.

[15] Cf. WOLF, *Die Irenik*, pp. 52 et suiv., 85 et suiv.

[16] BOTS – LEROY, *Correspondance Rivet-Sarrau*, I, p. 118, lettre du 18 avril 1642.

car dès la publication de son *Votum* en 1642, il fait savoir par Sarrau qu'il promet de ne plus repliquer, qu'il veut désormais se consacrer à "d'autres plus grandes œuvres."[17]

Si le témoignage de Sarrau est authentique, Grotius pressentait que ses idées sur la réunion de l'église ne pourraient être bien accueillies que dans un pays d'utopie. En effet, dans les Provinces-Unies, il ne pouvait plus se faire beaucoup d'illusion: le prince d'Orange n'avait pas apprécié la publication à la fin du *Votum* d'une lettre amicale écrite 20 ans plus tôt, ce qu'il avait jugé mal à propos et comme une "malice";[18] mais même dans le cercle étroit de ses amis fidèles, l'ouvrage avait déplu. C'est pourquoi Rivet conclut sa lettre à Sarrau en ces termes: "cet homme se faict tort et à ses amis, plusieurs desquelz le condamnent et mesme Utenbogaert et Mons. Vandermyle."[19] Même son propre frère Willem et son beau-frère Nicolaas van Reigersberch lui firent savoir que cette dernière publication les avait contrariés.[20]

En France il devait bien vite constater que ses amis érudits ne le suivraient pas dans son grand dessein. Jean Chapelain résume bien les sentiments du milieu intellectuel parisien: "Je ne scay par quelle bizarrerie un jurisconsulte, un critique, un poëte, un historien, un ambassadeur laisse le soin de toutes ses occupations pour devenir théologien et chercher l'Arminianisme dans le Nouveau Testament. Il n'y a pas de moyen de luy pardonner cette fantaisie qui recule l'accomplissement de tant de belles choses et prive le monde de ce qu'il desire il y a si long temps."[21] Il est étonnant de constater qu'il y a convergence de vues dans l'analyse de la démarche de Grotius entre le théologien orthodoxe de La Haye et le poète mondain

---

[17] Bots – Leroy, *Correspondance Rivet-Sarrau*, I, p. 247 et voir aussi p. 350: "M. le Legat veut pendre ses armes au croq…"

[18] Bots – Leroy, *Correspondance Rivet-Sarrau*, I, p. 285, lettre du 20 octobre 1642 et *BG* nos. 1183, remarque 7 et 1185, remarque 1, pp. 591–92.

[19] Bots – Leroy, *Correspondance Rivet-Sarrau*, I, p. 285. Cf. aussi p. 321, lettre du 24 novembre 1642: "Utembogard est aagé de 82 ou 83 ans, et ne seroit pas propre à cela, n'approuvant nullement ce que faict l'Ambas[sadeur] comme m'a asseuré feu Mons. Vandermyle…"

[20] Cf. lettre de Willem de Groot du 6 octobre 1642, *BW* XIII, p. 462: "Videtur enim aliqua iis fieri iniuria, quorum litterae se insciis et viventibus vulgantur. Reigersbergius etiam aegre fert nomen suum in ista epistola extare ideoque omnino editionem dissuasurus erat."

[21] Ph. Tamizey de Larroque (éd.), *Lettres de Jean Chapelain*, I, Paris 1881, p. 677, lettre du 2 septembre 1640; voir aussi un autre passage de cette même lettre: "Pour Mr Grotius (...). A vous en parler à cœur ouvert, cette dignité [d'ambassadeur] l'embarasse et embarasse ceux qui ont à traitter avec luy. Elle l'a tiré de l'ordre des sçavans et ne l'a pas mis dans celuy des grands politiques et il s'est fait un certain meslange de conditions en luy par cet employ qui le faict un homme médiocre d'un homme extraordinaire qu'il estoit."

parisien Chapelain qui souligne "l'orgeuil dans la fantaisie" de Grotius qui veut "composer une religion chrestienne à sa mode qui ne soit ni catholique, ni huguenote, et de faire une nouvelle église en raffinant l'arminianisme..."[22] Mais en outre, ce que Rivet craignait le plus, ces propositions risqueraient de déstabiliser les calvinistes et de mettre en péril leurs rapports avec le pouvoir politique.[23] Il est clair que de telles idées osées et en partie ambigues devaient isoler Grotius. Déjà dans une position difficile vis-à-vis de la couronne suédoise qu'il est censé servir et des autorités françaises qu'il fréquente le moins possible pour des raisons de préséance, l'ambassadeur se retrouve de plus en plus délaissé par ses amis.

Les réformés Sarrau et Saumaise expriment une position qui se rapproche facilement de celle du catholique Chapelain; Saumaise reçoit le *Votum*, lorsqu'il séjourne en Bourgogne; et on dirait qu'il perd immédiatement toute mesure à l'égard d'un ami qu'il avait tant estimé pour son érudition. Il croit déceler chez Grotius une tentation pour le papisme et il insinue aussitôt avec fiel: "je crois maintenant ce qu'on a dit de lui et de ceux de sa Secte en son pays que leur intention étoit sous pretexte d'arminianisme d'introduire le papisme et ensuite de remettre le pays à son ancien Maistre..." Saumaise lui reproche de flatter "l'auctorité du cardinal de Richelieu," dénonce ses amis jésuites et conclut "il est méchant et artificieux et nonobstant tout son artifice, il est un foible adversaire et fort aisé à enfoncer. Il n'a que des couleurs et du plastre..."[24] Pour l'érudit bourguignon l'attitude de l'ambassadeur est impardonnable et il se voit obligé de rompre l'amitié avec cet homme qui avait sapé "les fondements de la religion" sur laquelle il avait fondé tout son salut.[25] Même la mort de Grotius survenue en août 1645 ne redressera plus ce jugement de Saumaise. Il est vrai le monde des lettres y avait fait perte, dans son opinion, mais Grotius avait été "un homme pernicieux à la religion," car les sujets qu'il avait abordés à la fin de sa vie étaient "plustost à destruction qu'à edification" et

---

[22] PH. TAMIZEY DE LARROQUE (éd.), *Lettres de Jean Chapelain*, I, p. 692, lettre du 23 septembre 1640.

[23] C'est ce que les protestants français craignent toujours au cours du XVIIe siècle. Pour cela il fallait éviter le plus possible les tensions et les disputes internes. Cf. aussi à ce propos F.P. VAN STAM, *The Controversy over the Theology of Saumur, 1635-1650. Disrupting Debates among the Huguenots in Complicated Circumstances*, Amsterdam – Maarssen 1988, par exemple p. 290.

[24] P. LEROY, *Le dernier voyage à Paris et en Bourgogne 1640-1643 du réformé Claude Saumaise*, Amsterdam – Maarssen 1983, p. 178, lettre de Saumaise à Sarrau.

[25] P. LEROY – H. BOTS (éds.), *Claude Saumaise et André Rivet. Correspondance échangée entre 1632 et 1648*, Amsterdam – Maarssen 1987, p. 391, lettre du 13 novembre 1644.

non dépourvu de quelque cruauté il lui semble même que "Dieu en un instant ait soufflé sur toutes ses grandeurs et les a [*sic*] dissi-pées."[26]

Les sentiments éprouvés par Sarrau à l'égard de Grotius sont beaucoup plus complexes. Le parlementaire parisien ne cessera d'admirer l'homme de lettres qu'il rencontrait fréquemment au cabinet Dupuy, même s'il partageait les objections que Rivet oppo-sait aux idées de Grotius. On pourrait distinguer trois phases dans ses rapports quelque peu ambigus: *avant* le débat Sarrau est voué sans réserve à l'ambassadeur, *au cours de* la querelle il donne telle-ment de gages à Rivet, notamment en lui transmettant des "feuilles toutes mouillées"[27] du *Votum*, que Grotius devait lui fermer la porte de sa maison et enfin *après* la disparition de ce dernier, Sarrau va encore manifester un tel culte envers l'illustre savant qu'il se dépen-sera pour procurer une édition de ses *Epistolae ad Gallos*. Ces trois phases mettent sans doute bien en valeur la difficulté des érudits parisiens de confession réformée pour garder l'équilibre entre l'a-mour des belles lettres telles que les incarnait Grotius d'une part et la fidélité aux principes de leur confession de l'autre. Répondant aux reproches que Saumaise lui faisait perfidement d'avoir desservi ou même encouragé son ami Grotius, Sarrau se défend en ces ter-mes: "Vous dites que ie le loue de sa moderation en la religion. C'est ce que ie n'aye ni dit ni escrit ni pensé, dites moy où. Je n'ay garde de toucher cette chorde là, car je n'y trouverois pas ma satis-faction; et ne luy ay pas celé à lui mesme que quelque bon desseing qu'il dit avoir, il ne s'y prenoit pas de bonne sorte."[28] Mais quoi qu'il en soit, le comportement de Sarrau a été au moins discutable et on peut penser que c'est auprès d'hommes comme Sarrau que Grotius aurait pu trouver une oreille attentive. Peut-être a-t-il es-péré réunir une communauté de telles personnes qui s'en tiendrai-ent en matières religieuses à ce "qui doibt suffire aux doctes et equitables."[29] N'est-ce pas l'utopie après laquelle il court depuis la conception même de son *Meletius*?

Mais quel poids aurait pu avoir un tel groupe de personnes dans la France de Louis XIII et Richelieu au moment même où le car-dinal échafaudait son projet de réunir catholiques et réformés au

---

[26] Leroy – Bots, *Claude Saumaise et André Rivet*, p. 445, lettre du 17 septembre 1645.

[27] Paris, Bibliothèque Nationale, Ms Latin 10350, f. 178, lettre de Sarrau à Saumaise, s.d.

[28] *Ibidem*, même lettre de Sarrau à Saumaise.

[29] Bots – Leroy, *Correspondance Rivet-Sarrau*, I, p. 380, lettre du 23 janvier 1643.

sein d'une église plus spécifiquement gallicane?[30] On saisit bien le parallélisme possible entre le projet de Richelieu et celui de Grotius, leurs contemporains ne s'y trompèrent pas. On peut même admettre que cette coincidence n'est pas pour peu dans l'échec douloureux de l'ambassadeur. Cruelle ironie de l'histoire, notons-le en passant: Hugo Grotius qui avait pris position dès sa jeunesse en faveur d'une prédominance du magistrat politique sur les choses sacrées et qui avait dû s'exiler sous la pression du pouvoir politique de son pays, devait constater qu'à nouveau le pouvoir politique faisait de l'ombre à son ultime effort en faveur d'une réunion des églises; c'est que le soupçon d'un soutien du projet de la part de Richelieu ne manqua pas de discréditer l'ambassadeur et de dénaturer l'idéal même.[31]

Grotius n'avait toutefois obtenu que peu de résultats, lorsque la mort venait trancher le fil de sa vie, à l'instant même où selon ses contemporains de nouveaux choix semblaient s'annoncer. Saumaise n'écrit-il pas qu'"ayant eu son congé, il [Grotius] s'en retournoit en France où il eust fait abiuration pour y trouver de quoi occuper son ambition comme on lui avoit promis, et notamment le prince de Condé."[32]

Si la mort de Grotius a touché tous ses contemporains, elle n'allait pas retenir Rivet qui venait de prendre connaissance de la *Discussio*, dernière réplique de Grotius dans son débat avec Rivet. Après avoir souligné la malignité de cet ouvrage plein "d'invectives contre l'estat, le feu Prince Maurice, contre les Ministres, contre les Calvinistes sur tout...," Rivet ne peut s'empêcher de s'écrier: "il faut que la vérité soit defendue," même si Grotius ne pourra plus en tirer profit.[33] Sarrau l'y encourage d'ailleurs aussitôt, "pourveu qu'il plaise à Dieu vous continuer vie et santé..., vostre diligence ordinaire satisfera bientost à ces escrits cachés que vous saurés bien mettre au jour pour en faire veoir la foiblesse." Des écrits, comme cette

---

[30] Cf. H. BOTS – P. LEROY, "Hugo Grotius et la réunion des Chrétiens: entre le savoir et l'inquiétude," *XVIIe siècle* 35 (1983), pp. 451–70. Voir aussi R.J.M. VAN DE SCHOOR, *De irenische theologie van Théophile Brachet de la Milletière (1588-1665)*, Nijmegen 1991, pp. 102 et suiv.

[31] Cf. BOTS – LEROY, *Correspondance Rivet-Sarrau*, I, p. 310: "Le bruict est entre nous que Mr. le Cardinal songe autant que iamais à l'accommodement des religions, se voulant servir à cet effet du *Votum*..." Un tel renseignement ne pouvait être que très comprometteur.

[32] Cf. LEROY – BOTS, *Claude Saumaise et André Rivet*, p. 448. Rappelons qu'après la mort de Richelieu en décembre 1642, le prince de Condé reprit pendant un temps les projets du cardinal. Voir H. BOTS – P. LEROY, "La mort de Richelieu vue par des protestants," *Lias* 4 (1977), p. 93 et note 63 de cet article.

[33] BOTS – LEROY, *Correspondance Rivet-Sarrau*, III, p. 225, lettre du 25 septembre 1645.

Discussio, font tort, aux yeux du parlementaire, à la réputation de Grotius, sont en effet "indignes de son érudition et de sa piété."[34]

Tout en avançant une réfutation qui devait lui valoir à ses yeux la couronne de la victoire définitive, Rivet se croit cependant obligé de se disculper d'attaquer un mort. Il s'efforçait en effet de se tenir "dans les limites de la gravité chrestienne," mais les fraudes et malices demandaient qu'on les marque, d'autant plus que la dent de Grotius n'avait épargné "ni grands ni petis" et qu'il avait témoigné "une si grande haine contre nostre Eglise notamment, qu'il a merité d'estre traicté plus rudement" que l'humeur et l'inclination de Rivet ne l'y poussaient.[35] De même que Grotius avait essayé d'atteindre et de convaincre non pas Rivet lui-même, mais ceux que ce théologien au grand prestige pouvait entraîner,[36] Rivet de son côté voulait atteindre le parti de Grotius qu'il sentait déjà ébranlé. Certes, Grotius avait beaucoup de "fauteurs et de credit," bien que Rivet en ait "veu depuis peu quelques-uns" qui lui avaient avoué "qu'ilz n'eussent jamais creu qu'il [Grotius] en fust venu là."[37]

Dans l'ultime étape du cheminement parallèle de ces deux hommes, dans cette querelle sur la réunion des religions, Grotius et Rivet sont restés identiques à eux-mêmes: le grand homme d'esprit rêvait, la tête dans les nuages, à un paradis sur terre où guidés par les "doctes et equitables," parmi lesquels il se comptait, les chrétiens, toutes différences de dogmes aplanies, réussiraient à construire une église de piété. Depuis son plus jeune âge il conservait cet espoir au cœur, il avait nourri cette vocation dans ses vastes lectures, les épreuves de la vie l'avaient mûri et au cours de ses cinq dernières années il avait même tenté, ne cherchant plus les honneurs terrestres,[38] de forcer désespérément le destin. Le vieux pasteur et théologien de La Haye profondément marqué par sa longue fidélité à la cause de la foi calviniste en général et à celle des églises protestantes de France en particulier, chaque jour et en tous lieux menacées, devait se sentir comme mû par la main de Dieu. Pour

---

[34] Bots – Leroy, *Correspondance Rivet-Sarrau*, III, p. 230, lettre du 29 septembre 1645.

[35] Cf. Bots – Leroy, *Correspondance Rivet-Sarrau*, III, p. 397, lettre du 30 avril 1646: "... j'ay trouvé tant de venin, de virulence, et de malice en l'escrit adversaire, que quelques fois il m'a fallu appeler les choses par leur nom. Je ne touche point à l'erudition et à la celebrité du personnage en autre chose..."

[36] A.H. Haentjens, *Hugo Grotius als godsdienstig denker*, Amsterdam 1946, p. 136.

[37] Bots – Leroy, *Correspondance Rivet-Sarrau*, III, p. 397.

[38] *BW* XII, p. 607, lettre du 1 novembre 1641 à W. de Groot: "Ego legationis damno, si quid id mihi minetur, non moveor. Lucrosa res non est. Honorum sum satur. Senectus advenit et quietem aliquando postulabit. Non subtraham me negotiis, dum par sum, nec ea quaeram, si fugiant."

lui aussi c'était une véritable vocation de résister à tout changement doctrinal qui ne pouvait qu'engendrer trouble et division. Il n'est pas osé de dire que chacun d'entre eux désirait ardemment et avec la même sincérité la paix de l'église, mais que les moyens qu'ils croyaient devoir mettre en œuvre, étaient diamétralement opposés et même contradictoires.

PART THREE

THE INFLUENCE OF GROTIUS' THEOLOGICAL
THOUGHT

SOME ASPECTS OF THE SCOTTISH CONTRIBUTION TO APOCALYPTICISM IN THE SEVENTEENTH CENTURY AND THE REACTION TO GROTIUS

JAMES K. CAMERON

(St. Andrews)

In recent years considerable attention has been given by English historians, predominantly political writers, to the role of apocalypticism in both the sixteenth and seventeenth centuries. Particularly significant works are, Christopher Hill, *Antichrist in Seventeenth century England*, Oxford 1971, Bernard S. Capp, *The Fifth Monarchy Men: a study in 17th century millenarianism*, London 1972, William Lamont, *Godly Rule: Politics and Religion 1603–1660*, London 1969, and a collection of essays edited by Peter Toon, *Puritan Millenarianism and the Future of Israel; Puritan Eschatology 1600 to 1660*, Cambridge and London 1970. One of the most important recent studies is that of Katharine R. Firth, *The Apocalyptic Tradition in Reformation Britain 1530–1655*, Oxford 1979. English apocalyptic exegesis is the subject of a well researched study by Richard Bauckham, *Tudor Apocalypse*, The Courtnay Library of Reformed Classics, Appleforth 1978. With the exception of Dr. Firth, modern historical and theological scholars have paid little or no attention to the contribution made by Scottish writers, although some of them make reference to John Napier's *A Plaine Discovery of the whole Revelation of Saint John*, first published in Edinburgh in 1593[1] and to King James VI's *Ane Fruitful Meditatioun on Rev. 20, 7–10*, published in Edinburgh in 1588.[2] In this essay attention is concentrated on Napier's work, internationally well known in his day[3] and on the less well known theological commentary by the Scottish divine, James Durham (1622–1658), first published in 1658.[4]

Napier's work appeared toward the end of a period of concentration on Protestant apocalyptic thought and at the beginning of opposition to it set out primarily by Hugo Grotius[5] on the conti-

---

[1] W.A. JACKSON – F.S. FERGUSON – K.F. PANTZER (edd.), *A Short-Title Catalogue of Books Printed in England, Scotland and Ireland, 1475–1640*, London 1976[2], no. 18354.

[2] *Ibid.*, no. 14376; also printed in *The Works of ... Prince James*, London 1616.

[3] FIRTH, *The Apocalyptic Tradition*, p. 132 described it as "In Scotland, easily the most important contribution to the apocalyptic tradition provoked into print by the Armada and succeeding events."

[4] D. WING (ed.), *Short-Title Catalogue of Books Printed in England, Scotland, Ireland and Wales, 1641–1770*, New York 1972[2], vol. I, no. 2805.

[5] Grotius' interpretation is set out in his *Annotatationes in Apocalypsin*; see *OTh* II/2, pp. 1158 ff.

nent and Henry Hammond[6] in England. Durham's work, published almost half a century later, shows a considerable awareness of the European corpus of writings on the subject and in it he acknowledged his debt to earlier writers as well as setting out his disagreements with them. He did not, however, cite Napier and his discussion of Grotius and Hammond is brief and confined to the final section of his concluding synopsis. The dates within which Dr. Firth confined her study precluded her from dealing with James Durham's commentary.

Renowned as a mathematician and as the inventor of Logarithmic Tables, John Napier of Merchiston[7] devoted over a number of years considerable attention, skill, and ingenuity to the interpretation of the prophetic content of the Book of Revelation. His interest in the subject had, he acknowledged, been aroused while he was a student at St. Andrews in the early 1560s, where he had attended the sermons of Christopher Goodman (c. 1520–1603), one of the earliest protestant ministers in the city and one who had been strongly influenced by Swiss Protestantism. Napier had originally intended to publish his study in Latin, but in 1588 decided to present it to the public in English; his reasons are set out in his dedication to King James and in his address to his readers. The Book of Revelation, with its prophecy of the destruction of the "Antichristian seate, citie, and kingdom" had, he maintained, been directed to the kings of the earth, just as the writings of the Old Testament prophets had been directed to the rulers in their day in order that they might hold their commonwealth in good order.[8] It was undoubtedly the stressing of a contemporary relevance that largely accounted for its widespread popularity immediately on publication and in the following century. Three editions were printed in Scotland, in 1593, 1611, and 1645; two were printed in London, in 1594 and 1611. It was translated into Dutch and published at Middelburg in 1600 and 1607. A French translation was published at La Rochelle in 1602 and three times thereafter, in 1612, 1615, and 1627. A translation into German was published four times in rapid

---

[6] Hammond's interpretation is set out in his "Interpretation of the Apocalypse" in *A Paraphrase and Annotations upon ... the New Testament*, London 1675[4], pp. 855 ff.

[7] See MARK NAPIER, *Memoirs of John Napier of Merchiston, His Lineage, Life and Times, with a History of the Invention of Logarithms*, Edinburgh and London 1834; *DNB*, vol. XVI, pp. 255 f.; HEW SCOTT (ed.), *Fasti Ecclesiae Scoticanae*, New Edition, Edinburgh 1915, vol. III, p. 456.

[8] JOHN NAPIER, *A Plaine Discovery*, A3–7; see also FIRTH, *The Apocalyptic Tradition*, pp. 132–38.

succession, in 1611, 1612, 1615 and 1627. In all the work with some additions by the translators was published in the original English and in translation sixteen times.[9]

The immediate reason for its appearance in English was Napier's awareness of the intense national fear of the resurgence of the power of Roman Catholicism from the 1580s onwards. Despite the defeat of the Armada in 1588, a constant and deeply felt fear of a Spanish invasion of the country persisted, a fear that was nurtured from time to time by the apparent leniency of the King towards pro-Catholic sections of the nobility and his own predilection to include known crypto-Catholics and Catholic sympathisers in his political administration. Napier pleads with the King to reform his house, his court, and indeed the entire country as the great day of universal destruction of the antichristian seat of Rome, as prophesied in Revelation, chapter 17, is awaited. Indeed, he is convinced that the discovery, or rather the uncovering, of the antichristian and papistical kingdom, is the primary significance of this book, which had been especially written for "our age."[10]

The commentary is divided into two distinct parts. In the first — a series of propositions — he provides an analysis of the book that is clearly determined by Ramist method, and discusses the interpretation of the days, weeks and years. In this he follows several earlier writers from a wide ranging study that includes Philip Melanchthon, John Carion, and Joseph Justus Scaliger. He claims that it is possible to construct the main events in the church's history from the time of Christ's baptism down to the day of the last judgment. According to his calculations this event is to take place sometime between 1688 and 1700.[11] The second and principal part of the commentary contains a chapter by chapter, verse by verse commentary arranged in parallel columns, one of which sets out what the author describes as "the historical application." On this matter the reader is referred to Dr. Firth's detailed study, in which she writes:

> "When Napier applied his own particular reading of Ramist method to the text and found in the text itself propositions that resembled the old practice of conjecture, he brought to this practice the authority it

[9] For details see JOHN NAPIER, *Construction of the wonderful canon of logarithms*, which contains "A Catalogue of the various editions of Napier's works" by WILLIAM RAE MACDONALD, Edinburgh 1889, pp. 109–28. FIRTH, *The Apocalyptic Tradition*, p. 149, states that it gained its widest audience in the 1640s when it was abridged and reissued as *Napier's Narration*, London 1643, and *A Bloody Almanack*, London 1647.

[10] NAPIER, *A Plaine Discovery*, p. 75; FIRTH, *The Apocalyptic Tradition*, pp. 138 ff.

[11] For an exposition and discussion of Napier's chronological identifications see further FIRTH, *The Apocalyptic Tradition*, pp. 139 ff.

had lacked. If one accepts his propositions and follows his argument to the construction of a schema of world history, it is hard not to be persuaded also that his predictions carried an element of truth."[12]

How then does Napier understand the promised millennium? Despite the care which he has taken throughout his study to arrive at precise temporal interpretations, he does not follow this practice in interpreting "the thousand years of the great sabbath." Aware, as Dr. Firth remarks, of "the dangers of being classed as one of the millenarians" he goes out of his way to refute them. The period of "one thousand years" is "to be understood spiritually."[13] Thus, he maintained against the chiliasts and millenarians that the saints shall reign with Christ "for ever and ever." The millennium represents eternity and to take the term literally is to fall into error.[14]

In the matter of the understanding of the last judgment Napier also exercises an element of caution. The precise day and hour must remain unknown. It may be later than he had deduced or it may even be much earlier, as early as the year 1600. What he had to say of its nature is also noteworthy. Although he accepted the doctrine of election, he saw the need to attempt to reconcile the teaching of St. Paul with that of St. James. When Paul stated that we are saved by faith and not by works of the law, that, he claimed, did not mean without good works. Rather did Paul mean that we are justified by a lively faith with such good works as our weak nature will allow faith to produce. "We are justified," he wrote, "by fruitful faith or faith that produces works," for "a working faith and faithful works are inseparable."[15]

For Napier the Book of Revelation was essentially one of warning and especially of comfort for believers. Chapter 21 promises "The end of all miseries" and "yieldeth comfortable occasion to all God's servants, to endure patiently temporal and definite troubles, knowing that now shall follow the reward of infinite and eternal felicitie."[16] This is in line with his confident understanding of the Apocalypse as a prophecy of the imminent downfall and destruction of the enemies of the Gospel.

Between the publication of Napier's commentary in 1593 and that of Durham in 1658 the political and to some extent the theological scene in Scotland, had considerably altered. Protestantism was

---

[12] FIRTH, *The Apocalyptic Tradition*, p. 146.
[13] NAPIER, *A Plaine Discovery*, p. 235.
[14] The subject is briefly discussed by FIRTH, *The Apocalyptic Tradition*, p. 149.
[15] NAPIER, *A Plaine Discovery*, pp. 242 ff.
[16] NAPIER, *A Plaine Discovery*, p. 269.

more than ever deeply entrenched in the life of the nation although matters of ecclesiastical polity were far from settled. In these latter affairs Durham had not taken a leading role and was highly respected on both sides.[17] After undergoing his initial university education at St. Andrews he returned to his home and only later concentrated his attention on theology and entered the ministry of the church. For a time he was Professor of Divinity at the University of Glasgow and subsequently one of the ministers of the city. His theological publications are considerable, among which the extensive commentary on the Book of Revelation is the most significant.[18] In it he writes primarily as a dogmatic and practical theologian. Unlike many early Protestant reformers and theologians, Durham had a high regard for the Apocalypse. "It had," he maintained, "been written for the benefit of the church and ought to be welcomed thankfully."[19] He did not, however, allow the later Protestant interpretation of the book as intimating the imminent destruction of the antichristian, i.e., Roman, church to dominate his thinking. Originally composed as a series of lectures for the benefit of his congregation and his students, his commentary was intended to secure them in their faith and build them up in their spiritual lives. On the basis of the scriptural text he seeks to extract and develop practical lessons for his contemporaries.

In discussing, for example, the early chapters, which he believes to have been written by John for the benefit of the church in his own day, he stresses the importance of good government in the church and the need to exercise a rigorous discipline. Whenever he thinks it necessary to deal more at length with a dogmatic or a contemporary practical topic, he, in the manner of the mediaeval commentator, appends a dissertation, on that topic. For example chapters 2 and 3 provide the opportunity for a long discourse on church government and discipline.[20] The letters to the various churches in Asia Minor, he sees as providing an opportunity to expound the fundamentals of presbyterian church government.[21] Such dissertations, which appear at frequent intervals, virtually comprise when

---

[17] See further *DNB*, vol. XVI, pp. 255 f.

[18] See G. CHRISTIE, "A Bibliography of James Durham", in *Papers of the Edinburgh Bibliographical Society, 1922–1920*, Edinburgh 1921, pp. 37 ff. Durham's commentary was published in Scotland in 1658, 1680 (twice), 1739, 1764, 1788 and 1799; it was printed in Amsterdam in 1660; see also WING, *Short-Title Catalogue*, vol. I, nos. 2805–09. References in this paper are to the edition published in Glasgow in 1764.

[19] JAMES DURHAM, *A Commentary upon the Book of the Revelation*, p. 50.

[20] DURHAM, *A Commentary*, pp. 91–120.

[21] DURHAM, *A Commentary*, pp. 191–249.

added together a remarkable corpus of protestant dogmatic theology.

When dealing with what he regards as the "properly prophetical"[22] parts of the book, chapter 6 and following, he largely follows traditional contemporary protestant exegesis and emphasises the providence of God in all that concerns his church, especially in coping with all the troubles that have arisen from the activity of heathen and heretical forces. Unlike Napier, he is not specially interested in detailed calculations, yet he does recognise three explicatory prophesies. First, chapters 12, 13 and 14 describe the rise, reign, and ruin of the rule of Antichrist, which has already begun. Second, Chapters 17, 18 and 19, are concerned with a "particular explication" of that ruin. Third, chapters 20, 21 and 22 describe the happy estate of the church here and hereafter.[23] Durham acknowledges a remarkable agreement between the prophesies and the events of the church's history, of which he has a detailed knowledge from a variety of sources, but he does so primarily to derive practical lessons for his own day. For the church he foresees no temporal peace or millenarian kingdom altogether free from suffering before the great day of judgment, which is the day of redemption from those sufferings.[24] The happiness of God's people and the evidence of God's love for them does not consist in outward things. Their lot is more often one of suffering.[25] A flourishing Gospel must expect to be persecuted.[26] Much of what has happened in the history of the church had been foretold by John, but that is no ground for anyone indulging in prophesy in this day. The gift has ceased with the closing of the biblical canon. Yet that does not mean that God may not sometime reveal himself to some individual in order to foretell events before they come to pass. In illustration he cites some examples from early church history and includes from later periods John Hus, whom he regards as having foretold the coming of the Reformation. But this type of prophesy is in the nature of a "discerning of God's mind" and is properly one of the primary functions of the church's ministry.[27] Interpreting with any degree of specificity the times and seasons given in the Book of Revelation is neither edifying nor necessary. He notes that many have taken the one thousand years in chapter 20 literally and inter-

---

22 DURHAM, *A Commentary*, pp. 282 ff.
23 DURHAM, *A Commentary*, p. 341.
24 DURHAM, *A Commentary*, p. 385.
25 DURHAM, *A Commentary*, p. 375.
26 DURHAM, *A Commentary*, p. 364.
27 DURHAM, *A Commentary*, pp. 484 ff.

preted the period of 1260 days as so many years, but sees no justification for so doing.[28] He is, nevertheless not always consistent in such matters, as he agrees with Napier that the absolute tyranny of the Antichrist began to fall about 1559.[29]

How then does Durham interpret the millennium in chapter 20. He admits that there are difficulties, but essentially he sees it as marking the end of all the church's troubles. The period of one thousand years takes place on earth, but not immediately before the last judgment. It does not refer to a good condition of the church militant or to a period "absolute either for holiness, purity, peace, or length of time, while believers here reign in the world." It is not a period marked by an absolute freedom from suffering. "Whatever it be, it is not literally to be understood or properly as the words sound, but figuratively and spiritually." Words such as "souls sitting and reigning with Christ" cannot but be understood as figurative language.[30] Scripture promises no earthly temporal kingdom to Christ's saints, rather does it warn them always to be looking for the cross and affliction. A spiritual, not a temporal, kingdom has been promised, like the one which Christ himself exercised on earth. Any idea that Christ would come personally to earth, any idea that all the martyrs and saints would reign one thousand years before the general resurrection is totally rejected. Like Napier he too is anxious to disassociate himself from the millenarians, and consequently he rejects on these matters Irenaeus, Justin Martyr, and Lactantius among the ancients, and Piscator, Alsted, Archer and Patrick Forbes among the moderns. One should, however, stress his own particular positive teaching on the millennium.[31]

Durham interprets the one thousand years as referring to a flourishing and good condition for some time of the church militant. This period is recognisable by six distinguishing marks. 1. The pure preaching of the word and the administration of the sacraments or ordinances; 2. The power of such ministrations on believers to enable them to lead good lives. 3. An abundance of believers. 4. A visible, bold, public profession of faith, expressed in worship and discipline. 5. Outward freedom. 6. Length of time and good conditions.[32] This does not, however, amount to an absolute or uninterrupted period of freedom, of superiority in either temporal or

---

[28] DURHAM, *A Commentary*, p. 494.

[29] DURHAM, *A Commentary*, p. 511; NAPIER, *A Plaine Discovery*, pp. 62 ff and 148 f.; FIRTH, *The Apocalyptic Tradition*, pp. 144 ff.

[30] DURHAM, *A Commentary*, pp. 720 ff.

[31] DURHAM, *A Commentary*, pp. 723 f.

[32] DURHAM, *A Commentary*, pp. 724 ff.

spiritual privilege. As has been noted he considers that there are no grounds for expecting the Lord's personal, visible presence on earth, but rather a presence of the Spirit and its power in his ordinances with his saints living on earth, that is to say with the members of the church militant. The one thousand years thus signify a long time and a prosperous condition. Where days and years and months are mentioned no sound interpreter can take them literally. Indeed the church has already entered on this period, for it is "neither fully past nor yet fully to come."[33]

Durham's work was written towards the end of a century of intensive study of the Book of Revelation, particularly by protestants, but not exclusively so. Much of that material he had studied, as well as that of earlier writers and from time to time he discusses their interpretations with great respect, even when he considers it necessary to disagree. Among those to whom he specifically refers, apart from some writers mentioned above, are included Carion, Alsted, Foxe, Mede, Ussher and Patrick Forbes. He does not refer to the Geneva Bible to which he is indebted, nor, as has been said, does he cite Napier, although he was undoubtedly influenced by him. As was noted at the outset of this essay, he does not mention his rejection of Grotius, whom he links with Hammond, until he has reached his concluding synopsis.[34]

Durham's main objection to both of these contemporary interpreters is the fact that their exposition is different in character, to say the least, from what he regards as the true scope of the book, and not just in the interpretation of one vision or one prophecy. Throughout it is opposed to that of orthodox writers, even to that of papists. Nevertheless he admits there may be some who, when they have read what Grotius and Hammond have written and what others have written, and then compared both groups with the scriptural text, will require further help in order to see just how far out of harmony with the text are these new interpreters. Those with such a need, however, Durham confesses he would be unable to satisfy.[35]

The scope of the Book of Revelation is, as far as he is concerned, to set forth things that are to come in the future, things that belong to the church and Christ's servants, as is made clear in the inscription to the readers. These things include the confirmation of

---

[33] DURHAM, *A Commentary*, p. 736.
[34] DURHAM, *A Commentary*, pp. 794–98.
[35] DURHAM, *A Commentary*, p. 797.

the trials of the church from enemies within, such as the defection of some from the church, and especially the great defection of the Antichrist, of which so much is spoken in Scripture. The Apocalypse sets out the condition of the church under these trials. It is useful to its members in that it prophesies that they are blessed in such circumstances, even in his own day. It concludes with the last judgment, the condemnation of the reprobate and the glorification of the elect, and the promises of the last coming.[36] For Durham, Grotius and Hammond render all of these promises ineffectual when they say that the Book refers to things that are soon to happen and cite as their defence the phrase in chapter 1 verse 1 that states that "these things must shortly come to pass." Their interpretation of these words is the basis of all their teaching, yet Durham believes that they do not support this inference any more than the scriptural phrase "I come quickly" refers to a sudden, imminent return of Christ. Further he maintains that their interpretation is inconsistent·with what they later write in their exposition of Gog and Magog in chapter 20 as referring to the Turks. Both writers also maintain that the Apocalypse refers to civil events in the Roman Empire or events concerning the Jews, and not directly with events in the life of the church. They make no mention of spiritual enemies and heretics. What offended Durham most, however, was the fact that "there is not one word of Antichrist in it all, nor of the Pope of Rome."[37] Further – and this he regards as even more surprising – they date the one thousand years from the time of Constantine and reckon that the church has enjoyed peace throughout that time, except during the brief reign of the Emperor Julian. The fact that they consider that the church enjoyed uninterrupted peace, apart from those years and without enemies is unacceptable. Durham also maintains that the referring of the two witnesses in chapter 11 to the two bishops of the Jews and of the Gentiles at Jerusalem is without any foundation in history.[38] On account of these and such like matters Grotius and Hammond's conclusions are rejected, one might say out of hand.

It is a matter of regret that Durham did not attempt to deal more seriously with Grotius' exegesis. In no way can it be considered that he attempted a scholarly refutation. The two commentators were on entirely different wave-lengths, and their basic point of depar-

---

[36] DURHAM, *A Commentary*, pp. 797 f.
[37] DURHAM, *A Commentary*, p. 798.
[38] DURHAM, *A Commentary*, p. 798.

ture was different. Grotius, the Christian humanist and irenicist, was employing his skill as an historian and as a philological exegete to the interpretation of an ancient text. Durham, on the other hand, was a dogmatic theologian expounding an inspired text that for him contained the Word of God for his people and especially for his own day.

GROTIUS' VIEWS ON ANTICHRIST AND APOCALYPTIC THOUGHT IN ENGLAND[1]

JOHANNES VAN DEN BERG
(Leiden)

In a recent essay, Hugh Trevor-Roper depicts Grotius' attitude towards England as a love-affair, "a platonic love for an idealized England."[2] In many respects it was love on both sides, as appears in the field of theology: while Grotius sympathized with the theological climate of the Church of England (or rather with the ideal image he had formed of the *Ecclesia Anglicana*), quite a number of Anglicans highly esteemed him for his moderate and latitudinarian way of thinking. On the English side, however, the esteem was not unmixed: even in the circle of those who to a large extent sympathized with Grotius' theological approach there was criticism with regard to his interpretation of the figure of Antichrist. On this point, the ways sometimes parted.

Sixteenth and early seventeenth century Protestantism, however much divided on many theological and ecclesiastical issues, was marked by a broad consensus regarding the mysterious words in I John 2.18: "Little children, it is the last time: and as ye have heard that antichrist shall come, even now there are many antichrists."[3] In this context, II Thessalonians 2.3–4 also played an important part: "Let no man deceive you by any means; for that day shall not come, except there come a falling away first, and that man of sin is revealed, the son of perdition, who opposeth and exalteth himself above all that is called God, or that is worshipped; so that he as God sitteth in the temple of God, shewing himself that he is God." Furthermore, Antichrist and 'the man of sin' were often equated with the 'beast' of the Apocalypse with seven heads and ten horns, "and upon his heads the name of blasphemy" (Rev. 13.1). It is clear that the image of the 'beast' harks back to pre-Christian Jewish thought, as it is expressed in the prophecies of Daniel, where a 'beast' is depicted as speaking great words against the most High, and wearing out the saints of the most High, and thinking to change times and laws (Dan. 13.7). As we shall see, in the period of

---

[1] I thank Dr. N.E. Emerton, Cambridge, for her willingness to correct the English text.
[2] "Hugo Grotius and England," in HUGH TREVOR-ROPER, *From Counter-Reformation to Glorious Revolution*, London 1992, p. 47.
[3] Here, as elsewhere, I quote the *Authorized Version* (1611).

the Reformation these texts were generally projected upon the Pope or rather upon the papacy as an institution which manifested itself as 'antichristian.'

The 'papal' interpretation was not an invention of the Reformers: it occurred already in the later Middle Ages in heretical circles.[4] There is, however, a not inconsiderable difference between the late-medieval and the Protestant identification of the Pope with Antichrist. While certain medieval groups could see one specific Pope as Antichrist because his life and attitude were in radical conflict with the demands of the Gospel, the Reformers tended to identify the institution of the papacy with Antichrist. They saw the papacy as a manifestation of the spirit of Antichrist: it defended and maintained false doctrines which ran counter to the pure message of the Bible as it had been rediscovered by the Reformation, and it persecuted those who wanted to return to the pure and undiluted doctrine of the primitive church. When in Protestant circles 'the Pope' was denounced as Antichrist, the identification had not primarily a personal and incidental meaning; it was a pronouncement of an essentially theological nature, directed against an institution which was structurally and fundamentally evil, though of course the boundary-line between the personal and the structural aspects was sometimes blurred. Indignation at the persecution of the 'true believers' could lead to an identification of the person of the Pope with Antichrist.

Among the prominent Reformers, Luther was the first who used the term 'Antichrist' in connection with the Pope – explicitly in his reaction to his excommunication in 1520: *Adversus execrabilem Antichristi bullam*. In this context, Hans Hillerbrand remarks: "Luther's blunt identification of Pope and Antichrist constituted the watershed in the early Reformation controversy... The concept of the Antichrist was ... whatever it was theologically, a propaganda tool employed to repudiate the papacy in the strongest way possible."[5] There is with Luther a sideline: he saw the Turk or Saracen as a

---

[4] For the interpretation of the figure of Antichrist in the Middle Ages, see HANS PREUSS, *Die Vorstellungen vom Antichrist im späteren Mittelalter, bei Luther und in der konfessionellen Polemik*, Leipzig 1906, pp. 4–82; NORMAN COHN, *The Pursuit of the Millennium* (1957), London 1970; MARJORIE REEVES, *Joachim of Fiore and the Prophetic Future*, London 1976; RICHARD K. EMMERSON, *Antichrist in the Middle Ages*, Manchester 1981; furthermore GUSTAV ADOLF BENRATH's contribution to the article "Antichrist" in *TRE* 3 (1978), pp. 20–50.

[5] H.J. HILLERBRAND, "The Antichrist in the Early German Reformation: Reflections on Theology and Propaganda," in A.C. FIX – SUSAN C. KARANT-NUNN, *Germania Illustrata. Essays ... presented to Gerald Strauss* [Sixteenth Century Essays and Studies XVIII], Ann Arbor 1992, pp. 16 f.

minor Antichrist, but in the full sense the Pope was Antichrist, because he was active as persecutor of Christ within the church.[6] We meet the same identification between Pope and Antichrist with the other Reformers. Melanchthon wrote about the necessity to counteract the Pope "tamquam Antichristo,"[7] and Calvin described the Pope as the leader and head of the impious and execrable kingdom of Antichrist.[8] This view remained a constant element in the Protestant tradition. In the marginal notes to the Dutch 'States' translation,'[9] which first appeared in 1637, three years before Grotius' *Commentatio ad loca quaedam N. Testamenti quae de Antichristo agunt, aut agere putantur*[10] was published anonymously in Amsterdam, the 'Beast' or 'Antichrist' was identified as a long succession of persons who tried to suppress the true doctrine of Christ and his church. He would give himself splendid and alluring titles, such as 'Holy Father' and 'Vicar of Christ.' Some Popes could be singled out as pre-eminent representatives of the spirit of Antichrist, such as Gregory VII, no doubt primarily because of his affirmation of the doctrine of transubstantiation.[11] The 'Beast' and the 'False Prophet' signified the spiritual and worldly dominion of Antichrist "with all its mitred and armed substitutes."[12]

Similar notions prevailed in English Protestant circles.[13] The idea that the papal power was a manifestation of the spirit of Antichrist was a common opinion not only with puritanically-minded authors such as John Foxe (1516–1587), the martyrologist, but also with middle-of-the-road Anglicans such as the famous apologist Bishop John Jewel (1522–1571). The theme returns with seventeenth-century Anglican millenarians, of whom the Cambridge theologian Joseph Mede (1586–1638) is one of the most outstanding representa-

---

[6] GOTTFRIED SEEBASS, "Antichrist," *TRE* 3, p. 30.

[7] PREUSS, *Die Vorstellungen vom Antichrist*, p. 203.

[8] *Institutio religionis christianae* IV, VII, 25.

[9] In the Commonwealth period they were translated by Theodore Haak (one of the founders of the Royal Society) at the request of the Westminster Assembly: *The Dutch Annotations upon the whole Bible, together with, and according to their verse translation of all the text*, London 1657.

[10] *BG* no. 1100.

[11] *The Heidelberg Catechism* (1563) described the Mass, founded as it was on this doctrine, as a "damnable idolatry" (Answer 80).

[12] See the marginal notes to 2 Thess. 2.3; 1 John 2.18; Rev. 17.4; 20.8 and other places.

[13] For this, see in particular CHRISTOPHER HILL, *Antichrist in Seventeenth-Century England*, Oxford 1971; RICHARD BAUCKHAM, *Tudor Apocalypse*, Appleford [1978]; PAUL CHRISTIANSON, *Reformers and Babylon: English apocalyptic visions from the reformation to the eve of the civil war*, Toronto etc. 1978; KATHERINE R. FIRTH, *The Apocalyptic Tradition in Reformation Britain*, Oxford 1979.

tives; the scheme, which he expounded in his *Clavis Apocalyptica* (1627) and his *In Sancti Joannis Apocalypsis Commentarius* (1632) became the basis for practically all later apocalyptic and millenarian speculations in the English-speaking world. Mede was a consistent futurist: though he did not speculate on the exact date of the millennium, he expected the dawn of the thousand years of peace, predicted in Revelation 20, within a not too distant future. There is a connection between his (traditionally Protestant) conception of Antichrist and his millennial views: the fall of Antichrist (*i.e.* the ultimate defeat of the 'Roman' power) would ring in the millennium.[14]

As Christopher Hill points out, in the mid-thirties it had suddenly become unfashionable and unpopular to say that the Pope was Antichrist. A number of 'Laudians' – followers or supporters of William Laud, the 'Arminian' theologian who in 1633 became Archbishop of Canterbury and who, accused of treason and 'Popery,' was executed in 1645 – objected to a too easy identification between Pope and Antichrist. At his trial, Laud declared: "No man can challenge me that I hold the Pope not to be Antichrist; it is a great question even among learned protestants whether he be so or not."[15] His irenic attitude towards the Church of Rome was indeed one of the factors, if not the main factor, which led to his tragic fate. On this point, he fundamentally differed from Mede, who in spite of his tolerant and latitudinarian frame of mind was uncompromising in his anti-Roman demeanour. This is the reason why Mede, though he cannot be considered a Puritan, received posthumous recognition in the Commonwealth period. A first edition of his (largely unpublished) *Works* appeared in 1648. The third edition (1672) contains an anonymous 'Life,' probably written by John Worthington, the learned theologian who between 1650 and 1660 was Master of Jesus College, Cambridge and who in many ways was a kindred spirit. According to the 'Life,' Mede constantly asserted,

> That the *Great Apostasie* or *Antichristianism* did (as to one main part thereof) consist in *Spiritual Fornication* or *Idolatry*. Nor need any *Protestant* be disturb'd at the word *Antichristian* or *Antichrist*, so frequently used by our Author [Mede] when he had to doe with the *Roman* Polity and the Chief thereof...

---

[14] For his millenarianism and that of his pupil Henry More (to be mentioned below), see J. VAN DEN BERG, "Continuity within a changing context: Henry More's millenarianism, seen against the background of the millenarian concepts of Joseph Mede," in *Pietismus und Neuzeit* 14, Göttingen 1988, pp. 185–202.

[15] HILL, *Antichrist*, pp. 39 f.

Mede, the 'Life' continues, was well aware that the Antichrist or Antichrists mentioned in St. John's Epistles might primarily respect some impostors, who began to appear in the world about the end of the Jewish State, but he thought that what was said of those Antichrists might interpretatively (though not explicitly and directly) be applied to "that *Fatal and Great Apostasie* which was to surprise the Church"; to him of whom those other Antichrists were in some sense "Figures or Forerunners."

> For this was his Notion in this particular, He that sets up and substitutes in the room of *Christ* Saints and Angels, as so many Mediatours between us and God, (agreeably to the practice of the Heathens, who of old set up *Daemons* as Agents between the Sovereign Gods and Men,) *eo ipso negat Jesum esse Christum...*

Mede was not "fondly addicted" to the use of the word Antichrist. He also made use of other forms of speech, suggested to him from the style of that "Mysterious book," the Apocalypse, such as *"Bestia Bicornis, Pseudo-propheta Romanus, Meretrix Babylonica, Regnum Pontificale* etc." Yet "withall he was not so weakly nice, as wholly to decline that word [Antichrist] in his Apocalyptick labours."

The author of the 'Life' emphasizes that in this he was in line with the Anglican tradition. Archbishop Whitgift had, when he answered for the degree of D.D., defended the thesis: *Papa est ille Antichristus.* And Bishop Andrewes, "his ancient and constant friend," had stated that

> by *Babylon* in *Apocal.* chap. 17 and chap. 18, is meant, *non Roma Ethnica, sed Antichristiana;* and withall evinces the vanity of that poor subterfuge, (and yet made use of (as that other also of *Roma Ethnica*) by *H. Grotius* in his Annotations), That by the *Destruction of Babylon* there foretold is to be understood the *Burning of Rome* by the Goths and Vandals about the year 455. As afterwards he makes it clear that *Idolatry* ... is justly charged upon the *Roman* Church...[16]

The 'Life' of Mede was written at a time when the views of Grotius were well known in England. Though some of the Laudians had already called into question the traditional interpretation of Antichrist, Grotius' explicit rejection of the Protestant consensus was a shock to the great majority of English Protestants. Katherine Firth remarks:

> Grotius had done what seemed impossible to most Protestants – he had dispensed not only with the idea that the Revelation comprehended the history of the Church from Christ to the second coming

---

[16] *The Works of The Pious and Profoundly-Learned Joseph Mede, B.D.,* London 1672, pp. XXVI f. For Whitgift, the 'Life' refers to Whitgift's 'Life' by Sir George Paule (1609); for Andrewes to his *Tortura Torti* (1609), pp. 183; 188.

but also with the identification of the Roman papacy with Antichrist. This struck at the heart of the Protestant apocalyptic tradition.[17]
Grotius' *Commentatio ... de Antichristo,* which was published in 1640, two years after the death of Mede, appeared (as we saw) anonymously; at Grotius' own request, "ut quam minimo cum praejudicio legeretur."[18] Apparently, Grotius feared that the *Commentatio* would meet with strong opposition. His fears were not unfounded: in the same year appeared a refutation by Samuel Maresius, at that time professor at the 'Illustrious School' of Bois-le-Duc, later professor of theology at the University of Groningen: *Dissertatio de Antichristo;*[19] from the full title it becomes clear that Maresius was aware of Grotius' authorship.[20] In 1641 Grotius answered, now under his own name, in his *Appendix ad interpretationem locorum N. Testamenti quae de Antichristo agunt.* In his exegesis of the relevant texts he gave a historical explanation. He identified "the man of sin," "the son of perdition" of II Thessalonians 2.3 with the Emperor Caligula ('Cajus'), "that Wicked" in the same chapter (vs. 8) with Simon Magus (Acts 8.9–25) and "Antichrist" (I John 2.18) with the pseudo-Messiah Barkochba. The blasphemous Beast which rose up out of the sea represented the idolatry of heathen Rome (Rev. 13.1; "ex mari" is "ex populo Romano"), while "the great whore that sitteth upon many waters" (Rev. 17.1) was equally identified with "Roma gentilis."[21] The indefatigable Maresius, with whom Grotius had rather haughtily dealt in his *Appendix,*[22] reacted in a lengthy work: *Concordia discors et Antichristus revelatus. Id est Ill. Viri Hugonis Grotii Apologia pro Papa et Papismo* (2 vols., 1642). The sub-title reveals the core of the controversy. Maresius's accusation that Grotius' publications on 'Antichrist' were an apology for the Pope and for the 'papal' church was unfair. It is clear, however, that there was a connection between Grotius' irenicism and his view of Antichrist: "... eorum qui schisma esse perpetuum volunt, qui ad ipsum unitatis Ecclesiae ac concordiae nomen confremissent, interest Papam credi Antichristum."[23]

---

[17] FIRTH, *The Apocalyptic Tradition,* p. 246.
[18] *BG* p. 542.
[19] For this and what follows, see D. NAUTA, *Samuel Maresius,* Amsterdam 1935, pp. 168–72.
[20] Cf. *BG* p. 542.
[21] *OTh* III, pp. 458, 466, 471 ff., 490. See also the 'Annotationes' on the New Testament, *OTh* II/2, pp. 953 f., 113 f., 1200 f., 1214.
[22] He did not mention Maresius's name, but called him 'Borborita,' a contemptuous word which contained an allusion to the name of his opponent: Des Marets, 'of the bog'; see NAUTA, *Maresius,* p. 170 with reference to BAYLE's *Dictionnaire* III (ed. 1740), p. 323.
[23] "Appendix," *OTh* III, p. 475.

In Reformed circles in the Netherlands the idea that the Pope was Antichrist remained prevalent until far into the eighteenth century. Orthodox Lutherans, too, objected to Grotius' exegesis; thus the well-known polemicist Abraham Calovius tried to refute the "nugae Grotii de Caio" in his *Biblia Illustrata* (1676).[24] Even the Remonstrants did not follow Grotius: in his *Theologia Christiana* the leading Remonstrant theologian Philippus à Limborch defended the general opinion of the Reformers "per Antichristum designari Pontificem Romanum."[25]

In England Grotius was respected as a scholar, though even in the Laudian period, when the prevailing anti-Calvinist climate seemed favourable to the spread of his views, he did not meet with such response as he had hoped for. Laud was cautious and reserved, and Grotius' reputation was somewhat under a cloud, first because of the accusation of Socinianism, then because of his supposed 'popish' sympathies.[26] Still, his works were known and read. *De satisfactione Christi* (1617) was published in Oxford in 1636; *De veritate religionis Christianae* (1627) in 1639.[27] In the Commonwealth period his works seem to have been easily available. When in 1653 a friend of Richard Baxter complained that he had not been able to find the works of Grotius (and those of Du Plessis-Mornay and Cameron) in a Westminster library, Baxter wrote back: "Whereas you say that your library has not Grotius, Camero or Mornay, I answer they are common bookes as most in the shops."[28] In 1660 the *Commentatio* was published in England in the seventh volume of the *Critici Sacri*,[29] and thus within easy reach of scholars in the Universities.

Grotius had his critics, but also his supporters. One of the most outspoken among them was the Anglican theologian Henry Hammond (1605–1660), a Laudian, though not extreme.[30] He was on

---

[24] A. CALOVIUS, *Biblia Novi Testamenti Illustrata* II, Dresdae et Lipsiae 1719, pp. 901–18; cf. 1616 ff, 1624, 1841–59, 1880–96. In his criticism of Grotius, Calovius follows Maresius. See also PREUSS, *Die Vorstellungen vom Antichrist*, p. 265 n. 1.

[25] *Theologia Christiana ad praxin pietatis ac promotionem pacis Christianae unice directa,* Amstelaedami 1686, p. 833; cf. liber VII, cap. XII (pp. 841–45): "Examen sententiae H. Grotii de Antichristo."

[26] TREVOR-ROPER, "Hugo Grotius and England," pp. 70 f.

[27] *BG* nos. 925; 948.

[28] Baxter to Abraham Pinchbecke, 26 August 1653: N.H. KEEBLE – GEOFFREY F. NUTTALL, *Calendar of the Correspondence of Richard Baxter* I, Oxford 1991, nos. 127; 129.

[29] *BG* nos. 1142; 1143.

[30] See JOHN W. PACKER, *The Transformation of Anglicanism 1643–1660 with special reference to Henry Hammond,* Manchester 1969.

friendly terms with the Calvinist primate of Ireland James Ussher;
also with Baxter, who wrote: "I took the Death of Dr. Hammond
... just when the King came in [at his return from the Continent]
for a very great loss; for his Piety and Wisdom would sure have
hindred much of the Violence which after followed."[31] Hammond
was an admirer of Grotius. In a treatise on the Epistles of Ignatius
and the doctrine of episcopacy (1655) he inserted "A digression
concerning some jealousies spread of Hugo Grotius":

> This very learned, pious, judicious man hath of late among many fal-
> len under a very unhappy fate, being most unjustly calumniated,
> sometimes as a *Socinian*, sometimes as a *Papist*, and as if he had learn-
> ed to reconcile *Contradictories*, or the most *distant extreams*...

Hammond defended him against both charges. He saw him as a
friend and admirer of the Church of England, who sought nothing
but "a universal reconciliation" of the church:

> ... all that this very learned man was guilty of in this matter, was but
> this, his passionate desire of the unity of the Church in the bands of
> peace and truth, and a full dislike of all uncharitable distempers, and
> impious doctrines... All which notwithstanding, the temper of that
> learned man was known to be such, as rendred him in a special man-
> ner a lover and admirer of the frame and moderation observed in our
> Church of *England*, as it stood (shaken, but not cast down) in his life
> time, desiring earnestly to live himself in the Communion of it, and
> to see it copied out by the rest of the world.[32]

Hammond's best known work is *A Paraphrase and Annotations upon all
the Books of the New Testament* (1653); it was several times reprinted
and it became a classic of seventeenth century Anglican theology.
In his introduction to the annotations upon the Apocalypse he
claimed his interpretation was original:

> And it has been matter of much satisfaction to me, that what hath
> upon sincere desire of finding out the truth, and making my addresses
> to God for his particular directions in this work of difficulty ... appeared
> to me to be the meaning of this prophesie, hath, for this main of it,
> in the same manner represented it self to several persons of great
> piety and learning (as since I have discerned) none taking it from the
> other, but all from the same light shining in the Prophecie it self.
> Among which number I now also find the most learned *Hugo Grotius*,
> in those *posthumous* notes of his on the *Apocalypse*, lately publish'd.[33]

---

[31] *Reliquiae Baxterianae*, London 1696, II, 208, § 66; quoted in KEEBLE – NUT-
TALL, *Calendar* I, no. 582 (see also no. 581).

[32] *The Works of ... Henry Hammond* II (sec. ed., London 1684), section II, pp. 45;
47.

[33] *Works* III, p. 861. One may wonder who were the other 'persons of great
piety and learning.' Hammond will not have meant Catholic authors such as Luis
de Alcazar, a strong opponent of the Protestant interpretation of Antichrist; rather
they were English Protestant theologians – perhaps Richard Montagu or Gilbert
Sheldon (see HILL, *Antichrist*, esp. pp. 33–40).

From the Puritan John Owen this elicited the sarcastic remark, transmitted to Hammond by one of Owen's correspondents, "that there are many complaine of your secret vain-glory, in seeking to disclaime the direction from H. Grotius in reference to your comment on the Revelation."[34] However this may be, it is clear that Grotius and Hammond used the same method in their interpretation of the Apocalypse. Hammond's approach to the mysteries of the Book of Revelation was historical and rational, in line with the general trend of his hermeneutics: "... the understanding the Word of God contain'd in the Scripture is no work of extraordinary Illumination, but must be attained by the same means, or the like, by which other writings of men are expounded..."[35] Of course he did not deny the presence of a prophetic element in the Apocalypse: it would be anachronistic to expect with him or with Grotius a historical-critical approach in the modern sense, but regarded from the vantage-point of the seventeenth century their views of "the thousand years" (Revelation 20.3) were 'preterist.' Those thousand years, Hammond remarked, noted "the tranquillity and freedom from persecutions that should be allowed the Church of Christ from the time of Constantines coming to the Empire."[36] In his interpretation of II Thessalonians 2.3 and 9 and I John 2.18 Hammond sees "the man of sin," "the son of perdition," "that Wicked" and "Antichrist" as the same person, Simon Magus – here slightly deviating from Grotius, who only identified "that Wicked" with Simon Magus; but the difference is not essential. "The Beast" of Revelation 13.1 denoted "the heathen worship, as it stood at Rome"; the "whore" or "harlot" of Revelation 17.1 "the imperial dignity of Rome."[37] Fundamentally, Hammond agreed with Grotius in his interpretation of Antichrist, though it did not detract from his Protestant convictions: in more than one writing he firmly defended the claims of the Church of England over against the 'Romanists.'

Not all Anglicans of the post-Restoration period were prepared to follow Grotius and Hammond in their approach to the Antichrist problem. The traditional interpretation was strongly defended by the Cambridge Platonist Henry More (1614–1687), a pupil of Mede and, like his teacher, a Fellow of Christ's College, Cam-

---

[34] PACKER, *The Transformation of Anglicanism*, p. 96.
[35] "A Postscript concerning New light or Divine Illumination," *Works* III, p. IX.
[36] *Works* III, p. 937.
[37] *Works* III, pp. 678–83, 825–29, 911–15, 927–31. Though in his interpretation of Antichrist Hammond concentrated on Simon Magus, he emphasized that 'man of sin' etc. "should signifie more than one single person, viz. Simon and the Gnosticks" (p. 680).

bridge. Though on some minor points he deviated from Mede, yet essentially he agreed with him in his interpretation of the Apocalypse.[38] Over against Grotius' method of interpretation he championed that of his revered teacher, and while he respected Grotius as a scholar, he was convinced that (for perhaps excusable reasons) the latter had not penetrated as deeply into the mysteries of the Book of Revelation as Mede had done:

> And because there does nothing so much counterbalance the weight of Mr. *Mede*'s Reasons as the Autority [*sic*] and Luster of that worthily-admired Name of the Learned *Hugo Grotius*, who has interpreted the Revelations to quite another Sense; (the ingenuities and prettinesses of whose expositions had almost imposed upon my self to a belief that there might be some Sense also of the Revelation as he drives at) to make all clear I shall take the pains of exhibiting both to the view of the Reader. Who I hope will not take it ill that so Pious, so Learned and Judicious a Person as Mr. *Mede*, and that in a matter to which he may seem to be peculiarly selected and set apart to by God and nature, to which he mainly applied himself with all possible Care, Seriousness and Devotion, should see further than *Hugo Grotius*, who has an ample Harvest of Praise from other performances, and who by reason of his Political Employments could not be so entirely vacant to the searching into so abstruse a Mystery.[39]

More's fundamental objection to a mainly historical approach of the Book of Revelation such as practiced by Grotius was of a hermeneutical nature: if Grotius were right, and if in consequence the Book of Revelation did not cover the whole development of human history, then it would be "utterly *Useless*." On the contrary, the vindication of Mede's method "is really the rescuing of the Book itself into that Power and Use it ought to have in the Church: For it is a standing light to all the Ages thereof..."[40] More wanted to rescue the Apocalypse from what he considered a sterile explanation, without any use for the church of his own days, and to show that it functioned as a light that clarified the complex spiritual and political situation of the world with which contemporary England had to cope. He did so in particular in his work: *A Modest Inquiry into the Mystery of Iniquity*, which appeared in 1664 as a counterpart to his *Explanation of the Grand Mystery of Godliness*. Now the subject was what he also called "the Mystery of Antichristianism"; a subject, he realized, which at that time was not popular in more educated circles[41]

---

[38] See VAN DEN BERG, "Continuity," p. 191.
[39] From *An Explanation of the Grand Mystery of Godliness* (1680), in *The Theological Works of ... Henry More, D.D.*, London 1708, p. 119.
[40] "Mystery of Godliness," *Theol. Works*, p. 138.
[41] HILL, *Antichrist*, pp. 148 f.

(perhaps in reaction to Puritan times?) – but that made its treatment no less necessary.

To More, Antichrist (in the Apocalypse described as "the Beast" or "the whore of Babylon") was neither a figure from a far-away past nor of a distant future, but "Rome *Pagano-Christian*," or, "the *Roman Hierarchy* (taking *Roman* in the largest Sense) corrupting Christianity with the illicit Doctrines and Practices of Idolatry."[42] In his work on 'the Mystery of Iniquity' he devoted two chapters to a refutation of Grotius' interpretation of Apocalypse 13 and 17. He strongly opposed Grotius' identification of "the Beast' with the idolatry of pagan Rome, and declared he was astonished "that a Person of those admirable Parts and Learning, and, as I have always been prone to think, of great Ingenuity, should ever please himself in any such Performance as this." What, More asked, could be "the Cause of this strange Misadventure of his?" More could not believe that Grotius "was in good earnest in this Exposition," but neither did he want to believe that Grotius, a man of ingenuity and integrity, "would willingly and wittingly, in Favour of a Party ... adulterate the true Meaning of the Oracles of God."[43] The apocalyptic themes continued to occupy the mind of More. In 1680 appeared his *Apocalypsis Apocalypseos*, a commentary on the Book of Revelation. It appeared in the after-days of the 'Popish Plot' (1678), when in England anti-Catholic feelings ran high, but there was no direct connection. In a letter to Archbishop William Sancroft, to whom he sent a copy of his book, he wrote: "But that it is come out so seasonably in this grand tug between Protestantisme and Poperie, I must confesse that can not be ascribed to any prudence of mine but merely to Divine Providence."[44] More's fiercest attack on Grotius occurs in his commentary on Daniel (1681); there he declared that Grotius had excused the Pope from being Antichrist partly because of his distaste for the Reformed Church of Holland "for their usage of him," partly to "curry favour with the Pontifician party."[45] Apparently, to More it was no longer an open question why Grotius had deviated from the traditional interpretation of Antichrist.

In the same year in which More's *Apocalypsis Apocalypseos* appeared, one of the leading Latitudinarians, Simon Patrick (1625–1707), who in 1688 was appointed Bishop of Chichester, in 1691

---

[42] "Mystery of Iniquity," *Theol. Works*, p. 569.

[43] "Mystery of Iniquity," *Theol. Works*, pp. 630 f.

[44] More to Sancroft, 2 January 1679/80, Bodleian Library, MS Tanner 38, f. 115; see VAN DEN BERG, "Continuity," p. 201 n. 88.

[45] *A Plain and Continued Exposition of the several Prophecies or Divine Visions of the Prophet Daniel*, London 1681, pp. XXXVII f.

Bishop of Ely, published an English translation of Grotius' *De Veritate*.[46] As a Latitudinarian he admired Grotius, whom he defended against the accusations of heresy. To his translation he added a seventh, explicitly anti-Catholic chapter, perhaps in order to make clear that following 'the Grotian way' did not necessarily entail a sympathetic attitude towards the Church of Rome.[47] Shortly after the 'Glorious Revolution' Patrick encouraged the publication of a millenarian work by the Anglican clergyman Drue Cressener (1642–1718), vicar of Soham near Ely: *The Judgments of God upon the Roman-Catholick Church* (1689). In 1690 Cressener published a second work on the same subject; he realized that his work was "out of fashion," but it could appear thanks to the recommendation of Patrick. At one time, Cressener wrote, he was influenced by "the mollifying pleas of Grotius,"

> But when I came to be acquainted with Mr. Mede's Demonstrations, and had compared them with the monstrous evasions, and absurd strains of wit, that *Grotius* and others were fain to flye to, to turn off the force of them, I gave over all thoughts of the comprehending way.[48]

Richard Baxter (1615–1691) went the other way round. He was a man of an independent mind: a Puritan leader who in 1660 for conscience's sake had the courage to decline the offer of a bishopric; a theologian, who steered a middle course between 'High Calvinism' and Arminianism. As Geoffrey Nuttall writes, he "rarely agreed wholly with anyone."[49] Baxter's attitude towards Grotius was ambivalent. He was acquainted with the works of Grotius, and went as far in his appreciations as to write: "I must in Gratitude Profess that I have learnt more from Grotius then from almost any Writer ... that ever I read."[50] At the same time, however, in his *The Grotian Religion Discovered* (1658) he strongly objected to Grotius' irenicist attitude towards the Church of Rome. He warned "the Episcopal Party" against '*Grotianism*,' and in his *Grotian Religion* he

---

[46] SYMON PATRICK, *The truth of Christian Religion: In six books Written in Latin by Hugo Grotius. And Now Translated into English, With the Addition of a seventh book [Against the present Roman Church*: addition to the title in the 1689 ed.], London 1680 (*BG* nos. 1023, 1024 and 1025–28).

[47] For this, see J. VAN DEN BERG, "Between Platonism and Enlightenment: Simon Patrick ... and his place in the Latitudinarian movement," *NAKG* 68 (1988), pp. 175 f.

[48] *A Demonstration of the First Principles of the Protestant Applications of the Apocalypse*, London 1690, p. XIII.

[49] G.F. NUTTALL, "Richard Baxter and *The Grotian Religion*," in D. BAKER (ed.), *Reform and Reformation: England and the Continent c1500 – c1750 (dedicated ... to C.W. Dugmore)*, Oxford 1979, p. 245.

[50] *Calendar* I, no. 234 n. 1.

tried to prove that Grotius had turned 'Papist' and that "Popery was indeed his Religion."[51] John Maitland, Earl of Lauderdale, agreed. In 1658 he wrote to Baxter: "I was in Paris acquainted with Grotius ... and though I was then very yong yet some visits past among us. My discours with him was only in Humanities. But I remember well he was then esteemed such a Papist as you call Cassandrian..."[52]

Baxter himself deeply mistrusted the way of Cassander, which, he feared, would inevitably lead to Rome. "Cassandrian Papists," he averred, were "levelling all their doctrines to the advancement of the Papall interest."[53]

Still, his criticism of the 'Grotian religion' did not make him a supporter of More and Cressener in their rejection of Grotius' interpretation of 'Antichrist.' As a young man he had read millenarians such as Brightman and Mede, since then also More, Grotius and Hammond. The disparate interpretations brought him into confusion: "I confess despair." And though he did not become an outright follower of Grotius and Hammond in their view of Antichrist he refused to identify the Papacy with Antichrist: he thought it would be "far more dreadful to the Pope ... to be plainly condemned by the known Laws of Christ ... than to be under the Dread of a dark and controverted Prophecie."[54] On this point, too, Baxter demonstrated his independence.

More was deeply disappointed that Baxter did not follow Mede, and reacted in a rather bitter pamphlet; he accused Baxter of a sceptical attitude with regard to the "explanation of prophecy."[55] In 1691, Cressener asked Baxter for "a cautious examination" of his second book. He hoped Baxter would come over to his view by owning that the great adversary of the Reformation "is so Pompously set forth to the world in this Prophecy, As the Great Antichrist."[56] No reaction from Baxter is known; he died only a few months afterwards.

---

[51] *Reliquiae Baxterianae,* London 1696, part I, p. 280; cf. NUTTALL, "Richard Baxter," p. 249.

[52] The Earl of Lauderdaill to Baxter, 20 September 1658, *Calendar* I, no. 500.

[53] From BAXTER's *Christian Concord* (1653), quoted by NUTTALL, "Richard Baxter," p. 246.

[54] BAXTER, *A Paraphrase on the New Testament ... With an Advertisement of Difficulties in the Revelations,* London 1685, f. Q 2ᵛ; R 2ᵛ; 3ʳ, ᵛ; 4ʳ. See also W.M. LAMONT, *Richard Baxter and the Millenium,* London 1979, pp. 52 ff.; VAN DEN BERG, "Continuity," pp. 199 f.

[55] See his *Some cursory reflexions impartially made upon Mr. Richard Baxter his way of writing notes on the Apocalypse,* published in London in 1685 under the pseudonym Phililicrinis [*sic*] Parrhesiastes.

[56] Cressener to Baxter, 2 June 1691, KEEBLE – NUTTALL, *Calendar* II, no. 1245.

One may wonder whether millenarian speculations were indeed as 'unfashionable' as Cressener claimed in the dedication of his *Demonstration*. No less a person than Isaac Newton (1642–1727) sympathized with Mede's apocalyptic scheme.[57] He, too, believed that the predictions of things to come relate to the state of the Church in all ages, and though he did not explicitly identify the Pope with Antichrist, in his 'observations' on Daniel he explained the eleventh horn or king from Daniel 7.24–25, which would speak great words against the most High and would wear out the saints, as "the Church of Rome."[58] A similar approach we find with the famous scientist Joseph Priestley (1733–1804), who as a millenarian also stood in the tradition of Mede.[59] In his *Institutes of Natural and Revealed Religion* (1772–74) he declared he saw in a number of prophecies in the book of Daniel and of the Revelation "the plain characters of the *Church of Rome*," and in his *Notes on Revelation* (1804) he wrote: "The *blasphemy* of the beast, of which the papal power was a part, consists in the Pope's usurping the authority of God..."[60]

In his *Apologia* (1864) the later Cardinal John Henry Newman (1801–1890) writes that as a boy of fifteen he read Newton on the Prophecies,[61] and became most firmly convinced that the Pope was the Antichrist predicted by Daniel, St. Paul and St. John. "My imagination was stained by the effects of this doctrine up to the year 1843." Gradually, however, he came to other thoughts; but while his reason was convinced, he did not throw off, for some time after, the unreasoning prejudice and suspicion, which he cherished about the (Catholic) Church "at least by fits and starts."[62] Even in Newman's life the after-effects of the traditional Protestant view of Antichrist led a tough existence. In the second half of the nineteenth century, however, the identification between Pope and Antichrist

---

[57] See F.E. MANUEL, *Isaac Newton Historian*, Cambridge (Mass.) 1963, pp. 175 f.

[58] Sir ISAAC NEWTON, *Observations upon the Prophecies of Daniel, and the Apocalypse of St. John*, London 1733, pp. 15; 75.

[59] See J. VAN DEN BERG, "Priestly, the Jews and the Millenium," in D.S. KATZ – JONATHAN ISRAEL (edd.), *Sceptics, Millenarians and Jews*, Leiden [etc.] 1990, pp. 268 ff.

[60] J.T. RUTT (ed.), *The Theological and Miscellaneous Works of Joseph Priestley*, New York 1972 (repr. of the edition of 1817–32) II, p. 190; XIV, p. 476.

[61] Not Isaac Newton, but Thomas Newton, Bishop of Bristol, who between 1754 and 1758 published his *Dissertations on the Prophecies*.

[62] *Apologia pro Vita Sua*, ed. by M.J. SVAGLIC, Oxford 1967, pp. 20, 115; cf. IAN KER, *John Henry Newman*, Oxford 1990, pp. 5, 184 f.

just faded away, only to live on in extreme Protestant circles. At last, in his beloved England Grotius prevailed.

GROTIUS REMPLAÇA-T-IL CALVIN À GENÈVE?

Olivier Fatio

(Genève)

Le 24 février 1704, Elie Merlat, professeur de théologie à l'Académie de Lausanne, cachetait une lettre à l'intention de Jean-Alphonse Turrettini. Il y exprimait sa réaction après la lecture d'un discours académique de son jeune et déjà renommé collègue de Genève, l'*Oratio de saeculo 17. erudito et hodiernis literarum periculis.*[1] Merlat, septuagénaire arrivé au terme d'une vie mouvementée,[2] écrivait avec sa coutumière franchise à Turrettini:

> Vous êtes fils d'un homme que j'ay extremement estimé et honoré [*François Turrettini*], vous êtes chrétien: vous ne choisissez pas la bonne part; le monde vous trompe; vous perdez un précieux tems. Croyez un homme de soixante dix ans, qui a passé par l'état où vous êtes, et qui a eû autant de vanité que vous, quoyqu'il n'ait pas eû autant d'esprit, ni une aussi grande Bibliothèque. Ce vieillard maudit le jour qu'il a leû les Scaligers, les Casaubons et les Grotius, et encore plus les Saumaises et les Petaux. Il a appris plus de sottises, et qui pis est plus d'impiétés et de traits d'orgueil, dans ces auteurs-là, que de choses utiles. Il a reconnu que Dieu reveloit encore aujourd'huy ses mystères aux petits enfans, et les cachoit aux sages et aux entendus. Mais surtout Grotius, pour la Theologie, qu'a-t-il qui ne soit profane, corrompu, mocqueur ou imaginaire et outré? Je vous croy en très grand danger, par votre attachement au genre d'estude que vous suyvez; et si Dieu ne vous fait pas la grace d'en revenir enfin, j'ay peur qu'ayant longtemps bâty de la paille et du foin, vous ne veniez même à laisser le fondement. Hélas! quels dons vous ensevelissez ou vous gâtez par l'abus que vous en faites? *Une seule chose est nécessaire.* Vous dites vous-même que l'*une des causes de la décadence des sciences, c'est l'envie*

---

[1] Il s'agissait d'un discours que Turrettini avait prononcé comme recteur de l'Académie de Genève le 14 mai 1703. Nous citons d'après l'édition des *Orationes Academicae, quibus multa, ad Scientiarum incrementum, Christianae Veritatis illustrationem, Pietatis commendationem, Pacemque Christianorum, pertinentia continentur*, Genève, Barrillot et Fils, 1737, pp. 89–122. En éditant la lettre de Merlat à Turrettini, Eugène de Budé écrit à tort qu'il s'agit du discours intitulé *De studiis emendandis et promovendis*. Or ce discours fut prononcé par J.-A. Turrettini le 19 mai 1704 et la lettre de Merlat date du 24 février 1704 (J.-A. TURRETTINI, *Lettres inédites adressées de 1686 à 1737*, publiées et annotées par E. DE BUDÉ, t. 2, Paris-Genève 1887, p. 292 n. 1).

[2] Merlat était né en Saintonge en 1634; il avait fait ses études à Saumur et Montauban, exercé le ministère pastoral à Saintes pendant plus de 20 ans, avant d'en être banni en 1680 à cause de sa réplique à Arnauld: *Réplique générale au livre de M. Arnauld intitulé le Renversement de la morale de Jésus-Christ*, publiée à Saumur en 1676. Il s'était finalement réfugié à Lausanne où il enseigna à l'Académie de manière intermittente une théologie d'une orthodoxie souvent peu éclairée (FRANÇOIS LAPLANCHE, *L'écriture, le sacré et l'histoire. Erudits et politiques protestants devant la Bible en France au 17e siècle*, Amsterdam et Maarssen 1986, pp. 583–84, 686–88).

de vouloir trop savoir: votre Discours rend donc temoignage contre vous. Vous violez votre regle.[3]

Qu'avait bien pu dire Turrettini pour s'attirer une telle mercuriale? Avait-il fait une vibrante apologie de Grotius? Tant s'en faut. A l'intention d'un public académique, il avait dressé un tableau des progrès des diverses sciences pendant le XVIIe siècle. Il avait passé en revue la philologie, la philosophie, les mathématiques, la médecine, l'histoire, le droit, la théologie, les recherches sur l'antiquité, le développement des bibliothèques, avant de recenser les dangers qui menaçaient le développement des connaissances: négligence des études, nombre trop élevé de livres, volonté de trop embrasser, préjugés intellectuels, etc. Le recteur voulait exhorter ses collègues et ses étudiants à ne pas relâcher leurs efforts sur la route du progrès des sciences si brillamment ouverte au siècle précédent. De Grotius, il avait, à vrai dire, peu parlé – quatre fois en trente pages – et l'avait cité à côté d'autres noms célèbres. Une première fois il l'avait mentionné après Scaliger, Juste Lipse, Gruterus, Meursius, Casaubon, et avant Saumaise, Vossius, Heinsius, Gronovius, Graevius, Huet et Ezechiel Spanheim, et il avait fait un bref mais chaleureux éloge de son étonnante érudition, de l'acuité de son jugement et de l'ampleur de son champ d'activité: critique, éloquence, poésie, histoire, politique, droit humain et divin.[4] Il avait ensuite signalé l'histoire des Pays-Bas de Grotius, rappelé, en associant son nom à celui de Pufendorf, sa contribution au problème du droit de la nature et des gens.[5] Il avait enfin exprimé ses craintes que l'on ne retrouve avant longtemps des savants tels que Scaliger, Grotius ou Saumaise.[6] Somme toute, peu de chose, mais suffisamment pour déchaîner Merlat!

Dans ses papiers Jean-Alphonse Turrettini conserva une copie de sa réponse à Merlat, rédigée à la réception même de la lettre du professeur lausannois, le 26 février 1704. Le fait est suffisamment rare pour être significatif. L'attaque l'avait touché, sa justification mérite d'être citée.[7]

> ... Vos principales censures sont, que *je ne choisis pas la bonne part*, que je *perds un tems precieux*, que quand je m'amuse à fueuilleter *les Scali-*

---

[3] J.-A. TURRETTINI, *Lettres inédites*, t. 2, pp. 293–94.

[4] "Puta *Hugo* ille *Grotius*, cujus stupenda eruditio, cum acerrimo judicio certans, per omnem, sive Critices, sive Eloquentiae, sive Poëseos, sive Historiae, sive Politicae, sive Humani Divinique Juris campum sese diffudit" (TURRETTINI, *Orationes Academicae*, p. 97).

[5] "De Jure Naturae et Gentium, quis nescit eximias *Grotii* et *Puffendorfii* lucubrationes?" (*Ibid.*, p. 104).

[6] *Ibid.*, p. 109.

[7] J.-A. Turrettini à Elie Merlat, [Genève] 26 février 1704, Genève, BPU, Ms. fr.

gers, les Causaubons, les Saumaises, les Petaux, et surtout les *Grotius,* je ne prends pas garde qu'il n'y a rien de bon à apprendre dans tout ces autheurs, qu'on ni trouve que des *sottises* et qui pis est des *impiétés.* Tout cela, Monsieur, (souffrés que je le dize) me paroit un peu outré; et de l'air dont vous prenés les choses il faudroit fermer tous les auditoires et toutes les Académies. La science humaine a ses mauvais costés, elle est pleine d'inutilités, de sottises et d'incertitudes. J'en suis plus convaincu que qui que ce soit; et vous avez peu remarquer dans mon discours qu'entre les principales decouvertes de la Nouvelle Philosophie je compte pour une des premières, que nous sçavons mieux aujourd'huy combien nous sçavons peu de choses. Cependant il faut convenir que les sciences humaines ont aussi leurs utilités, et vous avez beau les décrier, je suis sûr que vous ne voudriés pas que nous rentrassions dans la barbarie du 9e, 10e et 11e siècles qui a été si funeste à la Religion, et que vous benissez Dieu incessamment du retablissement des sciences qui a si fort contribué à notre bienheureuse réformation.[8]

Mais Turrettini ne se borna pas à défendre son attitude à l'égard des sciences humaines. Il en vint à Grotius et réfuta en ces termes les attaques de Merlat:

Une des choses qui vous a le plus irrité contre mon discours, ce sont, ce me semble, les louanges que je donne à Grotius, qui selon vous n'a rien fait sur la Theologie qui *ne soit presque profanne, corrompu, moqueur, imaginaire ou outré.* Je n'en ay pas, je vous l'avoue, tout à fait la même idée. Son livre sur la Vérité de la Religion chrestienne le met bien à couvert du reproche de prophaneté, et son Commentaire sur les Evangiles donne du jour à une infinité de passages, par le moien des langues, de l'histoire, des coutumes anciennes que cet habile homme

---

481, fol. 19–20. Au début de la copie, J.-A. Turrettini a écrit: "Copie de ma Reponse à Mr Merlat."

[8] Fol. 19 v°. Turrettini poursuit en ces termes: "En mon particulier, Monsieur, vous me faittes plus d'honneur que je ne merite, quand vous conclués de mon discours que toutes ces sciences m'occupent beaucoup. Si je m'étans la dessus, ce n'est pas comme particulier; c'est comme ayant l'honneur d'avoir inspection sur nôtre Academie; et dans cette qualité, je ne croyois pas qu'il fut tout à fait hors de propos, dans un jour consacré aux sciences, de marquer les divers progrés qu'on a faits dans le dernier siècle, et d'encourager ceux qui les enseignent à ne se pas relacher. Voilà, Monsieur, mon unique but, car pour ce qui me regarde, je n'ay ni assez de tems, ni assez de genie, ni assez de santé, pour m'appliquer à toutes ces choses. Je me contente d'étudier l'Evangile par rapport à la predication et les Antiquités de l'Eglise, par raport à la Profession qu'on m'a donnée. Si je m'aquitte mal de ces deux emplois, si *je suis en tres grand danger dans le genre d'etude que je suis, si j'abuze de mes talens,* et que je les *gâtes,* si *je ne bâtis que de la paille et du foin,* et si je cours risque de *laisser même le fondement,* (car ce sont vos propres termes) permettés que je vous dize que vous en estes un peu cause, par l'approbation que vous donnâtes à ma manière de precher, lorsque vous m'ouïtes à Lausanne, et par l'approbation que vous donnâtes il n'y a pas plus de deux ans à ma manière d'etudier l'histoire, dans une lettre que vous me fistes l'honneur de m'écrire la dessus. Je n'ay point changé de methode depuis ce tems là. Ainsi si je suis une mechante route, c'est vous, Monsieur et tres honoré Pere, qui mi avez encouragé" (fol. 19 v°– 20 v°).

entendoit parfaitement bien. Du reste je n'ay gardes d'estre garant de
tous ces sentimens, et de toutes ses explications. Mais quoy qu'il en
soit, je ne vois personne qui luy refuse les eloges que je luy ay donnés
d'avoir eu un sçavoir presque universel accompagné d'un très beau
genie. Je ne le dis même, si vous y prenés garde, que dans l'article
des Belles Lettres, car sur la Theologie je ne parle de luy ni près ni
loin.[9]

Merlat ne se laissa pas convaincre. Le 6 mars 1704, il répliquait:

> J'ay des preuves en main de l'impiété de Grotius, et de son esprit
> moqueur sur des choses saintes; et son traité de la *Vérité de la religion
> chrétienne* n'est point capable de le disculper à cet égard, il peut même
> servir à l'en convaincre [...] Je suis seur de ce que je dis, et jamais
> homme ne fut, selon mon sentiment, ni si savant que Grotius, ni si
> grand corrupteur de la Religion chrétienne que luy.[10]

Laissons le vieux professeur remâcher sa rogne et intéressons-nous à
Turrettini. Chacun connaît l'importance de ce théologien né en
1671 et mort en 1737, intelligence précoce qui jouit dès son plus
jeune âge d'une réputation considérable dans la République des
Lettres. Liquidateur de l'œuvre de son père, François Turrettini,
parangon de l'orthodoxie réformée et co-auteur de la fameuse *Formula consensus helvetica*, Jean-Alphonse, à travers une production littéraire plutôt modeste, représente incontestablement, plus encore que
les deux autres théologiens auxquels on associe d'ordinaire son
nom, J.-F. Ostervald et Samuel Werenfels, l'adaptation de l'héritage
calviniste aux pressions induites par les premières manifestations des
Lumières. Dans une série d'études Maria-Cristina Pitassi a montré
les principaux axes de sa pensée, pas très approfondie ni très originale certes, mais soucieuse de défendre la théologie chrétienne contre les attaques de la philosophie et des sciences modernes.[11] A cet
effet Turrettini atténua ou se débarrassa même de ce qu'il y avait
de plus difficile à justifier au tribunal de la raison, comme la prédestination, l'interprétation salvifique de l'œuvre du Christ, la satisfaction pour le péché, l'imputation de l'œuvre du Christ au croy-

---

[9] Fol. 20 v°. Turrettini terminait sa lettre en disant à Merlat: "Je vous demande
très humblement pardon, Monsieur et très honoré Pere, si je prends la liberté de
me justifier auprès de vous. Je ne laisse pas d'avoir une extreme deference pour
vos conseils, et quelque idée que vous ayez de moy, je seray toujours avec une
profonde soumission, Monsieur et très honoré Père, votre tres humble et tres
obéissant serviteur."

[10] J.-A. Turrettini, *Lettres inédites adressées de 1686 à 1737*, t.2, p. 296.

[11] Cf. Maria-Cristina Pitassi, "L'apologétique raisonnable de Jean-Alphonse
Turrettini," dans *Apologétique 1680-1740. Sauvetage ou naufrage de la théologie?*, Actes du
colloque tenu à Genève en juin 1990 sous les auspices de l'Institut d'histoire de la
Réformation édités par Maria-Cristina Pitassi, Genève 1991, pp. 99–118;
Maria-Cristina Pitassi, *De l'Orthodoxie aux Lumières. Genève 1670-1737*, Genève
1992, pp. 41–50.

ant. Il avait compris que l'heure était à la théodicée, au Dieu dont les lois de la physique et les diverses civilisations prouvent l'existence et dont le besoin d'ordre social renforce la nécessité. Ce Dieu cautionne ici-bas le bonheur auquel les progrès de la raison donnent à chaque individu le droit d'aspirer; il assure en outre l'au-delà à tous ceux qui se seront efforcés de vivre selon une morale raisonnable.

Pour opérer cette évolution, Turrettini avait besoin de modèles. Sa dette à l'égard des Anglais, Locke et surtout Tillotson, a été mise en lumière par M.-C. Pitassi. Mais ces auteurs ne sont pas les seules sources de Turrettini et on ne peut s'empêcher de se demander si Grotius ne joue pas un rôle important dans la constitution de sa pensée. L'échange avec Merlat en est un signe, mais évidemment ténu. S'il marque ses distances, Turrettini n'en fait pas moins l'éloge de la *Vérité de la Religion chrétienne*. Certes il souligne qu'il n'en a pas parlé dans la section de son discours qui recensait les progrès de la théologie au XVIIe siècle. Mais aurait-il pu le faire? Certainement pas! Mentionner un des principaux agents de l'arminianisme au nombre des théologiens phares du XVIIe siècle eût été une provocation dans une Académie qui avait eu pour ligne de conduite la défense la plus stricte de Dordrecht. Il était déjà suffisamment étonnant que dans son discours le recteur de cette Académie n'évoque aucun des grands théologiens orthodoxes du XVIIe siècle et ne cite, au terme d'un développement aussi alambiqué qu'embarrassé, que trois noms: Daillé, Calixte et Stillingfleet, théologiens plus connus pour leur marginalité que pour leur orthodoxie au sein de leur confession respective.

L'absence de référence à Grotius dans cette partie du discours académique de Turrettini ne signifie pas qu'il ne marqua pas le professeur genevois. Nous serions évidemment plus à l'aise pour défendre l'hypothèse d'une influence de Grotius si dans le reste de son œuvre Turrettini en faisait de nombreuses citations. Or tel n'est pas le cas: on recense une dizaine de références explicites à Grotius qui généralement servent à appuyer tel point d'érudition exégétique ou historique.[12] C'est peu pour parler d'influence.

Pourtant ne pas citer – ou peu citer – un auteur ne signifie pas qu'on ne lui doit rien. Un examen de critique interne permet, me

---

[12] Cf. par exemple la leçon inaugurale de Turrettini en décembre 1705 intitulée *Oratio de theologo veritatis et pacis studioso*, dans *Orationes Academicae*, p. 32; *Disputatio theologica de veritate religionis christianae. Pars quarta, quae est de prophetiis*, Genève 1722, p. 28; *Disputatio theologica de veritate religionis christianae. Pars quinta, quae est De Evangelii propagatione*, Genève 1722, p. 15.

semble-t-il, de dégager entre Grotius et Turrettini des convergences qui dépassent l'érudition pour atteindre à ce que l'on pourrait appeler l'idéologie. Avant d'en montrer quelques exemples, comment ne pas remarquer que Turrettini a nommé la série des quinze thèses qu'il a publiées entre 1715 et 1728 et qui constituent l'armature de sa production théologique *De veritate religionis christianae*. Certes le titre est relativement banal – Jacques Abbadie l'avait employé pour son best-seller paru en 1687 –, mais pourquoi ne pas y voir un hommage à l'ouvrage auquel Grotius avait donné le même intitulé? De surcroît les analogies entre certains thèmes centraux du *De veritate religionis christianae* de Grotius et les positions de Turrettini sont impressionnantes.

On peut mentionner d'abord le rôle de la raison et de la théologie naturelle. Turrettini, comme Grotius, est confronté à la nécessité de transformer la théologie en apologétique. A cet effet les deux auteurs chargent la raison de démontrer la vérité du christianisme, aux non-croyants pour Grotius, aux incroyants pour Turrettini.[13] Certes ce rationalisme aboutissant à la démonstration rationnelle de l'existence de Dieu, de sa providence, de l'immortalité de l'âme et de la nécessité de la vie morale entre les hommes, était largement répandu dans l'Europe théologique du XVIIe siècle et Turrettini pouvait trouver de nombreuses autres sources, anglaise, hollandaise ou française, que Grotius pour le formuler à son tour.

En revanche la parenté de Turrettini avec Grotius est beaucoup plus étroite dès lors qu'il s'agit d'enraciner la certitude de la religion dans les faits historiques et non plus dans une vérité métaphysique telle que l'élection et la grâce. Grotius avait montré le chemin en établissant la vérité du christianisme dans l'historicité de son fondateur et de son expansion, d'une part, et dans la comparaison avec le judaïsme, le paganisme, voire l'islam, d'autre part. Les deux auteurs argumentent de manière analogue pour défendre la valeur des vérités de fait. Quand Turrettini écrit:

> Il est vrai que les preuves morales ou historiques n'ont pas une Evidence aussi claire, que les preuves mathématiques, mais elles ne sont pas moins solides et moins certaines dans leur genre, si elles sont bien maniées: par exemple, qu'il y ait aujourd'hui une ville qu'on nomme Rome etc., cela ne se prouve pas mathématiquement, cependant il n'y a point d'homme de bon sens qui ait quelques connaissances des choses du monde, qui revoque cette verité en doute,[14]

ne fait-il pas écho à Grotius qui dit:

---

[13] Cf. H. Grotius, *De veritate religionis christianae*, dans *OTh* III, pp. 3–4; Pitassi, "L'apologétique raisonnable de Jean-Alphonse Turrettini", pp. 101–02.

[14] Turrettini, "Abrégé de Leçons de Théologie," fol. 18, cité dans Pitassi, "L'apologétique raisonnable de Jean-Alphonse Turrettini," p. 105.

Si quis allatis hactenus argumentis pro Christiana religione satis sibi
factum non putet, sed magis urgentia desideret, scire debet, pro rerum diversitate diversa quoque esse probandi genera; alia in Mathe-
maticis, alia de affectionibus corporum, alia circa deliberationes, alia
ubi facti est questio; in quo genere sane standum est nulla suspicione
laborantibus testimoniis: quod ni admittitur, non modo omnis Historiae usus periit, Medicinae quoque pars magna, sed et omnis quae inter parentes liberosque est pietas.[15]

On chercherait en vain dans ces pages des allusions au témoignage
intérieur du Saint-Esprit. La doctrine traditionnelle est remplacée
chez Grotius comme chez Turrettini par un système de contrôle
rationnel qui détermine la véracité et la certitude de la religion. La
doctrine se dit en termes historiques; elle est d'autant plus certaine
qu'elle tire sa crédibilité des faits plutôt que des déductions théologiques. Turrettini à la suite de Grotius réduit donc la croyance à
une *fides historica* "dans laquelle l'assentiment est à la mesure de l'é-
vidence factuelle des éléments qui la composent."[16]

A cet égard il est frappant de constater le rôle que jouent dans
la démonstration de cette foi, non seulement la diffusion et l'effica-
cité du christianisme, mais également les miracles et l'accomplissement des prophéties. Pour Turrettini comme pour Grotius, les miracles, en particulier la résurrection, sont des preuves du caractère
divin de la religion chrétienne. Pourtant il est vrai que les deux auteurs ne résolvent pas la question de la même manière. Si Grotius
reconnaît sans difficulté que c'est Dieu lui-même qui a suspendu le
cours des lois naturelles pour rendre témoignage à la doctrine de
son Fils,[17] Turrettini ne peut régler la chose aussi simplement. Il
doit compter avec Spinoza qui avait démontré l'immutabilité des

---

[15] H. GROTIUS, *De veritate religionis christianae*, pp. 48–49. Il est intéressant de constater que la traduction française que P. Le Jeune donne de ce texte est plus une paraphrase correspondant aux préoccupations de la fin du XVIIe siècle et du début du
XVIIIe siècle qu'une traduction littérale de Grotius: "Si toutes ces preuves ne satis-
font pas, et qu'on en desire de plus convainquantes, on doit considérer que les preuves varient selon la diversité des choses que l'on veut établir. On ne peut conclurre
une vérité mathématique que par des raisons de la dernière évidence. Les disputes
de la Physique se doivent terminer par des arguments fondez sur des Principes natu-
rels. Lors qu'il s'agit de délibérer, il faut se déterminer par des argumens tirez des
maximes que le sens commun et l'expérience suggèrent. Les Faits ont aussi leurs
preuves, qui consistent dans la qualité de ceux qui les atestent; et c'est les avoir prou-
vez, que de faire voir que ces Témoins n'ont rien qui les rende suspects. Si l'on ne
s'en tient pas là, on annéantit la certitude des Faits historiques; on détruit celle des
expériences, qui font la partie la plus considérable de la Médecine, et l'on suspend
les devoirs réciproques des Pères et des Enfans, puisque ces rélations ne se connois-
sent que par ces sortes de preuves" (*Traité de la vérité de la religion chrétienne*, traduit du
latin par P. LE JEUNE, Nouvelle édition augmentée de deux dissertations de M. LE
CLERC qui ont rapport à la matière, Amsterdam 1728, pp. 175–76).
[16] Cf. PITASSI, "L'apologétique raisonnable de Jean-Alphonse Turrettini," p. 112.
[17] H. GROTIUS, *De veritate religionis christianae*, pp. 33–34, 36.

lois de la nature. Aussi pour continuer à soutenir que les miracles confirment la véracité de la doctrine, s'efforce-t-il laborieusement de démontrer la compatibilité entre l'intervention miraculeuse de Dieu et la non-altération des qualités essentielles de la nature.[18]

Dernier point de rapprochement: la vision que les deux auteurs ont de la personne et de l'œuvre de Jésus-Christ. L'essentiel pour Grotius est de démontrer l'existence historique de Jésus-Christ. Quant à son œuvre, elle se réduit aux avantages que la religion chrétienne présente sur les autres religions en promettant l'immortalité de l'âme et la vie éternelle et en prônant la sainteté de la morale.[19] Turrettini n'est pas aussi radical, mais le traitement rationnel qu'il impose aux diverses composantes de la christologie – incarnation, union hypostatique, mort expiatoire – fait singulièrement pâlir le caractère réformé de son Christ. Celui-ci passe de l'état de victime sacrificielle à celui de modèle de charité conforme au sens commun et aux données de la théologie naturelle.[20] Au terme de l'exercice, cette christologie se résout, comme chez Grotius, en une morale qui équilibre grâce et nature et dilue l'Evangile dans la bienséance profane.

Ces rapprochements entre Turrettini et Grotius sur des points fondamentaux, pour spectaculaires qu'ils soient, ne prouvent évidemment pas une influence directe de l'un sur l'autre. D'autres auteurs, dans les soixante ans et plus qui séparent leurs deux carrières, ont repris et développé les thèmes de la *Vérité de la religion chrétienne* de Grotius et ont pu ainsi fournir à Turrettini les concepts pour faire sortir la théologie réformée de l'impasse où son père François l'avait conduite avec la *Formula consensus*. Il n'empêche que les affinités idéologiques entre les deux auteurs sont frappantes et que la réponse à Merlat autorise à penser que Grotius fut pour Turrettini une référence centrale. Si seulement Turrettini avait fait à Genève un cours analogue à celui donné par son collègue bâlois, Johann Ludwig Frey, de 1717 à 1722, sur le *De veritate religionis christianae* de Grotius![21]

A défaut d'un témoignage si précieux, contentons-nous d'enregistrer les soupçons d'arminianisme qui pesaient sur J.-A. Turrettini.

---

[18] Cf. PITASSI, "L'apologétique raisonnable de Jean-Alphonse Turrettini," p. 115.

[19] H. GROTIUS, *De veritate religionis christianae*, pp. 33, 37, 38.

[20] Cf. PITASSI, "L'apologétique raisonnable de Jean-Alphonse Turrettini," p. 110.

[21] Le successeur de Frey, Johan Christoph Beck, fit également un cours sur le même sujet dans les années 1760 (cf. ERNST STAEHELIN, *Johann Ludwig Frey, Johannes Grynaeus und das Frey-Grynaeische Institut in Basel*, Basel 1947, pp. 42 et 140).

Dans une lettre du 4 juin 1711, le cousin de Jean-Alphonse, Samuel Turrettini, futur professeur de théologie à Genève, faisant sa tournée académique à travers l'Europe, écrit d'Amsterdam où il vient de rencontrer les ministres wallons:

> Tous ces Messieurs ont en général beaucoup de zèle pour ce qu'on appelle orthodoxie; Mr Boddens m'en donna des marques lorsque je le fus voir pour la première fois. Après les premiers compliments, il débuta par se plaindre du peu d'orthodoxie de Geneve; il me demanda s'il etoit vrai que tout le monde fut Arminien à Geneve, s'il etoit vrai que vous le fussiez, si je ne le serois point moi-même. Ces questions me firent un peu de peine, je m'en tirai le mieux que je pus et d'une manière qui le satisfit, car après ce début peu civil, il me fit toutes les honnêtetés wallones imaginables, m'offrant pipe, tabac, vin, thé, etc.[22]

Peut-on donner tort à la méfiance de ces pasteurs wallons? Certainement pas si l'on songe que dans les années 1710 l'on se ruait à Genève sur les stocks de Limborch et de Le Clerc mis en vente par les libraires et qu'on lisait ces ouvrages, non pas en cachette, mais au vu et au su de tout le monde, et que J.-A. Turrettini lui-même écrivait à Jean Le Clerc:

> Notre Suisse commence à s'epurer, et nos Académies sont, graces à dieu, sur un meilleur pied qu'autrefois. Vos ouvrages y contribuent beaucoup, j'en suis persuadé.[23]

A défaut de témoigner de l'influence de Grotius, ces indications montrent que Turrettini évoluait dans un milieu fortement marqué par l'arminianisme. Le climat intellectuel et théologique de Genève au début du XVIIIe siècle était devenu semblable à celui qui régnait à Londres un quart de siècle auparavant. Le pasteur genevois Pierre Mussard, que ses penchants pour la grâce universelle avait contraint à l'exil, écrivait en effet de Londres, le 24 mars 1676, à son ami, le pasteur et professeur Louis Tronchin:

> Le povre Calvin est extremement odieux à ceux qui ont à present le dessus, Grotius a succedé à toute l'estime que l'on avoit autrefois ici pour le premier. On m'a asseuré qu'on le cite en chaire avec les eloges de "divin" et d'"incomparable".[24]

La théologie de Jean-Alphonse Turrettini indique que l'esprit de Grotius occupait désormais la maison de Calvin!

---

[22] J.-A. TURRETTINI, *Lettres inédites adressées de 1686 à 1737*, t. 3, p. 357, cité partiellement dans M.-C. PITASSI, *De l'Orthodoxie aux Lumières*, p. 52.

[23] J.-A. Turrettini à J. Le Clerc, Genève, 29 septembre 1714, Genève, BPU, Ms. fr. 481, fol. 81, cité *ibid.*, p. 52 n. 5.

[24] Pierre Mussard à Louis Tronchin, Londres, 24 mars 1676, Genève, BPU, Archives Tronchin, vol. 47, fol. 173v°.

BETWEEN GROTIUS AND COCCEIUS: THE 'THEOLOGIA PROPHETICA' OF CAMPEGIUS VITRINGA (1659–1722)

ERNESTINE VAN DER WALL
(Leiden)

Introduction

In the late seventeenth and early eighteenth centuries Christianity came under heavy attack from a growing group of sceptics and atheists. These enemies of the Christian faith contributed to the growth of irreligion by directing their attack against the divine authority of the Bible. One of their main weapons was to show that the two traditional proofs of the Christian faith, miracles and prophecies, had no validity whatsoever. If it could be proven that both miracles and prophecies were of no use in the defence of the truth of Christianity, the divine authority of Scripture would be called into question and thus the foundations of Christianity itself would be shaken. This attack called forth a strong reaction from all kinds of theologians, enlightened as well as pietist, who made the apologetic validity of miracles and prophecies a hotly debated subject in the age of the (early) Enlightenment. It is well-known that in England a vehement debate on these apologetic proofs occurred in the first half of the eighteenth century. It is less known that in the Dutch Republic the same subject was being discussed already some time earlier, in the last decades of the seventeenth century. In this discussion Grotius' hermeneutical method concerning the biblical prophecies was one of the main issues.

In England the discussion actually started when Newton's successor at Cambridge William Whiston (1667–1752) delivered the Boyle Lectures in 1707 on the interpretation of scriptural prophecies, in which he stated that a prophecy could only have one meaning; he rejected the typological interpretation.[1] In the 1720s Whiston's publications on this subject provoked a reaction from the eminent deist – or rather, speculative atheist – the lawyer Anthony Collins (1676–1729), "the Goliath of Freethinking." Collins' views implied that the argument from prophecy as proof of the Christian religion did not have any validity. This argument was only valid if the prophecy was interpreted in an allegorical sense, but he obviously regarded

---

[1] WILLIAM WHISTON, *The Accomplishment of Scripture Prophecies*, Cambridge 1708. In 1722 Whiston published his *Essay Towards Restoring the True Text of the Old Testament*, which caused Collins to publish his *Discourse of the Grounds and Reasons*, 1724.

such an allegorical interpretation as absurd. He would have agreed wholeheartedly with the observation that "if we should once allow this typical or allegorical way of explaining Scripture, one might prove the history of Guy of Warwick out of the first chapters of Genesis."[2] Collins' publications, entitled *Discourse of the Grounds and Reasons of the Christian Religion* (1724) and *The Scheme of Literal Prophecy considered* (1727), called forth a stream of reactions. His attack on the prophecies was regarded as an assault on Christian belief as such.

Collins was well aware of the fact that he did not stand alone in his battle. There was one scholar in particular to whom he could appeal as a prominent supporter, Hugo Grotius, "the most Judicious of Interpreters," as Collins called him.[3] In his *Scheme of Literal Prophecy Considered* Collins devoted a whole chapter to the defence of Grotius. Collins' own position with regard to the interpretation of the prophecies was inspired by the views of Grotius as well as other Dutch Arminians such as Simon Episcopius and Jean Le Clerc.[4] Whether or not Collins had interpreted Grotius' observations accurately – Le Clerc expressed his doubts on that point – one thing was obvious: Grotius' ideas about the biblical prophecies could be most appropriately used in the enlightened assault upon scriptural authority and so challenge the traditional beliefs of Christianity.

It was precisely this use which could be made of Grotius that long rendered him so unpopular in the eyes of the orthodox divines. He, the author of the famous apologetic treatise *De veritate religionis christianae*, was considered one of those Christians who attempted to undermine Christianity from within the Church itself. He was ranged among the enemies of the Christian religion together with men such as Hobbes and Spinoza, who had also launched an attack against prophets and prophecies, the first in his *Leviathan* (1651), the latter in his *Tractatus theologico-politicus* (1670). At any rate, Grotius' disrespect for the prophetic word found no favour with the

---

[2] W. Nicholls, *Conference with a Theist*, London 1698, III, p. 19 (quoted by James O'Higgins s.j., *Anthony Collins. The Man and his Works*, The Hague 1970, p. 160).

[3] *Discourse of the Grounds and Reasons*, p. 42. For Anthony Collins, see O'Higgins, *Anthony Collins* (see note 2). See also H.W. Frei, *The Eclipse of Biblical Narrative. A Study in 18th and 19th Century Hermeneutics*, 1974, pp. 66–85; David Berman, *A History of Atheism in Britain: from Hobbes to Russell*, London – New York 1988, ch. 3, pp. 70–92. On the deist debate in England, see G.V. Lechler, *Geschichte des Englischen Deismus*, Stuttgart – Tübingen 1841; Henning Graf Reventlow, *Bibelautorität und Geist der Moderne. Die Bedeutung des Bibelverständnisses für die geistesgeschichtliche und politische Entwicklung in England von der Reformation bis zur Aufklärung* [Forschungen zur Kirchen- und Dogmengeschichte, 30], Göttingen 1980, pp. 363–65, p. 609 n. 119 (= *The Authority of the Bible and the Rise of the Modern World*, London 1984).

[4] O'Higgins, *Anthony Collins*, p. 156.

orthodox defenders of the Christian faith and so Grotius became a popular target in the apologetic literature of the age, Protestant as well as Roman Catholic.[5] It would be wrong, however, to view the judgement on Grotius as completely negative. Some theologians showed a certain open-mindedness towards Grotius' line of thinking. These included the Dutch theologian Campegius Vitringa.

Campegius Vitringa (1659–1722)

Campegius Vitringa was professor of oriental languages, theology and church history at Franeker university (Friesland) from 1680 until his death in 1722.[6] At the time Franeker's theological faculty bore a liberal stamp, occasioned by its open-mindedness towards Cocceian and Cartesian theology. Vitringa was no exception: he adhered to a moderate complex of Cocceian and Cartesian tenets. He was known for his vast scholarship that went hand in hand with a deep piety and an irenic mind. As a disciple of Johannes Cocceius Vitringa was an exponent of the federal theology, which possessed elements similar to Grotius' ideas on natural law. Belonging to the so-called 'serious' or pietistic Cocceians, he showed great interest in practical theology, mysticism, quietism and asceticism. Through his works, which were translated into various languages,

---

[5] For a Roman Catholic attack on Grotius' views on the prophecies, see for example JEAN-FRANÇOIS BALTUS S.J., *Défense des propheties*, I-III, 1737. A Dutch translation appeared in Leiden in 1747 (*Verdediging der profeetsien van den kristelyken godtsdienst ... tegen twee vermaarde mannen, Hugo Grotius en Richard Simon*) with a preface by the Leiden professor of theology Joan van den Honert, a fervent student of the 'theologia prophetica.'

[6] For Campegius Vitringa, see W.F.C.J. VAN HEEL, *Campegius Vitringa Sr. als godgeleerde beschouwd*, diss. Utrecht, 's-Gravenhage 1865; CHR. SEPP, *Johannes Stinstra en zijn tijd* I, Amsterdam 1865, pp. 39–44; HERMAN BAUCH, *Die Lehre vom Wirken des Heiligen Geistes im Frühpietismus*, Hamburg 1974; *Biografisch Lexikon voor de Geschiedenis van het Nederlandse Protestantisme* III, Kampen 1988, pp. 379–82 (K.M. WITTEVEEN); J. VAN SLUIS, *Herman Alexander Röell*, diss. Groningen, Ljouwert/Leeuwarden [1988], passim; K.M. WITTEVEEN, "Campegius Vitringa und die prophetische Theologie," in HEIKO A. OBERMAN et al. (edd.), *Reformiertes Erbe. Festschrift für Gottfried W. Locher zu seinem 80. Geburtstag*, Band II [= Zwingliana XIX/2], Zürich 1992 [= 1993], pp. 343–59. See also H.W.M. VAN DE SANDT, *Joan Alberti. Een Nederlandse theoloog en classicus in de achttiende eeuw*, diss. Utrecht 1984, passim. On Franeker theological faculty, see J. VAN DEN BERG, "Theologiebeoefening te Franeker en te Leiden in de achttiende eeuw," *It Beaken* 47 (1985), pp. 181–91 (= "Theology in Leiden and Franeker in the eighteenth century," in *Festschrift J. van den Berg* (forthcoming)). Twice Vitringa was appointed professor in Utrecht, but he never left Franeker: in 1698 his nomination as successor to his former teacher Herman Witsius was vetoed by stadtholder-king William III on account of his Cocceian-Cartesian ideas; in 1702 Vitringa himself refused to accept the appointment. Vitringa's son, like his father named Campegius (1693–1723), was also professor at Franeker.

and his many students from the Dutch Republic as well as from abroad (Hungary, Poland, France, Germany, Scotland), Vitringa's influence made itself felt for a long time, lasting well into the nineteenth century. Above all his eschatological ideas were influential among such famous pietists as Philipp Jakob Spener, August Hermann Francke, and Johann Albrecht Bengel. His dogmatic work, entitled *Aphorismi quibus fundamenta S. Theologiae comprehenduntur*, was reprinted several times. His *Commentarius in librum prophetiarum Jesaiae*[7] was highly praised by contemporary and later exegetes. So was his commentary on the Book of Revelation, entitled *Anacrisis Apocalypsios Joannis Apostoli*.[8] Vitringa was especially known for his exegetical achievements. He had acquired a great familiarity with philology, history, geology, archeology, and Jewish antiquities. Furthermore he was a prophetic theologian par excellence. Prophetic exegesis was most important to him, as is apparent from the long commentaries just mentioned as well as his methodological treatise, entitled *Typus doctrinae propheticae*.[9] Vitringa lends himself particularly well as an illustration of the open-mindedness of orthodox divines towards the Grotian line of prophetic thinking. In his prophetic theology he attempted to steer a middle course between the concepts of the two scholars who had formulated the main prophetic systems of his day: Hugo Grotius and Johannes Cocceius. In his own 'studium propheticum' Vitringa tried to connect the Grotian and Cocceian systems.

---

[7] *Commentarius in librum prophetiarum Jesaiae, quo sensus orationis ejus sedulo investigatur, in veras visorum interpretandorum hypotheses inquiritur, et ex iisdem facta interpretatio antiquae historiae monumentis confirmatur atque illustratur*. The first volume was published in Leeuwarden in 1714; second edition 1724. The second volume was published in 1720; reprinted with the first volume in 1724. Other editions: Herborn 1721; Basel 1732. A Dutch translation appeared in Leeuwarden in 1739; a German translation in Halle in 1739 (preface by Johann Lorenz von Mosheim). On the merits of this commentary, see ALBERT SCHULTENS, *Laudatio funebris in memoriam Campegii Vitringae*, in CAMPEGIUS VITRINGA, *Commentarius ... Jesaiae* I, Leeuwarden 1724, pp. 1–31, esp. pp. 19–20: "immortale illud in Jesaiam monumentum, opere magnifico conditum, perennibusque literis incisum velut, ac sempiternae gloriae dedicatum. Quicquid ab ingenio humano proficisci potest, huc congestum est et effusum." See also LUDWIG DIESTEL, *Geschichte des Alten Testamentes in der christlichen Kirche*, Jena 1869, pp. 436–38; HANS JOACHIM KRAUS, *Geschichte der historisch-kritischen Erforschung des Alten Testaments*, 3. erw. Aufl., Neukirchen – Vluyn 1982, pp. 91–92.

[8] First edition Franeker 1705; second, enlarged edition Amsterdam 1719; third edition Wittenberg 1721. A Dutch translation: Amsterdam 1728 (date of Vitringa's preface: 9 March 1719); the preface to this translation is an elaborated version of the Latin one.

[9] *Typus doctrinae propheticae, in quo de prophetis et prophetiis agitur, hujusque scientiae praecepta traduntur*. First edition: Franeker 1708. Usually together with his *Hypotyposis Historiae et Chronologiae sacrae a M.C. usque ad finem saec. I*, Franeker 1708; second edition: Leeuwarden 1716; third edition: Leeuwarden 1722.

Hugo Grotius and Johannes Cocceius on Scriptural Prophecies

As a well-known seventeenth-century saying went: "Cocceius found Christ everywhere in Scripture, while Grotius found Him practically nowhere."[10] This saying was inspired by their different views on the interpretation of the biblical prophecies. Hugo Grotius stressed the almost immediate fulfilment of the prophecies, advocating the so-called preterist view. This implied that he did not generally interpret the prophecies as referring to Christ; he thus believed that Isaiah 53 referred to Jeremiah instead of Christ. He parted company with current opinion of his day in his conviction that the Old Testament prophecies dealt first and foremost with the people of Israel. Besides the literal, primary sense of the text, Grotius nevertheless allowed for a secondary meaning, a 'sensus sublimior' or 'sensus mysticus,' which referred to Christ. This 'sensus mysticus,' however, would always remain the secondary meaning, the 'sensus primarius' being the literal, Israel-oriented one. In his annotations on the Book of Revelation Grotius saw the fulfilment of those apocalyptic visions in the days of the pagan Roman empire; a line of thinking which differed greatly from current Protestant interpretation of the Apocalypse. Grotius' exposition of the prophecies was not fully preterist: his interpretation was obviously not free from historicist elements.[11]

The most influential prophetic system of the (early) Enlightenment was Cocceianism. It stemmed from the German theologian and orientalist Johannes Cocceius, who, after having been professor of oriental languages and theology at Franeker, taught at Leiden

---

[10] Thus RICHARD SIMON, *Histoire critique des principaux commentateurs du Nouveau Testament*, 1693, p. 764: "On dit de lui (Cocceius) qu'il trouvait partout le Messie et que Grotius tout au contraire, qu'il combat ordinairement, ne le trouvoit presque en aucun endroit." Cf. J.F. BUDDAEUS, *Isagoge historico theologica* II, Lipsiae 1730, p. 1508: "Passim celebratur illud quorundam judicium: Grotium nusquam in sacris litteris invenire Christum, Cocceium ubique."

[11] See DAVID BRADY, *The Contribution of British Writers between 1560 and 1830 to the Interpretation of Revelation 13.16–18* [Beiträge zur Geschichte der biblischen Exegese, 27], Tübingen 1983, p. 168, and passim. For Grotius' exegetical ideas, see A. KUENEN, "Hugo de Groot als uitlegger van het Oude Verbond," in *Verslagen en Mededeelingen der Koninklijke Akademie van Wetenschappen, afd. Letterkunde*, 2e reeks, 12 (1883), pp. 301–32 (= "Hugo Grotius als Ausleger des Alten Testaments," in ABRAHAM KUENEN, *Gesammelte Abhandlungen zur biblischen Wissenschaft*, Freiburg i.B. – Leipzig 1894, pp. 161–85); H.J. DE JONGE, "Hugo Grotius: exégète du Nouveau Testament," in *The World of Hugo Grotius (1583–1645). Proceedings of the International Colloquium ... Rotterdam 6–9 April 1983*, Amsterdam – Maarssen 1984, pp. 97–115; HENNING GRAF REVENTLOW, "L'exégèse de Hugo Grotius," in JEAN-ROBERT ARMOGATHE, *Le Grand Siècle et la Bible* [= Bible de Tous les Temps 6], Paris 1989, pp. 141–55; J.P. HEERING, *Hugo de Groot als apologeet van de christelijke godsdienst*, diss. Leiden, 's-Gravenhage 1992.

University from 1650 till his death in 1669.[12] During his Franeker professorship Cocceius got involved in a debate with Grotius on the latter's interpretation of Antichrist. Grotius was of the opinion – which was quite unusual among Protestants at the time – that Antichrist should not be identified with the pope. In his *De antichristo* (1641) and other works Cocceius defended the current Protestant viewpoint. Cocceius wanted to be a biblical theologian; unlike his colleague from Utrecht, Gisbertus Voetius, he said farewell to the use of Aristotelian scholasticism in theology. Theology and philosophy each had their own field and we should not read Scripture with philosophical concepts in mind: "... necesse est, ut, qui ad Scripturarum disciplinam accedit, non habeat praejudicatam, quam ex sua Philosophia acceperit, sapientiae opinionem; sed, ut puer, se a Scriptura doceri expetat."[13] Yet among his followers many felt themselves attracted to philosophical studies, in particular to the novel philosophy of René Descartes. They even went so far as to formulate a kind of Cartesian theology, which, together with prophetic theology, would give rise to vehement quarrels in the Dutch Reformed Church in the early Enlightenment.[14]

Cocceius' basic hermeneutical principle was expressed in the following – and often misquoted – maxim: "Significatio sumenda est non ex aliqua potestate singulorum verborum, aut phraseos alicujus, aut enunciationis alicujus, sed ex tota compage sermonis... Id ergo significant verba, quod possunt significare in integra oratione, sic ut omnino inter se conveniant, ut appareat Deum sapienter ac apte ad docendum esse locutum."[15] Moreover, Scripture was seen by him as a harmonious system. On the basis of this important concept of

---

12 For Johannes Cocceius (1603–1669), see GOTTLOB SCHRENK, *Gottesreich und Bund im älteren Protestantismus, vornehmlich bei Johannes Coccejus*, Gütersloh 1923 [= Basel 1985]; HEINER FAULENBACH, *Weg und Ziel der Erkenntnis Christi. Eine Untersuchung zur Theologie des Johannes Coccejus* [= Beiträge zur Geschichte und Lehre der Reformierten Kirche, 36], Neukirchen – Vluyn 1973; W.J. VAN ASSELT, *Amicitia Dei. Een onderzoek naar de structuur van de theologie van Johannes Coccejus (1603–1669)*, diss. Utrecht, Ede 1988.

13 See JOHANNES COCCEIUS, *Commentarius in Epistolam ad Philippenses*, 1669, Praefatio, p. 7. Cf. RICHARD SIMON on Cocceius: "Toute son occupation etoit le simple texte de la Bible, sur lequel il meditoit sans cesse" (*Histoire critique des principaux commentateurs du Nouveau Testament*, p. 764).

14 See ERNESTINE VAN DER WALL, "Scepticism and Orthodoxy in the early Dutch Enlightenment," in R.H. POPKIN – A.J. VANDERJAGT (edd.), *Scepticism and Irreligion in the Seventeenth and Eighteenth Centuries* [= Brill's Studies in Intellectual History, 37], Leiden 1993, pp. 121–49; ERNESTINE VAN DER WALL, "Profetie en providentie. De coccejanen en de vroege Verlichting," in P. BANGE et al. (edd.), *Kerk en Verlichting. Voordrachten gehouden op het Windesheim Symposium te Windesheim op 18 november 1990*, Zwolle 1991, pp. 29–37.

15 See JOHANNES COCCEIUS, *Commentarius in Epistolam ad Romanos*, 1665, Praefatio.

scriptural harmony Cocceius discovered the same subject everywhere in the Bible, and especially in the prophecies: Christ and His Kingdom. The Bible became a prolonged prophecy of the history of the Christian Church; prophecy and history were closely linked. Thus Cocceius developed a dynamic theology of history: God's Kingdom gradually came to be revealed in the course of the centuries. History was divided into seven periods – the number seven being most important to Cocceius –, and he believed that the seventh and last period, the millennium, was imminent. Thanks to his prophetic theology, eschatological thinking with a light millenarian flavour gained admittance into the world of Reformed orthodoxy. Thus in the Dutch Republic a similar development occurred to what happened elsewhere in Europe: while at first millenarian thinking was mainly found among religious dissidents, this special form of eschatology became more or less respectable in orthodox circles in the latter half of the seventeenth century.[16]

Following in the footsteps of Cocceius, albeit in an independent way, his disciples developed, and intensely pursued, a specific genre, the 'theologia prophetica.'[17] Prophetic theology was concerned with the interpretation of the prophecies and so with biblical exegesis. Its students were no enthusiasts or fanatics who believed in new revelations to be disclosed in their own time – Vitringa himself emphasized this in the preface to his commentary on Isaiah –, but they occupied themselves with the scholarly study of the prophecies. They tried to formulate general rules for explaining the prophecies and wrote lengthy theoretical and methodological expositions on the topic. Typology (or, as their opponents liked to name it, "typomania"), allegory, emblematic theology: all were used in their hermeneutics. Prophetic theology was so popular because it bore witness to God's providence in history and so to His existence: the 'theologia prophetica' was intended as an apologetic instrument to show unbelievers that there was a God who, moreover, ruled history. Besides, prophetic evidence showed that the Bible was of divine origin. Time and again, until the end of the eighteenth century, this apologetic motive of prophetic theology was expressed by the adherents of the 'studium propheticum.' Prophetic theology soon be-

---

[16] See ERNESTINE VAN DER WALL, "'Antichrist Stormed': The Glorious Revolution and the Dutch Prophetic Tradition," in DALE HOAK – MORDECHAI FEINGOLD (edd.), *The World of William and Mary: Politics, Commerce, Ideas and Culture. Essays commemorating the Tercentenary of the Glorious Revolution*, California (forthcoming).

[17] On prophetic theology, see GRETE MÖLLER, "Föderalismus und Geschichtsbetrachtung im XVII. und XVIII. Jahrhundert," *Zeitschrift für Kirchengeschichte* 50 (1931), pp. 393–440.

came as popular as that other beloved apologetic weapon: physico-theology. Just as physicotheology appealed to God's work in nature, so prophetic theology appealed to His work in history. Both were meant to contribute to the refutation of sceptics and atheists.

For most divines in the (early) Enlightenment the choice between the preterist approach of Grotius and the historicist method of Cocceius was not a difficult one: there was a strong predilection for the latter. Campegius Vitringa was no exception to the rule. Though he often praised Grotius' philological achievements (as well as those of Erasmus) and seriously tried to connect Grotius' hermeneutics with those of Cocceius, he undoubtedly preferred the Cocceian view of history. Nevertheless he wanted to curb the typological extravagances of Cocceian exegesis. In this he surely followed in the footsteps of his teacher Herman Witsius.[18] Cocceian exegetes often lost themselves in intricate typological expositions in order to show the harmony of the Old and New Testament and its central theme: Christ and his Kingdom. Campegius Vitringa did not advocate such an extreme typological method. He had read Grotius and although he did not approve of Grotius' method in general, we get the impression that some of his exegetical notions were formulated with Grotius in mind. In what way did Vitringa use Grotius as a guide?

Being convinced of the absolute necessity of the 'studium propheticum' for theology as a whole Vitringa, like so many prophetic theologians, liked to write about the methodological aspects of prophetic theology. Thus he devoted his *Typus doctrinae propheticae* to this 'science,' in which prophecy and history were closely linked: "*Historia* enim ut est gestarum, sic *prophetia* rerum gerundarum narratio. *Historia* lucem foeneratur *prophetiae*; *prophetia* praevertit, et implementum nacta, vicissim illustrat ac confirmat *historiam*." What is a prophecy? "*Prophetia* est praedictio casus aut eventus contingentis futuri temporis ex revelatione divina, eaque immediate excepta."[19] He strongly emphasizes that a prophecy deals with contingent matters and events: "Cum enim *casus* omnes aut eventus rerum vel *necessarii* sint, qui a physicis et necessariis caussis secundum naturae legem atque ordinem pendent; ... vel *contingentes*, qui necessariam caussam habere non intelliguntur, ut sunt hominum volitiones et

---

[18] For Herman Witsius (1636–1708), see J. VAN GENDEREN, *Herman Witsius*, diss. Utrecht, 's-Gravenhage 1953. For Witsius' views on Cocceian exegesis, see esp. VAN GENDEREN, *Herman Witsius*, pp. 116–23.

[19] See *Typus doctrinae propheticae*, Praefatio, p. **3. (Quotations are from the edition Leeuwarden 1722).

actiones liberae, earumque consequentia, posterius hoc est prophetiarum verum ac proprium objectum."[20] He felt that in Grotius' preterist interpretation this element of contingency was more or less absent. To sum up: "Latius tamen recte dixeris, prophetiam esse *scientiam, declarationem, interpretationem ejus quod sciri nequit nisi ex revelatione divina.*"[21]

We may detect something of a Grotian approach in his rules for the correct interpretation of the prophetic word. The first thing that we have to do when we interpret a prophecy, Vitringa says, is to determine its subject. Does the prophet speak about himself or about other people? Does he talk about things of his own time or of the future? And does he talk about these things in a literal, grammatical sense or in a mystical, figurative one?[22] In other words, we need to be well informed about the historical context and the specific style of the various prophets. An exegete ought therefore to be a good historian; a requirement that was eminently fulfilled by Vitringa himself. If a subject in the prophecy has been given a proper name, then we should distinguish between three possible senses in order to determine the meaning of this subject: a grammatical meaning, a mystical one, or a mixture of the two.

Vitringa states that we should never deviate from the literal sense, if everything in the text agrees with such a literal meaning. Time and again he appeals to this 'canon certus et magni usus.' This rule reminds us of Grotius' insistence upon the literal sense. Vitringa, however, does not refer to Grotius, but to a theologian from Saumur, Etienne Gaussen, whose *De ratione studii theologici* (1670) enjoyed a certain popularity well into the eighteenth century.[23] Vitringa maintains that we can only start looking for a mystical meaning if the attributes in the text do not agree with the name of the subject. He adds that if a subject can be interpreted in a mixed sense, both literal and mystical, it will still be more correct to look first for the literal sense, and next for the spiritual meaning.

---

[20] See *Typus doctrinae propheticae*, p. 2.
[21] See *Typus doctrinae propheticae*, p. 2.
[22] See for this and the following, *Typus doctrinae propheticae*, pp. 175 ff.
[23] See *Typus doctrinae propheticae*, p. 176, where a passage is quoted from Gaussen's dissertation. For Etienne Gaussen (?–1675), see C.G. Jöcher, *Allgemeines Gelehrtenlexicon* II, Leipzig 1750, p. 889; E. and E. Haag, *La France protestante* IV (1853), pp. 235–36. Gaussen became professor of theology in Saumur in 1665. In 1670 he published *Quatuor dissertationes theologicae*, among them *De ratione studii theologici*. Other editions: Utrecht 1675 and 1678; Amsterdam 1697; Cassel 1697; Leiden 1698; Frankfurt 1707; Halle 1727 (preface by J.J. Rambach); Leiden 1792. Gaussen was highly praised by the Cocceian-Cartesian professor of theology at Utrecht Franciscus Burman as well as by August Hermann Francke.

One example may suffice here: the predictions about the state of the Jewish people after their return from the Babylonian exile refer to their situation in Israel at that time; however, these prophecies obviously bear such an elevated character that we cannot but assume that they also refer to the 'beneficia gratiae' of the New Testament. Criticism of Grotius' views is implied in this rule, since in the eyes of his opponents he had not respected the grandness of such predictions sufficiently with his denial of the mystical, elevated sense of biblical prophecies.

Commentarius in librum prophetiarum Jesaiae

These few theoretical notions give an idea of what Vitringa thought of Grotius' exegesis. For his judgement of Grotius, however, we do not need to browse through his works, but we can turn to the preface of his famous commentary on Isaiah in which he pays ample attention to Grotius' – and Cocceius' – method of interpretation. Vitringa first deals with the exegete's object of determining the grammatical sense of the text and points to the great use of the Masoretic, punctuated version. Yet there are, and will always remain, differences of opinion between interpreters of Isaiah, Jewish exegetes included. Vitringa has used the older Jewish commentators; he pays his particular respects to Abn Ezra and Kimchi. He warns, however, against relying too much upon the Jewish testimonies and ascribing too much to the Jews (as some Christians do), since they are sworn enemies of Christianity. The Christian religion and its proof are based on unshakable grounds and do not need the support of the Jews.[24]

In his survey of the different methods of interpretation in Christian history Vitringa first deals with the allegorical method of Origen and others in the early Church (Victorinus of Pettau, Eusebius of Caesarea, Cyrillus, Theodoretus, Procopius), who completely ignored the literal sense and interpreted the prophecies as only referring to a distant future: the coming of the Messiah and his Kingdom. Fortunately Jerome knew how to distinguish between the allegorical and the literal interpretation of the prophecies and most medieval and reformation commentators had followed him. Some exegetes, seeing this neglect of the literal meaning, had wanted however to interpret the prophecies in a more historical way as referring to events in the times of the prophets themselves (the Protes-

---

[24] See *Commentarius ... Jesaiae* I, Praefatio, p. 5.

tants Pellican, Calvin, Johannes Brentz, and Piscator; and the Roman Catholic expositors Estius, Sanctius and Tirinus).[25]

He then comes to Grotius who, as Vitringa observes, has adopted a new method which up till then no Christian exegete had used: "Hugo Grotius, praeclari nominis viri, et in universum de literis immortaliter meritus, cum ne in hac quidem sibi satisfeceret methodo, viam ingressus est novam, hactenus a nemine interpretum Christianorum calcatam, minus tritam, quam existimavit se iis maxime esse persuasurum, qui mysteria sublimiora in doctrinam religionis, et in ipso quoque verbo prophetico, gravantur."[26] Vitringa summarizes Grotius' hypothesis – which, as he emphatically points out, has been received with great indignation – that the prophecies generally refer to the Jewish people and the pagan nations of the prophets' own time. According to Grotius there is nothing to be found in Isaiah about the Messiah – or Jesus Christ and His Kingdom – "nisi ex sensu mystico et allegorico." Vitringa calls Grotius' way of thinking a novel method, because, he says, he does not know of any such interpretation having been advanced before Grotius' time; apparently Vitringa still clung to the idea that novelty implied heterodoxy. He points out that the medieval Jewish exegetes Abn Ezra and Moses Haccohen seem to have had similar ideas, but both of them deviated from the traditional Jewish line of thinking. In his famous review of the first volume of the commentary on Isaiah Jean Le Clerc observed that the controversy between some modern theologians and Grotius was not about whether there were two senses in Scripture – this was a common opinion – but whether various Old Testament prophecies which refer to Christ might have had a literal accomplishment less sublime and less precise before having been fulfilled more perfectly in Christ. Grotius answered this question in the affirmative, the others denied it.[27]

Vitringa next reviews Cocceius' line of analysis, showing how Cocceius interprets not in an allegorical but in a historical way the mysterious names in the prophecies as predicting the events of Jewish or Christian history.[28] So Cocceius has generally only agreed

---

[25] See *Commentarius ... Jesaiae* I, Praefatio, pp. 7–9.

[26] See for this and the following *Commentarius ... Jesaiae* I, Praefatio, p. 9.

[27] JEAN LE CLERC, *Bibliothèque choisie* 27/2 (1713), art. 3, pp. 378–423 (p. 390). He adds that Grotius' ideas are not as novel as is often assumed, referring to the Amsterdam professor of Hebrew and Greek Guilelmus Surenhusius (whose Βίβλος καταλλαγῆς appeared in Amsterdam in 1713), and to Simon de Muis' explication of Psalm 22 which resembles the one by Grotius. "La pensée de Grotius, touchant le double sense des prophéties, n'est pas nouvelle, et les plus outrez allégoristes ont reconnu un double sens." (p. 390).

[28] See *Commentarius ... Jesaiae* I, Praefatio, pp. 9–10.

with the literal, historical sense, being convinced that the prophecies speak directly about the Jews or the Romans. Vitringa remarks that in his time there are three different groups of exegetes: some who follow Grotius, others who follow Cocceius, and others again who want to steer a middle course between them. These exegetes of the 'via media,' among which Vitringa clearly reckons himself, acknowledge the historical sense of the prophecies on the one hand, while on the other they are aware of the fact that Christ and His Kingdom are the main subject of the prophecies. So when they find the attributes and characteristics of Christ and His Kingdom in a prophecy, they do not avert their eyes – as Grotius does, Vitringa seems to imply –, but they like to show that Christ is the figure referred to.[29]

In his opinion Grotius' hermeneutical method is not in accordance with the honour and truth of the Christian religion.[30] His main objection to Grotius is that, according to his hypothesis, Christ may not be found in the prophetic word in a direct and grammatical way. Grotius leads the reader away from Christ, even when Christ is clearly referred to. The fact that he prefers to interpret Isaiah 53 as referring to Jeremiah must be the result of shame: "Pudor, non ratio, virum doctum ad hanc sententiam compulisse videtur." It looks to Vitringa as if a certain heresy of Marcion has been revived according to which the Messiah of the prophets was other than our Jesus.[31] He points to a recent commentary on Isaiah by Samuel White; White's method of interpreting the prophecies echoes Grotius', but he is more liberal than Grotius, interpreting the last part of Isaiah 52 and the whole of Isaiah 53 as referring in a direct and grammatical sense to Christ.[32] If Grotius' hypothesis is correct, how should we interpret the sayings by the apostles that our Messiah was the one prophesied by the Old Testament prophets (John 1.46; Acts 10.43; Acts 3.24; 1 Peter 10.11; Luke 24.27; Acts 18.28)? Did not Christ himself refer to the Old Testament prophecies, as well as to those in Isaiah? Have Christ and his apostles interpreted the prophetic word in a sense other than the interpreters of later times?

---

[29] See *Commentarius ... Jesaiae* I, Praefatio, p. 10.

[30] See *Commentarius ... Jesaiae* I, Praefatio, p. 10: "Grotianam hyopthesin, et in ea fundatam methodum, cum honore et veritate sanctissimae religionis nostrae, aut cum auctoritate Christi Jesu et Apostolorum ejus, conciliari posse, aegre admiserim."

[31] See *Commentarius ... Jesaiae* I, Praefatio, p. 11.

[32] See *Commentarius ... Jesaiae* I , Praefatio, p. 11. It seems that Vitringa knew of Samuel White's commentary only through the review given by Le Clerc in the *Bibliothèque choisie* 23/2 (1711), art. 4.

Admittedly Grotius knows of a 'sensus sublimior,' but he pays so little attention to it and, if he does, talks about it in such a cold manner that it does not seem to play any particular role in his exegesis.[33] Other exegetes who belong to Grotius' party maintain that the mystical sense may only be found in those texts which are to be interpreted in such a manner according to the New Testament. The Remonstrant theologian Philippus van Limborch had expressed himself in this vein.[34] Moreover, as Le Clerc had pointed out, a recent British work contended that the apostles had accommodated themselves to the understanding of the Jews of their times when they talked about the mystical sense.[35] O we poor Christians, Vitringa exclaims, if we accept this thesis no proof whatsoever of the truth of our religion on the basis of the prophetic scriptures can be adduced against the Jews. Evidence of the truth of the Christian faith should be based upon general, rational principles. Only such a proof can be advanced against the Jews and other disbelievers. Belief in divine inspiration or the authority of the apostles cannot be its basis, since the Jews do not accept any of these arguments. All evidence concerning Christ out of the prophetic scriptures should be based on these two theses: 1) that the prophets prophesy about a certain lofty person more eminent than David, Solomon etc., that is the Messiah; and 2) that these eminent characteristics can be applied to Christ in every detail. This evidence is rational, understandable, being founded on general principles which cannot be made stronger by any inspiration or authority.[36]

Though sharply criticizing Grotius' exegesis, Vitringa, however, is not inclined to adopt the Cocceian line of analysis in detail. He cannot agree with the way in which Cocceius and his disciples interpret the biblical prophecies as only referring to events in Christian history. He again emphasizes the need of correct rules of interpretation; rules which common sense shows us to be valid. The interpretation of Scripture is a matter of 'demonstratio': "Nullus enim

---

[33] See *Commentarius ... Jesaiae* I, Praefatio, p. 12. Le Clerc adduces arguments to show that Grotius talks about this 'sensus sublimior' in several places, for example in his famous annotations on Matthew 1.22; Psalm 22.1; and in the fifth book of his *De veritate* (see *Bibliothèque choisie* 1713, pp. 389–90).

[34] See *Commentarius ... Jesaiae* I, Praefatio, p. 12, where Vitringa refers to Van Limborch's preface to his *Commentarius in Acta Apostolorum et in Epistolas ad Romanos et ad Hebraeos*, Rotterdam 1711. This preface contains a long passage in which Van Limborch attacks Cocceian prophetic theology, without mentioning any name. Vitringa seems to have known Van Limborch's commentary only through the review in Le Clerc, *Bibliothèque choisie* 23 (1711), which did not refer to the anti-Cocceian passages.

[35] See *Commentarius ... Jesaiae* I, Praefatio, p. 12.

[36] See *Commentarius ... Jesaiae* I, Praefatio, pp. 12–14.

sensus Scripturae S. me doctiorem et scientiorem facit, cujus veritas ex suis principiis demonstrari nequeat."[37] Without demonstration any science will remain vague and uncertain.

The first among the certain rules of interpretation is not to deviate from the primary, grammatical sense without any serious or necessary reason, that is "nisi *subjectis* illis aptentur *attributa*, quae secundum primum et proprium sensum iis non conveniunt."[38] Only if this is the case does reason allow us to look further and to think of an analogous subject. Similarly, and this the second rule, it is common sense that prescribes us to look for the fulfilment of a prophecy in its own time rather than in distant days. If a prophecy can be said to have been accomplished perfectly in the time closest to the prophet, then we need not look for another accomplishment. But if it is only imperfectly fulfilled in a time close to the prophet's days, then common sense again orders the exegete to look for a beginning of the fulfilment in the days close to those of the prophet and to seek for a more perfect accomplishment in later times. "Ab his canonibus si discesseris, omnis interpretatio prophetica vaga redditur, incerta, arbitraria, fluxae fidei ac dubiae, nemini demonstrabilis, infirmarum ac credularum mentium ludibrium."[39]

With these basic hermeneutical rules Vitringa wants to show Cocceian exegetes that they often unnecessarily interpret the prophecies as referring to later times. Some exegetes, such as Jean de Labadie and Jacob Alting, have even only seen the fulfilment of the prophecies in the end of days. Cocceius had shown more moderation in that respect. Vitringa himself does not want to set limits on the hopes of the Church. Why should we expect less than God has promised us? And He has promised us a glorious future. So, Vitringa confesses, I belong to those – and some resent that – who expect greater things to happen in the future than the Church has seen hitherto.[40]

---

[37] See *Commentarius ... Jesaiae* I, Praefatio, p. 16.

[38] See *Commentarius ... Jesaiae* I, Praefatio, p. 16. Cf. p. 18: "si subjecta orationis proprium et literalem admitterent sensum, absque gravi ratione et necessitate ad mysticum non transii..." See also *Commentarius ... Jesaiae* II, Praefatio, pp. 6–7, where Vitringa stresses the importance of the 'scopus' of the text: "At Scripturas propheticas, secundum primum et proximum earundem scopum, grammatice et historice interpretari, ad veram et perfectiorem intelligentiam plus olei et temporis poscit, et majoris operae res est. (...) Scopus enim orationis, judicio praetensus, omnes administrat interpretis cogitationes."

[39] See *Commentarius ... Jesaiae* I, Praefatio, p. 16.

[40] See *Commentarius ... Jesaiae* I, Praefatio, pp. 17–18.

Anacrisis Apocalypsios Joannis Apostoli

These 'greater things' were dealt with in his commentary on the Apocalypse, which was published several years before his commentary on Isaiah. Vitringa himself saw no difference between his ideas in his *Anacrisis Apocalypsios* and his commentary on Isaiah.[41] First of all he refuted the eschatological ideas of Grotius, who adhered to a novel way of interpreting the Apocalypse. In this he was "the Choragus and leads the Dance (a Dance which has made those of the Court of Rome no little sport)."[42] A Roman Catholic scholar who had followed Grotius' preterist interpretation was Jacques Bénigne Bossuet, Bishop of Meaux. In 1690 Bossuet had published his *L'Apocalypse avec une explication.* and it is this work that Vitringa seeks to refute in addition to Grotius. According to Vitringa Bossuet's interpretation, although in a Grotian vein, was preferable to Grotius' exegesis of the Book of Revelation.[43]

In the *Anacrisis Apocalypsios* we find a thorough theoretical exposition of the interpretation of the prophecies. Again he emphasizes that the most important matter is the formulation of correct rules of interpretation or of 'hypotheses' as he calls them. These hypotheses are the key to the Bible (Luke 11.52): if we use the right hypotheses, we will have no difficulty in acceding to the inner rooms of Scripture. With regard to the prophecies in the Book of Revelation Vitringa maintains that he has been more intensely engaged in finding the correct hypotheses than any of his predecessors, with the exception of Joseph Mede, who has devised the best method of interpreting the Apocalypse, though his hypotheses may not be without their faults.[44] It is Vitringa's firm conviction that there will never be any agreement among the interpreters of Revelation so

---

[41] *Anacrisis Apocalypsios Joannis Apostoli, qua in veras interpretandae eius hypotheses diligenter inquiritur et ex iisdem interpretatio facta, certis historiarum monumentis confirmatur atque illustratur. Tum quoque quae Meldensis Praesul Bossuetus hujus libri commentario supposuit, et exegetico Protestantium systemati in visis de bestia ac Babylone mystica objecit, sedulo examinantur.* Quotations are from the second edition, Amsterdam 1719. For other editions, see note 8. For Vitringa's judgement on both his commentaries, see the preface to the second volume of the commentary on Isaiah. Albert Schultens said of the *Anacrisis Apocalypsios* that it was the "praelusio ac praecursio" of the commentary on Isaiah (*Laudatio funebris*, p. 20). For Le Clerc's laudatory review of Vitringa's commentary on Revelation, see *Bibliothèque choisie* 6 (1705), pp. 334–41.

[42] Thus John Worthington in the "General Preface" to his edition of *The Works of the pious and profoundly-learned Joseph Mede*, London 1672.

[43] On Bossuet and Grotius, see J.A.G. TANS, *Bossuet en Hollande*, diss. Nijmegen, Maastricht 1949, pp. 12–51.

[44] See JOSEPH MEDE, *Clavis apocalyptica*, 1627. Vitringa was well informed about British writers on the Apocalypse, among them Francis Potter, Hugh Broughton, Patrick Forbes, Thomas Burnet.

long as they differ about the rules for explaining this book.[45] For
example, if it is certain that John received his prophecies some
years after the destruction of Jerusalem under Domitian, we will
thus not be easily persuaded by Grotius that Revelation 6.12 is a
prophecy about the downfall of the Jewish Republic.

One of the main causes to give rise to disagreement among interpreters is the abundance of remarkable events in history which
resemble one another and so make the expositors uncertain about
what event has been prophesied. It is not so much the obscurity of
the mysterious biblical images that bewilders us as the richness of
historical events. An intensive knowledge of history is therefore an
absolute requirement for interpreting the prophecies correctly, Vitringa concludes.

The duty of an exegete is twofold. First he has to choose proper,
that is sure or probable hypotheses. Secondly, he has to prove the
certainty or probability of those hypotheses. In doing so the exegete
will save the reader a lot of time, since we need not read all commentaries on Revelation extensively but need only check the hypotheses of the commentators. Vitringa mentions three principles for
choosing the correct hypotheses. (1) It is most important to pay
attention to the marks of the prophecy itself which show its intention. (2) Reason teaches us to distinguish between probable and less
probable matters, while it also shows us that the prophecies should
be interpreted in a particular sense; otherwise it would not have
been necessary to give this prophecy to the Church. And (3) we
should compare the visions of Revelation with the prophecies of the
Old Testament as well as with several parts of the prophecy itself,
which elucidate one another since they refer to the same period.[46]

Vitringa points out that with regard to Revelation this prophecy
is so full of varied emblematic figures that common sense urges us
not to look for an interpretation that sees the accomplishment of
the prophecies of Revelation in the time shortly after John, since
such an interpretation would detract from the dignity and glory of
these prophecies. Yet Grotius had taken this stance by interpreting
them as being fulfilled in the times of Nero and Domitian. Since,
however, only a few events occurred in those times which might be
compared with the glorious vision in the Apocalypse, Grotius is often obliged to resort to tiny details, explaining matters which are
great in the prophecies by historical events of little or no importance. Was the persecution by Domitian such a remarkable matter

---

[45] See *Anacrisis Apocalypsios*, Praefatio, p. ***2v.
[46] See *Anacrisis Apocalypsios*, Praefatio, p. ***3v–[4v].

that the Holy Spirit had to devote six chapters to this event, while according to Grotius' literal explanation this persecution did not even last 42 months? No rational man will welcome such a manner of interpretation as it is not in accordance with the dignity of the prophecies. Obviously for Vitringa the hermeneutical principle of dignity is most important. He notes that at times he has been angry with Grotius because the latter did so much to detract from the lustre of the prophecies. But he estimates his learning highly and was indignant when he saw that some commentators grabbed every opportunity not only to refute Grotius but also to slander him.[47]

Referring to Rev. 4.1, which says that only those things which will happen *afterwards* will be revealed to John, and to Rev. 22.12, which says that we have to wait for the glorious future of the Lord, Vitringa contends that according to reason it is probable that the Apocalypse contains a perfect prophecy which does not only refer to the churches in Asia, but also to the universal Catholic Church until the end of time. One of his main objections to Grotius, Bossuet and other preterist interpreters is that they remove consolation from the faithful: the general aim of Revelation, as of other prophecies, is to teach the Church about the changes in history and the signs of those changes. Knowing that its history of persecutions will one day come to a close, it will not abandon hope but look forward to the glorious end of history as determined by God.[48]

The Key to the Apocalypse: the Prophecy about the Beast

The key to the Book of Revelation is to be found in the correct interpretation of the prophecy about the beast. The Holy Spirit has devoted six chapters to the origin, reign, signs and downfall of the beast. If we can determine the true meaning of the prophecy about the seven-headed beast, we will have the key to the most important rooms of the whole prophecy. The appearance of the beast occurs in the days of the sixth trumpet. The marks of the beast are so various and remarkable that they cannot be applied to many kingdoms in the world. The king is expressly mentioned, Rome (Rev. 17.3). There are two ways of interpreting Revelation: 1) the beast is the pagan Roman empire; 2) the beast is anti-Christianity with Rome as its head. So it is a sure hypothesis that the beast is the Roman empire with its governors, whether pagan or Christian.

---

[47] See *Anacrisis Apocalypsios*, Praefatio, p. [***5ᵛ].
[48] See *Anacrisis Apocalypsios*, p. [***5ʳ–***5ᵛ].

There are many expositors, both Roman Catholic and Protestant, who maintain that the seven-headed beast refers to the pagan, idolatrous Roman empire. As a prominent representative of this opinion Vitringa mentions the Spanish Jesuit Luis de Alcazar. He then proceeds to expound Grotius' suggestion that both beasts refer to the time of Domitian, its seven heads being seven Roman emperors before Domitian. The hypotheses of Alcazar and Grotius are in themselves not unfounded, Vitringa admits, since the pagan empire has been a cruel beast. But is it possible to concord the marks of the beast as well as other circumstances of this prophecy with their view? If so, the interpretation of the beast as pagan Rome, and not as Christian Rome, should be preferred. It must be noted that Vitringa repeatedly says that he would rather side with Grotius and Bossuet than with the common Protestant interpretation. He would rather interpret the beast as pagan Rome than as Christian Rome, since it is a horrifying thought that the Christian Church should have been transformed into such a cruel beast as the one depicted in Revelation 13.[49]

Moreover, he hesitates to point to the faults of the Church of Rome, since the Reformed churches have also deviated from their first perfection and have often been unnecessarily driven apart by their polemics. He thinks it is hypocritical not to mention the sins of the Protestant churches, while exposing the faults of the Roman Catholic Church in sharp terms. He has therefore searched for another interpretation of the beast, such as the one advanced by Grotius and Bossuet. Bossuet's hypothesis is much more probable than Grotius's, since the persecution by Diocletian (which lasted ten years) shows more characteristics in agreement with the prophecy than Domitian's persecution. Grotius imagined that Revelation was a letter written to the Christians of that time: John warned the churches of Asia of the disasters that would befall them shortly.[50] If Grotius had given up that hypothesis, he would have been more fortunate in explaining the Apocalypse.

Vitringa thinks that any follower of Grotius will confess this after he has compared his views with those of Bossuet. To his regret, however, Vitringa has to admit that Bossuet's interpretation cannot

---

[49] See *Anacrisis Apocalypsios*, p. ****2ᵛ. For Luis de Alcazar, whose name only occurs in the Dutch version of the 'Praefatio,' see BRADY, *The Contribution of British Writers*, passim. Only in passing does Vitringa mention (in the Dutch version) the futurist interpretation of Franciscus Ribera, Cornelis a Lapide and other Roman Catholic expositors; their interpretation that Rome as depicted in Revelation has not yet appeared in history is rejected by him as absurd.

[50] See *Anacrisis Apocalypsios*, p. [****2ʳ].

explain the mysteries of previous and subsequent prophecies in Revelation and so has to be discarded too. Vitringa thus feels himself forced by the text to resort to the current Protestant, anti-papal exegesis of Revelation 13.

The Millennium

In his exposition of Revelation 20 Vitringa goes his own way, following neither Grotius nor Cocceius. He declares that this passage is the most difficult in the Book of Revelation. Among the expositors of this chapter he mentions Pierre Yvon, whose interpretation of Gog and Magog is similar to his own. Vitringa refers to Scaliger's opinion that, like Calvin, one should refrain from writing a commentary on the Apocalypse. However, it is wrong to mention Calvin in this respect, Vitringa says; the Genevan reformer must have had his own good reasons not to do so. He furthermore quotes Episcopius, who says that these prophecies are deliberately mysterious so that people might be prompted to investigate them.[51] According to Vitringa there are two systems of interpretation with regard to Revelation 20: some (Grotius and Hammond) see the beginning of the millennium with Constantine the Great and its end with the appearance of the Turks. Others (Vitringa) are firmly convinced that the millennial reign will follow upon the downfall of the beast. Here he parts company with Cocceius, who – like Grotius and Hammond, Forbes and Brightman – clung to the idea that the millennium was a matter of the past and had started with Constantine. Others (Augustine and all medieval commentators) think that it started earlier, with the era of the Christian Church. The presupposition of all these expositors is that in Revelation 20 a new story begins. Yet this is surely not the case, as Vitringa sets out to prove. He acknowledges the success of the Church since Constantine, but, as he points out, only three hundred years after Constantine Mohammed appeared. If such a monstrous thing could happen in a time in which Satan was bound, what would happen when Satan was let loose? Grotius had been aware of the difficulties involved in his solution of a past millennium; the Turk could not be Gog and Magog: where was the fire that had to destroy them? Grotius had obviously expected that judgement, even four centuries later.

So the millennial reign has to begin after the downfall of the beast. Revelation 20.4 makes it abundantly clear that this prophecy has to take place after the reign of the beast has collapsed. More-

---

[51] See *Anacrisis Apocalypsios*, p. [****4ᵛ].

over, the characteristics of the antichristian reign of the beast and those of the millennium are so different that they cannot exist simultaneously. Satan will be bound during those thousand years. This vision agrees with the vision in Daniel 7.9–10, as Mede had observed correctly. According to Vitringa the millennium refers to a long period of peace and well-being of the Church upon earth. God will not let the Kingdom of His Son on earth remain imperfect. Would the beast reign supreme and not Jesus Christ? Let nobody think that these ideas are novel and heterodox. Vitringa points to scholarly and pious men who embraced this millenarian view after the Reformation, such as Franciscus Lambertus, Carolus Gallus, Alfonsus Conradus Mantuanus, Caesius Pannonius, Jacobus Brocardus, and Albertus Leoninus; he also mentions later expositors such as Pierre de Launay, Joseph Mede, Matthieu Cottière and Thomas Burnet. The church fathers too had embraced this idea. It had also been the hope of the Jewish church. Yet we should not follow the 'chiliasts' in believing that the Temple in Jerusalem will be rebuilt and the Levitical cult restored; that the face of the earth will be transformed by fire and will be renewed, bringing forth many fruits without the aid of man. Neither should we believe that Christ will personally and visibly reign upon earth during the millennium: Christ's millennial reign will be a purely spiritual one. Still, Vitringa acknowledges that the Jews will be converted; he hopes that the malediction will be taken away from Canaan and that Jerusalem will be rebuilt. So Vitringa proves himself to be an exponent of the moderate millenarianism that characterized Dutch reformed orthodoxy in the early eighteenth century.

Conclusion

In the eighteenth century prophetic theology flourished in the Dutch Republic as it did elsewhere in Europe. The Book of Revelation enjoyed a great popularity and academic theologians immersed themselves in its interpretation. A host of publications on prophetic theology came from the press, advocating the expediency of the 'studium propheticum' for theology in general. Prophetic theology was deemed an effective weapon in the apologetic battle against the rising tide of unbelief as expressed by scholars such as Hobbes, Spinoza, and Collins.

On the continent Cocceius' influence was long to be felt; prominent pietists claimed to have been inspired by his insights. Yet Grotius' line of analysis gradually gained ground. This is illustrated by

Vitringa's exegetical notions. Like his teacher Witsius he chose to side with Cocceius, probably for the same reason, namely that it was less damnable to think we can find Christ where He may not be than to refuse to see Him when he shows Himself in full clarity. The first is proof of love of Christ, the other of slowness to believe.[52] Although Vitringa stands firmly in the line of Cocceius, he shows his independence, like most disciples of Cocceius, by formulating a prophetic theology of his own in which he appears to have incorporated Grotian ideas.

We may ask whether Vitringa ever succeeded in harmonizing the hermeneutics of Grotius and Cocceius. At times it seems as if the two systems run parallel in his own prophetic theology without actually growing into a whole. Like Witsius again, Vitringa has been described as "ein Zwei-Seelen-Mensch."[53] He strove for a synthesis. We may wonder, however, whether Le Clerc did not hit the mark when he observed that Grotius might have subscribed to Vitringa's hermeneutical rules, implying that Vitringa's position showed more affinity with his own than might appear at first glance. It could well be that Cocceius' insistence upon the 'sensus litteralis' was closer to Grotius' stand than Cocceian theologians assumed.

Vitringa's famous disciple, Herman Venema, his successor in Franeker, is another illustration of the affinity between the Grotian and Cocceian way of thinking. Venema incorporated Grotius' ideas in his own prophetic theology, while clinging to a Cocceian framework.[54] He is regarded as a typical representative of the moderate Dutch Enlightenment. It is perhaps an indication of the moderate character of the Dutch Enlightenment that Grotius' exegetical position never fully won the day. As is apparent from the seemingly unending stream of literature on biblical prophecies in the Enlightenment, Grotius had not put an end to the 'theologia prophetica' and its important role in Christian apologetics.

---

[52] See VAN GENDEREN, *Herman Witsius*, pp. 122–23.

[53] See BAUCH, *Die Lehre vom Wirken des Heiligen Geistes*, p. 24. Cf. CHR. SEPP, *Het godgeleerd onderwijs in Nederland gedurende de 16e en 17e eeuw* II, Leiden 1874, p. 302, who contends that Vitringa did not succeed in achieving a unity between the hermeneutics of Grotius and Cocceius. J.C. DE BRUÏNE, *Herman Venema. Een Nederlandse theoloog in de tijd der Verlichting*, diss. Groningen, Franeker [1973], pp. 43–46, sees Vitringa's position as closer to Cocceius' than to Grotius' system, though he is more moderate than Cocceius.

[54] For Herman Venema (1697–1787), see J.C. DE BRUÏNE, *Herman Venema* (see note 53).

BIBLIOGRAPHIES AND INDEXES

HUGO GROTIUS AS A THEOLOGIAN: A BIBLIOGRAPHY
(ca. 1840–1993)

Compiled by

HENK J.M. NELLEN and EDWIN RABBIE
(The Hague)

Preliminary Note – This bibliography aims at completeness as far as sections B, F, G, I, L and M are concerned. All other sections contain a selection of the most important contributions of the last 150 years. Although many studies of Grotius' works on international law also involve theological questions (e.g., the famous *etiam si daremus*-controversy), we have preferred to include only those contributions that primarily concentrate on Grotius as a theologian rather than as a lawyer. The bibliography is based on autopsy; an asterisk indicates those entries which we have not seen ourselves. We are grateful to Professor Henk Jan de Jonge (Leiden) and Dr. Johannes Trapman for their help in compiling this bibliography.

CONTENTS

A. BIBLIOGRAPHIES

1. Meulen, J. ter and P.J.J. Diermanse. *Bibliographie des écrits imprimés de Hugo Grotius.* La Haye: Nijhoff, 1950.

2. Meulen, J. ter and P.J.J. Diermanse. *Bibliographie des écrits sur Hugo Grotius imprimés aux XVIIe siècle.* La Haye: Nijhoff, 1961.

3. Rabbie, E. "Grotius' theological works (including the politico-religious works): a survey of available editions." *Grotiana* N.S. 11 (1990): 72–73.

220

B. Sources

1. Fruin, R., ed. *Verhooren en andere bescheiden betreffende het rechtsgeding van Hugo de Groot.* Werken van het Historisch Genootschap, gevestigd te Utrecht, N.R. 14. Utrecht: Kemink, 1871.

2. Pintard, R., ed. "Grotiana." In *La Mothe le Vayer – Gassendi – Guy Patin. Études de bibliographie et de critique suivies de textes inédits de Guy Patin.* 69–86. Publications de l'Université de Poitiers, Série des Sciences de l'Homme, 5. Paris: Boivin, [1943].

C. Related Sources

1. Bots, H. and P. Leroy, ed. *Correspondance intégrale, 1641–1650, d'André Rivet et de Claude Sarrau.* 3 vols. Amsterdam – Maarssen: APA – Holland University Press, 1978–82.

2. Leroy, P. and H. Bots, ed. *Claude Saumaise & André Rivet, Correspondance échangée entre 1632 et 1648.* Studies van het Instituut voor Intellectuele Betrekkingen tussen de Westeuropese landen in de moderne tijd, 15. Amsterdam – Maarssen: APA – Holland University Press, 1987.

D. Grotius' Library

1. Eekhof, A. "Grotiana in Noord-Amerika." *NAKG* N.S. 17 (1924): 127–44.

2. Molhuysen, P.C. "De bibliotheek van Hugo de Groot in 1618." *Mededeelingen der Nederlandsche Akademie van Wetenschappen, Afd. Letterkunde,* N.R. 6, 3. Amsterdam: Noord-Hollandsche Uitgevers Maatschappij, 1943.

3. Dovring, F. "Une partie de l'héritage littéraire de Grotius retrouvée en Suède." 1–14. *Mededelingen der Koninklijke Nederlandse Akademie van Wetenschappen, Afd. Letterkunde* N.R. 12, 3. Amsterdam: Noord-Hollandsche Uitgevers Maatschappij, 1949.

4. Meijers, E.M. "Boeken uit de bibliotheek van De Groot in de Universiteitsbibliotheek te Leiden." 15–43. *Mededelingen der Koninklijke Nederlandse Akademie van Wetenschappen, Afd. Letterkunde* N.R. 12, 3. Amsterdam: Noord-Hollandsche Uitgevers Maatschappij, 1949.

5. Dovring, F. "Nouvelles recherches sur la bibliothèque de Grotius en Suède et en Italie." *Mededelingen der Koninklijke Nederlandse Akademie van Wetenschappen, Afd. Letterkunde* N.R. 14, 10. Amsterdam: Noord-Hollandsche Uitgevers Maatschappij, 1951.

6. Eysinga, W.J.M. van and L.J. Noordhoff, *Catalogue de manuscrits autographes de Hugo Grotius, dont la vente a eu lieu à La Haye le 15 Novembre 1864 sous la direction et au domicile de Martinus Nijhoff, deuxième édition avec annotations.* La Haye: Nijhoff 1952.

7. Noordhoff, L.J. *Beschrijving van het zich in Nederland bevindende en nog onbeschreven gedeelte der papieren afkomstig van Huig de Groot welke in 1864 te 's-Gravenhage zijn geveild.* Groningen – Djakarta: Noordhoff, 1953.

8. Rademaker, C.S.M. "Books and Grotius at Loevestein." *Quaerendo* 2 (1972): 2–29.

9. Blok, F.F. *Contributions to the History of Isaac Vossius's Library.* Verhandelingen der Koninklijke Nederlandse Akademie van Wetenschappen, Afd. Letterkunde, N.R. 83. Amsterdam [etc.]: North Holland, 1974.

10. Rabbie, E. "The History and Reconstruction of Hugo Grotius' Library, A Survey of the Results of Former Studies with an Indication of New Lines of Approach." In *Libri, fonti, biblioteca ideale tra scienza, filosofia ed erudizione, da Cusano al Settecento,* ed. E. Canone. Lessico Intellettuale Europeo. Roma: Ateneo, [forthcoming].

E. ENCYCLOPÆDIAS AND COLLECTIONS; GENERAL BIOGRAPHIES

1. Glasius, B. "Hugo de Groot." In *Godgeleerd Nederland. Biographisch woordenboek van Nederlandsche godgeleerden.* 564–81. I. 's Hertogenbosch: Muller, 1851.

2. Rogge, H.C. "Grotius, Hugo." In *Realencyklopädie für protestantische Theologie und Kirche,* ed. J.J. Herzog and A. Hauck. 200–02. VII. Leipzig: Hinrich, 1899.

3. Lewalter, E. "Die geistesgeschichtliche Stellung des Hugo Grotius." *Deutsche Vierteljahrsschrift für Literaturwissenschaft und Geistesgeschichte* 11 (1933): 262–93.

4. *Spörl, J. "Hugo Grotius und der Humanismus des 17. Jahrhunderts." *Historisches Jahrbuch* 55 (1935): 350–57.

5. Hoenderdaal, G.J. "Hugo Grotius." In *Die Aufklärung,* ed. M. Greschat. 43–59. Gestalten der Kirchengeschichte, 8. Stuttgart [etc.]: Kohlhammer, 1983.

6. Benrath, G.A. "Die Lehre des Humanismus und des Antitrinitarismus." In *Die Lehrentwicklung im Rahmen der Ökumenizität,* ed. G.A. Benrath [et al.]. 1–70. Handbuch der Dogmen- und Theologiege-

schichte, ed. C. Andresen, III. Göttingen: Vandenhoeck & Ruprecht, 1984.

7. Guggisberg, H.R. "Grotius, Hugo (1583–1645)." In *TRE* ed. G. Müller. 277–80. XIV. Berlin [etc.]: De Gruyter, 1985.

8. Nellen, H.J.M. *Hugo de Groot (1583–1645): De loopbaan van een geleerd staatsman*. Erflaters. Weesp: Heureka, 1985.

9. "Grotius, Hugo." In *Biographisch-Bibliographisches Kirchenlexikon*, ed. F.W. Bautz. 361–62. II. Hamm (Westf.): Bautz, 1990.

10. Posthumus Meyjes, G.H.M. "Groot, Hugo de." In *Biografisch Lexicon van Protestantse Godgeleerden in Nederland*. IV. Kampen: Kok, [forthcoming].

F. Grotius as a Theologian in General

1. [Koenen, H.J.] "Hugo Grotius en zijne Godgeleerdheid." *Nederlandsche Stemmen over Godsdienst, Staat-, Geschied- en Letterkunde* 5 (1837): 29–36.

2. Dilthey, W. *Weltanschauung und Analyse des Menschen seit Renaissance und Reformation. Abhandlungen zur Geschichte der Philosophie und Religion*. Wilhelm Diltheys Gesammelte Schriften, 2. Leipzig – Berlin: Teubner, 1914.

3. *Schlüter, J. *Die Frömmigkeit und die theologischen Prinzipien des Hugo Grotius*. Diss. Rostock, Schwerin i.M.: Sengebusch, 1914.

4. Schlüter, J. *Die Theologie des Hugo Grotius*. Göttingen: Vandenhoeck & Ruprecht, 1919.

5. Schlüter, J. "Die Frömmigkeit des Hugo Grotius." In *Hugo Grotius; Essays on his Life and Works Selected for the Occasion of the Tercentenary of his "De iure belli ac pacis" 1625–1925 / Opinions sur sa vie et ses œuvres recueillies à l'occasion du tricentenaire du «De iure belli ac pacis» 1625–1925*, ed. A. Lysen. 90–100. Leyden: Sijthoff, 1925.

6. Haentjens, A.H. "Grotius." *Uit de Remonstrantsche Broederschap* 37 (1925/26): 41–47.

7. Roldanus, C.W. "De Groot als theoloog." *De Gids* 108 (1–2 1944–45): 103–25.

8. Haentjens, A.H. *Hugo de Groot als godsdienstig denker*. Amsterdam: Ploegsma, 1946.

9. Meylan, H. "Grotius théologien." In *Hommage à Grotius*. 19–41. Études et documents pour servir à l'histoire de l'Université de Lausanne, 4. Lausanne: Rouge, 1946.

10. Corsano, A. *Ugo Grozio, l'umanista, il teologo, il giurista.* Biblioteca di cultura moderna, 437. Bari: Laterza, 1948. Cf. Droetto, A. **Rivista di filosofia* 39 (1948): 178–83. Reprinted in Droetto, A. *Studi Groziani.* 191–97. Pubblicazioni dell'istituto di scienze politiche dell'Università di Torino, 18. Torino: Giappichelli, 1968.

11. Melzer, F. "Grotianisches Christentum." In *Völkerrecht beginnt bei Dir; Beiträge zur Verbreitung des Völkerrechts,* ed. H.K.E.L. Keller. 36–38. München: Grotius-Stiftung, 1952.

12. Voeltzel, R. "La méthode théologique de Hugo Grotius." *Revue d'histoire et de philosophie religieuses* 32 (1952): 126–33.

13. Ambrosetti, G. *I presupposti teologici e speculativi delle concezioni giuridiche di Grozio.* Pubblicazioni della Facoltà di Giurisprudenza dell'Università di Modena, 90–91 / 25–26. Bologna: Zanichelli, 1955.

14. Droetto, A. "L'alternativa teologica nella concezione giuridica del Grozio." *Rivista internazionale di filosofia del diritto* 33 (1956): 351–63. Reprinted in Droetto, A. *Studi Groziani.* 240–54. Pubblicazioni dell'istituto di scienze politiche dell'Università di Torino, 18. Torino: Giappichelli, 1968.

15. Beckwith, W.F. *The Theology of Hugo Grotius, Jurist – Theologian.* Diss. Boston University (microfilm): 1959.

16. Voeltzel, R. *L'actualité de Hugo Grotius.* Missio Grotiana. Munich: Fondation Grotius, [1964?]

17. De Michelis, F. *Le origini storiche e culturali del pensiero di Ugo Grozio.* Pubblicazioni della Facoltà di lettere e filosofia dell'Università di Milano, 45. Firenze: La Nuova Italia, 1967.

18. Posthumus Meyjes, G.H.M. "Grotius als theoloog." In *Het Delfts orakel; Hugo de Groot 1583–1645,* 111–20. Delft: Stedelijk Museum Het Prinsenhof, 1983. English translation: "Grotius as a theologian." In *Hugo Grotius, a Great European, 1583–1645. Contributions concerning his activities as a humanist scholar,* 51–58. Delft: Meinema, 1983.

19. Trevor-Roper, H. "Hugo Grotius and England." In *From Counter-Reformation to Glorious Revolution.* 47–82. London: Secker & Warburg, 1992.

20. Jonge, H.J. de. "Het belang van de uitgave van Grotius' theologische werken." In *Hoewel ick geen theologant en ben. Twee lezingen over het theologisch oeuvre van Hugo de Groot.* 5–11. 's-Gravenhage: Constantijn Huygens Instituut voor Tekstedities en Intellectuele Geschiedenis, Afdeling Grotius, 1994.

See also Lagrée, section G 3.1.2.

G. Editions, Translations and Studies of Theological Works

1 Collected Works

1. Grotius, H. *Opera omnia theologica, Faksimile-Neudruck der Ausgabe Amsterdam 1679*. 3 (4) vols. Stuttgart – Bad Cannstatt: Frommann – Holzboog, 1972.

2 In mortem Iacobi Arminii (1609)

2.1 Studies

1. Mallinckrodt, W. "Grotius' gedicht op het sterven van Arminius (1609, 19 October)." *Geloof en Vrijheid* 40 (1906): 29–80.

2. Nellen, H.J.M. and E. Rabbie. "Grotius' Fame as a Poet." In *Acta Conventus Neo-Latini Torontonensis, Proceedings of the Seventh International Congress of Neo-Latin Studies, Toronto 8 August to 13 August 1988*, ed. A. Dalzell [et al.]. 539–48. Medieval and Renaissance Texts and Studies, 86. Binghamton, New York: Center for Medieval and Early Renaissance Studies, 1991.

3 Meletius (1611)

3.1 Edition; Translations

1. Posthumus Meyjes, G.H.M., ed. *Hugo Grotius Meletius sive de iis quae inter Christianos conveniunt epistola, critical edition with translation, commentary and introduction*. Studies in the History of Christian Thought, 40. Leiden [etc.]: Brill, 1988.

2. Lagrée, J. *La raison ardente. Religion naturelle et raison au XVIIe siècle. Traduction en Appendice du Meletius de Hugo Grotius*. Philosophie et Mercure. Paris: Vrin, 1991.

3.2 Studies

1. Büch, B. "De waeraghtige bibliophiel." *Optima. Cahier voor literatuur en boekwezen* 2 (1984): 219–27.

2. Posthumus Meyjes, G.H.M. "Gij zult niet strijden met anderen maar met uzelf. Het eerste theologische tractaat van Hugo de Groot." *NRC Handelsblad* 10.8.1984, Cultureel Supplement p. 6.

3. Posthumus Meyjes, G.H.M. "Hugo de Groot's 'Meletius' (1611), his earliest theological work, rediscovered." *Lias* 11 (1984): 147–50.

4. Posthumus Meyjes, G.H.M. "Het vroegste theologische geschrift van Hugo de Groot herontdekt, zijn *Meletius* (1611)." In *Bestuurders en Geleerden. Opstellen over onderwerpen uit de Nederlandse geschiede-*

nis van de zestiende, zeventiende en achttiende eeuw, aangeboden aan prof. dr. J.J. Woltjer bij zijn afscheid als hoogleraar van de Rijksuniversiteit te Leiden, ed. S. Groenveld [et al.]. 75–84. Amsterdam – Dieren: De Bataafsche Leeuw, 1985.

5. Posthumus Meyjes, G.H.M. "De receptie van Hugo de Groots *Meletius.*" In *Kerkhistorische opstellen aangeboden aan Prof. dr. J. van den Berg*, ed. C. Augustijn [et al.]. 30–44. Kampen: Kok, 1987.

6. Besselink, L.F.M. "Hugo Grotius: Meletius sive de iis quae inter christianos conveniunt epistola." *Grotiana* N.S. 10 (1989): 97–103.

4 *Ordinum Hollandiae ac Westfrisiae pietas*

4.1 *Edition; Translation*

1. Rabbie, E., ed. *Hugo Grotius, Ordinum Hollandiae ac Westfrisiae pietas, edited, with an introduction and notes and an English translation.* Hugo Grotius, Opera theologica II. Assen – Maastricht: Van Gorcum, [forthcoming].

4.2 *Studies*

1. Woude, C. van der. *Hugo Grotius en zijn "Pietas Ordinum Hollandiae ac Westfrisiae vindicata".* Kampen: Kok, 1961.

2. Posthumus Meyjes, G.H.M. "De doorwerking van de Moderne Devotie, met name bij de Remonstranten." In *De doorwerking van de Moderne Devotie, Windesheim 1387–1987, Voordrachten gehouden tijdens het Windesheim Symposium Zwolle/Windesheim 15–17 oktober 1987*, ed. P. Bange, C. Graafland, A.J. Jelsma, and A.G. Weiler. 81–94. Hilversum: Verloren, 1988.

3. Rabbie, E. "Hugo Grotius's Ordinum pietas." In *Acta Conventus Neo-Latini Hauniensis, Proceedings of the Eigth International Congress of Neo-Latin Studies, Copenhagen August 1991*, ed. A. Moss. Binghamton, New York: Center for Medieval and Early Renaissance Studies, forthcoming.

5 *Brief D. Sibrandi Lubberti aenden Aertsbisschop van Cantelberch (1613)*

5.1 *Study*

1. Vollenhoven, C. van. "Een strijdschrift uit 1613." *Grotiana* 5 (1932): 17–20. Reprinted in *Mr. C. van Vollenhoven's Verspreide Geschriften*, ed. F.M. van Asbeck. I. 596–98. Haarlem – 's-Gravenhage: Tjeenk Willink – Nijhoff, 1934.

6 *Decretum pro pace ecclesiarum (1614)*

6.1 *Translation*

See Nocentini, section G 11.1.2.

6.2 *Study*

1. Rogge, H.C. "De resolutie der Staten van Holland tot vrede der kerk." *Bijdragen voor Vaderlandsche Geschiedenis en Oudheidkunde* N.R. 8 (1875): 79–122.

7 *Defensio decreti pro pace ecclesiarum (ca. 1614)*

7.1 *Translation*

See Nocentini, section G 11.1.2.

8 *Remonstrantie ... op de Joden (1615)*

8.1 *Edition*

1. Meijer, J., ed. *Hugo de Groot, Remonstrantie nopende de ordre dije in de landen van Hollandt ende Westvrieslandt dijent gestelt op de Joden, naar het manuscript in de Livraria D. Montezinos uitgegeven en ingeleid.* Amsterdam: 1949 – 5709.

8.2 *Studies*

1. Da Silva Rosa, J.S. *Geschiedenis der Portugeesche Joden te Amsterdam, 1593–1925.* Amsterdam: Hertzberger, 1925.

2. Prins, I. *De vestiging der Marranen in Noord-Nederland in de zestiende eeuw.* Amsterdam: Hertzberger, 1927.

3. Kuhn, A.K. "Hugo Grotius and the Emancipation of the Jews in Holland." *Publications of the American Jewish Historical Society* 31 (1928): 173–80.

4. Prins, I. "Huig de Groot's Jodenreglement." *Bijdragen en Mededeelingen van het Genootschap voor de Joodsche Wetenschap in Nederland gevestigd te Amsterdam* 4 (1928): 86–88.

5. Eysinga, W.J.M. van. "De Groots Jodenreglement." *Mededelingen der Koninklijke Nederlandse Akademie van Wetenschappen, Afd. Letterkunde,* N.R. 13,1 (1950): 1–8. Reprinted in *Sparsa Collecta, een aantal der verspreide geschriften van Jonkheer Mr. W.J.M. van Eysinga* ed. F.M. van Asbeck [et al.]. 423–29. Leiden: Sijthoff, 1958.

6. *Meijer, J. "Hugo Grotius' Remonstrantie." *Jewish Social Studies. A Quarterly Journal Devoted to Contemporary and Historical Aspects of Jewish Life* 17 (1955): 91–104.

9 *Oratio in senatu Amstelredamensi (1616)*

9.1 *Study*

1. Jong Hzn., M. de. "Hugo de Groot in den raad van Amsterdam." *Jaarboek van het Genootschap Amstelodamum* 25 (1928): 125–55.

10 *Defensio fidei catholicae de satisfactione Christi (1617)*

10.1 *Edition; Translation*

1. Rabbie, E., ed. *Hugo Grotius, Defensio fidei catholicae de satisfactione Christi adversus Faustum Socinum Senensem, edited, with an introduction and notes; with an English translation by H. Mulder.* Hugo Grotius, Opera theologica I. Assen – Maastricht: Van Gorcum, 1990.

Cf. also *BG* nos. 933–34.

10.2 *Studies*

1. Baur, F.C. *Die christliche Lehre von der Versöhnung in ihrer geschichtlichen Entwicklung von der ältesten Zeit bis auf die neueste.* Tübingen: Osiander, 1838.

2. Seisen, I.D. *Nicolaus Methonensis, Anselmus Cantuariensis, Hugo Grotius, quod ad satisfactionis doctrinam a singulis excogitatam, inter se comparati.* Diss. Heidelberg, Heidelberg: Groos, 1838.

3. Ritschl, A. *Die christliche Lehre von der Rechtfertigung und Versöhnung.* I. Die Geschichte der Lehre. Bonn: Marcus, *1870; 1882²; *1889³; 1903⁴. Reprint Hildesheim: Olms, 1978.

4. Rivière, J. *Le dogme de la rédemption, essai d'étude historique.* Études d'histoire des dogmes et d'ancienne littérature ecclésiastique. Paris: Lecoffre, 1905. 2nd and 3rd editions entitled *Le dogme de la rédemption, étude théologique.* Paris: Gabalda, *1914²; 1931³.

5. Kühler, W.J. *Het Socinianisme in Nederland.* Leiden: Sijthoff, 1912. Reprint Leeuwarden: De Tille, [1980].

6. Slee, J.C. van. *De geschiedenis van het Socinianisme in de Nederlanden.* Verhandelingen uitgegeven door Teyler's godgeleerd genootschap, N.S. 18. Haarlem: Bohn, 1914.

7. Franks, R.S. *A History of the Doctrine of the Work of Christ in its Ecclesiastical Development.* 2 vols. *London: Hodder & Stoughton, [1918]. Reprinted as Franks, R.S. *The Work of Christ: A Historical Study of Christian Doctrine.* Nelson's Library of Theology. London: Nelson, 1962.

8. Grensted, L.W. *A Short History of the Doctrine of Atonement.* Publications of the University of Manchester, Theological Series, 4;

Publications of the University of Manchester, 128. Manchester [etc.]: The University Press, 1920.

9. Ritschl, O. *Die reformierte Theologie des 16. und 17. Jahrhunderts in ihrer Entstehung und Entwicklung.* Dogmengeschichte des Protestantismus, 3. Göttingen: Vandenhoeck & Ruprecht, 1926.

10. Williams, G.H. *The Polish Brethren. Documentation of the History and Thought of Unitarianism in the Polish-Lithuanian Commonwealth and in the Diaspora 1601–1685.* I. Harvard Theological Studies, 30. Missoula, Montana: Scholars Press, 1980.

11. Rabbie, E. "Some remarks concerning the textual history of Hugo Grotius' *De satisfactione.*" *Grotiana* N.S. 7 (1986): 99–111.

12. Rabbie, E. "Grotius on Damages in Case of Homicide: *De iure belli ac pacis* 2,17,13 and *De satisfactione* 2,9." *Tijdschrift voor Rechtsgeschiedenis* 57 (1989): 109–16.

13. Rabbie, E. "Grotius als bestrijder van het Socinianisme." In *Hoewel ick geen theologant en ben. Twee lezingen over het theologisch oeuvre van Hugo de Groot.* 12–19. 's-Gravenhage: Constantijn Huygens Instituut voor Tekstedities en Intellectuele Geschiedenis, Afdeling Grotius, 1994.

11 *De imperio summarum potestatum circa sacra (ca. 1617)*

11.1 *Editions; Translations*

1. Grotius, H. *De imperio summarum potestatum circa sacra. Cui accedunt David Blondel, De iure plebis in regimine ecclesiastico, et De officio magistratus christiani alius autoris A.C.E.M.G. Neudruck der Ausgabe Frankfurt am Main 1690.* Aalen: Scientia, 1970.

2. Nocentini, L., ed. *Ugo Grozio, Il potere dell'Autorità Sovrana in ordine alle cose sacre e altri scritti.* Eirenikon, 6. Pisa: Del Cerro, 1993.

3. Dam, H.-J. van, ed. *Hugo Grotius, De imperio summarum potestatum circa sacra, edited, with an introduction and notes, and an English translation.* Hugo Grotius, Opera theologica III. Assen – Maastricht: Van Gorcum, [forthcoming].

11.2 *Studies*

1. Nobbs, D. *Theocracy and Toleration. A study of disputes in Dutch Calvinism from 1600 to 1650,* Cambridge: University Press, 1938

2. Solari, G. "Il 'jus circa sacra' nell'età e nella dottrina di Ugone Grozio." In **Studi filosofico-giuridici dedicati a Giorgio del Vecchio nel xxv anno di insegnamento,* 369–433. II. Modena: Società tipografica modenese, 1931. Reprinted in Solari, G. *Studi storici di filosofia del di-*

ritto, 25–71. Università di Torino, Miscellanea dell'Istituto giuridico, 2. Torino: Giapichelli, 1949; and in Solari, G. *La filosofia politica*, 65–130. I. Universale Laterza, 295. Roma – Bari: Laterza, 1974.

3. Vrankrijker, A.C.J. de. *De staatsleer van Hugo de Groot en zijn Nederlandsche tijdgenooten*. Nijmegen – Utrecht: Dekker & Van de Vegt, 1937.

4. Bohatec, J. "Das Territorial- und Kollegialsystem in der holländischen Publizistik des XVII. Jahrhunderts." *Zeitschrift der Savigny-Stiftung für Rechtsgeschichte, Kanonistische Abteilung* 35 (1948): 1–149.

5. Conring, E. *Kirche und Staat nach der Lehre der niederländischen Calvinisten in der ersten Hälfte des 17. Jahrhunderts*. Beiträge zur Geschichte und Lehre der Reformierten Kirche, 18. [Neukirchen]: Neukirchener Verlag des Erziehungsvereins, 1965.

6. Caspani, A. "Alle origine dello 'ius circa sacra' in Grozio." *Rivista di filosofia neo-scolastica* 79 (1987): 217–49.

7. Caspani, A. "Il *De imperio summarum potestatum circa sacra* di Grozio." *Rivista di filosofia neo-scolastica* 79 (1987): 382–419.

8. Dam, H.-J. van. "Grotius' Manuscript of *De imperio summarum potestatum circa sacra* Identified." *Grotiana* N.S. 11 (1990): 34–42.

9. Borschberg, P. "Zur Entstehung von Grotius' 'De Imperio Summarum Potestatum circa Sacra'." *Zeitschrift der Savigny-Stiftung für Rechtsgeschichte, Kanonistische Abteilung* 79 (110) (1993): 342–79.

12 *Disquisitio an Pelagiana sint (1622)*

12.1 *Edition*

1. Rabbie, E. and H.J.M. Nellen, ed. "The Unpublished Introduction to Hugo Grotius' *Disquisitio an Pelagiana sint ea dogmata quae nunc sub eo nomine traducuntur* edited with an introduction and notes." *Grotiana* N.S. 8 (1987): 42–79. Addenda and Corrigenda: *Grotiana* N.S. 9 (1988): 127–28.

13 *Apologeticus / Verantwoordingh (1622)*

13.1 *Studies*

1. Rogge, H.C. "De 'Verantwoordingh' van Hugo de Groot." *Bijdragen voor Vaderlandsche Geschiedenis en Oudheidkunde*, 3e reeks 7 (1893): 89–134.

2. Rogge, H.C. "Hugo de Groot te Parijs van 1621–1625." *De Gids* 57 (2 1893): 249–74; 405–78.

3. *Rijswijk, W. van. "The *Verantwoordingh* of Hugo de Groot." *Butterworths South African Law Review* (1957): 69–83.

14 *De veritate religionis christianae (1627)*

14.1 *Translation*

1. Pintacuda De Michelis, F., ed. *Ugo Grozio, Della vera religione cristiana.* Piccola biblioteca filosofica Laterza, 86. Roma – Bari: Laterza, 1973.

Cf. also *BG* nos. 1003–07; 1055–59; 1067; 1087.

14.2 *Studies*

1. *Roy, C. *Hugo Grotius considéré comme apologète.* Thèse Strasbourg, Colmar: Decker, 1855.

2. Millies, H.C. "Over de Oostersche vertalingen van het beroemde geschrift van Hugo Grotius: *De veritate religionis christianae.*" *Verslagen en Mededeelingen der Koninklijke Akademie van Wetenschappen, Afd. Letterkunde* 7 (1863): 109–34.

3. *Mary. *Le Christianisme et le libre examen, discussion des arguments apologétiques de Grotius, Pascal, Samuel Clarke, Paley, Chateaubriand.* 2 vols. Paris: Didier, 1864; 1865².

4. Bergman, J.T. "Hugo de Groot als apologeet beschouwd." *Godgeleerde Bijdragen* 43 (1 1869): 671–706.

5. Doedes, J.I. "Eene zeer weinig bekende, om de voorrede hoogstbelangrijke, Venetiaansche uitgaaf van Hugo Grotius, de veritate religionis Christianae. (1768)." *Godgeleerde Bijdragen* 43 (1 1869): 359–64.

6. Wijnmalen, T.C.L. *Hugo de Groot als verdediger des Christendoms beschouwd. Eene litterarisch-apologetische proeve.* Utrecht: Dannenfelser, 1869.

7. Wolters, W.P. "Hugo de Groot als verdediger van het Christendom." *De Gids* 33 (3 1869): 446–95.

8. Jager, A. de. "De verschillende uitgaven van De Groots *Bewijs van den waren godsdienst.*" In *Nieuwe taal- en letteroefeningen,* 37–45. Groningen: Wolters, 1876.

9. *Looten, C. *De Grotio christianæ religionis defensore.* Thèse Paris, Insulis: Le Bigot, 1889.

10. Norel Jzn., O. "Hugo de Groot's 'Bewijs van den waren godsdienst'." *Woord en daad, Tijdschrift voor inwendige zending* 4 (1925): 96–111.

11. Prins, I. "Ons welkom in Nederland. Hugo de Groot: Bewijs van den waren Godsdienst, 5de Boek: Tegen de Joden (1622)." *De Vrijdagavond, Joodsch Weekblad* 1 (vol. 2) (43 1924/25 [5685]): 258–61.

12. Roldanus, C.W. *Hugo de Groot's Bewijs van den waren godsdienst.* Arnhem: Gouda Quint [et al.], 1944.

13. Nauta, D. "Hugo de Groot als catecheet van Contra-remonstrantse zijde ingepalmd." *NAKG* N.S. 57 (1976/77): 16–30.

14. Gellinek, Chr. "Hugo de Groots und Martin Opitzens Glaubensverteidigungen von 1622 und 1631." In *Akten des VI. Internationalen Germanisten-Kongresses Basel 1980*, ed. H. Rupp and H.-G. Roloff. 33–39. III. Jahrbuch für Internationale Germanistik, Reihe A, 8,3. Bern [etc.]: Lang, 1980.

15. Gellinek, Chr. "Wettlauf um die Wahrheit der christlichen Religion. Martin Opitz und Christoph Köler als Vermittler zweier Schriften des Hugo Grotius über das Christentum (1631)." *Simpliciana, Schriften der Grimmelshausen-Gesellschaft* 2 (1980): 71–89. Reprinted in Gellinek, Chr. *Pax optima rerum: Friedensessais zu Grotius und Goethe.* 55–65. Germanic Studies in America, 49. New York [etc.]: Lang, 1984.

16. Gellinek, Chr. "Die Verteidigung der Wahrheit der christlichen Religion im Jahrhundert des Späthumanismus (1540–1631) bei Juan Luis Vives, Philippe Duplessis Mornay, Hugo Grotius und der Opitzschule." In *Sprache und Literatur. Festschrift für Arval L. Streadbeck zum 65. Geburtstag*, ed. G.P. Knapp and W.A. von Schmidt. 53–64. Utah Studies in Literature and Linguistics, 20. Bern [etc.]: Lang, 1981. Reprinted as "Die Frage nach der Wahrheit der christlichen Religion im Zeitalter des Späthumanismus (1540–1620)." In Gellinek, Chr. *Pax optima rerum: Friedensessais zu Grotius und Goethe.* 11–19. Germanic Studies in America, 49. New York [etc.]: Lang, 1984.

17. Laplanche, F. *L'évidence du Dieu chrétien. Religion, culture et société dans l'apologétique protestante de la France classique (1576–1670).* [Strasbourg]: Association des publications de la Faculté de théologie protestante, 1983.

18. Niemann, F.-J. "Die erste ökumenische Fundamentaltheologie: zum 400. Geburtstag von Hugo Grotius." *Catholica, Vierteljahresschrift für ökumenische Theologie* 37 (1983): 203–15.

19. Vet, J. de. "Jean Leclerc, an enlightened propagandist of Grotius' 'De veritate religionis christianae'." *NAKG* N.S. 64 (1984): 160–95.

20. Heering, J.P. *Hugo de Groot als apologeet van de christelijke gods-dienst. Een onderzoek van zijn geschrift De veritate religionis christianae (1640)*. Diss. Leiden, 's-Gravenhage: Pasmans, 1992.
See also Van Rooden and Wesselius, section M 18.

15 *Dissertatio de origine gentium Americanarum (1642)*

15.1 *Study*

1. Rubiés, J.-P. "Hugo Grotius's Dissertation on the Origin of the American Peoples and the Use of Comparative Methods." *Journal of the History of Ideas* 52 (1991): 221‑44.

16 *Annotationes in Novum Testamentum (1641‑50)*

16.1 *Studies*

1. W[itte] v[an] C[itters], J. d[e]. "Het lijden van een corrector in de zeventiende eeuw." *De Nederlandsche Spectator* (1866): 301‑02.

2. Leipoldt, J. *Geschichte des neutestamentlichen Kanons*. II: Mittelalter und Neuzeit. Leipzig: Hinrichs, 1908. Reprint Leipzig: Zentralantiquariat der Deutschen Demokratischen Republik, 1974.

3. Unnik, W.C. van. "Hugo Grotius als uitlegger van het Nieuwe Testament." *NAKG* N.S. 25 (1932): 1‑48. Reprinted in *Woorden gaan leven. Opstellen van en over Willem Cornelis van Unnik (1910‑1978)*, 172‑214. Kampen: Kok, 1979.

4. Köhler, W. "Die Annotata des Hugo Grotius zum Philemon-brief des Apostels Paulus." *Grotiana* 8 (1940): 13‑24.

5. Ros, J. *De studie van het Bijbelgrieksch van Hugo Grotius tot Adolf Deissmann*. Nijmegen – Utrecht: Dekker & Van de Vegt, 1940.

6. Kümmel, W.G. *Das Neue Testament, Geschichte der Erforschung seiner Probleme*. Orbis Academicus, Problemgeschichten der Wissenschaft in Dokumenten und Darstellungen. Freiburg [etc.]: Alber, 1970².

7. Jonge, H.J. de. *De bestudering van het Nieuwe Testament aan de Noordnederlandse universiteiten en het Remonstrantse Seminarie van 1575 tot 1700*. Verhandelingen der Koninklijke Nederlandse Akademie van Wetenschappen, Afd. Letterkunde, N.R. 106. Amsterdam [etc.]: North Holland, 1980.

8. Jonge, H.J. de. "Grotius als uitlegger van de Bijbel, speciaal het Nieuwe Testament." In *Het Delfts orakel; Hugo de Groot 1583‑1645*, 121‑28. Delft: Stedelijk Museum Het Prinsenhof, 1983. English translation: "Grotius as an interpreter of the Bible, particularly the

New Testament." In *Hugo Grotius, a Great European, 1583–1645. Contributions concerning his activities as a humanist scholar.* 59–65. Delft: Meinema 1983.

9. Jonge, H.J. de. "Hugo Grotius: exégète du Nouveau Testament." In *The World of Hugo Grotius (1583–1645), Proceedings of the International Colloquium organized by the Grotius Committee of the Royal Netherlands Academy of Arts and Sciences, Rotterdam 6–9 April 1983,* 97–115. Amsterdam – Maarssen: APA – Holland University Press, 1984.

10. Laplanche, F. *L'Écriture, le sacré et l'histoire. Érudits et politiques protestants devant la Bible en France au XVIIe siècle.* Studies van het Instituut voor Intellectuele Betrekkingen tussen de Westeuropese landen in de zeventiende eeuw, 12. Amsterdam – Maarssen: APA – Holland University Press, 1986.

11. Reventlow, H. Graf von. "Humanistic Exegesis: The Famous Hugo Grotius." In *Creative Biblical Exegesis, Christian and Jewish hermeneutics through the centuries,* ed. B. Uffenheimer and H. Graf von Reventlow. 175–91. Journal for the Study of the Old Testament, Supplement Series, 59. Sheffield: JSOT Press, 1988.

12. Reventlow, H. Graf von. "L'exégèse humaniste de Hugo Grotius." In *Le Grand Siècle et la Bible,* ed. J.-R. Armogathe. 141–54. Bible de tous les temps, 6. Paris: Beauchesne, 1989.

13. Rooden, P.T. van. *Theology, biblical scholarship and rabbinical studies in the seventeenth century. Constantijn L'Empereur (1591–1648), professor of Hebrew and theology at Leiden.* Studies in the History of Leiden University, 6. Leiden [etc.]: Brill, 1989.

14. *Seifert, A. *Der Rückzug der biblischen Prophetie von der neueren Geschichte: Studien zur Geschichte der Reichstheologie des frühneuzeitlichen deutschen Protestantismus.* Beihefte zum Archiv für Kulturgeschichte, 31. Köln – Wien: Böhlau, 1990.

15. Lang, M.H. de. *De opkomst van de historische en literaire kritiek in de synoptische beschouwing van de evangeliën van Calvijn (1555) tot Griesbach (1774).* Diss. Leiden: 1993.

17 *Annotationes in Vetus Testamentum (1644)*

17.1 *Studies*

1. Diestel, L. *Geschichte des Alten Testamentes in der christlichen Kirche.* Jena: Mauke, 1869. Reprint Leipzig: Zentralantiquariat der Deutschen Demokratischen Republik, 1981.

2. Kuenen, A. "Hugo de Groot als uitlegger van het Oude Verbond." *Verslagen en mededeelingen der Koninklijke Akademie van Wetenschap-*

pen, Afd. Letterkunde, 2e reeks, 12 (1883): 301–32. German translation: "Hugo Grotius als Ausleger des Alten Testaments." In *Kuenen, A. Gesammelte Abhandlungen zur biblischen Wissenschaft*, 161–85. Freiburg i.B. – Leipzig: Mohr, 1894.

3. Kraus, H.-J. *Geschichte der historisch-kritischen Erforschung des Alten Testaments*. Neukirchen-Vluyn: Neukirchener Verlag, 1982³.

See also Laplanche, section G 16.1.10; Reventlow, section G 16.1. 11 and 12; Van Rooden, section G 16.1.13; Seifert, section G 16.1.14.

H. Grotius and the Disputes During the Twelve-Year Truce

1. Nuyens, W.J.F. "De politieke en kerkelijke partijen in de Zeven Provinciën in het begin der XVII eeuw en het rechtsgeding van Hugo de Groot." *Onze Wachter* (1 1874): 4–41; 351–81; (2 1874): 129–48.

2. Brill, W.G. "Hugo de Groot als auteur van staatkundige strijdschriften." *Verslagen en mededeelingen der Koninklijke Akademie van Wetenschappen, Afd. Letterkunde*, 2e reeks, 12 (1883): 363–71.

3. Bots, P.M. *Van Erasmus naar Vondel, of de kern der vaderlandsche vrijheidshistorie*. Haarlem: St. Jacobs-Godshuis, 1893.

4. Harrison, A.W. *The Beginnings of Arminianism to the Synod of Dort*. Diss. University of London, London: University of London Press, 1926.

5. Tex, J. den. *Oldenbarnevelt*. 5 vols. Haarlem [Groningen]: Tjeenk Willink, 1960–72. Abridged English translation: *Oldenbarnevelt*. 2 vols. London: Cambridge University Press, 1973.

6. Melles, J. *Ministers aan de Maas. Geschiedenis van de Rotterdamse pensionarissen met een inleiding over het stedelijk pensionariaat 1508–1795*. Historische werken over Rotterdam, 3. Rotterdam – 's-Gravenhage: Nijgh & Van Ditmar, [1962].

7. Gerlach, H. *Het proces tegen Oldenbarnevelt en de 'maximen in den staet'*. Haarlem: Tjeenk Willink, 1965.

8. Deursen, A.Th. van. *Bavianen en Slijkgeuzen. Kerk en kerkvolk ten tijde van Maurits en Oldenbarnevelt*. Assen: Van Gorcum, 1974. Reprint Franeker: Van Wijnen, [1991].

9. Grayson, Chr. "James I and the religious crisis in the United Provinces 1613–19." In *Reform and Reformation: England and the Continent c1500–c1750. Dedicated and presented to professor Clifford W. Dugmore to mark his seventieth birthday*, ed. D. Baker. 195–219. Studies in Church History, Subsidia, 2. Oxford: Blackwell, 1979.

I. Irenicism

1. Joss, G. *Die Vereinigung christlicher Kirchen, eine von der Haager Gesellschaft zur Vertheidigung der christlichen Religion gekrönte Preisschrift.* Werken van het Haagsch Genootschap tot verdediging van den christelijken godsdienst, 5e reeks, 10. Leiden: Brill, 1877.

2. "Hugo de Groot in zijn streven naar het herstel der kerkelijke eenheid onder de Christenen." *De Oud-Katholiek, Godsdienstig maandblad* 20 (1904): 53–55; 59–60; 67–68; 75–77; 81–83; 92–95.

3. Rogge, H.C. "Hugo de Groots denkbeelden over de hereeniging der kerken." *Teyler's Theologisch Tijdschrift* 2 (1904): 1–52.

4. Jolles, N. "Vredesklanken van Willem en Hugo de Groot." *Geloof en Vrijheid* 48 (1914): 69–89.

5. Tex, J. den. *Locke en Spinoza over de tolerantie.* Diss. Amsterdam, Amsterdam: Scheltema & Holkema, 1926.

6. Muller, J. "L'œuvre de toutes les confessions chrétiennes (Églises) pour la paix internationale." *Académie de droit international, Recueil des cours* 31 (1 1930): 293–392.

7. Jordan, W.K. *The Development of Religious Toleration in England from the Accession of James I to the Convention of the Long Parliament (1603–1640).* London: Allen & Unwin, 1936.

8. Schiff, O. "Zur Literaturgeschichte der kirchlichen Einigungsbestrebungen. Eine Bibliographie von 1628." *NAKG* N.S. 30 (1938): 35–39.

9. Winkelman, P.H. *Remonstranten en Katholieken in de eeuw van Hugo de Groot.* Nijmegen: Centrale Drukkerij, 1945.

10. Blanke, F. "Pax ecclesiae: Hugo Grotius und die Einigung der christlichen Kirchen." *Reformatio* (1953): 595–609. Reprinted as "Hugo Grotius und sein Einsatz für die Einigung der Kirchen." In *Ökumenische Profile; Brückenbauer der einen Kirche*, ed. G. Gloede. 83–96. Stuttgart: Evang. Missionsverlag, 1961.

11. Blanke, F. "Grotius Papista?" In *Völkerrecht und Völkerpflicht. Beiträge zur Verbreitung des Völkerrechts*, ed. H.K.E.L. Keller. 16–18. München: Grotius-Stiftung, 1954.

12. Lang, H. "Grotius als Ireniker." In *Völkerrecht und Völkerpflicht. Beiträge zur Verbreitung des Völkerrechts*, ed. H.K.E.L. Keller. 13–16. München: Grotius-Stiftung, 1954.

13. Rouse, R. and S.Ch. Neill. *A History of the Ecumenical Movement 1517–1948.* London: SPCK, 1954. Second edition: Philadelphia: The Westminster Press, 1967.

14. Lecler, J. *Histoire de la tolérance au siècle de la Réforme*. 2 vols. Aubier: Montaigne, 1955. English translation: *Toleration and the Reformation*. 2 vols. New York [etc.]: Association Press, 1960. German translation: *Geschichte der Religionsfreiheit im Zeitalter der Reformation*. 2 vols. Stuttgart: Schwabenverlag, 1965.

15. Repgen, K. "Francesco Barberini, Hugo Grotius und die römische Vorgeschichte der Bulle In eminenti." *Römische Quartalschrift für christliche Altertumskunde und Kirchengeschichte* 58 (1963): 105‒32.

16. Droetto, A. "La formula giuridica dell'ecumenismo groziano." *Rivista internazionale di filosofia del diritto* 41 (1964): 515‒38. Reprinted in Droetto, A. *Studi Groziani*. 163‒88. Pubblicazioni dell'istituto di scienze politiche dell'Università di Torino, 18. Torino: Giappichelli, 1968.

17. Repgen, K. "Grotius 'papizans'." In *Reformata reformanda; Festgabe für Hubert Jedin zum 17. Juni 1965*, ed. E. Iserloh and K. Repgen. 370‒400. II. Münster Westf.: Aschendorff, 1965.

18. Haentjens, A.H. "Hugo de Groot als oecumenisch denker en werker." *Theologie en praktijk* 26 (1966): 97‒103.

19. Wolf, D. *Die Irenik des Hugo Grotius nach ihren Prinzipien und biographisch-geistesgeschichtlichen Perspektiven*. Schriften des Instituts für wissenschaftliche Irenik der Johann Wolfgang Goethe Universität Frankfurt am Main, 9. Marburg: Elwert, 1969. Reprinted as *Studia irenica, 9. Hildesheim: Gerstenberg, 1972.

20. Knieper, B. *Die Naturrechtslehre des Hugo Grotius als Einigungsprinzip der Christenheit, dargestellt an seiner Stellung zum Calvinismus*. Diss. Frankfurt am Main, Augsburg: Blasaditsch, 1971.

21. Posthumus Meyjes, G.H.M. "Jean Hotman's Syllabus of eirenical literature." In *Reform and Reformation: England and the Continent c1500‒c1750, dedicated and presented to professor Clifford W. Dugmore to mark his seventieth birthday*, ed. D. Baker. 175‒93. Studies in Church History, Subsidia, 2. Oxford: Blackwell, 1979.

22. Posthumus Meyjes, G.H.M. "Jean Hotman and Hugo Grotius." *Grotiana* N.S. 2 (1981): 3‒29.

23. Posthumus Meyjes, G.H.M. "Protestants irenisme in de 16e en eerste helft van de 17e eeuw." *Nederlands Theologisch Tijdschrift* 36 (1982): 205‒22.

24. Bots, H. and P. Leroy. "Hugo Grotius et la réunion des chrétiens: entre le savoir et l'inquiétude." *XVIIe siècle* 35 (141 1983): 451‒69.

25. Kuiper, E.J. "Hugo de Groot en de Remonstranten." *Neder-lands Theologisch Tijdschrift* 38 (1984): 111–25.

26. Peski, A.M. van. "Waarom Grotius als oecumenisch theoloog mislukken moest." *Nederlands Theologisch Tijdschrift* 38 (1984): 290–97.

27. Posthumus Meyjes, G.H.M. "Hugo Grotius as an irenicist." In *The World of Hugo Grotius (1583–1645), Proceedings of the International Colloquium organized by the Grotius Committee of the Royal Netherlands Academy of Arts and Sciences, Rotterdam 6–9 April 1983*, 43–63. Amsterdam – Maarssen: APA – Holland University Press, 1984.

28. Posthumus Meyjes, G.H.M. "Protestant Irenicism in the sixteenth and seventeenth centuries." In *The End of Strife, Papers selected from the proceedings of the Colloquium of the Commission Internationale d'Histoire Ecclésiastique Comparée held at the University of Durham 2 to 9 September 1981*, ed. D. Loades. 77–93. Edinburgh: Clark, 1984.

29. De Michelis Pintacuda, F. "Pour une histoire de l'idée de tolérance du XVe au XVIIe siècle." *Revue d'histoire et de philosophie religieuses* 65 (1985): 131–51.

30. Sutto, C. "Grotius et les querelles religieuses." *Canadian Journal of Netherlandic Studies/Revue canadienne d'études néerlandaises* 6 (1985): 23–39.

31. Nellen, H.J.M. "'Geene vredemaeckers zijn zonder tegenspreeckers,' Hugo Grotius' buitenkerkelijke positie." *De Zeventiende Eeuw* 5 (1 1989): 103–12.

32. Rotondò, A. *Europe et Pays-Bas. Évolution, réélaboration et diffusion de la tolérance aux XVIIe et XVIIIe siècles. Lignes d'un programme de recherches*. Firenze: Università degli Studi, Dipartimento di Storia, 1992.

J. Grotius Jurist-Theologian

1. Husik, I. "The Law of Nature, Hugo Grotius, and the Bible." *Hebrew Union College Annual* 2 (1925): 381–417.

2. Fortuin, H. *Hugo de Groot's houding ten opzichte van oorlog en Christendom*. Amsterdam: Ploegsma, 1946.

3. Hoffmann-Loerzer, G. *Studien zu Hugo Grotius*. Diss. München: 1971.

4. Rapp, H. "Grotius and Hume on Natural Religion and Natural Law." *Archiv für Rechts- und Sozialphilosophie* 68 (1982): 372–87.

5. Haggenmacher, P. *Grotius et la doctrine de la guerre juste*. Publications de l'Institut universitaire de hautes études internationales Genève. Paris: Presses Universitaires de France, 1983.

6. Todescan, F. *Le radici teologiche del giusnaturalismo laico*. I: Il problema della secolarizzazione nel pensiero giuridico di Ugo Grozio. Per la storia del pensiero giuridico moderno, 14. Milano: Giuffrè, 1983.

See also Ambrosetti, section F 13; Droetto, section F 14.

K. GROTIUS AND HIS CONTEMPORARIES

1 *Théophile Brachet de la Milletière*

1. Schoor, R.J.M. van de. *De irenische theologie van Théophile Brachet de la Milletière (1588–1665), Een wetenschappelijke proeve op het gebied van de Letteren*. Diss. Nijmegen: 1991.

2 *Isaac Casaubon*

1. Posthumus Meyjes, G.H.M. "Twee vrienden: Isaac Casaubon en Hugo de Groot." In *Voorbeeldige vriendschap. Vrienden en vriendinnen in theologie en cultuur. Aangeboden aan prof. dr. E.J. Kuiper ter gelegenheid van zijn afscheid als hoogleraar van het Seminarium der Remonstranten, 1 januari 1993*, 37–46. Groningen: Styx, 1993.

3 *Franciscus Gomarus*

1. Itterzon, G.P. van. *Franciscus Gomarus*. 's-Gravenhage: Nijhoff, 1930. Reprint Groningen – Castricum: Bouma – Hagen 1979.

4 *Festus Hommius*

1. Wijminga Jzn., P. *Festus Hommius*. Diss. Vrije Universiteit Amsterdam, Leiden: Donner, 1899.

5 *Franciscus Junius*

1. Venemans, B.A. *Franciscus Junius en zijn Eirenicum de pace ecclesiae catholicae*. Diss. Protestantse theologische faculteit te Brussel. Leiden: elve / labor vincit, 1977.

2. Jonge, Chr. de. *De irenische ecclesiologie van Franciscus Junius (1545–1602)*. Bibliotheca humanistica et reformatorica, 30. Nieuwkoop: De Graaf, 1980.

6 *Sibrandus Lubbertus*

1. Woude, C. van der. *Sibrandus Lubbertus. Leven en werken, in het bijzonder naar zijn correspondentie.* Diss. Vrije Universiteit Amsterdam, Kampen: Kok, 1963.

7 *Samuel Maresius*

1. Nauta, D. *Samuel Maresius.* Diss. Vrije Universiteit Amsterdam, Amsterdam: Paris, 1935.

8 *Dionysius Petavius*

1. Allard, H.J. "Hugo Grotius en Dionysius Petavius." *Jaarboekje van Jos. Alb. Alberdingk Thijm* 57 (1908): 217–44.

2. Hofmann, M. *Theologie, Dogma und Dogmenentwicklung im theologischen Werk Denis Petau's. Mit einem biographischen und einem bibliographischen Anhang.* Regensburger Studien zur Theologie, 1. Bern: Lang, 1976.

9 *Johannes Polyander*

1. Lamping, A.J. *Johannes Polyander, een dienaar van kerk en universiteit.* Kerkhistorische Bijdragen, 9. Leiden: Brill, 1980.

10 *André Rivet*

1. Honders, H.J. *Andreas Rivetus als invloedrijk Gereformeerd theoloog in Holland's bloeitijd.* Diss. Leiden, 's-Gravenhage: Nijhoff, 1930.

2. Klerk, C.R. de. *De grootste der "Great Hollanders".* Amsterdam: Mij. tot Verspreiding van goede en goedkoope lectuur, 1930.

3. Opstal, A.G. van. *André Rivet, een invloedrijk Hugenoot aan het hof van Frederik Hendrik.* Diss. Vrije Universiteit Amsterdam, Harderwijk: Flevo, 1937.

11 *Claude Saumaise*

1. Leroy, P. *Le dernier voyage à Paris et en Bourgogne, 1640–1643, du réformé Claude Saumaise; libre érudition et contrainte politique sous Richelieu.* Studies van het Instituut voor Intellectuele Betrekkingen tussen de Westeuropese landen in de zeventiende eeuw, 9. Amsterdam – Maarssen: APA – Holland University Press, 1983.

12 *Joost van den Vondel*

1. Bots, P.M. "Hugo de Groot en Vondel in de letteren." *De Katholieke Gids, Maandschrift voor het Katholieke Nederlandsche volk* 6 (1894): 11–39; 90–107; 174–83.

2. Brom, G. *Vondels geloof.* Amsterdam [etc.]: De Spieghel, 1935.

3. Frijns, W.M. "Vondel en Grotius als geestverwant." *Studiën, Tijdschrift voor godsdienst, wetenschap en letteren* N.R. 67 (123 1935): 202–21; 285–309.

4. Frijns, W.M. *Grotius in "Peter en Pauwels"?* Studiën-reeks, 3. 's-Hertogenbosch: Malmberg, [1938].

5. Vandervelden, J. "De vrienden Grotius en Vondel." *Vondelkroniek* 11 (1940): 64–70.

13 *Gerardus Vossius*

1. Roldanus, C.W. "Vossius' verhouding tot Hugo de Groot voor de Synode van Dordt." *Tijdschrift voor geschiedenis* 57 (1942): 241–53.

2. Roldanus, C.W. "Nederlandsch-Engelsche betrekkingen op den bodem van 'Arminianisme'." *Tijdschrift voor geschiedenis* 58 (1943): 6–21.

3. Rademaker, C.S.M. *Life and Work of Gerardus Joannes Vossius (1577–1649).* Respublica literaria Neerlandica, 5. Assen: Van Gorcum, 1981.

14 *Johannes Wtenbogaert*

1. Rogge, H.C. *Johannes Wtenbogaert en zijn tijd.* 3 vols. Amsterdam: Rogge, 1874–76.

L. GROTIUS AND CONTEMPORARY RELIGIOUS THOUGHT

1 *General*

1. Krogh-Tonning, K. *Hugo Grotius und die religiösen Bewegungen im Protestantismus seiner Zeit.* Köln: Bachem, 1904. Dutch translation: *Hugo de Groot en de religieuze stroomingen in het protestantisme van zijn tijd.* Rotterdam [etc.]: Van de Watering, 1905.

2. Pintard, R. *Le libertinage érudit dans la première moitié du XVIIe siècle.* 2 vols. Paris: Boivin, 1943.

3. Bleeker, C.J. "Hugo de Groot en de godsdienst van zijn tijd." *Theologie en praktijk* 32 (1972): 117–27.

4. Stelling-Michaud, S. "Grotius et les Genevois." *Musées de Genève* [N.S. 24] (240 1983): 20–25.

2 *Calvinism*

1. Nellen, H.J.M. "Grotius' relations with the Huguenot community of Charenton." *Lias* 12 (1985): 150–77.

3 *Lutheranism*

1. Creuzer, F. *Luther und Grotius; 1483–1546; 1583–1645, oder Glaube und Wissenschaft.* Heidelberg: Winter, 1846.

2. Nellen, H.J.M. "Grotius et les luthériens parisiens. Contribution à l'histoire des premières années de la communauté luthérienne de Paris." *NAKG* N.S. 67 (1987): 156–85.

4 *Socinianism*

1. Chmaj, L. "Hugo Grotius wobec Socynjanizmu." *Reformacja w Polsce* 4 (1926): 74–99.

2. Kot, S. "Hugo Grotius a Polska." *Reformacja w Polsce* 4 (1926): 100–20; 198–206.

5 *Roman Catholicism*

1. [Broere, C.] "De gezindheid van Hugo de Groot voor de Katholieke Kerk." *De Katholiek, Godsdienstig, geschied- en letterkundig maandschrift* 22 (1852): 201–29; 265–93; 23 (1853): 20–53; 129–47; 24 (1853): 1–20; 129–53; 193–231; 321–39; 25 (1854): 129–50; 265–86; 350–80; 26 (1854): 1–28.

2. Broere, C. *De terugkeer van Hugo de Groot tot het Katholieke geloof.* 's-Gravenhage: Van Langenhuysen, 1856. German translation: **Hugo Grotius' Rückkehr zum katholischen Glauben.* Trier: Lintz, 1871.

3. [Bosch Kemper, J. de.] *De terugkeer van Hugo de Groot tot het Katholieke geloof. Naar aanleiding van het werk van den heer Broere, hoogleeraar aan het Seminarie te Warmond.* Amsterdam: Witkamp, 1857.

4. Diest Lorgion, E.J. "Het Catholicisme van Hugo de Groot." *Waarheid in Liefde, Godgeleerd tijdschrift voor beschaafde Christenen* (1857): 105–64; 477–542. Also in book form, Groningen: Oomkens, 1857.

5. Gilse, J. van. "Is Hugo de Groot Roomsch geworden?" *De Gids* 22 (1 1858): 357–88. Reprinted in *Verspreide opstellen van Dr. J. van Gilse, ter hernieuwde uitgave bijeengebragt,* ed. P.J. Veth. 102–41. II: Verspreide opstellen van historischen inhoud van Dr. J. van Gilse,

ter hernieuwde uitgave bijeengebragt, tweede helft. Amsterdam: Van Kampen, 1860.

6. "Gezindheid van Hugo de Groot voor de Katholieke Kerk." *De Katholiek, Godsdienstig, geschied- en letterkundig maandschrift* 48 (1865): 383–84.

7. *Räss, A. *Die Convertiten seit der Reformation nach ihrem Leben und aus ihren Schriften dargestellt.* XI. Freiburg i.B.: Herder, 1873.

8. Philippona, Chr. "Guy Patin over Hugo de Groot." *De Katholiek, Godsdienstig, geschied- en letterkundig maandschrift* 90 (1886): 142–49.

9. Servaas van Rooijen, A.J. "Guy Patin over Hugo de Groot." *Stemmen voor Waarheid en Vrede, Evangelisch Tijdschrift voor de Protestantsche Kerken* 23 (1886): 314–19.

10. Klönne, B.H. "Leonardus Marius en Hugo de Groot." *De Katholiek, Godsdienstig, geschied- en letterkundig maandschrift* 95 (1889): 337–50. Reprinted in Klönne, B.H. *Amstelodamensia.* 183–97. Amsterdam: Bekker, 1894.

11. Klönne, B.H. "Nogmaals Leonardus Marius en Hugo de Groot." *De Katholiek, Godsdienstig, geschied- en letterkundig maandschrift* 96 (1889): 220–25. Reprinted in Klönne, B.H. *Amstelodamensia.* 198–203. Amsterdam: Bekker, 1894.

12. Görres, S. "Ist Hugo Grotius katholisch gestorben?" *Historisch-politische Blätter für das katholische Deutschland* 154 (1914): 1–11; 132–44; 161–73.

13. Sterck, J.F.M. "De bekeering van Hugo de Groot." *Historisch Tijdschrift* 1 (1922 [1923]): 22–38. Reprinted in Sterck, J.F.M. *Rondom Vondel. Studiën over den dichter en zijn kring.* 82–96. [Amsterdam]: Wereldbibliotheek, 1927.

14. Brom, G. "Grotius' testament." *Historisch Tijdschrift* 13 (1934): 303–31.

15. Hallema, A. "Is Hugo de Groot «bekeerd» of Roomsch geworden?" *De Protestant* 63 (1942): 26; 30.

16. Cornelissen, J.D.M. "Hugo de Groot en de vervolging der Katholieken." *Studia Catholica* 20 (1944): 201–08.

17. Polman, P. "Hugo de Groot in dienst van de verdediging der moederkerk." *Studia Catholica* 29 (1954): 134–51. Reprinted in *Adversaria Pontiani. Verspreide geschriften van P. Pontianus Polman,* ed. J.A.H. Bots [et al.]. 141–61 (cf. 310). Amsterdam: Holland Universiteits Pers, [1976].

18. *Stanley, C. of. "Father Archangel of Pembroke and the conversion of Grotius." In *Miscellanea Melchior de Pobladura, Studia Franciscana historica P. Melchiori a Pobladura dedicata, lx aetatis annum ... agenti*, ed. I. a Villapadierna. 313–26. II. Bibliotheca Seraphico-Capuccina, 24. Romae: Institutum historicum O.F.M. Cap., 1964.

See also Nuyens, section H 1; Winkelman, section I.9; Repgen, section I.15 and 17; Allard, section K 8.1.

6 Jansenism

1. Orcibal, J. *Jean Duvergier de Hauranne abbé de Saint-Cyran et son temps (1581–1638).* [= Les origines du Jansénisme, 2]. Bibliothèque de la Revue d'histoire ecclésiastique, 26. Louvain – Paris: Bureaux de la Revue – Vrin, 1947.

2. Orcibal, J. *Jean Duvergier de Hauranne abbé de Saint-Cyran et son temps (1581–1638). Appendices, bibliographie et tables.* [= Les origines du Jansénisme, 3]. Paris: Vrin, 1948.

7 Judaism

1. Löwenstamm, A. "Hugo Grotius' Stellung zum Judentum." In *Festschrift zum 75 jährigen Bestehen des jüdisch-theologischen Seminars Fraenkelscher Stiftung*, 295–302. II. Breslau: Marcus, 1929.

2. Balaban, M. "Hugo Grotius und die Ritualmordprozesse in Lublin (1636)." In *Festschrift zu Simon Dubnows siebzigsten Geburtstag (2. Tischri 5691)*, ed. I. Elbogen, J. Meisl, and M. Wischnitzer. 87–112. Berlin: Jüdischer Verlag, 1930.

3. *Meijer, J. "Hugo Grotius' Knowledge of Hebrew." *Historia Judaica* 14 (1952): 133–44.

4. Lachs, Ph.S. "Hugo Grotius' Use of Jewish Sources in On the Law of War and Peace." *Renaissance Quarterly* 30 (1977): 181–200.

5. Rosenberg, A.W. "Hugo Grotius as a Hebraist." *Studia Rosenthaliana* 12 (1978): 62–91.

M. RECEPTION

1. Boulan, É. "Pascal et Grotius." *Het Fransche Boek* 2 (1922/23): 148–50. Expanded version in Boulan, É. *De Pascal à Victor Hugo.* 26–32. Groningue – Batavia: Wolters, 1946.

2. Helm, E. van der. "Hugo de Groot's 'De jure belli ac pacis' en de Index." In *Annuarium der Roomsch-Katholieke studenten in Nederland*

A.D. 1926. 165–81. Amsterdam: Unie der R.K. Studentenvereenigingen in Nederland, [1926].

3. Wijnpersse, W.M.A. van de. "Grotius' 'De jure belli ac pacis' en de Index." *Studiën. Tijdschrift voor godsdienst, wetenschap en letteren* N.R. 58 (105 1926): 451–59. Cf. Wijnpersse, W.M.A. van de. "Grotius' de Jure belli ac pacis en de Index: een mise au point." *Studiën. Tijdschrift voor godsdienst, wetenschap en letteren* N.R. 60 (110 1928): 142–43.

4. Cornelissen, J.D.M. "Hugo de Groots Annales et Historiae de rebus Belgicis op den Index." *Mededeelingen van het Nederlandsch Historisch Instituut te Rome* 8 (1928): 161–72.

5. Henderson, G.D. "Dutch Influences in Scottish Theology." *The Evangelical Quarterly, A theological review, international in scope and outlook, in defence of the historic Christian faith* 5 (1933): 33–45.

6. Schiff, O. "Wallenstein und Hugo Grotius." *NAKG* N.S. 31 (1940): 23–32.

7. Cornelissen, J.D.M. "Lieuwe van Aitzema en Hugo de Groot." *Bijdragen voor de Geschiedenis der Nederlanden* 1 (1946): 47–71. Reprinted in Cornelissen, J.D.M. *De eendracht van het land. Cultuurhistorische studies over Nederland in de zestiende en zeventiende eeuw,* ed. E.O.G. Haitsma Mulier and A.E.M. Janssen. 151–65. Amsterdam – Dieren: De Bataafsche Leeuw, [1987].

8. Cornelissen, J.D.M. "Hugo de Groot op den Index." In *Miscellanea Historica in honorem Leonis van der Essen, Universitatis catholicae in oppido Lovaniensi iam annos XXXV professoris,* 757–68. II. Université de Louvain, Recueil de travaux d'histoire et de philologie, 3e série, 29. Bruxelles – Paris: Éditions Universitaires, 1947.

9. Droetto, A. "Ugone Grozio e l'«avversario» di Cartesio nella questione delle verità eterne." *Rivista internazionale di filosofia del diritto* 24 (1947): 58–80. Reprinted in Droetto, A. *Studi Groziani.* 35–63. Pubblicazioni dell'istituto di scienze politiche dell'Università di Torino, 18. Torino: Giappichelli, 1968.

10. Tans, J.A.G. *Bossuet en Hollande.* Diss. Nijmegen, Maastricht: Ernest van Aelst, 1949.

11. Lucas, J.J.A. "Grotius, Böhm-Bawerk en het kerkelijk renteverbod." *Maandschrift Economie* 29 (1965): 174–78.

12. Nuttal, G.F. "Richard Baxter and The Grotian Religion." In *Reform and Reformation: England and the Continent c1500–c1750, dedicated and presented to Professor Clifford W. Dugmore to mark his seventieth birthday,*

ed. D. Baker. 245–50. Studies in Church History, Subsidia, 2. Oxford: Blackwell, 1979.

13. Gellinek, Chr. "Politik und Literatur bei Grotius, Opitz und Milton: Ein Vergleich christlich-politischer Grundgedanken." *Daphnis* 11 (1982): 637–68 [= *Martin Opitz, Studien zu Werk und Person*, ed. B. Becker-Cantarino. 201–32. Amsterdam: Rodopi, 1982]. Reprinted as "Ein Vergleich christlich-politischer Grundgedanken bei den Späthumanisten Grotius, Opitz und Milton." In Gellinek, Chr. *Pax optima rerum: Friedensessais zu Grotius und Goethe.* 29–54. Germanic Studies in America, 49. New York [etc.]: Lang, 1984.

14. Le Brun, J. "La réception de la théologie de Grotius chez les catholiques de la seconde moitié du XVIIe siècle." In *The World of Hugo Grotius (1583–1645), Proceedings of the International Colloquium organized by the Grotius Committee of the Royal Netherlands Academy of Arts and Sciences, Rotterdam 6–9 April 1983*, 195–214. Amsterdam – Maarssen: APA – Holland University Press, 1984.

15. Bierzanek, R. "The Influence of the Personality and Ideas of Hugo Grotius on Religious and Political Struggles in the Polish-Lithuanian Commonwealth of the 17th and 18th Centuries." In *International Law and the Grotian Heritage. A commemorative colloquium held at The Hague on 8 April 1983 on the occasion of the fourth centenary of the birth of Hugo Grotius*, 298–309. The Hague: T.M.C. Asser Institute, 1985.

16. Rengstorf, K.H. "Hugo Grotius als Theologe und seine Rezeption in Deutschland." In *Theologische, juristische und philologische Beiträge zur frühen Neuzeit*, 71–83. Schriftenreihe der Westfälischen Wilhelms-Universität Münster, 9. Münster: Aschendorff, 1986.

17. Lesaulnier, J. "Témoignages Port-Royalistes sur Grotius 1670–1671." *Lias* 14 (1987): 277–90.

18. Rooden, P.T. van and J.W. Wesselius. "The Early Enlightenment and Judaism: The 'Civil Dispute' between Philippus van Limborch and Isaac Orobio de Castro (1687)." *Studia Rosenthaliana* 21 (1987): 140–53.

19. Trevor-Roper, H. "The Great Tew Circle." In *Catholics, Anglicans and Puritans. Seventeenth Century Essays.* 166–230. London: Secker & Warburg, 1987.

20. Lagrée, J. "Grotius, Stoicisme et Religion naturelle." *Grotiana* N.S. 10 (1989): 80–96.

See also Nauta, section G 14.2.13; Gellinek, section G 14.2.14 and 15; De Vet, section G 14.2.19.

BIBLIOGRAPHY OF THE WRITINGS OF GUILLAUME H.M. POSTHUMUS MEYJES

Abbreviations:

A&A	*Acta en Agenda*. Leids Universitair Weekblad
BLGNP	*Biografisch Lexicon van Protestantse Godgeleerden in Nederland* I, Kampen 1983²
Flambeau	*"Flambeau"*. Revue trimestrielle de théologie pour l'engagement de l'église dans le monde africain, Yaoundé (Caméroun)
Grotiana	*Grotiana*. A journal under the auspices of the Grotiana Foundation, New Series, Assen (The Netherlands)
KNAW	*Koninklijke Nederlandse Akademie van Wetenschappen*, Amsterdam
LIAS	*"LIAS"*. Sources and Documents relating to the Early Modern History of Ideas, Amsterdam – Maarssen
Mare	*"Mare"*. Leids Universitair Weekblad
NAKG	*Nederlands Archief voor Kerkgeschiedenis / Dutch Review of Church History*, Leiden
NTT	*Nederlands Theologisch Tijdschrift*, 's-Gravenhage
RhW	*"Rondom het Woord"*. Theologische Etherleergang van de NCRV, Hilversum
VC	*Vigiliae Christianae*. A review of early christian life and language, Amsterdam
VTh	*Vox Theologica*. Interacademiaal theologisch tijdschrift, Assen

1954/55

"De christologie van Theodorus van Mopsuestia I." *VTh* 24 (6 1954): 153–64; [idem] II. *VTh* 25 (1 1955): 9–22.

1956

Review: J.T. Bakker, *Coram Deo. Bijdrage tot het onderzoek naar de structuur van Luthers theologie*, Kampen 1956. *VTh* 27 (1 1956): 26.

1958

Review: B.J. Oldendaal, *Die kerklike betrekkinge tussen Suid-Afrika en*

Nederland (1652–1952) veral met betrekking tot die Ned. Geref. Kerk. Diss.
Vrije Universiteit Amsterdam, Franeker 1957. *VTh* 28 (6 1958): 156–
57.

1959

Review: Ernst Gerhard Rüsch, *Vom Heiligen in der Welt,* Zollikon
1959 (Beiträge zur Kirchen- und Geistesgeschichte). *VTh* 29 (2
1959): 59–60.

Review: Christoph Blumhardt, *Christus in der Welt. Briefe an Richard Wilhelm, herausgegeben von Prof. Dr. Arthur Rich,* Zürich [1958].
VTh 29 (3 1959): 92–93.

Review: Hellmuth Bandt, *Luthers Lehre vom verborgenen Gott. Eine
Untersuchung zu dem offenbarungsgeschichtlichen Ansatz seiner Theologie,* Ber-
lin 1958 (Theologische Arbeiten herausgegeben von Hans Urner,
VII). *VTh* 29 (6 1959): 183–84.

Review: G.C.P. van der Vyver, *Professor Dirk Postma 1818–1890,*
Potchefstroom 1958. *VTh* 29 (6 1959): 185.

"Bibliografie van Prof. Dr. J.N. Bakhuizen van den Brink." In
*Ecclesia. Een bundel opstellen aangeboden aan Prof. Dr. J.N. Bakhuizen van
den Brink...,* 252–56. 's-Gravenhage: Nijhoff, 1959.

1960

"Simon Episcopius en Johannes a Limborch." In *Documenta Reformatoria. Teksten uit de geschiedenis van kerk en theologie in de Nederlanden,*
327–29; 336. I. Kampen: Kok, 1960.

Review: Heinrich Schmidt, *Zwinglis Lehre von der göttlichen und
menschlichen Gerechtigkeit,* Zürich 1959 (Studien zur Dogmengeschichte
und systematischen Theologie, 12). *VTh* 30 (4 1960): 119–20.

1961

Review: D.W. de Villiers, *Reisbeskrywings as bronne vir die kerkge-
skiedskrywing van die Nederduitse Gereformeerde Kerk in Suid-Afrika tot 1853.*
Diss. Vrije Universiteit Amsterdam, Kampen 1959. *VTh* 31 (4 1961):
99.

1963

Jean Gerson. Zijn kerkpolitiek en ecclesiologie. Diss. Leiden, 's-Gravenhage: 1963 (344 pp.); appeared also, under the same title, as commercial edition in the series Kerkhistorische Studiën behorende bij

het Nederlands Archief voor Kerkgeschiedenis, 10, 's-Gravenhage: Nijhoff, 1963.

1964

"Évangile des chrétiens ou évangile de Jésus-Christ." *Flambeau* 4 (1964): 128–37.

Review: Jacques de Senarclens, *La réformation, hier et aujourd'hui. Avec un commentaire de K. Barth sur la première thèse de Barmen (1934)*, Genève 1964 (Collection "Les Cahiers du Renouveau", 35). *Flambeau* 4 (1964): 164.

Review: François Biot, *De la polémique au dialogue*, I: *L'Église face au chrétiens séparés*; idem II: *Les chrétiens séparés face à l'église*, Paris 1963 (Collection "L'Église aux cent visages"). *Flambeau* 4 (1964): 165–66.

1965

Review: Roland H. Bainton, *Notre église à deux mille ans*. Trad. André Péry, Genève [1964]. *Flambeau* 5 (1965): 119–20.

1966

Review: Boris Decorvet, *Le prix de la joie. Mémoires de Blanche Gamond. Héroïne de la Réforme*, Genève [1964]. *Flambeau* 5 (1966): 126.

1967

De controverse tussen Petrus en Paulus. Galaten 2:11 in de historie. Rede uitgesproken bij het aanvaarden van het ambt van gewoon hoogleraar in de geschiedenis van het christendom en van de leerstellingen van de christelijke godsdienst aan de Rijksuniversiteit te Leiden op 20 januari 1967. 's-Gravenhage: Nijhoff, 1967 (24 pp.).

1968

"Iconografie en Primaat. Petrus en Paulus op het pauselijk zegel." *NAKG* N.S. 49 (1 1968): 4–36.

1969

"Historische beschouwingen over de onfeilbaarheid der kerk." *RhW* 11 (1969): 75–87.

"De missionaire denkbeelden van Christoph Blumhardt." *NTT* 24 (1969): 105–17.

1970

Review: Aeneas Sylvius Piccolominus (Pius II), *De Gestis Concilii Basiliensis Commentariorum Libri II*. Edited and translated by Denis Hay and W.K. Smith, Oxford 1967 (Oxford Medieval Texts). *VC* 24 (1970): 80.

1971

"Paulus op de tweesprong tussen Oosterse en Westerse traditie." *RhW* 13 (1971): 29–38; appeared also in a commercial edition entitled: *De dertiende apostel en het elfde gebod. Paulus in de loop der eeuwen*, ed. G.C. Berkouwer and H.A. Oberman. 35–44. Kampen: Kok, 1971.

1972

"Nicolas de Dinkelsbühl à propos des auréoles des docteurs. Recherche fondée sur Melk, Stiftsbibliothek, cod. lat. 504 (autographe)." In *Texts & Manuscripts*, 47–55. Essays presented to G.I. Lieftinck, II, ed. J.P. Gumbert and M.J.M. de Haan. Litterae textuales. A series on manuscripts and their texts. Amsterdam: Van Gendt, 1972.

Review: Richard E. Weingart, *The Logic of Divine Love. A Critical Analysis of the Soteriology of Peter Abailard*, Oxford 1970. *NTT* 26 (1 1972): 99–100.

1973

"Het doctorenambt in Middeleeuwen en Reformatie." *RhW* 15 (1973): 21–45.

1974

"Berkhof en de dogmengeschiedenis." In *Weerwoord. Reacties op Dr. H. Berkhof's "Christelijk Geloof." Aangeboden aan prof. dr. H. Berkhof ter gelegenheid van zijn 60ste verjaardag*, 55–61. Nijkerk: Callenbach, 1974.

1975

"Richard Jean de Nerée en zijn 'Inventaire Général'." In *In het spoor van Arminius. Schetsen en studies over de Remonstranten in verleden en heden aangeboden aan Prof. Dr. G.J. Hoenderdaal ter gelegenheid van zijn 65e verjaardag*, 31–48. Nieuwkoop: Heuff, 1975.

"Gersons preek 'Diligite justitiam'." In *In Navolging. Een bundel studies aangeboden aan C.C. de Bruin bij zijn afscheid als hoogleraar te Leiden*, ed. M.J.M. de Haan, S.J. Lenselink, G.H.M. Posthumus Meyjes, and J. Trapman. 253–69. Leiden: [printed for private circulation], 1975 = *NAKG* N.S. 56 (1 1975): 253–69.

Geschiedenis van het Waalse College te Leiden, 1606–1699, tevens een bijdrage tot de vroegste geschiedenis van het fonds Hallet. Leiden: Universitaire Pers Leiden, 1975 (XV, 218 pp.).

"Le Collège Wallon." In *Leiden University in the Seventeenth Century. An Exchange of Learning,* ed. Th.H. Lunsingh Scheurleer and G.H.M. Posthumus Meyjes. 111–35. Leiden: Universitaire Pers Leiden, 1975.

Contribution. In *Leidse Universiteit 400. Stichting en eerste bloei 1575 – ca. 1650,* [Catalogus van de Tentoonstelling] 27 maart – 8 juni 1975 Rijksmuseum Amsterdam, 57. Amsterdam: Rijksmuseum, 1975.

1976

"In memoriam K.H. Miskotte." *A&A,* 16 Sept. 1976: 94.

1977

Review: Urban Pierius, *Geschichte der kursächsischen Kirchen- und Schulreformation,* [ed.] Thomas Klein, Marburg 1970. *NAKG* N.S. 57 (2 1977): 244–45.

"Het geschrift 'Examen Pacifique de la doctrine des Huguenots' (1589) en zijn auteur – Henry Constable in de kritiek." In *Kerkhistorische Studiën. Feestbundel uitgegeven ter gelegenheid van het 75-jarig bestaan van het kerkhistorisch gezelschap S.S.S.,* ed. E. Oort, H. Beck, and H. Wevers. 75–96. Leiden: [printed for private circulation], 1977.

1978

Jean Gerson et l'Assemblée de Vincennes (1329). Ses conceptions de la juridiction temporelle de l'Église. Accompagné d'une édition critique du De jurisdictione spirituali et temporali. Préface de Marcel Pacaut. Studies in Medieval and Reformation Thought, 26, Leiden: Brill, 1978 (XVIII, 148 pp.).

"Colonius (De Coulogne), Daniël." In *BLGNP,* 59–60. I.

"Gaillard, Jacques." In *BLGNP,* 80–81. I.

"Massis, Daniël." In *BLGNP,* 165. I.

"Nerée (Neraeus), Richard Jean de." In *BLGNP,* 279–80. I.

1979

Quasi stellae fulgebunt. Plaats en functie van de theologische doctor in de middeleeuwse maatschappij en kerk. Rede uitgesproken op 8 februari 1979 ter gelegenheid van de 404e dies natalis van de Leidse Universiteit. Leiden: Universitaire Pers Leiden, 1979 (20 pp.).

"Jean Hotman's Syllabus of eirenical literature." In *Reform and Reformation: England and the Continent c1500–c1750, dedicated and presented to professor Clifford W. Dugmore to mark his seventieth birthday,* ed. Derek Baker. 175–93. Studies in Church History, Subsidia 2. Oxford: Blackwell, 1979.

1980

"Autour d'une liste de Jean Hotman." In *La controverse religieuse (XVIe-XIXe siècles). Actes du 1er Colloque Jean Boisset. VIème Colloque du Centre d'Histoire de la Réforme et du Protestantisme,* ed. Michel Péronnet. 43–56. Montpellier: Université Paul Valéry, [1980].

1981

"Jean Hotman and Hugo Grotius." *Grotiana* 2 (1981): 3–29.

1982

In collaboration with G. Moreau. *Bibliographie de la Réforme 1450–1648.* Série publiée sur la recommandation du Conseil International de la Philosophie et des Sciences Humaines, huitième fascicule: *Benelux: Ouvrages parus de 1956 à 1975/76,* 83–151. Leiden: Brill, 1982.

"Het gezag van de theologische doctor in de kerk der middeleeuwen." In *Kerkhistorische Studiën, uitgegeven ter gelegenheid van het 80-jarig bestaan van het Kerkhistorisch Gezelschap S.S.S.,* ed. Joke Fabius, Arie Spaans, and Joke Spaans. 7–28. Leiden: [printed for private circulation], 1982.

"Protestants irenisme in de 16e en eerste helft van de 17e eeuw." *NTT* 36 (1982): 205–22.

1983

"De editie van Nicolaas van Clémanges, Opera Omnia, bezorgd door Johannes Lydius (Leiden 1613)." In *Boeken verzamelen. Opstellen aangeboden aan Mr J.R. de Groot bij zijn afscheid als bibliothecaris der Rijksuniversiteit te Leiden,* ed. J.A.A.M. Biemans, E. Braches, W.R.H. Koops, A.J.M. Linmans, and C. Reedijk. 231–48. Leiden: Bibliotheek der Rijksuniversiteit, 1983.

"Grotius als theoloog." In *Het Delfts orakel. Hugo de Groot 1583–1645*, 111–20. Delft: Stedelijk Museum Het Prinsenhof, [1983].

"Grotius as a theologian." In *Hugo Grotius, a Great European, 1583–1645. Contributions concerning his activities as a humanist scholar*, 51–58. Delft: Meinema, 1983.

"Jean Gerson." In *Gestalten der Kirchengeschichte, Mittelalter II*, ed. M. Greschat. 267–85. Stuttgart [etc.]: Kohlhammer, 1983.

"Inleiding tot de Serie Studies over de Geschiedenis van de Leidse Universiteit." In *Gedenkschriften Prof. mr R.P. Cleveringa betreffende zijn gevangenschap in 1940–1941 en 1944, voor het Leids Universiteits-Fonds uitgeg. door* L.E. van Holk en I. Schöffer. [VII]–VIII. Studies over de Geschiedenis van de Leidse Universiteit, 1. Leiden: Brill / Universitaire Pers Leiden, 1983.

1984

"Het gezag van de theologische doctor in de kerk der middeleeuwen – Gratianus, Augustinus Triumphus, Ockham en Gerson." *NAKG* N.S. 63 (2 1984): 102–28.

"Jean Hotman en het calvinisme in Frankrijk." *NAKG* N.S. 64 (1 1984): 42–77.

"Hugo Grotius as an irenicist." In *The World of Hugo Grotius (1583–1645), Proceedings of the International Colloquium organized by the Grotius Committee of the Royal Netherlands Academy of Arts and Sciences, Rotterdam 6–9 April 1983*, 43–63. Amsterdam – Maarssen: APA – Holland University Press, 1984.

"Gij zult niet strijden met anderen maar met uzelf. Het eerste theologische tractaat van Hugo de Groot." *NRC Handelsblad* 10.8. 1984, Cultureel Supplement p. 6.

"Hugo de Groot's 'Meletius' (1611), his earliest theological work, rediscovered." *LIAS* 11 (1 1984): 147–50.

"Protestant Irenicism in the sixteenth and seventeenth centuries." In *The End of Strife, Papers selected from the proceedings of the Colloquium of the Commission Internationale d'Histoire Ecclésiastique Comparée held at the University of Durham 2 to 9 September 1981*, ed. David Loades. 77–93. Edinburgh: Clark, 1984.

1985

"Het vroegste theologische geschrift van Hugo de Groot herontdekt, zijn Meletius (1611)." In *Bestuurders en Geleerden. Opstellen over onderwerpen uit de Nederlandse geschiedenis van de zestiende, zeventiende en acht-*

tiende eeuw, aangeboden aan prof. dr. J.J. Woltjer bij zijn afscheid als hoogleraar van de Rijksuniversiteit te Leiden, ed. S. Groenveld, M.E.H.N. Mout, and I. Schöffer. 75–84. Amsterdam – Dieren: De Bataafsche Leeuw, [1985].

In collaboration with H. Bots and F. Wieringa. *Vlucht naar de vrijheid. De Hugenoten en Nederland.* Amsterdam – Dieren: De Bataafsche Leeuw, [1985].

In collaboration with R. Bastiaanse, H. Bots, and F. Wieringa. *Catalogus van de tentoonstelling: De Hugenoten, de Herroeping van het Edict van Nantes en de Nederlanden, De Nieuwe Kerk, Amsterdam 15 juni – 20 augustus 1985.* 1985.

Verdrukking, vlucht en toevlucht. Het dagboek van Jean Migault over de geloofsvervolging onder Lodewijk XIV. Ingeleid en geannoteerd door G.H.M. Posthumus Meyjes. Kampen: Kok, [1985]. (89 pp.)

"La révocation de l'édit de Nantes et les Pays-Bas." In *Les Huguenots. Exposition nationale organisée par la direction des Archives de France, Ministère de la culture, à l'occasion du Tricentenaire de la Révocation de l'Édit de Nantes, 1685–1985,* 182–90. Paris: Archives Nationales: La Documentation, [1985].

1986

"Les rapports entre les Églises Wallonnes des Pays-Bas et la France avant la Révocation." In *La révocation de l'édit de Nantes et les Provinces-Unies, 1685. Colloque International du tricentenaire, Leyde, avril 1–3 1985,* 1–16. Amsterdam – Maarssen: APA – Holland University Press, [1986].

1987

"Het Westers Schisma vanuit Kerkhistorisch Gezichtspunt beschouwd." *Leidschrift Special: gescheurd geloven.* Uitgave van geschiedenisstudenten Leiden 3 (Jan. 1987): 17–28.

"L'Examen pacifique de la doctrine des Huguenots et son auteur (1589). Henry Constable et la critique." *LIAS* 14 (1 1987): 1–14.

"De receptie van Hugo de Groots *Meletius.*" In *Kerkhistorische opstellen aangeboden aan Prof. dr. J. van den Berg,* ed. C. Augustijn, P.N. Holtrop, G.H.M. Posthumus Meyjes, and E.G.E. van der Wall. 30–44. Kampen: Kok, 1987.

Review: *Getijden van de eeuwige wijsheid naar de vertaling van Geert Grote,* uitgegeven en ingeleid door Anton G. Weiler, [Baarn 1984]. *NAKG* N.S. 67 (2 1987): 202.

"In memoriam J.N. Bakhuizen van den Brink." *Mare* 19 Nov. 1987: 11.

1988

"In memoriam Jan Nicolaas Bakhuizen van den Brink (1896–1987)." *NAKG* N.S. 67 (1 1988): 93–94.

"In memoriam C.C. de Bruin." *Mare* 18 Nov. 1988: 12.

Review: Louis Desgraves, *Répertoire des ouvrages de controverse entre Catholiques et Protestants en France (1598–1685)*, t. I (1598–1628), t. II (1629–1685), Genève 1984/85. *NAKG* N.S. 67 (2 1988): 214–15.

Hugo Grotius Meletius sive de iis quae inter Christianos conveniunt epistola, critical edition with translation, commentary and introduction. Studies in the History of Christian Thought, 40. Leiden [etc.]: Brill, 1988 (XIX, 191 pp.).

"De doorwerking van de Moderne Devotie, met name bij de Remonstranten." In *De doorwerking van de Moderne Devotie, Windesheim 1387–1987, Voordrachten gehouden tijdens het Windesheim Symposium Zwolle/Windesheim 15–17 oktober 1987*, ed. P. Bange, C. Graafland, A.J. Jelsma, and A.G. Weiler. 81–94. Hilversum: Verloren, 1988.

1989

"Jan Nicolaas Bakhuizen van den Brink – 25 mei 1896 – 5 november 1987." In *Jaarboek KNAW*, 120–25. 1989.

"In memoriam C.C. de Bruin." *NAKG* N.S. 69 (1 1989): 1–2.

In collaboration with J.P. Heering "Cassander, Georgius." In *Literatur Lexikon. Autoren und Werke deutscher Sprache*, ed. Walter Killy. 386–87. II. Gütersloh – München: Bertelsmann Lexikon Verlag, [1989].

1990

"Quasi stellae fulgebunt: the Doctor of Divinity in Mediaeval Society and Church." In *In Divers Manners. A St Mary's Miscellany to commemorate the 450th anniversary of the founding of St Mary's College, 7th March, 1539*, ed. D.W.D. Shaw. 11–28. [St Mary's College, University of St. Andrews: 1990].

Jean Hotman's English Connection. Mededelingen KNAW, N.R. dl. 53 no. 5, Amsterdam [etc.]: North Holland, 1990 (pp. [161]–222).

"Les relations entre les églises réformées des Pays Bas et les églises Vaudoises au 17ième siècle." In *Atti del XXIX Convegno Storico In-*

ternazionale: "Il Glorioso Rimpatrio 1689 1989, Contesto Significato Immagine", 83–93. Torino: 1990.

1991

"Charles Perrot (1541–1608). His opinion on a writing of Georg Cassander." In *Humanism and Reform: The Church in Europe, England and Scotland 1400–1643. Essays in Honour of James K. Cameron*, ed. James Kirk. 221–36. Studies in Church History, Subsidia 8. Oxford: Blackwell, 1991.

"Pierre d'Ailly's verhandeling *Utrum indoctus in iure divino possit iuste praeesse in ecclesiae regno.*" In *Kerk in Beraad. Opstellen aangeboden aan prof. dr. J.C.P.A. van Laarhoven bij gelegenheid van zijn afscheid als hoogleraar aan de Katholieke Universiteit Nijmegen*, ed. Gian Ackermans, Adelbert Davids, and Peter J.A. Nissen. 87–101. Nijmegen: Faculteit der Godgeleerdheid, Katholieke Universiteit Nijmegen, 1991.

"Exponents of Sovereignty: Canonists as seen by Theologians in the Late Middle Ages." In *The Church and Sovereignty c590–1918. Essays in Honour of Michael Wilks*, ed. Diana Wood. 299–312. Studies in Church History, Subsidia, 9. Oxford: Blackwell, 1991.

"Les débuts de l'Église Wallonne de Rotterdam." *Echo Wallon. Mensuel des Églises Réformées Wallonnes aux Pays Bas* 44 (5 1991): 5–13.

"De studentenjaren van Fredrik Pijper." In *Quisque Suis Viribus 1841–1991. 150 jaar theologie in dertien portretten*, ed. R.B. ter Haar Romeny and Joh. Tromp. 109–25. Leiden: Collegium Theologicum c.s. "Quisque suis viribus", 1991.

1992

Geloven en lachen in de historie. Enkele opmerkingen over de waardering van de lach in de geschiedenis der kerk. Rede uitgesproken ter gelegenheid van zijn afscheid als hoogleraar in de geschiedenis van het christendom en van de leerstellingen van de christelijke godsdienst aan de Rijksuniversiteit te Leiden op 5 juni 1992. Leiden: Rijksuniversiteit Leiden, [1992] (33 pp.).

"Charles Perrot (1541–1608), een onbekend advies van zijn hand over een werk van Georgius Cassander met, in appendix, iets over zijn *De extremis in ecclesia vitandis.*" *NAKG* N.S. 72 (1 1992): 72–91.

1993

"Twee vrienden: Isaac Casaubon en Hugo de Groot." In *Voorbeeldige vriendschap. Vrienden en vriendinnen in theologie en cultuur. Aangebo-*

den aan prof. dr. E.J. Kuiper ter gelegenheid van zijn afscheid als hoogleraar van het Seminarium der Remonstranten, 1 januari 1993, 37–46. Groningen: Styx, 1993.

"Die Beziehungen zwischen Jean Hotman und Theodor Beza." In *Reformiertes Erbe. Festschrift für Gottfried W. Locher zu seinem 80. Geburtstag,* ed. Heiko A. Oberman, Ernst Saxer, Alfred Schindler, and Heinzpeter Stucki. 315–26. II. Zwingliana XIX, 2. [Zürich]: Theologischer Verlag, [1993].

"Het Sypesteyn-handschrift te Leiden: BPL 2899." In *Miscellanea Gentiana. Een bundel opstellen aangeboden aan J.J.M. van Gent bij zijn afscheid als bibliothecaris der Rijksuniversiteit te Leiden,* ed. C. Berkvens-Stevelinck and A.Th. Bouwman. 263–75. Leiden: Brill / Universitaire Pers Leiden, 1993.

"50 jaar Historische Kring." In *Herinneringen aan een halve eeuw "Historische Kring" te Leiden,* 1942–1992, 7–17. Leiden: [printed for private circulation], 1993.

1994

"Some Remarks on Grotius' *Excerpta Theologica,* Especially Concerning his *Meletius.*" In *Hugo Grotius Theologian, Essays in Honour of G.H. M. Posthumus Meyjes,* ed. Henk J.M. Nellen and Edwin Rabbie. 1–17. Studies in the History of Christian Thought, 55. Leiden [etc.]: Brill, 1994.

IN THE PRESS

"Les années de Jacques Gaillard à Leyden et son sermon *l'Echole saincte des femmes* (1667)." In *De l'Humanisme aux Lumières: Bayle et le protestantisme. Mélanges en l'honneur d'Elisabeth Labrousse.* I. Universitas, 1994.

"Groot, Hugo de." In *BLGNP.* IV.

"Lydius, Johannes." In *BLGNP.* IV.

INDEX OF NAMES

INDEX OF SUBJECTS

INDEX OF BIBLICAL REFERENCES

LIST OF CONTRIBUTORS

JOHANNES VAN DEN BERG
Professor emeritus of Church history
Leiden University

HANS BOTS
Professor of intellectual relations in the early modern times
Catholic University of Nijmegen

JAMES K. CAMERON
Professor emeritus of Church history
University of St. Andrews

HARM-JAN VAN DAM
Research fellow, Grotius department
Constantijn Huygens Institute for Text Editions and Intellectual History
The Hague

OLIVIER FATIO
Professor of Church history
Université de Genève

JAN PAUL HEERING
Research fellow
Leiden University

HENK JAN DE JONGE
Professor of New Testament
Leiden University

FRANÇOIS LAPLANCHE
Centre national de la Recherche scientifique, Paris
Angers

HENK J.M. NELLEN
Senior research fellow, Grotius department
Constantijn Huygens Institute for Text Editions and Intellectual History
The Hague

GUILLAUME H. M. POSTHUMUS MEYJES
Professor emeritus of Church history
Leiden University

EDWIN RABBIE
Research fellow, Grotius department
Constantijn Huygens Institute for Text Editions and Intellectual History
The Hague

JOHANNES TRAPMAN
Senior research fellow, Erasmus department
Constantijn Huygens Institute for Text Editions and Intellectual History
The Hague

ERNESTINE VAN DER WALL
Professor of Church history
Leiden University

Studies in the History
of Christian Thought

EDITED BY HEIKO A. OBERMAN

50. HOENEN, M. J. F. M. *Marsilius of Inghen*. Divine Knowledge in Late Medieval Thought. 1993
51. O'MALLEY, J. W., IZBICKI, T. M. and CHRISTIANSON, G. (eds.) *Humanity and Divinity in Renaissance and Reformation*. Essays in Honor of Charles Trinkaus. 1993
52. REEVE, A. (ed.) and SCREECH, M. A. (introd.) *Erasmus' Annotations on the New Testament*. Galatians to the Apocalypse. 1993
53. STUMP, Ph. H. *The Reforms of the Council of Constance (1414-1418)*. 1994
54. GIAKALIS, A. *Images of the Divine*. The Theology of Icons at the Seventh Ecumenical Council. With a Foreword by Henry Chadwick. 1994
55. NELLEN, H. J. M. and RABBIE, E. *Hugo Grotius – Theologian*. Essays in Honour of G. H. M. Posthumus Meyjes. 1994

Prospectus available on request

E. J. BRILL — P.O.B. 9000 — 2300 PA LEIDEN — THE NETHERLANDS

DATE DUE

			Printed in USA